CELEBRATING

50 YEARS

Texas A&M University Press
publishing since 1974

"WE WANT BETTER EDUCATION!"

Elma Dill Russell Spencer Series in the West and Southwest

"WE WANT BETTER EDUCATION!"

The 1960s Chicano Student Movement, School Walkouts, and the Quest for Educational Reform in South Texas

JAMES B. BARRERA

Texas A&M University Press | College Station

Copyright © 2024 by James B. Barrera
All rights reserved
First edition

⊗ This paper meets the requirements of ANSI/NISO Z39.48–1992
(Permanence of Paper).
Binding materials have been chosen for durability.
Manufactured in the United States of America

LIBRARY OF CONGRESS CATALOGING-IN-PUBLICATION DATA

NAMES: Barrera, Baldemar James, 1974–author.
TITLE: "We want better education!": the 1960s Chicano student movement, school
walkouts, and the quest for educational reform in South Texas / James B. Barrera.
OTHER TITLES: Elma Dill Russell Spencer series in the West and Southwest.
DESCRIPTION: First edition. | College Station : Texas A&M University Press, [2024]
| Series: Elma Dill Russell Spencer series in the West and Southwest | Includes
bibliographical references and index.
IDENTIFIERS: LCCN 2023019182 | ISBN 9781648430886 (hardcover) | ISBN
9781648430893 (ebook)
SUBJECTS: LCSH: Mexican Americans—Education—Texas, South—History—
20th century. | Mexican American high school students—Political activity—Texas,
South—History—20th century. | Student movements—Texas, South—History—
20th century. | Chicano movement—Texas, South. | Educational change—Political
aspects—Texas, South.
CLASSIFICATION: LCC LC2687.T4 B375 2024 | DDC 371.8/109764—dc23/eng/20230526
LC record available at https://lccn.loc.gov/2023019182

For my parents, Baldemar and Yolanda A. Barrera

Contents

Preface
ix

Acknowledgments
xvii

Introduction
1

CHAPTER 1.
Historical Background of South Texas Prior to the 1960s
24

CHAPTER 2.
Mexican American Civil Rights Activism and
the Rise of the Chicano Student Movement in South Texas
46

CHAPTER 3.
The Chicano Student Movement in South Texas
Begins in San Antonio's West Side
81

CHAPTER 4.
The 1968 Edcouch-Elsa High School Walkout
Chicano Student Activism in Deep South Texas
125

CHAPTER 5.
The 1969 Kingsville School Walkout
Chicano Student and MAYO Activism Spreads to Mid-South Texas
150

CHAPTER 6.
The 1969–70 Crystal City School Walkout
The Climax and Decline of the Chicano Student Movement in Rural South Texas
179

CHAPTER 7.
Conclusion
205

APPENDIX A.
Lanier High School Walkout Demands
219

APPENDIX B.
Edgewood High School Walkout Demands
222

APPENDIX C.
Edcouch-Elsa High School Walkout Demands
224

APPENDIX D.
Kingsville Gillett Junior High School Walkout Demands
226

APPENDIX E.
Crystal City High School Walkout Demands
228

Notes
231

Bibliography
269

Index
283

Preface

I am a third-generation Texan and native of McAllen, Texas, which is 10 miles north of the US-Mexico international boundary in the Rio Grande Valley ("Valley" for short) and 230 miles south of San Antonio, the largest city in south-central Texas. Although I grew up in the same region where the 1960s Mexican American student "walkouts" or protests took place, the student protest movement had already faded into history prior to my birth. I am a member of the so-called Generation X of Americans born in the 1970s, and the history of the 1960s occurred a few years before my lifetime, when de facto segregation according to race was in effect, dividing both "mexicanos" (ethnic Mexican people) and "gringos" (Anglo-Americans). McAllen and most other South Texas towns had segregated schools, neighborhoods, cemeteries, theaters, restaurants, stores, and hospitals for many years until the 1970s. I grew up in the 1980s, a decade characterized by the policies and Cold War ideology of President Ronald Reagan, the rise of social and political conservatism, the flamboyant display of materialism, the expansion of television cable networks such as MTV and innovative TV sitcoms such as *The Cosby Show*, and the advent of the computer information age. As a historian born after the 1960s, I gathered much of my research data and knowledge of this period from class lectures, secondary literature, government reports, films, newspaper articles, oral history records, and conversations or interviews with former movement activists. I first became curious about researching the history of the student movement as a twenty-four-year-old graduate student when I first learned of the 1968 walkout at Edcouch-Elsa High School, just fifteen miles away from my hometown.

Although I did not experience the historic events of the nation prior to the 1970s, I will always remain proud of the sacrifices, achievements, and successes of the previous generations of Latin Americans. Unfortunately for me, the 1960s were a part of history I just missed living, much like the Great Depression was for those of the baby boom generation born in the 1940s and 1950s. However, if I could somehow transport through time to experience certain events for myself, I would travel to the Edcouch-Elsa High School campus on November 14, 1968, the first day of the protest. Feeling the cold breeze, I see students walking into their school after unloading from buses and cars. I notice the clothing, shoes, and hairstyles made popular during the 1960s, which I have never seen before.

A few students salute each other with the peace sign and say "groovy," a common expression during this period. Many also converse using words and phrases in both English and Spanish.

It appears to be another typical day at school until classes begin at 8:00 a.m. Suddenly, I see approximately two hundred Chicano students rise from their desks and walk out of their classrooms.[1] After walking out, student protesters congregate in front of the school and outside the campus across an unpaved dusty road, US Highway 107. After greeting each other, the students engage in a peaceful protest, exclaiming, "Boycott classes!" I see them carrying picket signs with slogans such as "We want better education." As I notice protesters march, clap, chant, and exclaim "Viva la Raza," I am curious why they left class and became so vociferous and energetic. After observing the beginning of the student boycott in my daydream, I suddenly awaken and see the current-day neighboring towns of Edcouch and Elsa.

As I look around the Edcouch-Elsa of the early twenty-first century, I notice how much this community has changed since 1968. I see the newly paved roads, modern-day cars, national chain businesses, corporate buildings, and people wearing the latest designer clothes conversing on iPhones. Popular culture, fads, fashion, music, clothing, and the most recent television ads of the current decade further distinguish the Edcouch-Elsa of today. The local population is different as well. The community now has very few Anglo-American residents since most moved away after the walkout. I see billboards and signs displaying the Spanish surnames of people running for city and school board positions, rather than the names of Anglos. How did the political power structure of this community and its school system change so drastically over time? This book seeks to answer this question and will provide flashbacks or "snapshots" of the major events of the Chicano student movement in Edcouch-Elsa and throughout South Texas. The Edcouch-Elsa walkout occurred only eight months after the Edgewood and Lanier High School protests in San Antonio, but it ended before the famous Crystal City school boycott of 1969. The year 1968 marked the beginning of the Chicano student movement, which gradually began to decline by the early 1970s. This book offers the reader a greater awareness and understanding of the history of Mexican Americans in South Texas who were at the forefront of one of the most important social movements of the twentieth century, the 1960s Civil Rights Movement.

Chicano Movement activists are not the only ones who exemplified extraordinary courage, perseverance, and fortitude in promoting the value of education. For me, such people include my mother and father, who became the first in their families to graduate from high school and college in the 1960s. Although they never protested during the movement, they faced and overcame challenging circumstances in school including racial prejudice, inadequate counseling, living a long distance from family, and the lack of student financial aid. Both were told by their respective high school counselors that they were not college material, yet they still enrolled and eventually completed their education despite the obstacles and long odds of successfully navigating a four-year university. My father, Baldemar Barrera, a native of the South Texas border town of Pharr, attended Texas A&M University, one of the two flagship universities of Texas, where he received a bachelor of science degree in architectural engineering. Very few Hispanics were admitted to the main campus of Texas A&M during his years as a student from 1965 to 1968. According to the most recent admissions report for 2022, Hispanics continue to remain a minority (16,885 out of 74,829, or 22.5%) at Texas A&M University.[2]

My mother also moved away from her hometown of Corpus Christi, Texas, to enroll in Texas Woman's University, just north of the Dallas–Fort Worth area, where she earned a bachelor of science degree in biology in 1970. She worked for two years as a nurse in Houston and retired as a public-school educator after teaching biology and English as a second language for twenty-two years in the Mission and Pharr–San Juan–Alamo public schools. She then helped manage the family business until her year-long terminal illness and untimely death in 2009. Prior to starting his own small business, Balde's Auto Sales, in 1972, my father was employed as a licensed engineering professional for the Brown and Root Engineering and Construction Company of Houston, where he planned, designed, and oversaw the construction of twenty-five bridges near Saigon for eighteen months during the Vietnam War.[3] I will always admire my mom and dad for overcoming formidable obstacles to achieving their educational and life goals, and for raising me to believe in the importance of hard work, integrity, compassion, faith, and family. Furthermore, I credit them for motivating me to complete my education, teaching me the importance of serving others and helping those in need, and instilling in me a desire to learn that began in childhood. Their examples of strength, courage, persistence, discipline, and unwavering determination in the face of adversity continue to inspire me, and they will always remain my most important role models in this world.

As a present-day college educator at South Texas College (STC), a regional community college and Hispanic-Serving Institution in McAllen, Texas, I appreciate the opportunity to teach my students the history of the Chicano Movement as part of US history. Although the student population of South Texas College is more than 94 percent Hispanic, most students possess very little knowledge of the movement, or they have heard only of César Chávez and the farmworkers' movement, but not of Antonio Orendain or the Texas Farm Workers Union. For most students, the Chicano Movement is as distant as World War I and the 1920s were to those who were of high school and college age during the late 1960s. Some individuals barely recall the movement from brief mention in high school history courses or in the media, while others may know a few basic facts but fail to understand its relevance in their lives. Furthermore, most did not learn the significance of the Chicano Movement as part of the overall history of the United States early in their lives. In both my US and Mexican American history courses, I specifically emphasize the role of movement activists and their supporters who willingly sacrificed themselves to advocate for equality, social justice, political inclusion, and better-quality education in the public schools. Throughout my discussions with students, I encourage them to understand how the Chicano Movement significantly impacted and improved the educational system for Mexican Americans and made worthy contributions to the nation as a whole. Many are surprised to learn that mainstream society once regarded people of Mexican origin as culturally inferior, ignorant, foreign, or illegal, and incapable of achieving much in life beyond manual labor.

My main contributions to student success at STC include advising first- and second-year students on their degree plans and career goals, adopting student-centered learning strategies, serving as faculty adviser of the history club, and planning special events throughout the school year such as STC's annual Hispanic Heritage Month Lecture Series and Veterans Day Lecture Series. Working closely with undergraduate students has been one of the most rewarding aspects of my academic career. I especially enjoy this part of my job, as I have the opportunity to establish meaningful mentoring relationships, thus positively impacting the lives of students and their ability to succeed in college and beyond. I sincerely believe that being a good role model to students includes sharing my own academic and professional experience, being approachable and sensitive to their educational needs, and remaining committed to their academic progress and sustained growth. I am always happy to facilitate the learning of history and ignite enthusiasm in students as they increase their knowledge about the breadth and diversity of the American experience. Overall, I strive to instill in students a desire to learn regardless of the course content and to continue learning throughout their college career and beyond, and I try to help them better understand the relevance of history in their lives.

The completion of this book has truly been a dream come true for me because not many thought I could complete high school, much less college and graduate school. Working on this book allowed me to reminisce about my own academic experience in high school during the early 1990s. I was never considered a "top-notch" student or the cream of the crop in my graduating class at Memorial High School in McAllen, Texas. Most of my high school teachers never encouraged me to apply for college, nor do I recall the school counselor, a

Mexican American woman, showing me how to fill out college application forms or register for college entrance exams, or recommending me for scholarships. She summoned me into her office only to inform me of my course schedule and evaluate my progress in each class, especially in math and science, my weakest subjects. A few weeks into the second semester of my freshman year, I spoke to the counselor about transferring to new math and science classes with different teachers who were willing to offer a supportive learning environment appropriate to my learning style. My parents knew the switch was necessary because of my low grades in math and science throughout my first semester. After the counselor refused to fulfill my request, claiming that "it was too late," my father took time off from work to visit the school and insist that she change my schedule. My grades in both subjects improved after the counselor finally agreed to move me to courses taught by teachers who gave me more constructive feedback, encouragement, and praise. History and English were among my two favorite subjects, and I enjoyed learning with dedicated teachers who were approachable and instilled in me a desire to learn. One of my English teachers, Mrs. Cowley, nominated me for Memorial's Blue and Gold Award as a student of the week to acknowledge my participation in her class.

At the beginning of my senior year at McAllen Memorial High, my parents were the only ones who helped me apply to Texas A&M University, or "Aggieland," in College Station. They encouraged me to enroll at Texas A&M rather than the nearby University of Texas–Pan American in Edinburg, where most of my classmates chose to attend to remain close to home.[4] After submitting my application, I honestly thought Texas A&M would not accept me and was expecting to receive a rejection letter to show as proof to my parents, teachers, and high school counselor that I had given it my best shot. Two months before I graduated from high school, the university accepted me into its summer provisional admission program, which offered prospective students from underserved areas the unique opportunity to gain full admission after completing and passing two or more summer courses prior to the fall semester. I will always remain thankful to my mother for phoning the university admissions office and speaking on my behalf, which helped me gain acceptance into Texas A&M's provisional program. Both my parents took time out of their busy schedules to help me apply to the university from start to finish, and they made all the necessary arrangements for my transition to college. Memorial High never offered me this type of assistance or support. I remember the counselor congratulating me on my acceptance into Texas A&M just prior to my graduation, but neither she nor anyone else at the school informed me about the admissions requirements or campus tours or offered instruction in filling out application forms. Although a few teachers encouraged my academic growth in high school, none suggested higher education. Perhaps, in retrospect, I should have "walked out" of my school to protest this lack of support, as students did in the 1960s.

During my high school years in the 1990s, "college readiness" was not a buzzy trend or norm. Most faculty and counselors were unable to identify students like me who showed potential for greater scholastic achievement given the proper guidance, mentorship, and training in forming long-term occupational goals suited to their academic strengths, thus positively impacting their ability to attain greater success in high school and beyond.[5] Thus, I regret not demanding that my school provide me more direct assistance and preparation for college. If given the opportunity to relive my high school years, I would focus more on becoming a dedicated learner, achieve a higher class rank so I could compete for valedictorian, insist that the counseling staff assist me in planning a challenging course schedule and completing college application requirements, request information on colleges that supported my learning interests, and apply for scholarships. Although I was not one of the highest-ranking graduates of my class, I strongly believe I was one of the most improved students, earning mostly As and Bs during my senior year.

In the spring of 1993, I chose to attend Texas A&M because my parents took me to College Station to visit Aggieland during my adolescent years. After I gained full admission to Texas A&M, my initial reaction was not what you would expect. I thought, "I am not going to be able to fit in. I am not sure how I will finish. I am not going to be able to afford it." However, my parents helped me secure enough funding to cover the complete cost of my education, and I am proud to say I earned my bachelor of arts degree in history and graduated from the university debt-free without taking out a loan. During my senior year at Texas A&M, I met Professor Armando Alonzo, who encouraged me to apply to graduate school after I enrolled in his Mexican American history course. My parents supported my decision to pursue graduate studies in history at the University of Texas at El Paso from 1998 to 2001 (where I earned an MA), and at the University of New Mexico in Albuquerque from 2001 to 2007 (where I earned a PhD). This improbable "Cinderella story," my uncommon academic journey from an introverted learner and underachieving high school freshman to a dedicated college educator and emerging scholar, will always remain one of my greatest achievements and one of the most important transformative experiences of my life.

One of the most inspiring movies in motion picture history is *Rudy* (1993), starring Sean Astin, which closely reflects my attitude and work ethic as a young student and scholar. *Rudy* tells the story of Daniel "Rudy" Ruettiger, a young man from the working-class city of Joliet, Illinois, who aspired to play football at the University of Notre Dame. However, Rudy's poor grades in high school, working-class background, skeptical family, struggle with dyslexia, and small physical stature prevented him from achieving immediate success and recognition. Despite such formidable obstacles, Rudy personified the virtues of persistence, desire, commitment, courage, and undaunted character. He simply refused to believe those who told him to forgo his seemingly impossible dreams, and he became a trailblazer who forged his own path of success in the classroom and on the football field at Notre Dame. After the death of his best friend Pete, Rudy began his miraculous journey from being a walk-on player and transfer student to participating in the last two plays of the final home game as a graduating senior at Notre Dame in 1975.[6] I can certainly relate to Rudy's real-life story because his experience reminds me of some of my own struggles in academia; I was also an "underdog," or least likely to succeed after high school. Most student activists of the 1960s across South Texas were academic underdogs as well prior to achieving their goals and dreams later in life. I believe their greatest triumph was rising above the status quo and beyond the low expectations set for them in school, since most were determined to voice their desire for educational reform, graduate, and pursue a college education despite their marginalization.

Students participating in the movement for educational reform at their schools were seeking equal opportunity, college readiness, and greater recognition of their cultural heritage during the late 1960s. Today, parents, teachers, and school administrators must avoid stereotyping students and should support them in accomplishing their goals and dreams regardless of their test scores, racial background, national origin, gender, or socioeconomic background. Do all you can to help everyone excel in the classroom regardless of the course content. Evaualte who your students are, what they need and what they already know, and how their education can provide greater opportunities in life. Refuse to categorize students according to your expectations or make assumptions about them without actually getting to know them beyond what you read in their academic file. Do not be quick to give up on them, but believe in their ability to rise to the level of expectations and instill in them a desire to improve their performance in school. Support your students, children, or grandchildren in their school activities and communicate with their teachers and administrators throughout the school year. Schedule time to attend open house events and other public activities at school and vote for candidates in school board elections who support student-centered learning, equal opportunity for all students, up-to-date educational technology, and a college-going culture. For those who teach or serve in school administration, always believe in your students' ability to learn from their mistakes, and assist them in realizing their potential to become more proficient learners and productive members of society. Educators must commit to being "coaches" who transform "athletes" (underperforming students) into "playoff contenders," or active learners who are trained to use effective study and critical thinking skills and who are motivated to achieve academic goals, both short and long term, to measure their success.

If you are a high school or college student reading this book, please do not take your education for granted or allow yourself to fail because of lack of effort, participation, and commitment on your part. The purpose of school is to promote your intellectual growth and prepare you to serve in the professional or skilled workforce in the future. Students walked out of their schools during the Chicano Movement to avoid being tracked into low-wage vocational fields or dropping out to work in migratory farm labor. Do you take advantage of the variety of educational resources available to help you thrive and achieve in school, resources that did not exist before your lifetime? What do you think your school, faculty, counselors, parents, and community need to do to support your interests, ability to learn, and academic goals? If you lack adequate resources and support to accomplish your goals, how will you address those concerns at your school? As this book will attest, if you seek to reform or improve conditions at your school, you must do it for yourself with the support of your family and community. *"We Want Better Education!"* seeks to inspire readers toward that end.

Acknowledgments

Without a doubt, the completion of this book has been a tremendous undertaking and represents the culmination of countless hours of exhausting work. I owe much gratitude to numerous people who made it possible. First, I would like to acknowledge and thank the members of my dissertation committee, including Professors Bárbara O. Reyes, Sam Truett, Durwood Ball, and Felipe Gonzáles at the University of New Mexico (UNM). They provided me intellectual guidance, suggestions for revision, moral support, and cooperation that helped me eventually turn my dissertation into a book. Other professors who took time to share their expertise, critical insights, and scholarly advice throughout my years of graduate study include David Farber (former UNM professor), Virginia Scharff (UNM), Linda Hall (UNM), Charles Martin at the University of Texas at El Paso (UTEP), Oscar Martinez (visiting professor at UTEP), and John Wunder (visiting professor at UNM). Various fellow history graduate students at UNM took an interest in my work and showed me moral support and friendship as well. They include Wallace Begay, Robert Carriedo, Frank Tellez, Joe Lenti, Scott Meredith, Kim Klimek, Laurie Hinck, Sarah Payne, Bill Convery, Richard Sanchez, and Brad Schreve. I am very grateful to Professor Ernesto Chávez, my master's thesis adviser at UTEP, for his suggestions and encouragement to follow up on my research after finishing my thesis, which further motivated me to finish this book as well.

I would like to acknowledge and thank Tobias Duran for sponsoring and funding graduate student fellowships on behalf of the UNM Center for Regional Studies. The center awarded me the Dennis Chavez and Fabiola Cabeza de Baca Gilbert fellowships during the 2002–03 and 2003–04 school years, respectively. The fellowships not only provided me funding during the last two years of my graduate education at UNM but also allowed me to work part time in the Center for Southwest Research and Special Collections at the UNM Zimmerman Library. Throughout the course of both my fellowships, I received training in the practice and methodology of public history that significantly enhanced my research skills. Those who provided me instruction and supervision at the Center for Southwest Research include Kathlene Ferris, Teresa Marquez, Nancy Brown-Martínez, and Ann Massman. It was a pleasure working with these fine professionals (archivists and reference librarians) who assist research scholars in more ways than one could imagine.

Unknown to me at the time, I began drafting the overall plan for this book while I was a master's student at UTEP. In the fall of 1998, I wrote a research paper on 1960s Chicano/Mexican American student protests in South Texas in Professor Charles Martin's US history graduate seminar class. During the initial stage of my research, I discovered a reference to the student strikes in South Texas in Armando Rendon's *Chicano Manifesto* and soon found a lot of newspaper coverage, which eventually convinced me to undertake a comprehensive study and write this book. I also completed a small part of this writing in a modern US history graduate seminar course taught by Professor Farber in the fall of 2003.

I greatly appreciate the scholarly dialogue and professional support of various colleagues at South Texas College (STC), where I have worked since 2005. They include Benjamin "Mark" Allen, Margaretha E. Bischoff, Bill Carter, Chris R. Davis, Esther Garcia, Victor Gomez, Trinidad Gonzáles, Robert Sean Kennedy, Darrell Muckleroy, Elizandro Muñoz, Chris Nelson, Gilberto Reyes, Joel Rodríguez, Adrian J. Salazar, Rene Zuniga, and the late Charles Robinson III. They encouraged me to think more clearly about the value of researching, teaching, and promoting history. The Hispanic Heritage Month Lecture Series and the José de la Luz Sáenz Veterans Day Lecture Series at STC featured numerous scholars from around the country who shared their perspectives on their research and offered me new ideas for revising a few parts of this book. Serving as a member of the Américo Paredes Book Award Committee at STC has further enhanced my assessment of recent scholarly works in Chicano and Latino studies as well. My discussions in the classroom and during office hours at STC allowed me to further promote the study of history among my students. I am especially grateful for the opportunity to advise and serve as a mentor to STC history majors as they progress in their academic studies and transfer to a university of their choice to earn bachelor's and graduate degrees as the next generation of historians. A few of them include Romeo Rosales, Claudia Espinoza Rosales, Jeremy Gonzales, Jessica De La Rosa, Rafael Soto, Rey Castañeda, and Frank Fuentes.

Special thanks go to Professors Patricia Portales of San Antonio College, David Montejano of the University of California, Berkeley, and Mario Longoria of San Antonio, who provided me additional information on the whereabouts of former Chicano student activists in the San Antonio area. History professor Emilio Zamora from the University of Texas at Austin took time to share his commentary via email, suggesting additional contacts and new research data. Cynthia E. Orozco, professor of history and humanities at Eastern New Mexico University–Ruidoso, used her extraordinary editing skills to significantly enhance the clarity, structure, style, and overall quality of the final draft. I am also indebted to the readers of the final drafts of the book, including the anonymous peer reviewers as well as Professor Andrés Tijerina and Jay Dew at Texas A&M

University Press. They offered valuable feedback and recommendations for revision during the last stage of the project. However, I am solely responsible for the interpretation and analysis of the history in this work, as well as its shortcomings.

Finally, I would like to express my deepest gratitude to my parents, Mr. and Mrs. Baldemar Barrera, for their encouragement, assistance, consideration, and belief in me in finishing this book. I regret that my mother, Yolanda A. Barrera, did not live long enough to see the finished product because of her untimely death in 2009. I will always cherish her kindness, encouragement, compassion, humor, and love for me. She would have enjoyed reading this book and would have purchased a few extra copies to distribute to relatives and friends. The only way I can begin to thank her is by dedicating this book in her memory.

I must admit there were many times I thought this book would never come to fruition, especially during a serious health crisis that required major surgery, extensive rehabilitation, and a six-month healing period beginning in December 2013. This condition required me to take a medical leave of absence from STC before returning to work in the fall of 2014. I am very thankful to numerous people who helped me make a full recovery, including the medical staff at Doctors Hospital at Renaissance in Edinburg, Texas; the physical therapists and nurses at the Briarcliff Nursing and Rehabilitation Center in McAllen, Texas; and my family and friends who kept me in their thoughts and prayers. If I had been unable to fully recover, you and other readers would not have had the opportunity to read this book. Please remember to take good care of yourself and never take the gift of life for granted. The peer review process required additional time to complete as well. I hope the readers of this book will acknowledge this work as one of the main highlights of my career as a scholar in the fields of Latino/Mexican American studies and US civil rights history. The completion of this work has truly been a dream come true for me after spending over twenty years of my time, skill, labor, and resources locating information in numerous places across South and Central Texas. I will always appreciate the honor of sharing this history with my readers and hope they enjoy reading and learning from it.

"WE WANT BETTER EDUCATION!"

Introduction

Come mothers and fathers throughout the land
And don't criticize what you can't understand
Your sons and your daughters are beyond your command
Your old road is rapidly agin'
Please get out of the new one if you can't lend your hand
For the times, they are a-changin'
—"The Times They Are a-Changin'" by Bob Dylan, 1963

This part of American singer-songwriter Bob Dylan's unforgettable hit song reveals the nature of youth rebellion and the generational gap that was evident across the United States when the times were indeed "a-changin'" because of mass protest movements, social revolutions, and political upheavals in the 1960s. This tumultuous decade, marking one of the most unforgettable epochs in US history, culminated in the emergence of Third World struggles, the Women's Rights Movement, the American Indian Movement, and other mass demonstrations for equality, freedom, and civil rights in the streets and on school campuses throughout the nation. A new generation of young people in the United States and around the world suddenly became outspoken in the 1960s, the dawn of hope and idealism for them. As the 1960s progressed, widespread tensions and divisions continued to develop concerning the expansion of the US government's role in the Vietnam War and Civil Rights Movement. Many young people grew skeptical of the traditional modes of authority, including church and state, while embracing new forms of cultural expression, lifestyles, and values. Protest became progress, signifying a national awakening during a decade that profoundly transformed America. Thus, the participants in these movements forged their own destinies toward greater self-determination, social justice, political participation, cultural awareness, and institutional reform.

In 1968, the Chicano Movement, also called the Chicano Civil Rights Movement or El Movimiento, suddenly burst onto the national scene and emerged as one of the most significant social protest movements and consciousness-raising events of the civil rights era. This movement was part of the larger Civil Rights Movement, which sought social, political, cultural, and economic empowerment for Mexican Americans as well as African Americans and other minority groups. This mass movement, characterized by numerous organized campaigns of nonviolent protest and civil disobedience, encompassed a broad cross section of issues, from farmworkers' rights to the restoration of land grants, voting and political rights, new employment opportunities, and educational equality. Therefore, the Chicano Movement fits into the rich tradition of civil rights and social protest movements in modern US history. Like many grassroots social movements, this movement began with the youth of the afflicted community seeking the recognition of rights, opportunities, and representation in US society.

The most important participants of El Movimiento included both Chicana and Chicano[1] students who protested at their schools in South Texas in such notable places as San Antonio's West Side, Edcouch-Elsa, Kingsville, and Crystal City. South Texas, originally a Spanish-Mexican cultural province, is still known for its strong ethnic Mexican cultural influences and Spanish language usage because of its proximity to Mexico. Many people born in this area continue to share a common identity rooted in small-town ambience, strong family values, cultural loyalty, the Catholic religion, and land usage. The region includes and lies south of the city of San Antonio, north of the Texas-Mexico border along the Rio Grande between Brownsville and Del Rio, and east of the coastal city of Corpus Christi on the Gulf of Mexico.[2] Prior to the 1960s, however, many outside the US Southwest regarded Mexican Americans as a rather obscure ethnic minority group compared to African Americans, who received more government attention and extensive media coverage for school desegregation efforts, bus boycotts, and sit-in strikes. Chapter 3 will highlight the major events of the Mexican American struggle for equality and civil rights in Texas during the twentieth century and will further reveal a long tradition of labor and political activism that predated the 1960s.

This book will demonstrate how Chicano students organized and sustained their own grassroots movement from 1968 to 1970. Examining the diverse perspectives and real-life situations of students from a different time, background, and place offers a better glimpse into their reality and experiences at school. This work will further underscore how Chicano students played a central role in the struggle for justice, educational reform, and equal opportunity in South Texas. Activists

Map of Texas showing the location of the four school walkout cases described in this book: San Antonio, Crystal City, Kingsville, and Edcouch-Elsa.

operated on the local, grassroots level and openly expressed their dissatisfaction with differential treatment by certain school educators, segregation of schools, lack of curriculum acknowledging the contributions of people of Mexican origin, inadequate counseling and academic support, and low academic achievement among students of Mexican descent. To seek redress for these injustices at their schools, Chicano students employed nonviolent, direct action that culminated in a boycott of classes, or "walkout," a common form of protest in the 1960s. Walkouts occurred throughout the nation during the Civil Rights Movement and have been recognized as a standard manifestation of grievance and protest in African American as well as Latino movements in US history. Unlike other student protests of this era, Chicano school walkouts occurred in economically poor communities with a predominantly ethnic Mexican population. Most students attending the schools were either the children of Mexican immigrants or immigrants themselves. They often used ethnic nationalism and nonviolent, direct-action protest as the central vehicle to achieve self-determination and educational reform while engaging in the gender and ethnic identity politics of the times.

As a study of the Chicano student movement in Texas, *"We Want Better Education!"* considers these student protests as one mass movement while examining the demonstrations as individual case studies by attempting to reconstruct the major events of each walkout in chronological order: West Side San Antonio (April 1968), Edcouch-Elsa (November 1968), Kingsville (1969), and Crystal City (1969–70). Each case study underscores the major historical influences and development of Mexican American student insurgency.[3] Adolescents between the ages of fourteen and eighteen were among the most active and important actors in their own protest movement. This work focuses on ordinary, working-class Chicano students whose activism reshaped the course of their lives as they sought to participate in the decision-making process of their local school system. Moreover, this book contends that the Chicano student movement in South Texas was not an isolated outburst of an irrational form of insurgency, but part of an ongoing historical process of social and political transformation of the overall Civil Rights and Chicano Movements. As young actors in this process, student protesters purposely defied and challenged the existing power structure or educational system at their school in order to gain inclusion within it. This book reveals the collective methods and strategies of Chicano student activists who attempted to engage in the political process by which power could be attained within the school system.

A better understanding of this student movement will require seeking answers to the following main questions: What were the inequities and circumstances in and out of school that motivated Chicano students in South Texas to protest? What educational issues did Chicano students endorse by formulating their own demands and grievances against their school system? What were the common experiences that politicized students to promote their own movement for public school reform? How did the student protests lead to a grassroots, region-wide movement? Did Chicanos gain political control of the public schools after the walkouts? Is it significant that the protests involved Mexican Americans? What is the walkouts' larger significance in Mexican American history and in US history? The importance of ethnic identity, language, and culture raises additional questions that are just as relevant in our understanding of the movement. To answer such questions, we must explore the societal and political forces of the 1960s. These include the conditions of the schools, the common educational experiences of students of Mexican origin, the catalyst of radical student activity, and the impact of Chicano student insurgency on society.

Chicano students sought political clout by negotiating collectively with school officials before and during the walkouts for genuine respect and

4   INTRODUCTION

nondiscriminatory treatment in the decision-making policies that impacted their education. They specifically demanded that their school system better accommodate the educational needs of ethnic Mexican students. School-related issues became an important element of the students' political and cultural struggle to gain a better-quality education and equal treatment. Thus, *"We Want Better Education!"* underscores the nature of Chicano student educational experiences in each school and describes the student protesters' collective behavior, motives, and strategies.[4] This book further reveals the public interactions between school administrators and students while underscoring certain community members' and educators' viewpoints and reactions to the protests. Chicano student activism emerged as a mass movement typical of the 1960s that merits the same attention and recognition as the historic protests of the larger US Civil Rights Movement.

Although scholarly works mention the occurrence of walkouts in Texas as part of civil rights history, most discuss the protests in general without focusing on any particular event. Most references to the walkouts appear in books and articles that discuss community-based political events associated with the larger Chicano Movement, the acceptance of Chicano cultural nationalism, the adoption of the militant ethos known as chicanismo, and the rejection of the liberal agenda.[5]

Historian Ignacio M. García, author of *Chicanismo: The Forging of a Militant Ethos among Mexican Americans* (1997), explores Chicano political identity and activism during the Chicano Movement. Interestingly, he is a former student of Lanier High School in San Antonio's West Side, the first reported site of the Chicano student movement in Texas. García uses the term "militant ethos" to refer to a body of ideas, strategies, tactics, and rationalizations used in response to external challenges. His main argument is that the development of the Mexican American political ethos or consciousness became the impetus for social upheaval during the Chicano Movement. Although García's work does not specifically discuss the Chicano student movement in South Texas, he analyzes the process by which the Mexican American community in the Southwest, including students, constructed a political ethos that identified them as a distinct ethnic minority group. By adopting the political ideology known as chicanismo, Chicano Movement activists chose to identify with certain symbols, events, rhetoric, and other forms of resistance that gave value to the term "Chicano."[6] This term came to identify young Mexican Americans who favored a more direct and aggressive approach to civil rights and sought to combat racism, discrimination, poverty, segregation, and powerlessness. The ideology of chicanismo also sparked a new sense of identity through the belief that one should be proud to be "brown" or a person of color, and it taught Chicanos to refrain from utilizing Eurocentric terms of racial classification such as "Hispanic" or "Latino." Chicanos developed this political ethos in response to self-victimization and

INTRODUCTION ～ 5

limitations on empowerment imposed by Anglo-Americans who promoted bigotry.[7] Other circumstances shaping the influence of this ethos included disputes against ethnic-group solidarity and strategies to gain the attention of the race-conscious American mainstream.

García notes that Chicano Movement participants from different walks of life sought to express pride in their ethnic Mexican ancestry, culture, and ethnic heritage vis-à-vis direct-action protest. The decline of this movement in the late 1970s marked a new era in which these reformers started to establish their own community organizations and programs that did not emphasize chicanismo, and by the 1980s they began publicly referring to themselves as Hispanic or Latino. García's work provides background details concerning student involvement in the Chicano Movement, but it underscores the development and expression of chicanismo exclusively rather than Chicano student-led protests. Nevertheless, his work offers a comparative framework for analyzing the significance of Chicano activism in the South Texas community of Robstown.

"We Want Better Education!" offers a much more detailed analysis and historical coverage by fully examining the emergence of movement politics and its related school reform efforts in key sites throughout South Texas. It also promises to strike the best balance of any book in analyzing specific walkouts while also expanding its review across a part of Texas where the community of Mexican origin has been, and continues to be, the largest minority population.

Conceptualization

Social movements throughout history have significantly changed the societies in which they occurred on the local, national, or even global scale. Some movements have been revolutionary in their aims, some have advocated reforms to the existing system, and others have worked to oppose changes in society. The student walkouts evolved from the development of a localized social movement and conformed to the political processes and poor people's movement of the time. Therefore, *"We Want Better Education!"* analyzes Chicano student activism within the context of a student-led social movement. This book also examines the intricacies of student activism while exploring the key factors and dynamics central to the evolution of 1960s social protest movement activity. Key elements that shaped the character and course of the social movement are evident in the 1960s student insurgency in South Texas. These elements included the rise and decline of the social movement; grassroots organizing; community empowerment; behaviors and expressions that enhanced movement solidarity; the emergence of movement-bred identities; and the communication of movement ideas, values, and goals. The so-called movement culture of Chicano students involved shared values, behaviors, language, and ideology that was shaped from their experience of being political and taking direct action by organizing school walkouts or boycotts. The tangible, identifiable markers of the movement culture included slang, ritualized behaviors, symbols, remembrances of major movement events, movement-identified wording on protest picket signs, and identification with ethnic Mexican tradition.[8] The emergence of such elements indicates how student activists pursued power through collective action.

The analytical framework of this book acknowledges unequal power relationships between people agitating for empowerment in the educational system and officials inside the system who controlled it. Chicano students represented an aggrieved population whose collective needs and interests were not being satisfied. Upon formulating grievances addressing such needs and interests, student activists in the movement were able to form or join viable organizations, mobilize resources, and attract supportive followings. The source of inequality differentiates the elite from the excluded group, or those seeking to influence and add input to the decision-making process. Chicano students and the parents who supported them sought political power and recognition of their educational needs in the school system. Thus, these students sought to overcome their marginalized status in the school system and became agents of their own social movement as part of an explosion of protests and demonstrations during the ongoing Civil Rights and Anti–Vietnam War Movements.

A social movement is difficult to define in precise terms, but it is not a political party, popular clique, or interest group, nor is it a fleeting mass fad or trend that lacks clearly identifiable goals. A truly viable movement strives to promote an organized yet informal network of committed activists oriented toward a desirable goal. This goal can involve a specific policy change or be more broadly focused on cultural change. The main objective of the Chicano student movement of South Texas encompassed both. It opposed school policies and practices that segregated students of Mexican origin or prevented them from pursing college preparatory coursework, and it advocated for ethnic Mexican cultural awareness and bilingual education as part of the school system's curriculum. By forming a smaller, localized movement, Chicano students had a better chance of achieving their goals, although assessing how successful they were remains difficult to this day. Nevertheless, their social movement was a major force across South Texas by the late 1960s. Understanding how social movements form, develop, solidify, and decline helps us understand the society and political climate, as well as the major changes and trends that play out during such movements.

Three key factors lead to the emergence of a social movement. These include the expansion of political opportunities, the rise of collective consciousness (cognitive liberation), and resource mobilization.[9] Political opportunity refers to the institutional context and "the degree of openness of a political system to the social and political goals, and tactics of social movements."[10] The rise of collective consciousness involves the transformation of both the consciousness and behavior of a large group that is socially marginalized and politically powerless. Moreover, this group acknowledges its situation as unjust or intolerable and therefore desires change through collective action.[11] Both material and nonmaterial resources (moral commitment, trust, friendship, knowledge, and skills) can be mobilized in the pursuit of movement goals.[12] Exploring these dynamics of a social movement will enhance our understanding of the ways Chicano student activists formed their own movement in South Texas. This movement involved a purposeful, organized group of students who strived toward the common goal of improving the quality of education and the treatment of ethnic Mexican students in the public school system.

"We Want Better Education!" highlights three stages of social movements. These include the emergence of the movement and the formulation of goals and activist identities, the formation of an organization that mobilizes and unites activists, and the decline of the movement when its activities decrease.[13] This book attempts to trace the three movement stages that are evident from the first to the last major student walkouts in South Texas, demonstrating that the student movement became self-directed by grassroots or community-based, school-issue politics. This movement significantly influenced the restructuring of the school system's decision-making to address the educational needs of ethnic Mexican students, thus altering the electoral process and hiring practices of the public schools in South Texas where the protests occurred. Examining the development of Chicano student activism as a social movement serves to substantiate the significance of the case studies in this work.

Various scholars have studied the development of the 1960s Chicano Movement in one locality or state, and the main narrative of Chicano student walkouts has been broadly examined in news articles and the media as well as in textbooks. Yet scholarly knowledge of the school walkouts of the 1960s is fragmentary and disconnected. While most people know a fair amount about a few significant areas (Los Angeles, Denver, Houston, and yes, Crystal City), they know very little about the whole. Scholarly literature still lacks a more national, comprehensive understanding of what transpired, how it was connected, and why it is an important part of the Chicano history, educational history, Texas history, and US history of the 1960s. Although *"We Want Better Education!"* is a regional study, it is the first attempt to promote such an understanding of how Chicano student activists publicized their cause to the region and nation by comparing the West Side San Antonio, Kingsville, Edcouch-Elsa, and Crystal

8 ～ INTRODUCTION

City school walkouts. Chicano youth activists really did make a difference in transforming their communities and the institutions that served them by participating in the student movement at their schools to express their longing for educational reform. Far from homogeneous, Chicano student walkouts varied by region and phase, as well as by the peculiarities of community involvement or resistance. The major contribution of this work is to expand the mantle of agency to a new group of historical actors in US society—the youth. And minority youth, indeed. This age group has traditionally been excluded from independent action, and even historians have rarely identified youth as agents of meaningful social and political reform.

American historians, for example, have focused on pamphlets, taverns, mobs, and patriot statesmen as primary agents for promoting independence in the American Revolution, but there were no teenage Thomas Paines, John Hancocks, Thomas Jeffersons, or Samuel Adamses in 1776. However, a few lesser-known teen patriots became revolutionary heroes, such as sixteen-year-old Sybil Ludington, who rode forty miles by herself on horseback to warn American colonists of the impending arrival of British troops at Danbury, Connecticut, on April 26, 1777.[14] Another teen patriot, sixteen-year-old Laodicea "Dicey" Langston, willingly crossed the icy waters of the Enoree River in South Carolina to warn her brother James's military camp of enemy troop movements.[15] Thus, Ludington's and Langston's courageous actions marked the start of a new era in the emerging nation's history; the Revolution gave legitimacy to women who found themselves stepping out of familiar prescribed roles. Like Ludington and Langston, Chicano youth were seeking to transcend their commonly prescribed stereotyped destinies as indolent, docile, low-skilled members of US society. However, Luis Alvarez and Marc Simon Rodríguez are among the few historians who have produced major works examining the social, political, and cultural influences on the lives of American youth from diverse backgrounds during the mid- to late twentieth century.[16] As *We Want Better Education!* will demonstrate, teenagers, both young men and women, became the most determined and aspiring participants seeking better-quality education, educational equity, and access to college and professional career pathways in their local communities. Furthermore, this book attempts to fill the gaps in the historical literature and combines the findings and interpretations of various relevant works to construct a new history of the Chicano student movement in four South Texas communities. The goal is not to sensationalize this protest movement but to reconstruct as fully as possible the experiences of those it touched, and the social and political reality in which it occurred. Thus, *We Want Better Education!* attempts to provide the most comprehensive analysis of the walkouts to date.

Methodology: Archival and Documentary Sources

In-depth documentation for this book comes from archival records pertaining to the major historical events of the South Texas student walkouts. The documents informed me about the important actors, occurrences, and developments of each protest. Archival records that provided essential data for this study include the José Angel Gutiérrez Papers, 1954–1990, in the Nettie Lee Benson Latin American Collection at the University of Texas at Austin; the Hector P. García Papers at Texas A&M University–Corpus Christi, the *San Antonio Express-News* photograph collection at the Institute of Texan Cultures in San Antonio, and the José Angel Gutiérrez Papers, 1959–1991, at the University of Texas at San Antonio. I completed additional archival research in the South Texas Archives at Texas A&M University–Kingsville, at the Kleburg Public Library in Kingsville, and the Crystal City Public Library. The Oral History Collection of the Mexican American Project, in the Texas Collection and University Archives at Baylor University in Waco, Texas, offered me new and insightful data as well. This university archival collection contains the oral memoirs of people who recall the major events of the Crystal City school protest, including José Angel Gutiérrez, former school superintendent R. C. Tate, ex-schoolteacher Joyce Langenegger, and former teacher's aide Rebecca Pérez. These memoirs provided some important details for this book since the interviews were conducted in the early 1970s. Special acknowledgment goes to former Edcouch-Elsa High School principal Robert Rodríguez and his library staff for allowing me to view a few of the school's old yearbooks. Additional sources of insightful information include school district records, telegrams, written material from student activists, city and county records, newspaper accounts, census data, and federal court documents. These research findings underscore the major social, political, and economic changes throughout South Texas from the late 1960s to early 1970s. I also gained access to items from the personal collections of three former activists, including Nelda Villareal Treviño, a participant in the Edcouch-Elsa walkout; Richard Herrera, a walkout participant at Edgewood High School in San Antonio; and Homer D. García, a graduate of Lanier High School in San Antonio.

Methodology: Oral Interviews

Collective experiences and community memory were especially important for this research, which aimed to recover firsthand knowledge from those familiar with the Chicano student movement in South Texas. Lynn Abrams, in her book *Oral History Theory*, refers to memory as a key source of oral history practice that involves "a process of remembering: the calling up of images, stories, experiences and emotions from our past life, ordering them, placing them within a narrative or story and then telling them in a way that is shaped at least in part by our social and cultural context." She further notes that the use of memory is an "active process of reconstruction whereby traces of the past are placed in conjunction with one another to tell a story... not just about the individual; it is also about the community, the collective."[17] The stories of respondents further represent examples of memory narratives based on their personal recollections of experiences that significantly impacted their lives. They shared their own stories by piecing together their memories and imparted their knowledge of how they saw various events transpire over time while being influenced by the context or environment in which they were retrieving their memories.[18] This book underscores the respondents' experiences at school and in their communities that shaped how they remembered the events of the student movement. Thus, a significant part of this book's analysis relies on primary source data from interviews in order to help us understand the ways in which people remember and the ways in which they relate their memories.

Much appreciation goes to the numerous former students, teachers, school officials, community members, and Chicano Movement activists who took time out of their busy schedules to conduct personal interviews. Many people were instrumental in reconstructing this history by consenting to interviews or finding interview recordings throughout this research. Over forty former walkout participants and longtime community members shared their recollections, perspectives, and opinions about their role in the protests. These in-depth interviews help us visualize how the student movement transpired and provide a better understanding of the historical significance of the student-led protests as they related to the Chicano Movement and larger Civil Rights Movement. *We Want Better Education!* further examines each informant's feedback, recollections of protest activity, or perceptions of school faculty and administrators' performance in educating Mexican American students. By privileging oral history interviews with key student activists, this work underscores their experiences, their reasons for risking their standing at the schools, and how the local walkout affected them. Such information provides lesser-known details of the protests not mentioned in archival records.

Unknown to me at the time, I began to conceive the overall framework for this book when I was a graduate student in history at the University of Texas at El Paso. Shortly after beginning my research, I discovered a reference to the student strikes in South Texas in Armando Rendon's *Chicano Manifesto*. My parents helped me research and identify a lot of newspaper coverage highlighting the activism of key walkout participants in the late 1960s, which eventually convinced me to undertake a comprehensive study and write this book. One case study in particular that attracted much attention was the walkout at Edcouch-Elsa High School, approximately twenty miles from my hometown of McAllen, Texas.

INTRODUCTION ⟿ 11

Locating former student activists and other prospective interviewees at the start of this research was challenging because I was born after the 1960s, started conducting research with very limited funds, and did not know anyone living in the communities where the protests occurred. After much trial and error during the initial stage of the research, I almost decided to quit and pursue a new topic, but then my mother showed me two newspaper articles commemorating the thirtieth anniversary of the Edcouch-Elsa High School walkout in December 1998.[19] As I read the accounts of a few former students and community members in both articles, two names caught my attention: R. P. "Bob" Sánchez, attorney-at-law in McAllen, and Maricela Rodríguez Lozano, an Elsa native and a school district secretary at the time.[20] These articles featured the commentary of a few former students and community leaders and gave valuable clues that helped confirm the identity of two people whose landline phone numbers were listed in the phone book. Sánchez, the civil rights attorney who provided legal counsel to Edcouch-Elsa students during their protest, continued to practice law in his office in McAllen. The Edcouch-Elsa School District office put me in touch with Lozano. Sánchez was the first interviewee of this book, and then I interviewed Maricela Lozano, who was one of the youngest participants in the Edcouch-Elsa walkout as an eighth grader.

Lozano was instrumental in verifying the whereabouts of one of the former walkout leaders, Freddy Sáenz, who offered information on two other former student protesters, Mirtala Villarreal and her younger sister, Nelda Villarreal Treviño. Thus, these initial meetings had a "snowball effect" because the early interviewees led to other potential participants and community members in Edcouch-Elsa and in the other locations. I would also like to express special thanks to Francisco "Frank" Guajardo, founder and executive director of the Llano Grande Center for Research and Development at Edcouch-Elsa High School, for granting access to other essential primary sources and videotape recordings containing documentaries of interviews with a few former students who participated in the Edcouch-Elsa walkout. Nelda Villarreal Treviño first informed me of Guajardo's project with his students, involving oral history documentaries with various informants in Edcouch-Elsa in 1999. Early informants and archival documentation at the Llano Grande Center for Research and Development helped locate other former students and community members from Edcouch-Elsa in 2000 and 2001.

This scope of this research began to expand outside Edcouch-Elsa in the fall of 2004 after I contacted Annette Guerrero Lehman, a former student and nonparticipant observer of the 1969 Crystal City High School walkout, at the Crystal City Public Library. After an impromptu interview with her in the library, Lehman identified a few local walkout participants, including Diana Palacios and

Severita Lara. Both were willing to take time from their busy schedules for interviews. However, this work relies on archival and oral history records, as well as published works on the Crystal City walkout, one of the most popular case studies of the Chicano Movement. Most Crystal City walkout participants and key organizers such as José Angel Gutiérrez no longer live in the community.

This book also includes research data based on the protest movement in Kingsville, Texas. Longtime community members who contributed to this study in Kingsville include Antonio Bill, a former student activist at Texas A&I University (now Texas A&M University–Kingsville); Ward Albro, professor emeritus of history at Texas A&I; former Kingsville school administrator Raúl G. Garza; community member Mario Salazar; and one elderly person in Kingsville who requested anonymity. Former activists and organizers of the Mexican American Youth Organization (MAYO) who were available for interviews included Carlos Guerra, Alberto Luera, Mario Compean, and Viviana Santiago Cavada. Juan Rocha Jr., former attorney of the Mexican American Legal Defense and Educational Fund (MALDEF), founded in San Antonio in 1968, also agreed to meet for an interview to discuss the role of MALDEF and the student movement in Kingsville. I found the names of most former students and longtime community activists in archival records and looked up their landline phone numbers in a telephone directory. I completed some interviews by phone because of distance and my limited travel funds.

Former students contributed significantly to this work after it initially took shape, adding new data and suggestions for revision. In 2010, former Edcouch-Elsa student Felix Rodríguez agreed to participate in this research. Although he was not a participant in the Edcouch-Elsa school walkout, Rodríguez offered an alternative view of the protest as a former student who favored a more diplomatic approach during negotiations with school officials to meet student demands for educational reform. In February 2015, former Kingsville student activist Faustino Erebia responded to a newspaper ad in the *Kingsville-Bishop Record News* requesting information on the local student movement. His commentary on the Gillett Junior High School walkout in Kingsville was insightful and detailed, including his memories of the local MAYO activities. Former Kingsville student Cecilia Cortez also shared her recollections of the local walkout and was able to provide a few significant details on the student movement in Kingsville.

Patricia Portales, Mario Longoria, and Patricia Muñoz Jacobs assisted in contacting former students at Edgewood and Lanier High Schools in San Antonio. Portales, professor of English at San Antonio College, contacted San Antonio community activist Mario Longoria. Longoria was instrumental in offering a list of phone numbers of a few former students from Edgewood High School, including Richard Herrera, who was eager and proud to share his story. Herrera firmly believes that historians need to "get the story out" about the Edgewood walkout. When I contacted Herrera, he agreed to invite ten other former students, including his wife and high school sweetheart Diana Briseño, for a group interview in July 2013. This research includes data from follow-up interviews with Edgewood activists Richard and Diana Herrera, and Rebecca Campos Ramírez and Rosendo Gutiérrez in July 2016. Longoria also provided the whereabouts of key activists from Lanier High School in San Antonio, including Edgar Lozano and Homer D. García, 1968 class reunion organizer Patricia Muñoz Jacobs, and female classmates Rosie Peña and Irene Yañez.

Special thanks go to all who consented to interviews and provided valuable insights and perspectives on the walkouts. These informants' insights offered a better understanding of the walkout's major events and provided vital information about each interviewee's personal experience. Hearing their passionate, articulate, and emotional stories was truly inspirational, as was learning about the dissenting opinions of community members who did not support the student movement. Conversations with former students and community activists helped put together some of the missing pieces of this narrative by illuminating their interests, beliefs, and understandings related to their experiences. By focusing on individual lives and memories, these oral histories acknowledge the crucial interactive relationship between the informants' school communities, their perceptions and experiences, and social contexts and events. Thus, these oral histories, along with other primary and secondary sources, allow for a more in-depth assessment and unique glimpse into the development of the student movement.

This research analyzes information from walkout participants and community activists who were willing to contribute to this study. The intent was not to write a definitive oral history narrative based on the daily accounts of every walkout participant across South Texas, but rather to underscore their common experiences and collective actions during the student movement. Therefore, I used qualitative interviews as a methodological and research tool that allowed me to ask questions on specific topics or issues while the interviewees responded based on their recollections of events at their school. The structure of the interviews was informal and laid back, conversational at times, and based on a detailed list of questions. The primary topics of discussion included the interviewees' life experiences in the community of their school, and their personal involvement with or impressions of the protests. Each interviewee had time to give a complete response before I moved on to the next question, and there was flexibility in the framing and asking of each question. The interviews usually lasted between one and two hours and allowed me to probe for answers to questions concerning the extent of the person's participation or recollections of the student movement, and to pursue a line of discussion opened up by the interviewee.

The process of engaging people with memories of their lives, especially after so much time had passed since the 1960s, required patience, careful listening, adaptability, and sensitivity. By privileging oral history interviews with participants, *"We Want Better Education!"* assesses their experiences to explain how the walkouts impacted them and their local school communities. Each interviewee could answer on his or her own terms rather than following a set structure, though I did facilitate some structure for comparison across informants by covering the same topics, even in some instances using the same questions. For example, to understand the motivations for students choosing to walk out of school, I needed to ask a few questions about the interviewee's knowledge of the conditions at his or her school and about the feedback of administrators reacting to Chicano student demands for reform. I asked these questions of all walkout participants in the same general format.

Interviewees could explain their ideas, perspectives, interpretations, and meanings in their own words and discuss any relevant issues that emerged throughout the research. Each interview was respectful and cordial, and the interviewees were not pressed for responses. The walkouts were very real, personal, and memorable for all interviewees because they happened during their adolescence. Even though I introduced myself as the principal investigator and academic researcher, I was seeking to learn from them rather than educate them. They shared their unique life experiences and memories. Thus, one major goal of this work was to preserve and show appreciation for such firsthand knowledge and documentation.

This research seeks to fill a gap in the scholarly assessment of the student movement, and this proved challenging at times. A few key student activists were difficult to locate because they had moved away from their hometowns or chose not to communicate with their fellow classmates after high school. Certain people refused to speak about their school experiences because they conjured up unpleasant memories or dissatisfaction. Some who agreed to speak preferred not to discuss controversial topics about the walkouts, and others had passed away during the past several years. Because of the lapse of time, most informants were unable to remember every single detail of the student movement, and their memories of certain events while they attended high school in the 1960s remained hazy or incomplete. The most common details they forgot or could not confirm included exact dates of events, names of certain school educators and politicians, and names of a few classmates. Despite such lapses of memory, the informants did not hesitate to remember and articulate what was important to them concerning the student movement's significance in history. Nonetheless, this work attempts to reconstruct a story involving collective action and persistence in the school communities that I examined, and to reveal how the informants recalled

INTRODUCTION ～ 15

the key events and experiences of the past. I recorded most of the interviews, depending on the consent of each person, but some recordings and field note-books were lost or misplaced over the years. Only a few handwritten documents and personal collections exist on the walkouts. Therefore, no one can possibly know all the precise details of the student movement from start to finish.

"We Want Better Education!" intends to bring greater attention to the Chicano student movement in South Texas as part of the larger struggle for public school reform and cultural recognition in US history. It offers a means by which readers can transport themselves into someone else's reality while underscoring the historical background of the school communities where the walkouts occurred in West Side San Antonio, Edcouch-Elsa, Kingsville, and Crystal City. Such data allow readers to discover how Mexican American students forged their own movement for educational equity and Mexican cultural awareness in South Texas. No work of history is ever complete or beyond argument, and for that reason, historiographic engagement is a necessary part of this book's analytical framework and enables a clearer understanding of how this topic has been examined over time. What have scholars said about the history of Mexican American education or the role of Chicano students during the student movement of the 1960s? What are the key concepts and interpretations of major studies in Chicano education? Previous scholars' works have examined the historical significance of Mexican American education and Chicano student activism in Texas, providing a more analytical discussion of these subjects and their major interpretations.

The Chicano Struggle for Better Education and Its Relevant Issues

Within the historiographic narrative of Mexican American education in Texas, the role of school walkouts has been briefly mentioned, but there has not been a comprehensive study. Scholars have argued that the Chicano struggle for better education during the twentieth century involved grassroots community organizing, ethnic leadership, political consciousness raising, and student-led mobilizations for empowerment.[21] Major works on the Chicano Movement further explore the formation of a new social identity, the changing perceptions of ethnicity, and the role of student activism as part of the movement. Historian Guadalupe San Miguel, for example, has written at length on educational policy making, and the history of Mexican American political activism in education as part of the overall Civil Rights Movement, but he focuses mainly on Chicano activism in Houston in *Brown, Not White: School Integration and the Chicano Movement in Houston* (2001). Additional works by San Miguel, Carlos Kevin Blanton, and other Chicano education scholars help explore the major concepts relevant to this book. These concepts include student activism,

16 ∾ INTRODUCTION

bilingual-bicultural schooling, English-only or subtractive Americanization, school segregation, and the transition from the community to district school system in Texas. Historiographic engagement further assesses the significance of ethnic Mexican students' educational experiences and activism as an essential part of understanding both educational neglect and the community struggle for better-quality education.

Only a few works fully explore the Chicano struggle for better education during the 1960s and 1970s in Texas and in a few other regions throughout the US Southwest.[22] Scholars generally agree that Chicano student activism of this time was a product of the larger forces of the 1960s, and an integral part of the Chicano Movement. These works on Chicano student activism also explore significant influences and conditions affecting Chicano youth. Education scholar Rubén Donato confirms that before and during the civil rights era, students of Mexican origin were often tracked into vocational education programs and low-level curricula. Vocational training became the norm for most Mexican American schoolchildren, who were denied access to quality schooling based on race. This "dual system of education" meant that "working-class and minority youth were given the skills necessary for the lower echelons of the labor market while white middle-class youth received an academic education that coincided with the social and cultural hegemony they already possessed."[23] Consequently, most Mexican Americans were left on the fringes of American society as menial laborers prior to the Civil Rights and Chicano Movements.

Chicano studies scholar Gilbert G. González suggests that restrictions on speaking Spanish in school, widespread across the US Southwest in that era, reveal how US public school officials identified "the Spanish language and Mexican culture as contradictory to educational success."[24] He further identifies three rationales for the segregation of ethnic Mexican schoolchildren in the history of the United States. First, school administrators and faculty deemed it necessary to segregate white and ethnic Mexican students because of their cultural differences, including their modes of learning. Second, Mexican American students scored lower on IQ tests than white children, and thus it was believed that white students should attend separate schools to learn at a more accelerated pace. Third, school officials believed it was "socially inevitable" for Spanish-surnamed children to pursue the same occupations in the lowest echelons of society as their parents: farm work and domestic servitude.[25]

Most educators and school administrators in San Antonio's West Side, Edcouch-Elsa, Kingsville, and Crystal City, as elsewhere in the nation, often advised Mexican American students to engage in the same type of work as their parents, which normally was migrant farm labor. According to Donato, "Mexican migrant children in the Southwest were not being served equally to whites

INTRODUCTION ~ 17

because of indifference, because local economies depended on their labor, and because they were ethnically distinct."[26] González also contends that the "educational experience of migratory children represented the social aspect of the economic system."[27] The late Thomas P. Carter, one of the foremost scholar-activists in the field of Mexican American education, concludes that the school system often mirrored the community it served according to the demands of the local socioeconomic and labor systems: "If what is needed is a docile, low-skilled worker, the school provides individuals with these characteristics ... in rural areas where the population is composed of isolated and parochial groups of Mexican Americans, youngters are hampered by not being aware of the greater rewards and higher status afforded their ethnic group outside the immediate area; they tend to judge their future on the basis of the restricted local model."[28] Such circumstances motivated Chicano student activists to organize their own movement to promote educational reform and ethnic Mexican cultural awareness as part of El Movimiento or the Chicano Movement.

Most scholars examining the participation of students during the movement focus their attention on the Mexican American community in large urban areas such as Houston, Phoenix, San Diego, or Los Angeles. This book instead examines the common educational experiences and social protest activity of ethnic Mexican students in rural or low-income areas of South Texas during the 1960s, including what was then the predominantly segregated Mexican American community of San Antonio's West Side. It further highlights the role of the Chicano student activist group MAYO and points to the role this movement played in the founding of La Raza Unida, a political party. Engaging with the interpretations of other secondary studies opens a more analytical discussion that will help elucidate the key issues and concepts relevant to this book. Chapter 3 briefly discusses the major literary works on Chicano student activism in Los Angeles, California, where thousands of Chicano students walked out of five East Side high schools in March 1968. A clearer overview of the Mexican American educational experience can be achieved because of this narrower geographic concentration.

Most scholarly works tend to regard 1960s Chicano student activism as a peripheral aspect of the larger historical narrative, except for Darius Echeverría's *Aztlán Arizona: Mexican American Educational Empowerment, 1968–1978* (2014). This excellent book expands the current literature by analyzing the "Arizonan-Mexican" educational experience and the Chicano Movement in Arizona. As the first full-length text on the subject, Echeverría's work connects Arizona to the national Chicano Movement by arguing that "the majority of Mexican Americans in Arizona endured long-standing educational discrimination similar to ethnic Mexicans across the nation" and "were equally active in combating such discrimination as their Chicano counterparts" in Texas and California.[29]

Echeverría examines student-oriented political movements during the Chicano Movement at Tucson High School, Phoenix Union High School, the University of Arizona, Arizona State University, and surrounding communities. Underscoring the significance and unity of Arizona's student movement, he argues, "I posit that Arizonans, notably of Mexican descent, coalesced around regional interests, especially educational concerns."[30] However, it is never apparent how regional interests in Arizona differed from those in other southwestern states. Nevertheless, *Aztlán Arizona* largely succeeds in revealing how Mexican American community activism and student movements in general have shaped current educational debates. Scholars examining the Chicano educational experience and student movement in Texas in the twentieth century discuss these types of debates as well.

Relevant Studies on Mexican American Activism in Education in Texas

Guadalupe San Miguel investigates the Chicano educational experience, and how the Mexican American community promoted educational reform in Texas throughout the twentieth century. His first major work on Mexican American education is *"Let All of Them Take Heed": Mexican Americans and the Campaign for Educational Equality in Texas, 1910–1981* (1987). This is the first full-length text on the subject to demonstrate that the pre-1960s generation of Mexican American community activists promoted school integration and fought educational inequality through the organizing efforts of the League of United Latin American Citizens (LULAC), the American GI Forum, and the Mexican American Legal Defense and Educational Fund. He also offers a comprehensive analysis of the historical origins of inequality and discrimination among Mexican Americans in Texas who advocated for public school reform, discussing the socioeconomic factors affecting ethnic Mexicans, examining how law and policy enabled educational inequity, and underscoring their strategies and aspirations in reaching their goals.

San Miguel often depicts Chicano schoolchildren as victims of racial discrimination and prejudice in the educational system by describing what he calls a "victim-oppressor" relationship. He argues that Anglo school officials were responsible for sanctioning school segregation based on educational grounds such as English-language proficiency, and for reproducing the patrón-peón or dominant-subordinate system between the white and Mexican communities in Texas. Segregated school districts throughout Texas increased substantially because of "popular demands, legal mandates, increasing financial ability, and a greater acceptance of the idea of common schooling by local and state political leaders."[31] The so-called Mexican Schools often consisted of overcrowded, dilapidated buildings with inadequate resources and incompetent teachers who were paid less, including some who lacked the proper credentials, especially compared to schools for white students, as noted in the works of Rubén Donato, Gilbert G. González, and Guadalupe San Miguel. Although the federal court case *Plessy v. Ferguson* legally sanctioned separate but equal facilities for whites and African Americans in 1896, segregated schools for nonwhite schoolchildren were never equal, including those for Mexican Americans. Chicano activist-scholar José Angel Gutiérrez commented on this type of unequal condition in his autobiography: "The combination of white administrative and instructional personnel, English only, an Anglo-centered curriculum, and a preferential social setting dominated by Anglos for Anglos in the public schools made for systematic discrimination and exclusion of Chicanos."[32] Additional factors justifying the need for school segregation included the racial ideology of white supremacy as well as intelligence or IQ testing to prepare ethnic Mexican students for manual labor jobs or vocational work in order to maintain the economic and political dominance of the white community elite.

In his work examining Chicano activism in Houston, San Miguel maintains that "for [Anglo] public school officials, the schools became instruments of social control aimed at reproducing the existing social class structure and dominant-subordinate relations found between Anglos and Mexicans in the larger society."[33] He uses the term "subtraction" to indicate that the public school system did not allow the use of the Spanish language or support the learning of Mexican heritage and history. Thus, Mexican American students throughout the US Southwest were poorly served by the school systems that had traditionally accommodated white, middle-class, college-bound students before and during the 1960s. As this book will reveal, the unequal allocation of resources, Americanization policies involving the cultural and linguistic assimilation of students of Mexican origin, and inadequate school funding underscored the fact that Mexican American students were racialized as nonwhite and viewed as subordinate to their European American classmates.

One of San Miguel's assessments in *Brown, Not White* identifies the historical origins of grassroots ethnic leadership that promoted Chicano control of the city's schools, and the racial classification of Mexican Americans as a distinct minority group, or rather their recognition as "brown, not white," which he indicates was a popular protest slogan during the 1970 Houston school boycott. This protest gained momentum from resistance toward the school district's classification of Mexican Americans as "white" to initiate the desegregation of African American schools. Local Chicano activists gained much political clout thanks to their increased participation in the city's civic and social affairs and their involvement in ethnic-based organizations by the early 1970s. Although San Miguel's book does not examine the larger student movement outside Houston, he reveals how both students and adult community members played key roles in a new development reflecting "a shift in the [Houston] community's identity from one based on the politics, culture, and social change strategies of the Mexican American Generation [1930–60] to one based primarily on those of the Chicano Generation."[34] Therefore, San Miguel's work offers an examination of an educational reform movement initiated by Chicanos in a major urban site that was part of the overall Chicano Movement in Texas.

In his 2013 work, *Chicana/o Struggles for Education: Activism in the Community*, San Miguel assesses the Mexican American experience in the twenty-first century by underscoring the effects and aftermath of the Chicano Movement on public education in the Southwest. He seeks to identify the impact of Chicano activism in overcoming adverse conditions such as de facto segregation and low academic achievement among Mexican American students at all levels of education. The Mexican American educational reform agenda since the 1960s has "both extended and intensified the historic struggle for education that earlier activists had initiated."[35] San Miguel maintains that this struggle evolved beyond the desegregation efforts of the early twentieth century, and toward the three major activist strategies of "contestation, advocacy and alternative forms of education."[36] These activists included a community-wide coalition of "parents, students, community activists, civil rights leaders, educators, scholars, and a host of others who dared to speak up on behalf of improved schooling."[37] He also notes that the educational struggle was broader than previously documented, as demonstrated by various activists' attempts to maintain culture and language, as well as a grassroots movement. Various social, political, cultural, and economic factors after the 1960s led to gradual changes in the school setting. This was a transitional period, he points out, when "activism did not die down" but "ebbed and flowed over decades" and "continues to this day."[38] Such circumstances meant that the Mexican American community's search for quality education, and the recognition of cultural and linguistic diversity, occurred outside the public school system.

San Miguel further discusses the significance of students' academic achievement, cultural heritage, and the political autonomy of the larger school community to argue in favor of the activists' agenda for the Chicano Movement. While he believes the movement did not fulfill all its goals because of internal strife and limitations, he does acknowledge that "the struggle for education then was not one monolithic, unified movement focused only on eliminating discrimination in the schools. Rather, it was a series of overlapping and staggered movements aimed at accomplishing a variety of goals."[39] San Miguel's work, however, does not fully analyze the conditions of assimilation and acculturation of US-born

Mexican Americans during and after the 1960s. Yet it is worth mentioning that San Miguel's *Chicana/o Struggles for Education* stands as a pioneering work in Mexican American educational history for exploring relevant themes such as ethnic identity, grassroots activism, mass mobilization, unequal funding of schools, Spanish-language retention, limitations toward higher education access, and opposition to a culturally subtractive curriculum.

Historian Carlos Kevin Blanton analyzes the ramifications of an Americanization curriculum and the Nativist Movement first targeting German immigrants before shifting to Mexicans in Texas during the early twentieth century. This era in the state's history also witnessed a shift in the method of school organization from the community system, which allowed minorities to establish bilingual schools under local administrative control, to the district system, which was favored by Progressive educators because of centralized supervision over the curriculum. Societal and institutional factors including nativism, racism, segregation, English-only instruction, and the implementation of the subtractive Americanization model served to facilitate the full Americanization of immigrant children during World War I.[40] Blanton's book *The Strange Career of Bilingual Education in Texas (1836–1981)* (2004) discusses the justification of the segregation and Americanization that affected Mexican Americans, stating: "Segregation and Americanization for Mexican American children became synonymous with and based upon the increasing racialization of Mexican Americans in the early twentieth century.... The inability of many Tejano and immigrant children from Mexico to speak English in school reinforced preexisting racist ideology."[41] In the Progressive Era, American educators "championed different forms of Americanization in response to perceptions that immigrant children were not sufficiently quick in their assimilation to American culture."[42] In an effort to combat this nationalistic, anti-immigrant movement, the ethnic Mexican community in South Texas used the press to defend bilingualism via Spanish-language newspapers such as *La Cronica* in Laredo. This newspaper promoted the establishment of new schools that supported the linguistic and cultural needs of students, beginning in 1910. Blanton further validates the inclusion of a bilingual curriculum as one of the key demands of Mexican American community activists promoting education throughout the twentieth century, arguing: "Such demands bear a striking resemblance to Chicano-era demands in the 1960s for bilingual-bicultural education."[43] By the 1960s and 1970s, the Civil Rights Movement, antisegregation court cases, and federal support for bilingual programs led to the breakdown of institutional barriers obstructing bilingual education in Texas. Bilingual education and the right of ethnic Mexican students to speak Spanish freely on school grounds was one of the goals of the Chicano student movement in South Texas that is underscored in this book.

There is no single interpretive study of the Chicano school walkouts in South Texas despite the growing body of literature investigating the role of high school students in the Chicano Movement, mostly in the form of essays and books since the 1970s. Various aspects of the history of the Chicano Movement regarding its connections, ramifications, and meaning have yet to be detailed. This work offers another model for examining the 1960s social protest activism of ethnic Mexican students in the public school system in Texas. Still, this book attempts to evaluate the regional student movement's nature, influence, and effectiveness as part of the larger movement for public school reform in the nation's history. My 2004 article in *Aztlán: A Journal of Chicano Studies*, titled "The 1968 Edcouch-Elsa High School Walkout: Chicano Student Activism in a South Texas Community," features the Edcouch-Elsa walkout as the original case study. This larger comprehensive study, including three additional case studies, examines the walkouts as a product of the 1960s Chicano Movement. Thus, this work traces the origins, development, and legacy of the student movement in South Texas and provides insights into its historical ramifications. This student movement is critical to understanding the emergence and implications of other Chicano student protests occurring throughout the US Southwest, and their role in bringing about greater awareness of educational and cultural issues as a vital aspect of Chicano Movement insurgency. Before exploring the Chicano Movement, which began in 1968, we must first examine and understand the region's major cultural, social, and political developments over time. A historical overview of the region provides a glimpse into the ethnic makeup, social and cultural fabric, and political instability that led to the Chicano student protests of the late 1960s.

1

Historical Background of South Texas Prior to the 1960s

South Texas was originally a rural grassland in a bushy, flat valley with dense thickets and forest features during the earliest development of the Texas-Mexico borderlands. Spanish and Mexican land settlement, a vibrant Tejano ranching community with fertile soils, the US annexation of Texas, capitalist economic ties and foreign trade, and major demographic changes in the 1880s significantly shaped its society prior to the twentieth century.[1] The region still has abundant rich farmland and a subtropical climate and serves as a major agricultural center. Thus, the land is well known as an area of plains vegetation in a semi-arid landscape that is suitable for a variety of crops such as vegetables, citrus fruits, and cotton. Various indigenous tribes first settled this region prior to the arrival of the Spaniards and other European colonizers of the New World.[2] Spanish conquest brought European disease, religious conversion to Roman Catholicism, and cultural assimilation into the empire of New Spain, which gradually led to the disappearance of these once thriving indigenous people's hunting and gathering way of life. Residing on both sides of the river, Spanish settlers formed a unique Texas-Mexico borderlands culture characterized by the Spanish ranching tradition, patriarchal society, strong family ties and compadrazgo (godparenthood), and the preservation of ethnic Mexican cultural practices.[3] Furthermore, the Spanish introduced livestock, horses, guns, and metal from Europe.

The end of Spanish rule in 1821 marked the birth of Mexico as a nation, and South Texas became part of the state of Tamaulipas. Shortly after gaining independence, Mexico began opening its northern lands—the land that is now Texas—to settlement by foreigners, drawn primarily from the United States. The Mexican provinces of Nuevo León, Coahuila, and Texas were united as one state under the Constitution of 1824. Mexico offered land to American settlers such as

Sam Houston, who would later participate in the Texas Revolution in the 1830s. The land between the Nueces River and Rio Grande remained under Mexico's rule before it became disputed territory shortly after Texas gained its independence from Mexico in 1836.

In 1845, Texans voted overwhelmingly in favor of annexation to the United States, and the US Congress officially admitted Texas to the Union in a joint resolution in 1846. Consequently, the annexation of Texas contributed to the outbreak of the Mexican-American War over a disagreement concerning the southern boundary of Texas: Mexico claimed the boundary was at the Nueces, while the United States recognized the Rio Grande. The Treaty of Guadalupe Hidalgo in 1848 ended the war and set the official border at the Rio Grande. Furthermore, Mexico relinquished all claims to Texas and gave Mexican residents the right to remain in the southwest territories, formerly the northern province of Mexico. The overwhelming majority chose to stay and become US citizens of Mexican descent, Mexican Americans. Consequently, Mexican Americans were regarded as a hybrid, mongrel race because of extensive intermarriage with the "savage" Indian race, which had the status of a conquered people.[4] Most were also despised for their cultural distinctiveness and racial otherness. In his book *Race and Manifest Destiny: The Origins of American Racial Anglo-Saxonism*, historian Reginald Horsman acknowledges Anglo-Saxonism as "the concept of a distinct, superior Anglo-Saxon race, with innate endowments enabling it to achieve a perfection of governmental institutions and world dominance."[5] This ideology, or belief that Anglo-Saxons were a superior race destined to rule over other races, became the foundation of westward expansion as Mexican territory from Texas to California came to be seen as land meant to be owned by the United States.

Historian Arnoldo De León argues that Anglo Texans used their system of racial domination to classify Tejanos (the descendants of the original Spanish and Mexican settlers residing in Texas) as those "grouped together alongside blacks and Indians in a category of animal-like people, and racial antipathy toward Mexicans frequently matched hatred of the other two groups."[6] Anglo newcomers and observers in the West commented frequently on the "backwardness" of the Mexican culture. They also denounced Catholicism for its hierarchical priestly structure because of their notion of superiority, promulgated by the ideology of Manifest Destiny to spread "civilization" among "barbarians" and "savages."[7] For example, Noah Smithwick, a blacksmith who moved to Texas in 1827, wrote a very disparaging remark stereotyping the entire Mexican race: "I looked on the Mexicans as scarce more than apes."[8] The early to mid-nineteenth century marked the climax of US Manifest Destiny, which proclaimed the proexpansionist notion of America's divine right to occupy the entire North American continent.

This type of racially biased system has often characterized politics, socio-economic status, and social relations in the United States since its founding as a nation. Dark-skinned Tejanos, in particular, were condemned to the bottom of society, especially by certain white American transplants whose prejudice toward people of color originated with their ideological need to control the livelihood and freedom of African Americans.[9] Many Tejanos led the life of a working-class laborer or agricultural field hand well into the twentieth century. Even with the aftermath of the Mexican-American War and the impact of the Treaty of Guadalupe Hidalgo, they remained the majority of the population in various South Texas towns along the Texas-Mexico border, and they negotiated some measure of political influence despite the growing number of Anglo elected officials in local and county elections.[10] For example, only nineteen Tejano politicians won elections or were named to represent their districts in the state legislature between 1846 and 1961 despite the emergence of so-called machine party politics throughout South Texas.[11]

One such person, who attempted to challenge machine politics in the South Texas city of Laredo after serving three terms (1879–84) in the Texas House of Representatives, was former Confederate Army colonel and one-time county judge Santos Benavides.[12] As a supporter of the Guaraches (Sandals), or citizen's party, which was an affiliate of the Democratic Party, Benavides opposed the dominant rival faction called the Botas (Boots), led by local political patrons Raymond Martin and José Maria Rodríguez beginning in 1884.[13] In that year, Rodríguez defeated Juan V. Benavides, son of Santos Benavides, for county judge despite various allegations of voter fraud and frequent outbreaks of violence. Both groups often contested each other for political control until they merged to form the Independent Club, or Old Party (Partido Viejo) by 1895. This unified party continued to dominate Laredo politics under the patrón (boss) system for decades until its demise in 1978.[14] Over the years, Tejanos would learn to organize together to exercise their political power as a collective force apart from machine politics. Nevertheless, the development of political machines (political bossism) affecting Tejanos along the Texas border region was evident by the 1880s.

Political Bossism and Anglo-American Control in South Texas

Political bossism dominated much of the local politics and society across the region. Political bosses often coerced or secretly bribed voters, the majority of whom were Mexican American. This type of political order or semifeudal arrangement derived from the patrón system, which first emerged in Texas during the Spanish colonial era. Under this system, the patrón or political authority figure governed ranch peones (peons) by offering social and economic incentives or patronage. In his study of labor in South Texas, historian John Weber argues that the region's agricultural economy mirrored "the system of jefaturas políticas in Porfirian Mexico, through an uneasy system of overlapping mechanisms of coercion and accommodation."[15] He further asserts that "fraudulent poll tax payments, payoffs, and intimidation of political opposition marked each election cycle as the machine balanced the need to woo Mexican American voters against the fear of Mexican and Mexican American numerical superiority in South Texas."[16] However, most Tejanos and Mexican immigrants lived as tenants or peons on ranches and small farms and often promoted or represented the political clout of Anglo bosses throughout the region. Thus, the subordinate position of Mexicans and Mexican Americans in the hierarchical structure of this new agricultural society "became the justification for their banishment from full citizenship in the farm society," and "their supposed unfitness for full citizenship validated their political and economic powerlessness."[17] Two methods of subjugation became apparent in this social environment: instituting the so-called white primary to disenfranchise Mexican American voters in such places as Maverick and Dimmit Counties, both in the Winter Garden Region southwest of San Antonio; and the creation of thirteen new counties across South Texas, which allowed white farmers and ranchers to maintain their dominance of old machine politics.[18] Scholar David Montejano also asserts: "This was a new [agricultural] society, with new class groups and class relations, with the capacity to generate an 'indigenous' rationale for the ordering of people. The duality of the farm society . . . served to preserve a cheap Mexican labor force . . . through the construction of separate and subordinate institutions that rigidly defined their position as farm laborers."[19] As historian Evan Anders has argued, the political boss "centralized government authority by filling city offices with men willing to follow his orders. Patronage became the lifeblood of the machine."[20] One early pioneering work by Tejana educator and folklorist Jovita González assesses the major characteristics of peones. In comparison to the patrón, she comments that "the peón on the other hand was of Indian blood, immigrant from Mexico whom the landowner had brought to Texas to work. He was submissive to his master's orders, obeyed blindly and had no will of his own. . . . The master exercised complete control over the peón, economically and socially as well as in religious matters. He might be the possessor of a goat, a few chickens, and a pig, and these only if he kept them within his own enclosure."[21] Thus, the patrón exerted a tremendous amount of paternalism over the lives of the peones, who lacked the means to achieve self-sufficiency and gain political autonomy.

The most notable Anglo and Mexican American bosses in South Texas included Jim Wells (Cameron County), Archie Parr (Duval County), Manuel Guerra (Starr County), and John Nance Garner (Uvalde County). Such machinations were based on the social and economic structure of the region's Hispanic ranching system, which was later transformed by white Texan control of land in the region.[22] This system relegated many Mexican Americans in the region to low-wage and unskilled employment in the predominantly agricultural economy managed by Anglo newcomers. Mexican American peons (hired hands or servants) were often destitute because they owed large debts to Anglo landlords, and they "developed a spirit of hopelessness and despair."[23] According to US census figures, the percentage of Tejano workers rose from 32.4 percent to 47.6 percent between 1850 and 1870, while their share of accumulated wealth dropped from 33 percent to 10.6 percent during the same period.[24] Moreover, Tejanos' per capita wealth decreased substantially within this twenty-year period, from $926 to $122.[25]

Many Tejanos were deeply impacted by the economic developments of the Gilded Age, which transformed the United States from an agrarian nation to an industrial giant. Thus, Tejanos became *jornaleros*, or journeyman workers, employed in menial service jobs and other types of unskilled work when they shifted from farm and ranch ownership to hired labor as ranch hands, migrant farm laborers, and blue-collar industrial workers.[26] Meanwhile, white Texans' share of accumulated wealth increased from 66.95 percent to 89.4 percent, and their per capita wealth grew from $899 to $942 between 1850 and 1870.[27] US economic development and the influx of Anglo-American newcomers to Texas who gained employment in skilled trades downgraded the occupational status of Tejanos, who struggled to escape inequities in the workplace and overcome obstacles to upward mobility.

The 1880s and 1890s were a time of unprecedented technological innovation, urbanization, immense growth of corporations, population increase, and intense political partisanship. Despite the advent of commercial farming, cattle ranching and the patrón-peón (employer-employee) relationship remained vital to the regional economy.[28] This type of working relationship was mutually beneficial and was linked to politics, since many ethnic Mexican people were economically dependent on their Anglo-American supervisors.[29] Therefore, Anglo employers often instructed their Mexican American employees to vote for a political boss in exchange for paying their poll taxes and for providing transportation to the voting precinct.[30] White Texans who adhered to the ideology of social Darwinism believed that ethnic Mexicans were culturally and intellectually inferior, and therefore fit only for unskilled manual labor in agriculture, ranching, and mining.[31]

Political bosses also provided protection from violent activity, legal titles to land claims, food, money, and jobs.[32] Most Mexican Americans from middle-'class and low-income neighborhoods received employment in exchange for their loyalty and political support. Members of the middle class gained jobs in public education, law enforcement, city and county government, and the customhouse.[33] Wealthy political bosses also maintained control of the political system by funding or hosting social gatherings such as parties and dances, and intermarriage among the upper class.[34] This type of political arrangement was commonplace in the region well into the twentieth century.

In response to the exploitative conditions of bossism, Mexican Americans established *sociedades mutualistas,* or mutual aid societies, which offered insurance, promoted fraternal and cultural activities and community service, and endorsed private *escuelitas* (small community-based schools), which offered more affordable tuition and provided Spanish-language instruction. According to historians Carlos Kevin Blanton and Philis Barragán Goetz, county judges and school superintendents in various South Texas counties questioned the feasibility of private and parochial schools that supported bilingual instruction.[35] In her pathbreaking work *Reading, Writing, and Revolution,* Barragán Goetz assesses the development of *escuelitas* in Texas that influenced ethnic Mexican students' bicultural, bilingual, and bieducational experiences from the late nineteenth to mid-twentieth centuries. She and other Chicano education scholars further assert that Mexican Americans were not apathetic toward education but rather were resolute in establishing a more inclusive educational system for themselves and their communities. Nevertheless, these schools continued to actively recruit and hire bilingual faculty members who successfully passed the English examination as part of the state teacher certification. In regard to how late-nineteenth-century bossism affected the delivery of public education, Blanton notes: "The use of Spanish in the classroom was deemed essential to securing the patronage of these [Mexican-origin families] and ultimately to the acquisition of English, then equated with the requisite degree of 'Americanization.'"[36] He further argues: "Those schools choosing to educate Spanish speakers in an English-Only manner paid the price of losing Tejano patronage."[37] Thus, political bosses and county officials who wished to placate their Tejano constituencies supported bilingual public schools rather than a full-fledged instructional system of Americanization.

In his pioneering work *The Tejano Community, 1836–1900,* historian Arnoldo De León examines the conditions of countywide ranch schools in remote areas of South Texas, such as Duval County (ninety miles west of Corpus Christi), that held numerous public performances, including dramas and concerts, and had extracurricular activities in both languages.[38] In the 1880s, the Duval County school system included five Spanish-surnamed teachers. Luis Puebla, a former world languages and mathematics professor at Lagarto College, served as the director of schools in San Diego, the county seat.[39] Other countywide school systems across South Texas also hired Spanish-surnamed faculty who served as community schoolteachers in ethnic Mexican communities that had "an abiding faith in schooling" and "subscribed to the values of [social, political, and occupational] advancement and enterprise."[40] However, historian Jovita González's study commented on the deplorable conditions and educational deficiencies that had plagued the rancho schools in other counties along the border of South Texas where patrones forbade Tejano children from attending more formal public schools. According to her recollections: "The rural school buildings were jacales, thatched-roofed huts with dirt floors. There were neither blackboards nor desks of any kind, the pupils wrote on slates and sat on crude backless benches or boxes. The numbers and alphabet were learned in English, and 'America' was sung in a pronunciation that would not have been recognized by any English speaking person."[41] The certification of teachers "became a political issue and a means of controlling votes" for political bosses, and "the taxpayer who assured the political boss the greatest number of votes was sure of getting [teaching] certificates for all his sons and daughters."[42] Despite this type of underhanded activity involving political patronage, the preservation of bilingualism, cultural orientation, and the establishment of educational facilities can be attributed to the long history of Tejano activism.

New farm towns and large-scale mechanized irrigation emerged in the region and led to a substantial increase in agricultural productivity shortly after the turn of the twentieth century. Newly arrived Anglo-American industrialists soon invented the term "Magic Valley" to characterize this important economic transformation of the period.[43] The agricultural industry involved the cultivation of major cash crops such as sugarcane, corn, cotton, and a variety of vegetables. This industry continued to flourish well into the twentieth century thanks to the growing ranks of land-dispossessed Mexican American laborers and the growing influx of Mexican immigrant workers along the border counties of South Texas. Approximately thirty-four thousand resided in counties such as Cameron, Hidalgo, Starr, and Willacy by 1900.[44] Transportation advancements and the burgeoning agricultural and ranching industries culminated in not only economic transformation but also new sources of political power. Such power sanctioned the establishment of segregation in public accommodations, including in the public school system. Farm towns in South Texas built separate schools for Mexicans and Mexican Americans to keep them from attending the same schools as Anglos, thereby replicating the racial divisions of society. John Stone, a resident of Dimmit County who lived twelve miles south of Crystal City, expressed his sentiments on the need for separate schools in his local area: "Reasons for separation? They're [Mexicans and Mexican Americans] low morally, and many of their children aren't clean; either they would be left behind by the faster progress of white children, or the white children would be held back.

The Mexicans could go to the white schools if they knew enough and insisted; they're Caucasians. But they are satisfied; they know that the white children would make it pretty hard for the Mexican children and would probably get the best of them."[45] Another Anglo farmer supported the use of separate schools, "because a damned greaser is not fit to sit side of a white girl . . . if they separate in school the children learn the difference and they won't mix with Mexicans."[46] The educational history of Texas since the end of Mexican rule in 1836 reveals the origins of the public school system that led to the creation of separate schools for Anglos and students of Mexican origin.

The Development of Public Schools from 1836 to the Early Twentieth Century

On April 21, 1836, the final battle of the Texas Revolution took place at San Jacinto, near present-day Houston, securing Texas independence from Mexico after the surrender of Mexican president General Antonio López de Santa Anna. One of the major reasons for the rebellion and the declaration of independence from Mexico was the lack of support for public education. According the newly established Declaration of Independence of the Republic of Texas: "It [Mexico] has failed to establish any public school system of education, although possessed of almost boundless resources, the public domain, and although it is an axiom in political science, that unless a people are educated and enlightened, it is idle to expect the continuance of civil liberty, or the capacity for self-government."[47] The republic's first president, Sam Houston, supported private charter schools, but the Texas legislature under President Mirabeau Lamar first approved a proposal calling for the creation of a public school system by granting 17,712 acres to each county.[48] Lamar began to promote the development of public education shortly after his election as president of the Republic of Texas in 1838: "To patronize the general diffusion of knowledge, industry, and charity, has been near to the hearts of the good and wise of all nations. . . . A suitable appropriation of land to the purpose of general Education, can be made at this time without inconvenience to the Government or the people."[49] Despite his endorsement of the development of a comprehensive public school system, thirty-eight counties failed to survey their land because of low property values during the Lamar administration, yet the republic's undeveloped educational system included private, religious, and other self-directed academic institutions.[50] Many of these institutions first opened during and after the Spanish colonial era.

In 1845, Texans voted overwhelmingly for annexation to the United States and approved the establishment of tuition-free schools under a new state constitution. The constitution also required the Texas legislature to set aside 10 percent of annual state tax revenue for school funding.[51] During its formative years, the state legislature approved the 1854 Act to Establish a System of Common Schools, which significantly altered the structure and organization of education by converting private schools into common schools modeled on the US public school system.[52] It further created a school fund by allocating $2 million of the $10 million received from the sale of lands to the United States.[53] The Texas legislature began formally establishing its public school system by reinforcing Americanization and English-only instruction during the mid- to late nineteenth century. An 1856 law intended to promote the assimilation of ethnic Mexican students stated: "No school shall be entitled to the benefits of this act unless the English language is principally taught therein."[54] The Texas legislature once again ratified this amendment in 1858.[55] Tejanos rarely observed this restrictive law mandating English-language instruction and instead opted to establish their own community schools in the remote rural areas of Texas, since most regarded education as a private matter and resented interference from the state government.

During the post–Civil War era, Governor Edmund J. Davis approved a law to formally organize a public school system in Texas, and to establish a state board of education by 1871.[56] Jacob C. De Gress, a German Texan and the first superintendent of public instruction of Texas, along with the State Board of Education adopted a rather flexible, albeit regulated, approach toward maintaining some semblance of bilingual instruction in the schools. One state education code that compromised on language policies for minority schoolchildren states: "Teachers are permitted to teach the German, French, and Spanish languages in the Public Schools of this State, provided the time so occupied shall not exceed two hours each day."[57] Historian Carlos Kevin Blanton comments on the ambiguity and unspecified application of this code: "It is not clear that the language provision meant for those languages to be taught as mere subjects or, more significantly, as a medium of instruction. Could two hours of German or Spanish be stretched over a six- or seven-hour school day as the medium of directions and general conversation while the rest of the day was spent in an all-English environment of written English grammar exercises, oral recitations, and silent reading? Or would the medium of instruction not count toward the two-hour time limit?"[58]

State policy could not deter bilingualism in Texas during the late nineteenth century. One 1872 educational record reveals that "of the population three-fifths are Mexicans, still speaking their own language and observing their own customs, and the remainder a mixture of all classes and creeds."[59] In 1886, many Texas residents complained that some schools still provided instruction in Spanish or German despite the state superintendent's announcement that "schools shall be conducted in the English language."[60] Thus, Tejanos maintained the use of Spanish in the Texas public school system, which they recognized as essential to preserving their cultural identity and traditions during the transitional years between the 1850s and 1890s. However, the Texas public school system began to impose Jim Crow segregation on Mexican Americans by establishing separate Mexican schools not long after the turn of the twentieth century. Chicano scholar David Montejano reveals that "the first 'Mexican school' was established in 1902 in Central Texas (in Seguin) and the practice continued unabated until Mexican ward schools existed throughout the state."[61] By the turn of the twentieth century, the educational system in Texas began to further witness a shift from the socialization of a diverse and heterogeneous population to the imparting of knowledge and skills to meet the demands of the rapidly emerging modern economy of increased mechanization, corporate growth, urban development, and technological innovation.

Public schools began to adopt Americanization programs to assimilate ethnic-minority schoolchildren to the dominant Anglo-American mainstream culture and schooling in the English language during the Americanization movement of the 1910s and 1920s.[62] This national phenomenon and movement facilitated the cultural integration and assimilation of thousands of foreign-born immigrants who faced resistance toward multicultural integration, the influence of nativism, and the passage of patriotic legislation after America's entry into World War I. English-only curricula and the implementation of the subtractive Americanization model served to stigmatize Mexican American schoolchildren's cultural heritage and the Spanish language as un-American and contrary to the idea of democracy.[63] Furthermore, Americanization policies did not improve the status quo of ethnic Mexican students since such policies "tended to preserve the political and economic subordination of the Mexican American community."[64] Progressive education and Americanization at this time were interconnected and thus redefined the role of schools in expediting acculturation, as Carlos Kevin Blanton indicates: "Through the use of IQ tests, which tracked students in the name of 'efficiency,' along with the implementation of a 'socially relevant' curriculum of vocational education, civics, and patriotism lessons, and education in health and hygiene, progressives also sought to facilitate the full Americanization of immigrant children."[65] Historian Guadalupe San Miguel concurs by stating: "The Americanization movement rapidly shifted its emphasis from promoting an understanding of America's traditions and fostering positive aspects of the foreign-born population to forcefully teaching immigrants the 'American' way of life."[66]

Educators during the Progressive Era adhered to different notions of immigrant assimilation, supported a more rigid control of schools, and rarely agreed on a standard form of Americanization. However, most scholars of this era, such as Ellwood P. Cubberley and Emory S. Bogardus, believed that "Americanization was a state-sponsored form of social reconstruction that would eradicate the native cultures and languages of immigrants and impose a new set of English loyalties."[67] Annie Webb Blanton, state superintendent of public instruction in Texas, furthered expressed the era's nativist sentiments of school officials favoring Americanization in 1923: "If you desire to be one with us, stay, and we welcome you; but if you wish to preserve, in our state, the language and customs of another land, you have no right to do this. . . . You must go back to the country which you prize so highly and rear your children there."[68] Although Americanization proponents such as Blanton favored the cultural and linguistic assimilation of Mexican Americans, no concerted effort was made to elevate their economic and political positions in US society. As part of their efforts to adopt Americanization, other school officials throughout Texas often promoted the recruitment of "capable English speaking Mexicans" since "the work of Mexican education can best be done by the intelligent Americanized Mexicans themselves."[69] The Americanization of the Mexican community further perpetuated the stereotype of the "Mexican home . . . as a reinforcer of the 'Mexican educational problem.'"[70] Chicano education scholar Gilbert G. González believes educators promoting Americanization frequently rationalized their efforts to assimilate the Mexican community: "The Anglo image of the culture in Mexican communities appears to have instilled in educators an exaggerated sense of guardianship of the American way of life."[71] Thus, Mexican Americans continued to live in substandard housing in low-income, segregated neighborhoods with very little opportunity for socioeconomic mobility.

The Development of South Texas during the Early Twentieth Century

The expansion of the railroad and irrigation transformed the South Texas border region into a major agricultural center within a few years after 1900 before the advent of the automobile. In 1903, the St. Louis, Brownsville and Mexico Railway constructed rail lines that extended from Kingsville, Texas, to the border cities of Harlingen and Brownsville.[72] Commercial-scale irrigation began after the building of the Hidalgo Pumphouse in Hidalgo, Texas, off the shore of the Rio Grande in 1909. The pumphouse first operated by steam prior to the use of coal and electricity, distributing water to thousands of acres of crops throughout Hidalgo County.[73] The county's population, including the communities of Edcouch and Elsa, rose from 6,534 in 1900 to 38,110 in 1920.[74] This sudden increase was attributed largely to ambitious Anglo farmers and land developers from the upper Midwest states who moved to the "Magic Valley" during the early 1900s because of its fertile delta soil and irrigation networks.[75] Towns started growing and becoming more modernized as banks, stores, houses, schools, churches, and businesses were built. The technological era also emerged as telephones, electric lights, phonographs, and automobiles became more widespread. Meanwhile, Mexican Americans living throughout the Lower Rio Grande border region continued to identify themselves as "Mexicans" or "México Texanos" while embracing Mexican liberalism and residing in what they called *México perdido* (lost Mexico).[76] Most did not acknowledge or claim "American" identity, usually spoke Spanish at home and in public, and read Spanish-language newspapers.

As the county seat of Bexar County, San Antonio became the largest city in the region and the state in 1900, with a population of 53,321, and remained the most populous urban area in Texas in 1910, when there were 96,614 inhabitants thanks to the rapid increase of Mexican, German, and Anglo-American settlers.[77] The population of San Antonio continued to swell, until there were over 161,000 people by 1920.[78] Crystal City, located 120 miles southwest of San Antonio in Zavala County, became known as the main shipping point for winter vegetables.[79] Crystal City's population was fewer than 600 during its founding and incorporation as a city in 1910.[80] The vast majority of agricultural laborers in Crystal City, and throughout the entire southern region of Texas, were Mexican immigrants.

Most Mexican immigrants came to South Texas during the Mexican Revolution, from 1910 to the early 1920s. During the revolution, various Mexican Americans in Texas drafted the Plan of San Diego, which called for the formation of a "Liberating Army of Races and Peoples." Key articles of the plan called for the return of Mexican rule in the Southwest, a redrawing of the map of North America, and the summary execution of all white males over the age of sixteen.[81] The Plan of San Diego was a revolutionary manifesto allegedly written and signed at the South Texas town of San Diego on January 6, 1915. This manifesto, drafted in a jail in Monterrey, Mexico, influenced numerous Mexican Americans to take up arms against Anglo settlers, leading to vigilantism and murder. Armed raids were led by Venustiano Carranza, a revolutionary general; and Aniceto Pizaña and Luis de la Rosa, residents of South Texas. Mexicans residing throughout the region and in northern Mexico used guerrilla tactics to disrupt transportation and communication in the border area and reportedly killed twenty-one Anglos.[82]

Mexicans supporting ousted Mexican dictator Victoriano Huerta, who had been overthrown by Carranza in 1914, were responsible for numerous raids throughout the region as well. In response, the US Army sent reinforcements into the area, eventually subduing the raids by the late 1910s. One local historian surmises that factors such as poverty, discrimination, and inequality stimulated the raids across the region.[83] According to state representative J. T. Canales, who headed a legislative investigation, the Texas Rangers murdered an estimated three hundred to two thousand Mexican Americans.[84] To this today, many elderly Mexican Americans who reside in South Texas blame the Texas Rangers for the deliberate murder of hundreds of ethnic Mexican people throughout the region. They also refer to the Rangers as *los rinches*, a derogatory moniker characterizing this law enforcement group's reputation for wanton violence. Upheavals such as the Mexican Revolution and the Plan of San Diego uprising prompted Mexican Americans to mobilize and speak out against social injustice and discrimination in small, obscure locations such as Edcouch-Elsa, Crystal City, and Kingsville.

History of Edcouch-Elsa

Located in the middle of Hidalgo County, Edcouch-Elsa was and remains a small, rural farming community with a population of fewer than ten thousand. It is part of what is called the Delta area, located near Delta Lake. Both towns stand on land that was part of the Llano Grande land grant given to Spanish settler Juan José Hinojosa de Ballí in 1790.[85] The first Spanish and Mexican settlers began building and working on small family-owned ranches. After the signing of the Treaty of Guadalupe Hidalgo in 1848, which officially established the Rio Grande as the permanent international boundary, land tracts in the Delta area began to be transferred from Mexican to Anglo ownership through legal and extralegal means.

The historical literature examining South Texas briefly mentions the contributions of native Mexicans who have resided in the region for generations. According to Edcouch-Elsa native and education specialist Francisco Guajardo, longtime Mexican residents such as Isabel Gutiérrez tell counterstories that differ from the traditional historical narratives. In a 1997 interview with Guajardo and an Edcouch-Elsa High School student, Gutiérrez proudly proclaimed that ethnic Mexican people founded Edcouch. In response to the student's question concerning this type of alternative narrative, Gutiérrez stated: "Joven ... ¿tú has tomado agua en este pueblo? En 1926, yo escarbé los diches para sentar las paipas de agua para este pueblo. ... Yo soy fundador de Edcouch." (Young man ... have you ever drunk water in this town? In 1926, I dug the ditches to lay down the water pipes for this town. ... I am a founder of Edcouch.)[86] This bold statement from Gutiérrez, ninety-seven years old at the time of his interview with Guajardo, reflected his pride and dignity as an anonymous pioneer. His account suggests the lack of recognition of people of Mexican origin who provided necessary labor. However, very few of these local pioneers left behind written records to further validate the establishment of their community throughout their lives. Another little-known member of the community, 103-year-old Luisa Garza, described the early years of Edcouch-Elsa's existence. She recalled: "We just lived in the brush. There was nothing else here. ... There were no stores, no churches, no priests; there was nothing" except for sprawling brush and

36 ～ CHAPTER 1

wildlife.[87] Gutiérrez's and Garza's oral accounts indicate that Mexican people in rural South Texas were born and raised in a sparsely populated ranch country prior to the arrival of the land development companies, which by the 1920s were purchasing large tracts of land.

In the early twentieth century, numerous Anglo-American entrepreneurs began moving into the Delta region and purchasing property in the area, including R. R. Hill, who developed a produce empire by the mid-twentieth century.[88] In 1927, white settlers began to racially segregate Edcouch and Elsa when the Elsa townsite was auctioned. Land developers placed red, white, and green tags in different land sectors. Red tags designated business lots, white tags residence lots, and green tags land space for the Mexican part of town.[89] Segregation that adversely affected Mexican Americans came in different forms, whether spatial, vocational, or institutional.

According to scholar Jennifer Nájera, whose work examines segregation in the South Texas town of La Feria, "Anglo settlers strategically developed farm towns along the [Texas-Mexico] border in ways that amplified their economic strengths in farming while keeping their local Mexican populations socially, economically, and politically subordinate through the practices of segregation."[90] She underscores how de facto segregation or spatial separation between Anglos and ethnic Mexicans was most apparent in the school system and local Catholic Church because of the increased hiring of Mexican farmworkers who worked for Anglo landowners, and the acceptance of segregation as a social custom between whites and nonwhites. These standards of early town development designated separate land for Anglo and Mexican American communities. The railroad split the town; Mexicans lived north of the tracks, while whites settled on the south side. Esperanza Salinas, one elderly resident, revealed that "lots on the Mexican side were tiny . . . Mexicans were set up to live in small lots, and real close to each other, while the gringos [Anglos] built their houses in lots two to three times bigger than ours."[91] Ezequiel Granado of Elsa described why Anglo city planners chose to place the Mexican colony on the north side of the tracks: "The gringos were smart . . . they put themselves south from us because they didn't want to be downwind from us."[92] Granado explained another important reason why Anglos selected the south side of town. In South Texas, the wind blows from the southeast, and "we [Mexican Americans] had hogs and outhouses" that emitted foul odors. This type of segregation became a major adverse influence on the lives of Mexican Americans because their section of town had low-income or substandard housing that separated them from the more affluent southern part of Elsa.

By the mid-twentieth century, Edcouch-Elsa had a strong agro-industrial sector as a result of increased population, industrialization, and migration from Mexico. The Vahl'sing Packing Shed, specializing in the production of broccoli, employed many Mexican American residents, including men, women, and children. This vegetable factory, which is no longer in operation, was built in Elsa and founded by Fred Vahl'sing, a native of Long Island, New York. The Vahl'sing enterprise contributed much to the economic growth and prosperity of the Delta area, which became a produce empire by the mid-twentieth century.[93] The Vahl'sing Packing Shed eventually gained national and international acclaim. During the Great Depression, it created over three thousand jobs in both the shed and the fields, where laborers of Mexican origin picked vegetables. *Reader's Digest* magazine named Vahl'sing "The Henry Ford of Vegetables" in 1947.[94] World War II veteran Ezequiel Granado remembered seeing the name of the company on boxes of produce shipped from the Vahl'sing shed while serving in Germany.[95] Mexican Americans contributed significant labor to America's food demands by the 1940s thanks to the wide distribution and shipment of produce from the Vahl'sing shed.

Mexican Americans in Edcouch-Elsa had little access to educational opportunities. Between 1920 and the early 1930s, the Common School system governed rural schools. The San José Ranch Common School and the Carlson Common School established clear rules of segregation; the San José School enrolled Mexican children, and the Carlson School accepted only Anglo-American children. In 1929, Carlson was important in the early development of the Edcouch-Elsa Independent School District and perpetuated segregation.[96] Education scholar Francisco Guajardo argues: "The racial division and broader thinking process upon which both Edcouch and Elsa were founded supported the established segregationist culture of the schools, and the profitable agricultural interests further defined a political economy where Mexicans were viewed as a critical part of the manual labor force." During an interview with Guajardo, local elder William Foerster commented on his and other Anglos' interests in the community: "We came to buy land, to manage the sheds, and to run the schools . . . yeah, some of us white folks were poor, but there was no question who was in control of the politics and of the jobs."[97] Foerster further suggests the emergence of the early-twentieth-century power structure that fashioned segregation. However, a few Mexican Americans owned small businesses in the community. Tila Zamora and her husband owned Farmacia Zamora (Zamora's Pharmacy), located on the Mexican side, and Pablo Ramírez owned and operated his own barbershop across from Edcouch Elementary School.

English-only policies also adversely affected students of Mexican origin. Students often repeated the first and second grades because they lacked English proficiency and fluency. Lupita Guzman, who attended Elsa's Mexican school in the 1930s, stated, "Many Mexicans repeated the first grade" and "just stopped going when they were 11 or 12 years old and still in the first or second grade."[98]

Monolingualism continued to impact students into the 1960s and became one of the reasons why Chicano students walked out of Edcouch-Elsa High School in 1968.

History of Crystal City

Crystal City has a unique history of settlement and possibly some of the harshest oppression and exploitation of ethnic Mexican workers. Located on the far southwest edge of Texas, 120 miles southwest of San Antonio and 45 miles from the US-Mexico border, Crystal City is situated in the heart of the Winter Garden Region. It has served as the county seat of Zavala County since 1928, named for 1836 Texas vice president Lorenzo de Zavala.[99] The county traces its history to the establishment of the Republic of Texas before the annexation of Texas in 1845.[100]

Spanish explorer Alonso de León first settled the land of present-day Zavala County and introduced ranching in the area in 1689.[101] Thus, early Spanish exploration laid the groundwork for the development of the cattle ranching industry in the county. The Cross S, Chaparrosa, and Mangum Ranches emerged when multimillion-dollar ranches dominated the economy after the latter part of the twentieth century.[102]

Suitable for growing vegetables such as sugar beets, cotton, onions, and spinach during the winter, the area is known as the Winter Garden. During the 1920s and early 1930s, residents called Crystal City the "Spinach Capital of the World."[103] Crystal City first celebrated the harvesting of this local cash crop in 1936. The Crystal City Spinach Festival featured a parade, spinach cook-off, coronation of a queen, and various other events publicizing the positive aspects of the community. In 1937, the town erected a statue of the popular cartoon character Popeye to promote the city's reputation as a major producer of spinach.[104] This celebration ceased in 1941 but was reestablished in 1982. Anglo-American community members coordinated the festival during its early years, but by the 1980s Mexican Americans were planning the event as a result of their increasing political clout in civic affairs during the years after the local school walkout.

Crystal City first became a town in 1907 when E. J. Buckingham and Carl Groos agreed to divide sections of the land into ten-acre farms. The two developers arranged for engineers to place the town close to the Nueces River. Anglo economic development increased substantially throughout the twentieth century shortly after Crystal City was founded. As a result, ethnic Mexican people served as the city's low-wage labor force and harvested the Winter Garden crops.

Land ownership was a political issue early on, as it was in many places in South Texas, when Anglo-American newcomers often fraudulently purchased, extorted, or stole lands once owned by people of Mexican origin. Economist

Paul S. Taylor reported that "many of the Mexican property owners were 'run out' of the country and their lands obtained cheaply."[105] Chicano scholar-activist José Angel Gutiérrez, a native of Crystal City, recalls this type of disparity linked to land ownership and labor: "The gringos [Anglo Americans] owned almost everything and controlled everybody, especially those associated with the Del Monte plant. Mexicans lived physically apart from Anglos, and the two groups did not mix socially. Mixing was limited to economic relations. Anglos *worked* Mexicans, but no Anglo *worked for* a Mexican."[106]

The first developers of Crystal City, founded in 1907, named the town for the clear artesian water discovered in the region in the late 1800s.[107] Buckingham and Groos were the first land developers of ten thousand acres of the Cross S Ranch in Zavala and Dimmit Counties.[108]

The rise of large-scale agriculture in Crystal City in the early twentieth century provided employment for many Mexican immigrant laborers. The spinach industry became a vital part of the economy, attracting hundreds of Mexican workers beginning in the 1920s. Moreover, the demand for labor led to dramatic social and economic transformation of the area when Crystal City's agro-industrial sector made significant improvements in transportation and packing methods.[109] As Mark Odintz indicates, "As soon as the railroad reached Crystal City, the community became a major shipping point for winter vegetables."[110] According to historian Marc Simon Rodríguez, the population of Crystal City more than tripled between 1920 and 1930, when it grew from 3,108 to 10,349.[111] One 1930s study suggests the symbiotic relationship between Mexican migrant labor and agribusiness in the early twentieth century: "The situation of the Mexican migratory workers of Crystal City is a striking example of the relationship between low-paid labor and the development of certain types of agriculture. Spinach and onion farming reached their present proportions in south Texas largely because of the presence of thousands of Mexicans who have customarily worked for wages of a dollar a day or less."[112] The report detailed the socioeconomic conditions of three hundred Mexican migrant families. Over 90 percent were migratory laborers. The sugar beet, cotton, and onion seasons began in April and ended in November, and the spinach harvest occurred during the first or last few months of the year. As far as unemployment, fewer than 4 percent of the families studied were unemployed for more than half of any given month except for an idle period between the spinach harvest and the cotton and sugar beet seasons in April.[113]

Factors leading to the decline of spinach production in Crystal City after 1932 included poor soil management resulting from a fungal disease known as "blue mold," reduction in crop shipments, and the lowering of agricultural work wages.[114] In the early 1930s, the ethnic Mexican population outnumbered Anglos for the first time.[115] Zavala County had the highest percentage of laborers (1,430 per 100 farms) of all counties in South Texas at this time as well.[116] In 1938, the average income of three hundred Mexican migrant families, averaging approximately 5.5 people each, totaled $506, or roughly $100 per person.[117] One study described their housing conditions: "The Mexican sections of Crystal City form a large semi-rural slum. More than half of the Mexicans own their own houses or shacks, but most of the dwellings in the Mexican quarter are crudely built and in very bad repair. Few have electricity or plumbing. The houses are badly overcrowded; there was an average of 2.6 persons per room at the time of the survey." Tuberculosis and diarrhea were rampant among people of Mexican origin in Crystal City, and education for their children was at a "low level."[118] Unemployment, low wages, and an unstable agricultural economy plagued Mexican Americans.[119]

During World War II, an alien internment camp was built on the edge of Crystal City. It held hundreds of people of Japanese and German descent from throughout the country.[120] After the war ended, the city received the deed to the land. In 1945, the California Packing Corporation, later renamed Del Monte, relocated to the city.

In 1942, Mexican contract workers entered the US Southwest to work under the Bracero Program, a formal binational labor agreement negotiated between the United States and Mexico. This program, authorized by both nations, was intended to alleviate labor shortages and provide low-paying temporary jobs in the agricultural and industrial sectors during World War II. However, Crystal City and the rest of Texas did not participate in this program because Mexican-born workers were banned from coming into the state after negotiations between the Mexican and US governments in August 1942.[121] This blacklisting of Texas was part of the Emergency Farm Labor Supply Program, which prohibited discrimination against such workers by employers in any town or region in the state. The agreement further restricted growers from hiring undocumented workers.[122] However, the Immigration and Naturalization Service (INS) provided Texas with a federally sanctioned open-border policy until 1943. The Mexican government agreed to terminate this policy in response to complaints about alleged discrimination against Mexican workers.[123] As historian Emilio Zamora has argued, "[US] State [Department authorities] usually minimized the extent of discrimination at the same time they announced that the Good Neighbor Commission (GNC) was resolving individual complaints and leading an 'educational' campaign to improve racial understanding among Anglos. They insisted that the GNC's 'gradualist' approach avoided disruptions that Anglo segregationists would surely cause if pushed too hard. Mexican government officials and [League of United Latin American Citizens] LULAC officers, on the other hand, preferred an immediate solution in the form of civil rights legislation."[124]

Historian Arnoldo De León also notes that in an effort to combat the exploitation of bracero workers, LULAC and other labor rights groups lobbied to deport undocumented immigrants, terminate the Bracero Program, and stop the influx of undocumented immigration from Mexico.[125] However, the Texas legislature approved the Caucasian Race Resolution, also known as House Concurrent Resolution 105, a law that protected Mexicans and outlawed discrimination in "all public places of business or amusement."[126]

Regarding the state's Good Neighbor Commission investigation into discrimination, Mexican American educator and civil rights advocate George I. Sánchez complained that the commission represented nothing more than a "glorified tourist agency" meant for Texas to save face in order to uplift the bracero blacklist.[127] According to historian John Weber, "This nonbinding proclamation did not change the minds of officials in Mexico," despite its good intentions on paper.[128] As many as 445,000 Mexicans entered the United States during the height of the postwar Bracero Program in 1956. The need for more agricultural labor led Texas to participate in the program by the mid-1950s before its termination in 1964. Approximately four and a half million workers likely participated in the Bracero Program.[129] It fostered a symbiotic relationship between the United States and Mexico that served to fulfill wartime needs.

History of Kingsville

The city of Kingsville, the county seat of Kleberg County, is situated in the northeastern part of the region known as the Coastal Bend in the heart of Texas cattle country. The city, named after cattle and land baron Richard King, was founded after the first passenger train began operation in 1904.[130] The first inhabitants of the area cultivated its black, fertile, sandy loam to grow numerous vegetables, citrus fruits, grapes, and cotton.[131] The land between the Nueces River to the north and Rio Grande to the south was known as the Wild Horse Desert because of the large herds of untamed mustangs, or mesteños, that once freely roamed the region.[132] The Wild Horse Desert is the once-disputed area in southern Texas, the initial site of open hostilities between the United States and Mexico in 1846. Kingsville is approximately 40 miles southwest of Corpus Christi and 155 miles southeast of San Antonio. It originated as a railroad town with a small farming community.

Kingsville was founded along the St. Louis, Brownsville and Mexico Railway near the famous King Ranch, the economic and political hub of Kleburg County. The King Ranch began in 1853 when former steamship captain and ranch baron Richard King and Gideon K. Lewis purchased a Spanish land grant, Rincón de Santa Gertrudis, of 15,500 acres on Santa Gertrudis Creek in present-day Nueces County before acquiring the Santa Gertrudis de la Garza grant, a Mexican land

42 ～ CHAPTER 1

grant of 53,000 acres.[133] Both business partners bought more landholdings around Santa Gertrudis Creek by the mid-1850s. All land titles were eventually put under the business name R. King and Company.[134] King Ranch heiress Henrietta M. King arranged for the building of a railroad line linking the county to the border city of Brownsville shortly after the turn of the twentieth century. King designated a large tract of land belonging to the King Ranch, half of which was deeded to the construction company for building the local railroad. The Kleberg Town and Improvement Company, established by Robert Justus Kleberg, later sold the property on behalf of King and the railroad construction company, leading to the founding of the town in 1903. Thus, King donated approximately 75,000 acres of land for the benefit of the railroad and the creation of a new townsite, located three miles east of the King Ranch headquarters.[135]

Before the town's first passenger train began running in 1904, Kingsville existed in open, flat cattle country covered with cactus and mesquite.[136] This sparsely populated area also had a few cowboy huts and corrals, which were the only remains of permanent human settlement just prior to the founding of Kingsville.[137] John D. Finnegan, secretary-treasurer of the St. Louis, Brownsville and Mexico Railway, described the area as "a mass of tents and a bundle of shacks."[138] The first railroad workers who began moving into the Wild Horse Desert referred to the new town as the "townsite of the Santa Gertrudis Ranch" in 1904.[139] Robert J. Kleberg, general manager of the King Ranch, along with local ranchers John Kenedy and Major John B. Armstrong, met with B. F. Yoakum to plan and draft the charter to construct the railroad, which was subsequently approved by the state secretary of Texas in 1903.[140] The construction of the railroad contributed greatly to Kingsville's population growth and emerged as the economic center of town during its early years.

Businesses included general stores, drugstores, furniture stores, small factories, and the King's Inn, "the most modern hotel in south Texas" at the time.[141] Doctors, lawyers, and other professionals were predominantly Anglo-American. Farmers of the Santa Gertrudis Growers were among the first to ship onions and other vegetables via the local train station.[142] Approximately 4,000 lived in Kingsville in 1912 according to local historian George O. Coalson, and by 1930 the population had gradually risen to 6,815, of whom 2,000 were Mexican Americans and 524 were African Americans.[143] Kingsville was incorporated as a city in 1911 and became officially established as the county seat of Kleberg County in 1913. Racial segregation began shortly afterward, dividing Anglo, Mexican American, and African American neighborhoods and businesses. The Mexican American section began in the northernmost part of the city, from Corral Street south to Kleberg Street, and extended east to west from Fourteenth Street to Sixth Street.[144] Residential segregation eventually led to racially segregated schools as well until the local school board voted unanimously to desegregate Henrietta M. King High School on July 15, 1955.[145] However, during the 1960s Mexican American students continued to attend segregated elementary and junior high schools until they enrolled in grades nine through twelve at King High School.

Kingsville began to experience a flurry of railroad construction, industrialization, and agribusiness proliferation, and it gained greater recognition during the early to mid-twentieth century. The city first appeared in the national spotlight for one brief moment in 1920, when Republican presidential nominee Warren G. Harding made a whistle-stop campaign speech outside the local train station prior to his election as president.[146] The oil, gas, and cotton industries hired many local residents throughout the area in the early 1920s before establishing its first institution of higher learning, the South Texas Teachers College.[147] In 1929, the institution changed its name to the Texas College of Arts and Industries before becoming Texas A&M University–Kingsville. As in other towns during the Great Depression, economic turmoil hit Kingsville. During this time, the railroad industry continued to serve as Kingsville's lone steady employer.[148] The local railroad first received acclaim at the outset of World War II for transporting troops out of Kingsville to cities for shipment overseas. In the early 1940s, the city's railroad played another critical role when it was contracted by the federal government to ship raw materials and goods as part of America's war effort. Kingsville's population growth increased substantially when the Naval Auxiliary Air Station Kingsville, now known as the Naval Air Station Kingsville, opened in 1942. The naval base was closed in 1946 and reopened in 1951. The influx of naval personnel boosted the local economy.[149] The Celanese Corporation of America added more jobs to Kingsville's local economy in 1944. During the 1950s, the trucking and passenger bus industries cut severely into the city's railroad business. The steam engine became obsolete, leading to a substantial loss of jobs for the Kingsville Locomotive Shop.

Summary and Conclusion

Ethnic makeup, political bossism, racial discrimination and segregation, and labor exploitation provide the context for the school protests. The insurgent movements of the last two centuries, although vying for divergent interests at different points in time, attest to the revolutionary fervor that also characterized the Chicano student movement in South Texas. Additionally, the region played a significant role in major wars, with the most notable battle sites including Palo Alto, the site of the first major skirmish of the Mexican-American War; and Palmito Ranch, the site of the last known military engagement of the Civil War.

Zachary Taylor commanded the US military at Fort Brown near present-day Brownsville prior to the outbreak of the Mexican-American War in 1846, and General Robert E. Lee lived for a short time at Fort Ringgold in the South Texas border town of Rio Grande City just before the start of the Civil War in 1860. Historic developments influenced and inspired Chicano students throughout the region to form their own protest movement during the late 1960s. In the aftermath of the Mexican Revolution and the Plan of San Diego uprising, a thriving Mexican American middle class emerged and began promoting civil rights activism, integration, greater political participation, and equal educational opportunities for people of Mexican origin from the 1910s to the 1950s.

2

Mexican American Civil Rights Activism and the Rise of the Chicano Student Movement in South Texas

The entry of the United States into World War I in April 1917 marked the beginning of cultural assimilation of Mexican Americans into US mainstream life, which instilled in them a strong sense of American patriotic values and national pride. Adhering to President Woodrow Wilson's call to make the world safe for democracy, men fought in the US military abroad, and women served on the home front in various civilian roles as seamstresses, laundresses, and operators of boardinghouses, which further facilitated their integration into US society and the acceleration of acculturation.[1] Mexican American veterans such as José de la Luz Sáenz volunteered in the US Army and served with the 360th Infantry Regiment of the 90th Division in the American Expeditionary Forces of World War I. Sáenz recorded his personal recollections in a diary published in 1933 as *Los Mexico-Americanos en la Gran Guerra y su contingente en pro de la democracia, la humanidad y la justicia: Mi diario particular* (Mexican Americans in the Great War and their contingent in the defense of democracy, humanity and justice: My diary). The diary describes the author's enlistment, service in France, and other wartime accounts of ethnic Mexican soldiers from 1918 to 1919.[2] Approximately 197,000 Texans served in the military, including an estimated 5,000 with Spanish surnames.[3]

While recalling his observations and the military contributions of fellow soldiers, Sáenz compared the Mexican American struggle for equal rights and integration at home with their fight to uphold American democracy, freedom, and justice in the US armed forces abroad.[4] Regional newspapers such as *La Prensa* (San Antonio, Texas), the *San Antonio Express,* and the *Laredo Weekly News* provide various examples of Tejano community members expressing ethnic pride, patriotism, and other such motivations for enlisting in the US military and supporting the war effort.[5] Military service during World War I allowed Tejano soldiers to adopt an American identity, acknowledge the importance of US citizenship, and gain greater proficiency in the English language.[6] Historian José A. Ramírez further comments on the common experiences of Tejano soldiers in the military: "The evidence suggest that their general experiences were akin to those of other 'white' ethnic troops—positive and worthwhile in the main, but by no means devoid of the occasional derogatory name-calling (wop, dago, and bohunk, e.g.) and other forms of hostility from intolerant peers. . . . In Sáenz's case, military life, though arduous, still allowed sufficient time for the cultivation of friendships."[7] After returning home from the war, Sáenz began collaborating with community activists Alonso S. Perales, José Tomás "J. T." Canales, and Adela Sloss Vento to promote greater civic participation and civil rights advocacy among Mexican American community leaders across South Texas from San Antonio to Brownsville.[8] Their grassroots organizing efforts eventually led to the creation of a new statewide civil rights organization known as the League of United Latin American Citizens (LULAC) by 1929.

During the 1920s, middle-class Mexican Americans established their own civic groups to exercise civil rights and acknowledge themselves as full-fledged Americans. Groups such as the Sons of America, the Knights of America, and the Latin American Citizens League merged to form LULAC in 1929.[9] The founding members of LULAC, Mexican American men who were US citizens employed as skilled laborers and small business owners, were from various cities throughout South Texas including Brownsville, Harlingen, McAllen, Laredo, Alice, Corpus Christi, and San Antonio.[10] Prominent leaders such as Ben Garza and Alonso S. Perales led the unification convention at Obreros Hall in Corpus Christi, Texas, on February 17, 1929.[11] These community activists founded LULAC at a time when numerous public establishments throughout Texas displayed "No Mexicans Allowed" signs. Therefore, most participants of the group chose to downplay their ethnic Mexican background to avoid exclusion from mainstream US society, often identified as legally "white" and English speaking, and focused on a strategy of integration to exercise their rights as US citizens.[12] Members of the new organization further sought to promote the group's ethos of solidarity and unity by choosing the motto "All for one and one for all." They also selected a shield resembling the American flag, with white stars on a navy blue background and red stripes, with the words "LULAC" in the middle, as the group's emblem, signifying a defense against racism.[13] However, those in attendance agreed to formal unification mainly in response to political disenfranchisement, resistance to bossism, racial segregation, the lack of Mexican American representation on juries, poverty among Mexican Americans, and the mistreatment of ethnic Mexican people in the workforce.[14] Striving to achieve first-class citizenship and human dignity, they determined to "work within the system" and accepted political accommodation in order to achieve equal status and gain the respect of Anglo society.

The LULAC constitution reflected the organization's adherence to American patriotism and group members' promotion of human and civil rights through the legal system. It also emphasized its members' middle-class goals of economic, social, and political rights for Mexican Americans, yet LULAC members began to identify increasingly as "México Texano" or "Mexican Texan," separate from the persona of the Mexican immigrant working class that was perceived in a different way.[15] Historian Cynthia Orozco contends that "México Texanos were US citizens who identified with Texas as a state, with a regional culture, and with the United States" and "operated in Mexican, México Texano, and European American [or Anglo] worlds," thus representing a unique and flexible hybridity.[16] México Texano became the most prevalent identity among the Mexican American community.

Among the LULAC constitution's most important stipulations were proclaiming English as its official language, educating others about American customs, and developing "within the members of our race the best, purest and most perfect type of a true and loyal citizen of the United States of America."[17] In accordance with one of its core values, LULAC advocated the belief that young children had to learn English in order to "think and act like Americans."[18] LULAC leader Alonso Perales summed up the organization's position on education, stating: "If we, the Mexican American and the Mexican citizens raised in the United States, are to occupy the honorable place that we merit, it is indispensable to educate ourselves."[19] Thus, LULAC contended that promoting higher educational attainment among students of Mexican origin would improve Mexican Americans' socioeconomic status and living conditions. This organization was also instrumental in conducting numerous poll tax drives, initiating school desegregation efforts, and supporting the election of many Mexican American politicians. Such political activity enabled LULAC to establish local chapters across the nation.

Various scholars use the term "Mexican-American Generation" to identify this type of ethnic leadership by those residing mainly in the US Southwest from the 1930s to 1950s.[20] This generation comprised mainly middle-class professionals and small numbers of working-class people who were the American-born sons and daughters of Mexican immigrants. They espoused liberal political reform and sought greater political participation and socioeconomic mobility in America.[21] Moreover, individuals of this generation directed their activities toward educational endeavors, political collaboration, acculturation within or affinity for American mainstream culture, mastery of the English language, and public recognition as patriotic Americans. In expressing their ideology or liberal agenda, they often emphasized their status as permanent US residents and their national loyalty, collaboration with liberal groups, confidence in government, cultural assimilation, and contributions to American society.[22] Political activists of the Mexican-American Generation developed strategies to combat racial discrimination, resist exclusion from American politics, and oppose economic exploitation of ethnic Mexican workers within their communities. They did so to resist their subordinate position in society as second-class citizens or those regarded as racially inferior. However, their political struggles for democracy and social integration focused on gradual and incremental reform within society during the formative years of the late 1920s early 1930s.

The Great Depression in South Texas

The Great Depression of the 1930s adversely affected Mexican Americans in South Texas, as it did so many others throughout the nation. Unemployment skyrocketed to thirteen million, or 25 percent of the US labor force.[23] Father Carmelo Tranchese, known as the "apostle of the poor," became the first Jesuit priest of Our Lady of Guadalupe Catholic Church in the heart of the West Side of San Antonio in 1932. In assessing the living and health conditions of the West Side, he confessed, "I am familiar with the slums of San Francisco, New York, London, Paris, and Naples, but those of San Antonio are the worst of all."[24] A public welfare survey of San Antonio reported in 1939 and 1940 that "there has been mass unemployment, between 15,000 and 20,000 unemployed persons, for over a decade in San Antonio."[25] Many Mexican Americans became poverty stricken and left the cities in search of jobs in rural areas, but they lost even low-paying menial work in the agricultural sector.[26] One other significant event of the 1930s involved the US government's repatriation of undocumented Mexicans, and even some American citizens of Mexican descent. More than 270,000 people of Mexican origin were repatriated through the government's attempt to reduce welfare loads and open jobs to white American workers.[27] Very few Mexican Americans qualified for employment under relief programs such as the Works Progress Administration and Civilian Conservation Corps. No known source offers data regarding how many of those repatriated during the 1930s were from South Texas.

The 1930s, however, were also a time of increased labor unrest. Labor protests occurred in the pecan industry in the West Side of San Antonio in the mid-to-late 1930s. The Texas pecan industry, dominated by the San Antonio–based Southern Pecan Shelling Company, accounted for roughly half the nation's production.[28] The pecan-shelling industry was one of the lowest-paying industries in the nation. The protest began when approximately five thousand ethnic Mexican workers, mostly women, went on strike for higher wages before gaining an income of fifteen cents per hour in 1934.[29] In her book *Women of the Depression*,

Julia Kirk Blackwelder writes: "Hispanic women dominated jobs as seamstresses and pecan shellers, while other women held numerical advantages as servants and waitresses . . . but pecan shelling and hand sewing were the lowest paid jobs in San Antonio. . . . Mexican Americans in San Antonio initially entered into pecan shelling and provided an attractive labor supply for shellers because the work was seasonal and could be taken up after the agricultural harvest. Shelling plants were concentrated on the West Side, where Mexican American residence centered and population density was highest."[30] Pecan industry workers initiated another strike four years later after a drastic reduction in wages. Emma Tenayuca Brooks, a key figure in local politics and in the Communist-affiliated group Workers Alliance, emerged as the prominent strike leader.[31] In addition to low wages, workers protested the deplorable working conditions, including the lack of restroom facilities and insufficient ventilation. The high amount of pecan dust contributed to the high tuberculosis rate in San Antonio, 148 deaths per 100,000 people, compared to the national average of 54.[32]

As many as twelve thousand pecan shellers, mostly ethnic Mexican women, went on strike. The labor union representing the pecan shellers and endorsing the strike was the United Cannery, Agricultural, Packing, and Allied Workers of America (UCAPAWA). Local police arrested an estimated seven hundred strikers, attracting national attention.[33] Strike leaders and the American Civil Liberties Union sought an injunction against the strike-related violence by police, but a local judge denied the request.[34] This action also led Texas governor James Allred to call for a state government investigation, led by the Texas Industrial Commission, into allegations of civil rights violations by the pecan industry. The investigation charged that the police had interfered with the strikers' right to peaceful assembly before the Fair Labor Standards Act established a minimum wage of twenty-five cents per hour in 1938.[35] One Hispanic woman who participated in the strike alleged that a policeman had deliberately hit her in the stomach with a baton while she remained on the picket line.[36] In examining the ramifications of Mexican American labor activism in San Antonio, Blackwelder notes, "While the strike of 1934 and the more protracted and violent strike of 1938 closed down several plants, they [striking workers] were ineffective in interfering with home shelling and encouraged plant owners to adopt the contract system." By the early 1940s, more than ten thousand pecan shellers had lost their jobs because of a significant increase in mechanization (cracking machines) in the San Antonio pecan industry.[37]

Mexican Americans during World War II and Postwar Activism

World War II marked another major turning point for Mexican Americans that fundamentally redefined their status as US citizens in mainstream society.

Hispanic men enlisted and fought alongside Anglo-American soldiers in the military, and US factories recruited Hispanic women to work in male-dominated trades such as welding, riveting, and engine repair. The wartime experience further reinvigorated Mexican Americans' sense of national pride, loyalty, and "Americanness." Approximately four hundred thousand had served in the armed forces, "were awarded a notable record of commendations," and "had proven their tenacity in every major battle of the war" when the term "Mexican American" was first popularized.[38] Despite their heroism in combat, Mexican American veterans returned home after defeating Hitler and the Japanese, only to find that "Mexicans" were still second-class citizens in the land they had fought so bravely to protect. Nevertheless, wartime industry offered better jobs, "with more [Mexican American] workers than ever before entering skilled and semi-skilled positions."[39] During the postwar years, Mexican American activists began their own campaign for civil rights to oppose the second-class citizenship that had been their lot before the war. More specifically, they demanded equality, launching political and legal campaigns to secure better treatment at the same time that they attempted to assert that Mexicans were racially white.[40] Historian Ricardo Romo underscores how Mexican American veterans' wartime service had accelerated their Americanization: "Nationwide, Mexican-Americans returned as the most decorated ethnic group in the armed services, winning seventeen Medals of Honor. Those who did not receive Medals of Honor often gained in other ways from their experiences in the service. Many soon applied the skills that they learned while in uniform to civilian life . . . the postwar years were also marked by increased political activism aimed at obtaining local political representation, metropolitan services and improvements, and equity in the judicial system."[41] Thus, Mexican Americans, especially war veterans, gained a renewed sense of patriotism shortly after the establishment of the American GI Forum during the post–World War II era. The fight against fascism had taught them important concepts such as sacrifice and perseverance as they began their quest toward middle-class economic stability and respectability upon receiving the GI Bill.

Hector P. García, a physician of the South Texas city of Corpus Christi who served as an army medic during World War II, founded the organization in 1947. After García organized a group of Mexican American veterans from throughout the Corpus Christi area, they chose the name "American GI Forum" to emphasize their allegiance and service to the United States.[42] The organization's name not only suggested a connection to US military service, a requirement for membership, but had a symbolic association with American patriotism that García and group members valued as their passion for working together.[43] García emerged as the "general," or key leader who unified Mexican Americans in becoming politically active to gain recognition of their rights and privileges as US citizens during the post–World War II era. One important part of García's "battle plan" or reform agenda to remedy injustice involved seeking the benefits and privileges outlined in the GI Bill of Rights, as well as demanding that the Veterans Administration (now the Department of Veterans Affairs) provide compensation for Hispanic veterans' medical treatment. However, García and the American GI Forum first gained national attention when they led a protest campaign during the so-called Felix Longoria incident in Three Rivers, Texas, in 1948.[44] This event involved the denial of Private Felix Longoria's funeral wake in his hometown of Three Rivers, seventy miles south of San Antonio.

The incident began when funeral director Tom Kennedy denied Longoria's spouse, Beatrice, the wake, claiming that the "whites [Anglo Americans of the local community] wouldn't like it."[45] García learned of Kennedy's refusal to allow the funeral service upon discussing the matter with Longoria's widow and her sister. He received the same refusal and rationale when he talked to the funeral director by phone. García then sent numerous telegrams and letters to Texas senator Lyndon B. Johnson in an appeal for a resolution to the situation.[46] Johnson sympathized with García and Beatrice Longoria's dilemma and responded by arranging the burial of Private Longoria's remains at Arlington National Cemetery in Washington, DC, in 1949. This controversial case served to unify and consolidate the political power base of Mexican Americans in South Texas and throughout the nation. Most Mexican Americans were already active supporters of the Democratic Party in Texas; however, according to historian Juan Gómez-Quiñones, they "were not widely recognized electorally as a significant factor in the national presidential elections."[47] Many Mexican American political activists of the postwar era such as García publicized their struggle for civil rights through the awareness of this incident. Although numerous Chicano history texts underscore the post–World War II era as the birth of modern Mexican American civil rights activism, historian Cynthia E. Orozco contends that such activism encompassed a broader social movement between 1920 and 1965 comprising numerous smaller movements across the decades in different states and regions.[48] She further argues that previous studies of LULAC failed to use social movement theory to analyze the league's development and history and did not fully postulate the meaning of the "Mexican American civil rights movement."[49] According to her research, most activist-scholars who once participated in the 1960s Chicano Movement do not view LULAC as a successful Mexican American civil rights advocacy group and remain reluctant to acknowledge pre–World War II activism as part of "the" Mexican American civil rights movement.

Like LULAC, the American GI Forum highly valued and endorsed the educational interests of Mexican Americans. One statement in the organization's

52 ～ CHAPTER 2

informational pamphlet indicates that members considered education an important issue: "Education is the principal weapon to fight the many evils affecting our people."[50] Thus, the GI Forum joined the struggle to combat racial discrimination in the public schools. It emerged as a key financial supporter of ethnic Mexican student education by conducting school drives, canvassing house to house, and raising scholarship funds to help young Mexican Americans finish high school and attend college.[51] This organization joined LULAC in initiating litigation in the courts to seek redress for the educational deficiencies of schoolchildren of Mexican origin.

Four major Chicano school litigation cases, two of which were supported by LULAC and the GI Forum in the 1940s and 1950s, called for such redress by seeking the desegregation of public schools. Prior to the famous *Brown v. Board of Education* desegregation school case pertaining to African Americans in 1954–55, the *Del Rio Independent School District v. Salvatierra* case was filed in 1930. This historic case challenged the segregation of schools in the small rural Texas border town of Del Rio. More importantly, this landmark case represented the first significant legal challenge to school segregation in America. The Texas Court of Civil Appeals ruled in the Del Rio case that segregation based on national origin was unconstitutional, but it allowed segregation based on the "pedagogical wisdom" of the educators to separate children with "language problems."[52] A 1923 report on illiteracy in Texas by University of Texas professor Everett E. Davis underscores the insensitive and prejudicial nature of Americanization literature in favor of school segregation: "The American children and those of the Mexican children who are clean and high-minded do not like to go to school with the dirty 'greaser' type of Mexican child. It is not right that they should have to. There is but one choice in the matter of educating these unfortunate [Mexican American] children and that is to put the 'dirty' ones into separate schools till they learn how to 'clean up' and become eligible to better society."[53] Another historic study further elaborates the rationale concerning the segregation of Mexican American students in 1970: "Separate schools gave Mexican American children the opportunity to overcome these deficiencies and protected them from having to compete with Anglos and thus feeling inferior . . . segregation seemed to be maintained out of fear of intermarriage with inferior people and a feeling that if Mexican Americans were educated, they would not be so easy to manipulate and would no longer work for low wages."[54] Thus, many students of Mexican origin continued to attend segregated schools because educators presumed that Mexican American children lacked the ability to master the English language upon entering school, and they associated Mexican dirtiness or dirty "greasers" with racial inferiority, low-class status, ignorance, and poverty.

In 1946, *Mendez v. Westminster School District* outlawed the continued segregation of Mexican American schoolchildren in California. Judge Paul J. McCormick ruled in the case that the segregation of Mexican American students was illegal since they were not an officially recognized ethnic/racial group under the law.[55] Scholar Ian Haney-López argues that Mexican American activists of the mid-twentieth century were "employing what they termed the 'other white' strategy," when "these groups [LULAC and the American GI Forum] insisted that Mexican Americans were members of the white race and that, consequently, no basis existed for subjecting Mexicans to racial segregation of the sort imposed on blacks."[56] As in the Mendez case, segregation of schoolchildren of Mexican ancestry was unconstitutional according to the rulings of *Delgado v. Bastrop Independent School District* (1948) and *Hernandez v. Driscoll Consolidated Independent School District* (1957).[57] *Alvarez vs. the Board of Trustees of the Lemon Grove School District* was the first successful school desegregation court decision in the history of the United States, made in 1930. Lemon Grove was a rural suburb of San Diego, California. This landmark case served as the legal precedent for later desegregation court cases.[58] Despite these efforts toward educational reform via court rulings, racial segregation and discrimination against students of Mexican ancestry in the public schools continued. However, Mexican American activists persisted in their fight against school segregation after the postwar years.

Chicano Desegregation Cases during the Latter Twentieth Century

In *Chapa v. Odem* (1967), Mexican Americans living in the small South Texas town of Odem near Corpus Christi filed a case alleging school segregation based on the testing of English-language proficiency. The plaintiffs argued that the school district's basis for separating Mexican American schoolchildren was invalid because it could not assign a qualified educator to teach the allegedly English-deficient students.[59] In his final ruling, Judge Woodrow Seals ordered the Odem School District to cease the segregation of Mexican American schoolchildren. James De Anda, a pioneering civil rights lawyer, tried the *Chapa v. Odem* case along with fellow activist George I. Sánchez, who offered legal advice and testimony.[60] However, De Anda had previously played a key role in *Hernandez v. Texas*, a US Supreme Court decision in 1954 that prohibited the Texas courts from systematically excluding Mexican Americans from jury duty while granting them equal protection under the Constitution as a class apart. De Anda used the "class apart" strategy in *Chapa v. Odem.*[61]

The first case to extend the US Supreme Court's *Brown v. Board of Education of Topeka* (Kansas) decision (1954) to Mexican Americans was *Císneros v. Corpus Christi Independent School District* (1970). This decision recognized Tejanos in Corpus Christi, Texas, as a separate race, reaffirmed by the ruling of the US Supreme Court in *Hernandez v. Texas* (1954), which acknowledged their constitutional rights based on class discrimination.[62]

In 1968, José Císneros, bothered by his children's descriptions of "broken windows and dirty bathrooms" at their school, and twenty-five other Mexican American and African American parents filed suit against the Corpus Christi Independent School District (CCISD).[63] This was the first desegregation lawsuit funded by a labor union; all the plaintiffs were members of the United Steelworkers of America.[64] The plaintiffs, assisted by the Mexican American Legal Defense and Educational Fund (MALDEF), alleged that school officials operated a de facto dual school system at all levels.

James De Anda, the attorney in *Hernandez* and *Chapa*, served as cocounsel in the *Cisneros* case, arguing that CCISD illegally segregated Mexican American students according to state law, whereas school officials, the defendants, claimed that no such law allowed segregation based on race or permitted the establishment of a dual school system.[65] The plaintiffs accused CCISD of violating the Fourteenth Amendment of the US Constitution and Title VI of the 1964 Civil Rights Act.[66] Woodrow Seals, who had previously served as judge in the *Chapa* case, considered data from expert testimony and rulings from previous Mexican American desegregation cases before issuing his ruling. Citing the "other white" argument, Judge Seals found that "Mexican American students are an identifiable, ethnic-minority class sufficient to bring them within the protection of Brown [v. Board of Education]."[67] He also believed that Mexican Americans were "more susceptible to discrimination" based on physical, cultural, religious and language usage.[68] Thus, he declared that CCISD was responsible for operating a dual or segregated school system that "has its real roots in the minds of men."[69] School officials were reluctant to draft a new zoning plan to satisfy constitutional requirements for school integration until 1975.[70] Historian Carlos Kevin Blanton assesses the ramifications of the *Cisneros* case: "The Cisneros decision opened the door for legal activists to push the boundaries of civil rights law. As the history of educational discrimination against Mexican Americans involved curricular justifications for segregation, it only followed that notions of school integration for Mexican Americans involved not just shifting bodies but also a complete overhaul of the standard curriculum that had enabled such discrimination in the first place. Bilingual-bicultural education was viewed as a possible remedy along with busing and the redrawing of school districts in school integration plans."[71] American GI Forum leader Hector P. García and seventeen Chicano activists were arrested during a sit-in protest at CCISD headquarters.[72] The next major court decision that occurred shortly after *Císneros* concerned the implementation of bilingual education and school desegregation.

In *United States of America v. State of Texas* (1971), Judge William Wayne Justice handed down one of the most extensive desegregation orders in the state's history, endowing the Texas Education Agency (TEA) with the arduous task of integrating the entire Texas public school system. A key part of the case declared that the San Felipe Del Rio Consolidated Independent School District had failed to obtain federal funding for a comprehensive educational plan mandated by the court.[73] This plan also supported the educational needs of language-minority students and called for "sufficient educational safeguards to insure that all students in the San Felipe Del Rio Consolidated Independent School District will be offered equal educational opportunities" such as "bilingual and bicultural programs" along with other appropriate curriculum modifications.[74] During the previous year, on May 25, 1970, the Office for Civil Rights had issued a memo in support of bilingual education that restricted school districts with more than 5 percent language-minority students from placing students in special education or low-ability courses based on language proficiency. Additional directives of the memo included requiring schools to "take affirmative steps to rectify the language deficiency," and giving parents prior notice of school activities in their own native language.[75] The *United States of America v. State of Texas* decision and the Office for Civil Rights memo intended to reduce segregation and ethnic isolation and acknowledged the linguistic diversity of language minorities.

Other landmark cases contesting the segregation of Mexican American schoolchildren during the latter twentieth century include *Ross v. Eckels* (1970), *Keys v. School District No. 1 of Denver Colorado* (1973), *Soria v. Oxnard School District Board of Trustees* (1974), and *Diaz v. San Jose Unified School District* (1985).[76] Mexican Americans were classified as an "other white" group in order to circumvent *Brown v. Board of Education of Topeka* until *Císneros v. Corpus Christi Independent School District* in Texas officially recognized them as an identifiable ethnic group. Segregation had stagnated the intellectual development of Mexican American students, which meant that they became vulnerable to poor academic achievement, were often assigned to non-college-bound curriculum tracks, and received less equitable learning opportunities. Attending racially and socioeconomically segregated schools negatively affected the educational opportunities of Mexican Americans, thus perpetuating the stereotype of ethnic Mexicans as a culturally inferior people. Separate schools were also deemed necessary in order to prevent students of Mexican descent from supposedly holding back the academic progress of Anglo students based on the ideology of white supremacy, as argued by Carlos Kevin Blanton, Rubén Donato, and Gilbert G. González. Race, culture, and language were seen as detrimental to learning for students of Mexican origin and provided the basis for establishing segregated schools. Therefore, desegregation lawsuits represented an important part of the

56   CHAPTER 2

Mexican American struggle for better education, fought in the courts rather than on the picket line in an effort to uphold Chicano students' legal right to integrated schooling.

Major cultural, social, and political developments throughout the history of South Texas must be understood to contextualize the environment in which the Chicano student walkouts occurred. This historical synopsis provides a glimpse into the ethnic makeup, social and cultural fabric, political instability, and environment of discrimination and exploitation that led to the protests. The insurgent movements of the last two centuries, although vying for divergent interests at different points in time, attest to the progressive character and political fervor that also characterized the Chicano student movement in South Texas. These movements include the Texas Revolution, Mexican-American War, Juan Cortina raid, Civil War, Mexican Revolution, and Plan of San Diego uprising. Such armed conflicts resulted in the dramatic transformation of the region's society, system of government, and struggle for land and its resources. The civil rights activism of LULAC and the American GI Forum served in part to promote betterquality education for Mexican Americans through community action. The pecan shellers' strike and Felix Longoria incident emerged as important twentieth-century protest movements organized by ethnic Mexican people in South Texas. These pre-1960s upheavals prompted Mexican Americans to mobilize and speak out against social injustice and racism. Such historic events would influence and inspire Chicano students in South Texas to do the same during the 1960s, thus continuing a long tradition of grassroots activism while promoting their own brand of ethnic solidarity and community control in South Texas. An overview of the American Civil Rights Movement reveals the broader historical influences that would further motivate Chicano students to take action for social and political change in their communities.

The Broader Historical Influences on Chicano Student Activism

The 1960s ushered in a liberal political era in national politics under Presidents John F. Kennedy and Lyndon B. Johnson, who appealed to the political aspirations of Mexican Americans. Both presidential candidates and their respective campaigns successfully mobilized Mexican American voters with the formation of "Viva Kennedy" and "Viva Johnson" clubs. Kennedy received approximately 85 percent of the vote among this new electorate because he "shared with most of them a Roman Catholic religious heritage, and had a wife who spoke to them in Spanish."[77] Many characterize the major events of this memorable decade in America as tumultuous, chaotic, and virtually earth shattering. The Civil Rights Movement of this era impacted most events across the nation. Numerous people formed their own social protest movements for political change and equality. The African American Civil Rights and Anti–Vietnam War Movements were major influential forces that stimulated a parallel movement among Mexican Americans during the 1960s. The burning desire for civil and human rights served as the fuel that kept the fires of each movement alive throughout the entire decade. Those participating in the larger Civil Rights Movement sought freedoms, liberties, and political rights denied them because of their race, ethnicity, gender, sexual orientation, or country of origin. The most significant part of the movement pertained to the peaceful, nonviolent protests influenced by the teachings of civil disobedience introduced by Mahatma Gandhi, César Chávez, and Martin Luther King Jr. The modern Chicano political movement, most scholars agree, began during the mid-1960s, a time coinciding with the African American Civil Rights Movement.

One can trace the roots of the Civil Rights Movement in America to the major historical events of the mid- to late 1950s. Beginning in 1954, the US Supreme Court outlawed school segregation in the landmark *Brown v. Board of Education of Topeka* (Kansas) ruling. Oliver Brown, the plaintiff, sued the Topeka school system, arguing that his daughter should attend a nearby white school rather than a predominantly black school that was distant from their home. Thurgood Marshall, the plaintiff's lawyer from the National Association for the Advancement of Colored People (NAACP), contended that the concept of "separate but equal" did not promote equality and inhibited black students' academic progress. Prior to the court's decision, President Dwight D. Eisenhower appointed Earl Warren as chief justice in 1952. Although Warren was a conservative, the Warren-led court ushered in pathbreaking, historic decisions supporting liberal activism in racial issues and individual rights. Thus, the *Brown* decision declared that "separate educational facilities are inherently unequal," and the court called for the integration of schools "with all deliberate speed." This pro–civil rights case not only overruled the "separate but equal" decision of the 1896 *Plessy v. Ferguson* case but represented one means to eradicate racial segregation in society.[78]

Not long after the conclusion of the *Brown* case, African Americans waged another important challenge against racial segregation. The confrontation began when seamstress Rosa Parks refused to give up her seat on a public bus in Montgomery, Alabama, on December 1, 1955. Her refusal subsequently led to her arrest and the beginning of the Montgomery bus boycott by African Americans. The birth of nonviolent civil rights resistance began when a young and relatively unknown Baptist preacher named Martin Luther King Jr. emerged as the leader of the boycott movement. He also formed the first major 1960s civil rights advocacy group, known as the Southern Christian Leadership Conference (SCLC). Meanwhile, the boycott involved a citywide effort by African Americans to deliberately avoid public buses. Instead, many organized carpools or walked to their destinations around town as a means to pressure city officials to integrate the bus system. The boycott lasted one year, until the Supreme Court officially outlawed segregation on the city's public buses in the landmark case *Browder v. Gayle* in 1956. The boycott represented the first mass movement of the civil rights era that succeeded in propelling racial equality in the South. Rosa Parks summed up the historical significance of her arrest by simply stating, "The direct-action civil rights movement had begun."[79]

Throughout the 1960s, the rising numbers of marches, boycotts, sit-ins, and picket lines in response to racial inequality and discrimination within mainstream American society vastly influenced Mexican Americans. In August 1963, King delivered his famous "I Have a Dream" speech before an estimated quarter of a million people in Washington, DC, and in front of a nationwide television audience, bringing broader attention to civil rights issues and challenging the nation to live up to its founding principles of freedom and equality. His speech further endorsed the end of segregation and the advancement of civil rights, and he exhorted the country to make racial equality a reality.[80] On November 22, 1963, the nation endured one of the most tragic moments in its history when an assassin, Lee Harvey Oswald, shot President John F. Kennedy in a motorcade in downtown Dallas, Texas. Kennedy was an enormously popular president before his assassination, and many young people felt that their hopes died with him. Upholding Kennedy's pledge to support civil rights legislation, President Lyndon B. Johnson signed into law the Civil Rights Act of 1964 and the Voting Rights Act of 1965. These laws represented the most far-reaching and comprehensive civil rights legislation passed by Congress in the twentieth century. Both laws were passed as a way to honor President Kennedy after Johnson used his connections with key congressional leaders to secure their approval. However, the passage of these laws did not come easily. Johnson faced much criticism and opposition while winning bipartisan support and congressional approval for both laws. The Civil Rights Act banned racial discrimination and segregation in public establishments and workplaces on the basis of race, color, religion, sex, or national origin. After he officially signed the Civil Rights Act, President Johnson turned his attention to voting rights the following year.

In his eloquent "We Shall Overcome" speech, delivered to Congress on March 15, 1965, President Johnson spoke on the importance of passing the Voting Rights Act a week after African Americans were brutally attacked by white police officers while marching peacefully from Selma to Montgomery, Alabama.[81] While pledging his commitment to voting rights before a national TV audience, Johnson also began to introduce his unconditional "War on Poverty" domestic program along with social welfare initiatives endorsing government support for job training, a higher minimum wage, housing and urban renewal initiatives, and greater access to health care and educational programming.[82] Johnson also made public the conditions of poverty that plagued Mexican American students in segregated schools, describing his first job as a twenty-year-old teacher in training at the Welhausen "Mexican" Elementary School in the South Texas town of Cotulla, ninety miles southwest of San Antonio:

> My students were poor and they often came to class without breakfast, hungry. And they knew, even in their youth, the pain of prejudice. They never seemed to know why people disliked them. But they knew it was so, because I saw it in their eyes. I often walked home late in the afternoon, after the classes were finished, wishing there was more that I could do. But all I knew was to teach them the little that I knew, hoping that it might help them against the hardships that lay ahead. And somehow you never forget what poverty and hatred can do when you see its scars on the hopeful face of a young child. I never thought then, in 1928, that I would be standing here in 1965. It never even occurred to me in my fondest dreams that I might have the chance to help the sons and daughters of those students and to help people like them all over this country. But now I do have that chance—and I'll let you in on a secret—I mean to use it.[83]

His remarks on Cotulla, which linked the voting rights struggle with the hardships of his poorest students, were met with rousing applause from the congressional chamber.

Cotulla school superintendent W. T. Donaho had offered Johnson the teaching position after they met at Southwest Texas State Teachers College (present-day Texas State University in San Marcos) in 1928, which included the supervision of five other teachers, teaching sixth and seventh grade, and directing various extracurricular activities.[84] Johnson first demonstrated compassion for the poverty of others when he used most of his first month's salary ($125) to buy sporting equipment for the school, and he instilled in his students a desire to learn by organizing debate and spelling bee competitions with neighboring schools.[85] Historian Gene Preuss sums up how Johnson's experience in Cotulla likely influenced his desire to exert the strong leadership he later exhibited during his presidency: "Although his parents had been poor, when Lyndon Johnson moved to Cotulla he found a level of poverty and discrimination he had probably never experienced before, and one that certainly made a lasting impression upon the young teacher."[86] Other scholars such as Julie Leininger Pycior characterize Johnson as being paternalistic and condescending in his role as a

60 ～ CHAPTER 2

teacher: "Even while he stood out as a tireless advocate on behalf of his students, Johnson acted for them, rather than with them. He enjoyed the authority his professional position commanded; he would help his students, but on his terms, drawing them into his world."[87] Nevertheless, Johnson's experience as an educator involved his adherence to the values of Americanization, which focused on assimilation, English only, and patriotism. In 1966, Johnson returned to Cotulla as president to honor National Education Week, and as part of the celebration, he spoke of his role as a young teacher at Welhausen Elementary School. His experience in Cotulla was one of the most important influences for his War on Poverty: "Right here I had my first lessons in poverty. I had my first lessons in the high price we pay for poverty and prejudice right here."[88] Thus, Johnson's visit to Cotulla helped solidify his civil rights legacy as a former educator who once served students from one of the most impoverished areas of the country, which formed a key part of his domestic reform agenda for the nation, promising young Mexican Americans a better education.

Mexican American youth watched the major events of the larger Civil Rights Movement unfold and saw their aftermath on the evening news and in the newspapers. Such events inspired them to ignite their own movement for social and political change in South Texas. By the late 1960s, young Chicanos along with older movement activists took direct action—public marches, boycotts, pickets, sit-ins, and rallies—in response to the harsh and unjust circumstances involving racial inequality, violence, poverty, and discrimination. Amid the ever-growing societal and political transformations of the country, Chicanos emerged as actors in forging their own movement for civil rights, political change, and social justice beginning in 1968. As in many other places throughout the Southwest, Chicano students in South Texas were awakened to the need for reform within their schools and longed for dignity and respect, especially in making the Spanish language and ethnic Mexican culture an integral part of their education. Indeed, the role of students was unique in the 1960s. Thus, the Chicano student walkouts evolved much like the other major historical, nonviolent grassroots protests throughout this era.

The Coming of Age of Chicano Movement Activists

The baby boomer generation, a new politicized generation of activists born and raised during the 1940s and 1950s, initiated their own social movement for ethnic awareness, social justice, and civil rights during the Chicano Movement. Most activists claimed that this movement began after the end of the Mexican-American War in 1848, when most Mexicans living in the newly acquired US territories (California, Arizona, Nevada, Utah, Colorado, and New Mexico) agreed to become American citizens under the Treaty of Guadalupe Hidalgo. They further argued that Mexican Americans had always struggled for recognition as full-fledged citizens because of the denial of their civil and property rights under the treaty and the US Constitution since 1848. This struggle had convinced young Chicanos that they were a colonized people economically exploited by conquest, like most nonwhite groups, because of the expansion of American imperial control since the nineteenth century. They also began embracing a new political consciousness and a unique cultural identity apart from whiteness: "This generation—the Chicano Generation—would no longer accept invisibility, irrelevance, marginalization, discrimination, racism, and second-class citizenship . . . [they embraced] a new empowered identity and a new sense of their human worth."[89] During their childhood and adolescence, Chicano students lived through the early Cold War period and Vietnam War era characterized by McCarthyism, the Atomic Age, conservative values and conformity, national economic prosperity, the popularity of the automobile, the glamor of rock 'n' roll music, and the burgeoning Civil Rights Movement. The eight-year presidency of Dwight D. Eisenhower was a relatively peaceful one after he ended the Korean War with an armistice in 1953.

The Eisenhower-era campaign known as Operation Wetback involved the large-scale deportation and mass-arrest roundup of an unknown number of ethnic Mexican people in the United States in a way that was both indiscriminate and selectively targeted against such people. Historian Jerry Cunningham notes, "Caught up in the campaign were many Mexican-American citizens, arrested and deported without charge or warrant and delivered, along with the mass of undocumented Mexican nationals, by rows of buses and crowded trains into Mexico's interior, and shipped on the ships named *The Emancipator* and *The Mercurio* from Port Isabel, Texas, over 500 miles south to Veracruz, Mexico."[90] However, the Chicano Movement was made possible by the massive migration of Mexican immigrants and Mexican Americans in major cities such as Los Angeles, San Diego, Denver, Phoenix, Albuquerque, El Paso, Houston, and San Antonio. Historian George J. Sánchez wrote of the Mexican American family as a multifaceted unit with divergent interests, in which "some immigrants settled in largely Mexican communities along the border; others ventured further inland where the Anglo American population dominated." He also revealed that the Mexican-origin family unit was an amalgam of migrant and resident populations, with some families composed of Mexican and American unions and each "acculturated and adapted in a multitude of ways." By the 1960s, the Mexican American community became much more urban, leading to the creation or expansion of Mexican barrios, usually in the poorest section of the city. Family ties, cultural heritage, and common language and values became the foundations for the emergence of a highly concentrated Mexican American population in East Los Angeles and in other cities in the US Southwest where segregated schools existed.[91] The ethnic Mexican population vastly outnumbered Anglo-American residents in most rural farming communities where the agricultural industry thrived. Chicano activists further challenged "the assumptions, politics, and principles of the established political leaders, organizations, and activity within and outside the [Mexican American] community."[92] The Chicano Movement called for immediate reform through increased political action, cultural regeneration, and greater attention toward addressing the needs of the Mexican American working class.

In 1962, Mexican American labor activists César Chávez, Dolores Huerta, and members of the National Farm Workers Association (later named the United Farm Workers of America, or UFW) became the first major participants in Mexican American protests during this era.[93] The UFW attracted national attention to farmworkers' struggles for basic workers' rights such as collective bargaining and minimum wages, beginning in California. The union eventually achieved greater success through nonviolent protest tactics (strikes, boycotts, pickets, and marches), including the adoption of civil disobedience practiced by leaders Mahatma Gandhi in India and Martin Luther King Jr. in the South. King adapted Gandhi's idea of civil disobedience to the Civil Rights Movement. The Chicano Generation took notice of the farmworkers' movement and the events and forces behind the Civil Rights Movement that promoted social and political change around the nation. Television news coverage showing various UFW protesters carrying red flags with the black eagle symbol, and banners with the words *huelga* (strike) and *viva la causa* (long live our cause), soon became unifying symbols for the Chicano Movement, thus inspiring Chicano students to initiate their own protests.[94] The movement further raised a collective cry of "Ya basta!" (We have had enough!)

By the time the school walkouts in South Texas began in 1968, the Civil Rights Movement had already emerged as a nationwide campaign that explicitly demonstrated the power and effect of nonviolent social protest action by the masses. One aspect of the movement politicized Mexican American youth by calling attention to the inequities of the US public school system. Ethnic Mexican students who became movement activists because of the social forces and political climate of the sixties pursued a different approach in seeking acceptance of and respect for their cultural distinctiveness, claiming a need for quality education access and reform at their schools. Armando B. Rendón, in his *Chicano Manifesto*, expressed the new political fervor of Chicano activists: "The Chicano insists that the Anglo respect his language and grant it equal value in any educational system where Chicano students are dominant. The Chicano insists that his culture, his way of life, and that he as a person be taken into account when housing is built, when industry offers jobs, when political parties caucus."[95] Many such activists refuted the conventional methods of political negotiation of the so-called Mexican American Generation, which they viewed as too passive, ineffectual, and accommodating. They did not call for social integration, cultural assimilation, or allying themselves with liberal Democratic politicians, as had the Mexican American Generation; rather, they favored a militant version of cultural and political self-determination, and community control of US institutions beginning with their local schools. Thus, many Mexican American activists "faced . . . a juncture between integration and self-determination" because of the seemingly paltry gains or tokenism applied to civil rights since the World War II era.[96] Sharp tongued, energized, and defiant, young Chicano activists became vociferous in expressing their frustrations and urged their peers to protest en masse.

These movement participants also rejected the proassimilationist creed of LULAC and the American GI Forum, denounced the authority of gringo (white American) society, and refused to use such pre-1960s euphemisms as "Latin American" or "Spanish American," choosing instead the term "Chicano."[97] Chicanos in the late 1960s became quick to criticize the so-called accommodationist approach of their activist predecessors, and they rarely acknowledged the social and political context of their elders' times despite building on their activist traditions.[98] They further believed that LULAC and the American GI Forum catered only to a small, politically active middle class in urban areas, and that the socioeconomic gains made by the Mexican American Generation had been woefully inadequate. Although both traditional reformers and militant ones like those of the Chicano Generation believed that educational reform ranked as one of the most important issues of their community, both camps pursued their own objectives. Chicano historian Ignacio M. García argues: "Protesting educational inequalities was not new to Mexican American reform activity, but unlike the educational battles fought from the 1930s to the 1950s by middle class reformers, which were mostly about segregation and ending the 'Mexican schools,' these ones called for more funding for predominately Mexican American schools, the firing of racist teachers and administrators, the end of the ban on Spanish, and a curriculum that prepared Mexican American students for college and taught them their history."[99] Thus, this new generation of political radicals sought to develop a true Chicano identity emphasizing ethnic solidarity among all Mexican Americans while reconstructing a new narrative of their own shared history vis-à-vis numerous cultural icons. These icons included imagined Aztec deities, Our Lady of Guadalupe or the Virgin Mary, Mexican revolutionary leaders, the eagle and serpent of the Mexican flag, and the reconquest of Aztlán, the mythical homeland of the pre-Columbian Mexican indigenous civilization.[100] Implicit in their Mexican cultural affinity was the affirmation of their ancestral Aztec Indian roots, with its emphasis on masculinity, virility, and brute force.[101]

Chicanos turned to cultural nationalism as a means to define their shared culture, imagined Mexican nationalism that proclaimed unity across borders, and embraced an idealized indigenous past grounded in Aztec folklore such as that of Aztlán. Benedict Anderson's highly acclaimed *Imagined Communities* refers to shared national identity as an imagined community where "the members of even the smallest nation will never know most of their fellow-members, meet them, or even hear of them, yet in the minds of each lives the image of their communion," because despite coming from diverse upbringings, they are still members of the same community.[102] American identity was suppressed to prevent a loss of ethnic identity and history by rejecting the melting pot integrationist model involving the fusion of nationalities, cultures, and ethnicities. This form of nationalism allowed Chicanos to define themselves on their own terms and instilled a greater sense of ethnic solidarity when they began viewing themselves as a colonized people. However, such nationalism failed to unify ethnic Mexican people from different religious, political, class, and economic backgrounds.

By incorporating more radical and forceful confrontational tactics, Chicanos sought to liberate themselves from the marginalized status they held in the United States, and they wanted "equality with white America; demanded an end to racism, and asserted their right to cultural autonomy and national self-determination."[103] Most activists adopted the militant ideology of chicanismo while rejecting the term "Mexican American" and its proassimilationist philosophy:

> Chicanismo involves a crucial distinction in political consciousness between a Mexican American and a Chicano mentality. The Mexican American is a person who lacks respect for his cultural and ethnic heritage. Unsure of himself, he seeks assimilation as a way out of his 'degraded' social status. Consequently, he remains politically ineffective. In contrast Chicanismo reflects self-respect and pride in one's ethnic and cultural background, Thus the Chicano acts with confidence and with a range of alternatives in the political world. He is capable of developing an effective ideology through action.[104]

Thus, Chicanos regarded those of the Mexican American Generation as *vendidos* (sellouts), or acculturated Mexican Americans accused of selling out their ethnic culture (Mexicanness) in favor of acquiescing to Anglo society. Chicano activist Carlos Guerra, a native of Robstown, Texas, offered his personal views on the radical and assertive approach, which differed from the conservative style or accommodating nature of the Mexican American Generation: "There was a great dissatisfaction building within the youth over the old-line organizations like the [American] G.I. Forum and LULAC who had by this time [late 1960s] been reduced to social clubs, and did little. They would go out and never really protest anything because they didn't want to compromise their dignity. If you can't be an activist, if you can't risk everything, join the G.I. Forum, join LULAC, because we [Chicano activists] were looking for people [new recruits] who could take on tactics that were in every way confrontational."[105]

José Angel Gutiérrez, one of the foremost leaders of the Chicano Movement, rejected "the LULAC example of assimilationist thought."[106] Mario Compean, a Chicano leader from San Antonio, expressed his interest in adopting new political strategies during the late 1960s: "What we [Chicanos] needed was an approach similar to what the Black Movement was using . . . demonstrating, marching in the streets. To that we incorporated a Saul Alinsky component of confrontation politics. And we said that was going to be the strategy. . . . Use confrontational politics based on information . . . well-researched, but also foregoing the use of nice language."[107] This young generation opposed the so-called lone wolf approach of the LULAC and GI Forum generation: "writing letters, [calling] press conferences, [utilizing] the style of diplomacy . . . very proper, very formal, raising substantive issues, but in a nice voice."[108] Gutiérrez claimed that "such tactics are ineffective and the results obtained through them are too meager."[109] Chicanos also became impatient with the slow or delayed process of legal cases and viewed the federal government as remote and unresponsive toward the injustices facing Mexican Americans.

Chicano activists esteemed Mexican indigenous roots yet did not completely orient themselves toward Mexico, and they valued American socialization, socioeconomic mobility, and citizenship. Thus, they constructed a new mestizo (mixed Indian and Spanish) identity that became a source of ethnic pride, cultural distinctiveness, self-determination, group unity, and political empowerment. Although they embraced the history of their Mexican and Indian heritage, they did not completely forsake the Spanish language and the cultural traditions of Spanish origin. They further explored and expressed pride in their ethnicity and its roots in Mexican history, including the Texas Revolution, the Mexican-American War (1846–48), the Mexican Revolution (1910–1920), and the history of Mexican immigration to the United States. However, most young Mexican Americans grew up feeling ashamed, ridiculed, or insecure regarding their cultural heritage and mother tongue (Spanish), and they had been taught that Mexican identity was synonymous with racial inferiority or cultural weakness. Furthermore, many came from working-class homes or migrant families and were raised in the United States, educated in American schools, and socialized according to American cultural norms. Historian Arnoldo De León

66 ∼ CHAPTER 2

explains the political agenda for militant activists of the Chicano Movement in contrast to middle-class reformers of the previous generation: "The Movement represented a phase in Chicano history during which Mexican Americans—many with working-class roots—opted for militant tactics as part of the continued struggle for self and group improvement. Activists and their supporters during the era came mainly from the ranks of those who had experienced barrio or migrant life, and thus spoke from firsthand knowledge: in the process, they even reproached Mexican-American politicians who represented the old guard and who, presumably because of their middle-class upbringing, did not understand the needs of poor folks."[110]

Various Chicano student activists demanded that public schools better serve the needs of ethnic Mexican students who came from low-income homes and were seasonal migrant workers. They endorsed their own radical version of an educational reform agenda that had not been actively pursued by Mexican Americans in the past.[111] Their political aims focused on bringing about immediate institutional change within the public school system.[112] José Angel Gutiérrez summed up the main objective for Chicano institutional control: "We [Chicanos] were convinced that we were the generation that was going to recover the land in the Southwest [from Texas to California] not by taking the land, but by taking political control of the institutions in the land."[113] The pursuit of and approach to achieving this monumental undertaking was perhaps the greatest challenge of the Chicano student movement and larger Chicano Movement. Institutional and political control was deemed necessary in large part because of Mexican American students' poor performance and the substandard conditions at their schools during the 1960s, issues that Chicanos contested during their protest movement.

Both women and men were active in the Chicano Movement in Texas, yet sexism and misogynistic attitudes were sometimes evident within the movement in grassroots organizing groups such as the Mexican American Youth Organization (MAYO).[114] San Antonio MAYO leader Carlos Guerra acknowledged the ingrained patriarchal tendencies among men during the group's formative years: "We would like to think that in the old days [late 1960s] we were progressive about it [the role of women], but we were not. We were pretty sexist. They [women] were essentially second-class participants by and large."[115] Luz Bazan Gutiérrez, Chicana activist and former wife of MAYO organizer José Angel Gutiérrez, further commented: "Women were not necessarily in a leadership capacity because at the time we really didn't demand to be recognized as leaders as we do now. We were just partners in the whole development of MAYO. . . . [Chicanas] didn't want the feminist issue to divide us. So we tended to want to be united for la causa [Chicano cause] as a family and not divided. We wanted to go forward together."[116]

Historian Ramón A. Gutiérrez recounts the sense of powerlessness among women in the movement, who started noticing that "although the movement persistently had advocated the self-actualization of all Chicanos, Chicanos still actually meant only males."[117] According to scholar Adelaida del Castillo, men often demanded "sexual cooperation as proof of commitment to the struggle, by gratifying the men who fought it."[118] Luz Bazan Gutiérrez further noted: "Within the Chicano student movement, women were denied leadership roles and were asked to perform only the most traditional stereotypic roles—cleaning up, making coffee, executing the orders men gave, and servicing their needs. Women who did manage to assume leadership positions were ridiculed as unfeminine, sexually perverse, promiscuous, and all too often, taunted as lesbians."[119] Thus, certain Chicano men were reluctant to accept Chicanas as leaders because their inclusion was viewed as a transgression against the masculine Chicano culture and machismo (male chauvinism). In seeking to resist the gendered expectation of female domesticity in the larger Mexicano and Chicano societies, Chicanas formed their own feminist movement, known as Xicanisma, to promote their liberation from oppression in US society, including their exclusion from the mainstream feminist movement because of their race and class.[120] In 1969, the San Antonio–based newspaper *El Rebozo* promoted the cultural image of "La Adelita," or soldadera (ethnic Mexican female soldier), to illustrate Chicanas' multiple roles according to its figurative description of the traditional Mexican women's garment: "El Rebozo— the traditional garment of Mexican women, with its many uses, symbolizes the three roles of the Chicana, portraying her as 'la señorita' [single woman], feminine yet humble; as 'la revolucionária' [revolutionary], ready to fight for 'la causa' [the cause of the movement], and finally portraying the role of 'La Madre' [mother] radiant with life."[121] Chicanas such as Gutiérrez who supported the formation of MAYO prior to establishing La Raza Unida in the early 1970s expressed their desire to fight for the Chicano cause, in a more integrated and egalitarian community: "We actually had to walk in to one of the meetings . . . and said, 'Hey we don't want to be the tamale makers and . . . the busy bees. We really want to be part of the decision-making process.'[122] The student movement revealed the conditions of Chicanas, especially those in MAYO, who fought for inclusion in both the Chicano and the mainstream feminist movements. Nevertheless, the actions of Chicano students became front-page news and aroused a greater sense of awareness and sympathy toward the educational needs of ethnic Mexican students in South Texas than in any other era in history.

Three months prior to the first major Chicano student political activity at Lanier High School in San Antonio, approximately 1,500 middle- and working-class Mexican Americans from the city and other South Texas towns held a historic meeting—the La Raza Unida Conference—at John F. Kennedy High

School in San Antonio.[123] A key issue discussed at the meeting concerned a proposed consumer boycott of the Humble Oil Company (which later changed its name to Exxon Oil) at the district office in Kingsville, Texas. Conference attendees agreed to protest the company's hiring practices, alleging the lack of employment of Mexican Americans. At one point during the meeting, conference participants shredded their Humble Oil credit cards as a symbolic gesture of their frustration. Various people who attended the conference later held a picket-sign protest outside the Humble Oil district office for several days. In retaliation for the demonstration, many Anglo community members in Kingsville boycotted El Jardín (The Garden) Restaurant, owned by the family of protest organizer Efrain Fernández.[124] Although the protest against Humble Oil had no direct connection to the Lanier High School walkout, the La Raza Unida Conference and subsequent demonstration influenced Chicano student political activism in South Texas during the late 1960s.

Mexican American Academic Assessment in the 1960s

Statistical data regarding the academic progress of ethnic Mexican students in the Texas public schools suggest in part the Chicano students' urgent need for change at their schools. In 1950, the Spanish-surnamed population in Texas had approximately 3.6 years of schooling, compared to 9.7 for whites.[125] By 1960, these figures jumped to 6.1 for Mexican Americans and 10.8 for Anglos.[126] The dropout rates for Mexican Americans in the rural population of Texas were much higher than the total for all Spanish-surnamed people living elsewhere in the United States. Moreover, the number of Spanish-surnamed sixteen-to-seventeen-year-olds not attending school was nearly double that of all people in the comparable age group residing in the United States during the 1960s. According to another source, 34.1 percent of the total Mexican American population, and 53.1 percent of Mexican Americans who lived below the poverty level, had four years or less schooling.[127] Exactly 30.4 percent of the total Mexican American population aged twenty-five years and older in all educational groups (ranging from no years of schooling completed to more than five years of college) lived in poverty.[128]

At the beginning of the 1960s, an astonishing 78 percent of Mexican American children dropped out and failed to graduate from high school.[129] Another such abysmal figure indicates that only 46 percent of Mexican American youngsters were enrolled in school during this time.[130] The median number of years of educational attainment for Mexican Americans in Texas who were fourteen years of age and over was 4.5 in 1950 and 6.2 in 1960.[131] One former Chicano student activist describes the so-called weeding out of ethnic Mexican students from the educational system:

Census data of the 1960s (which is when I was a junior high and high school student) clearly demonstrate that, by the time Hispanic students attended high school during my youth, most of my ethnic classmates had already dropped out during elementary or junior high school. We, the survivors, tended to be the more acculturated, at least in a bicultural if not an Anglo-conformist manner. All the resistors had, by now, left school, flunked out, or been kicked out. We were also the ones who had learned to deal with the predominantly white-oriented school system, as well as learned to cope with all the prejudices and lower expectations that were inherently part of [the] US apartheid educational system of the era.[132]

In summarizing the consequences of these educational deficiencies of the 1960s, the Texas State Advisory Committee to the US Commission on Civil Rights concluded that "the schools of Texas have generally failed at the job of educating their Mexican American children."[133] Historical factors such as low-wage employment, poverty, and poor performance in school serve as the prior context of student protests. By the late 1960s, a new student group had organized under a charismatic and articulate leader and sought to focus awareness of such educational deficiencies. José Angel Gutiérrez emerged as one of the foremost leaders of Chicano youth activism in Texas when he cofounded the MAYO student group to promote educational reform and cultural awareness. In 1968, he and other MAYO activists began traveling to numerous cities across Texas to assist Chicano students in gaining equality and political power within the public school system.

José Angel Gutiérrez and MAYO

Most social movements promoting political, civil, and human rights throughout the world have been known for outspoken, dynamic, and influential leaders. Such leaders cultivate a strong symbiotic relationship with their followers, stimulate devotion, and promote group identity. José Angel Gutiérrez, a native of Crystal City, Texas, and former leader of the 1960s Chicano student movement in Texas, was no exception. He emerged as one of the most radical and well-known organizers of the larger Chicano Movement as well because of his unique talent for public speaking and debating in both English and Spanish. Chicano scholar-activist Ignacio M. García accurately notes: "He was a cunning, always-in-control strategist with a sharp tongue, able to curse heavily in either language, and even more capable of being charming when necessary. He was a political chameleon, able to fit in almost any environment he chose; although unyielding in those he did not. It was not beyond him to tell someone to step outside to settle a discussion."[134] Historian Tony Castro further portrays Gutiérrez as the most distinct among the protest leaders: "José Angel Gutiérrez is not like other leaders of the Chicano movement.... Young, college-educated, the son of a doctor, Gutiérrez may have the most brilliant mind of any of the civil rights leaders of his lifetime. He represents the new breed of Chicano professionals produced by the colleges and universities, but he is still a Chicano with the old dream of revolution.... Gutiérrez is a Chicano prodigy, a well-read intellectual by Anglo standards who can just as comfortably organize barrio youth to counter the very system that taught him."[135] Gutiérrez was the first generation in his family born in the United States, after his father had served as a doctor in Pancho Villa's army during the Mexican Revolution (1910–1920s). His father moved to Crystal City in the 1920s, married, and practiced medicine in the town's ethnic Mexican community until his death in 1957. The younger Gutiérrez was only twelve at the time. Shortly after his father's death, Gutiérrez remembers that the "Anglo social doors" were shut tightly on him and his mother.[136] He further contends that Anglo educators adopted measures to deliberately strip Mexican American students of their Mexicanness (Mexican cultural identity) and discourage use of the Spanish language in public schools during his years of schooling. One of Gutiérrez's writings illustrates this type of condition:

> At the Anglo school, the teachers were also trying to make Anglos out of us. That is the whole point of public education in the United States. Students of all kinds have to learn how to be of one kind, Anglo, to stay in and succeed in that system. This was very contradictory for me because the teachers first subtracted from me all of my Mexicanness. They took away my language. I was punished if I spoke Spanish in school or on the playground during recess. They took away my culture. I had to eat Anglo food, speak English, learn their stories, songs, and dances. They took away my history. They didn't want to hear about my dad and Pancho Villa—he was a bandit to them. They made me choose between Davy Crockett and Mexican President Antonio López de Santa Anna. They took away everything that was important to me and certainly important to my father. In its place they put in shame and rejection for everything Mexican, me included.[137]

Many Chicano students experienced similar conditions at their schools and subsequently formed their own social and political movement to oppose English-only assimilationist policies meant to "subtract" from them their ethnic culture and language.

During his high school years, Gutiérrez became the student body president, won a state championship in declamation, and was respected even by Anglo students. Former Crystal City school superintendent R. C. Tate recalls that Gutiérrez "was outstanding in every way and every one of his teachers were very fond of him [and] . . . all during high school, his friends had been mostly Anglos."[138] Gutiérrez graduated from Crystal City High School in 1962, briefly attended Southwest Texas Junior College in Uvalde in the mid-1960s, and received a BA degree from Texas A&I University in 1966. While at Southwest Texas Junior College, he unsuccessfully ran for student body president and would later establish a chapter of the Political Association of Spanish-Speaking Organizations (PASSO) at Texas A&I University in Kingsville in the mid-1960s.[139] Gutiérrez discovered and put into practice the political concept of bloc voting, first in high school and then when he ran for student body president at Southwest Texas Junior College.[140] He applied bloc voting by convincing Mexican American students to vote only for him rather than for their favorite Chicano or Anglo candidates. Thus, Gutiérrez learned at an early age how to organize and mobilize politically with this concept. This political practice enabled him and other Chicano activists to attain electoral success in the city government and the school system of Crystal City during the local student movement.

Gutiérrez's 1998 autobiography, *The Making of a Chicano Militant: Lessons from Cristal* (Crystal City, Texas), is the first insider's view of the important political and social events that occurred in various Mexican American communities throughout South Texas during the 1960s and 1970s. Gutiérrez's memoir further explains why he "never became a Hispanic" and offers his interpretation of the events of his life during the Chicano Movement by simply proclaiming that this "work is my truth about Chicano militancy."[141] As the most well-known activist leader in Texas, Gutiérrez first emerged as a self-made militant beginning with the formation of MAYO in 1967. The most vivid recollections of his early years in school include how the local educational system regarded Chicanos as inferior in the classroom, on the playground, and around Anglo teachers and students. His memoir further discusses the events and impetus for establishing La Raza Unida, a unique third political party that promoted Chicano political autonomy where Mexican Americans were the majority, beginning in his hometown of Crystal City, Texas (almost one hundred miles southwest of San Antonio in Zavala County). Crystal City was key in the development of the Chicano Movement in Texas. His recollections of the student activism in South Texas reflect the ways he exerted his influence, charisma, and organizing skills throughout his time as a significant leader of the movement.

In his discussion of his activist days in MAYO, Gutiérrez tends to give this organization too much credit for encouraging Chicano students to protest or walk out of their schools in Texas. Like most Chicano scholars, Gutiérrez offers a general analysis of why Chicano students walked out of their schools. Yet he provides only a brief overview of the unequal conditions they faced in their school system. Although Gutiérrez examines the role of Crystal City student leadership before and during the local walkout, he and other Chicano scholars do not fully analyze the conditions and circumstances that incited Chicano students to walk out of their schools throughout South Texas. In a statement regarding the extent of his involvement in other Chicano student protests, Gutiérrez indicates, "I participated in thirty-nine of them [school boycotts] between 1967 and 1969. . . . By 1969, I had participated in Texas walkouts in Plainview, Lubbock, San Antonio, Kingsville, Uvalde, Hondo, Edcouch-Elsa, Alice, El Paso, Del Rio, San Marcos, and Houston to name a few locations." However, he argues that Chicano students in Crystal City did not benefit greatly from making certain concessions with the local school board before ending their walkout. He states, "I felt bad about the agreement. The school board got too much."[142] Despite Gutiérrez's pro-Chicano perspective, his scholarly work serves to highlight the role he played as a prominent activist leader in the larger student movement throughout South Texas.

After completing his studies at Texas A&I, Gutiérrez earned an MA from St. Mary's University in 1968 and a PhD in political science from the University of Texas at Austin in 1976. One of his former professors at St. Mary's, Charles Cotrell, knew Gutiérrez as a young graduate student who was just starting to research and identify new methods and strategies that would stimulate electoral, economic, and social revolution.[143] Gutierrez's master's thesis ("La Raza and Revolution: The Empirical Conditions of Revolution in Four South Texas Counties") analyzes the economic and political inequality as well as the social segregation of Mexican Americans in South Texas by evaluating statistical and empirical data underscoring the low levels of income and education, evidence of rural poverty, and substandard housing. His thesis also promotes the theory that Mexican Americans could achieve control of the political and institutional power structures in South Texas by grassroots organizing, and by establishing a third political party to generate more active campaigning and voter turnout for Chicano candidates at the local, county, and state level.[144] Despite being the most flamboyant and vociferous of the principal Chicano leaders in the movement, Gutiérrez felt perplexed about his personal identity as a college-educated, middle-class American and an ethnic Mexican person raised in a barrio in Crystal City, Texas. His autobiography conveys this personal struggle:

> Since it was important to be liked, as a Chicano I had to choose which group to be liked by first and foremost. Which is preferred, groups of other Chicanos or groups of Anglos? Anglos liked me only when I was identical to them. That is to say, I had to learn how to stop being my Chicano self and acquire a new posture, identity, attitude, and traits, all of which were anti-Mexican! I had to learn to dislike myself enough to

reject my bilingual being and become a clone of Anglos as a rite of cultural passage into gringolandia [White American society]. Anglos did not let me be both, even if I was able to and could.[145]

Although Gutiérrez faced this dilemma, his personal experiences involving racial prejudice as an adolescent helped make him a Chicano militant eager for revolutionary-type transformation in America.

During his years as a Chicano Movement activist, Gutiérrez acknowledged that the social, economic, and political conditions impacting ethnic Mexican people in the United States necessitated an immediate and radical change. In remarking about the conditions Mexican Americans faced in the Texas public schools, Gutiérrez noted that "the combination of white administrative and instructional personnel, English only, an Anglo-centered curriculum, and a preferential social setting dominated by Anglos for Anglos in the public schools made for systematic discrimination and exclusion of Chicanos."[146] In the summer of 1967, Gutiérrez discovered the "vehicle," or means to put his vision for change into action, by helping to form MAYO in San Antonio.

Gutiérrez, along with cofounders William "Willie" C. Velásquez, Mario Compean, Ignacio Pérez, and Juan Patlán, initially organized MAYO at St. Mary's University, a small Catholic liberal arts college on the West Side of San Antonio. During their meetings at the Fountain Room, a bar several blocks away from St. Mary's, the five read and discussed books on the political theory and ideology of African American nationalists such as Stokely Carmichael, Eldridge Cleaver, and Malcolm X.[147] According to historian and scholar-activist Ignacio M. García, "No one bothered to record that date [of the meeting], yet it was then that the seeds were planted for a Chicano social and electoral movement that was to shake the state's political and educational foundations, and which was to have a profound effect on the future of Mexican American politics in Texas and other parts of the Southwest and Midwest."[148] Although MAYO emerged as an offshoot of the older Mexican American political activist and civil rights groups such as LULAC and the American GI Forum, it promoted an aggressive, confrontational strategy to combat systematic inequality toward Mexican American students in the public schools. García further notes, "The five also concluded that they were not interested in forming another mass membership organization, of which several already existed; but rather they were interested in organizations such as the Students for a Democratic Society (SOS) or the Students Non-violent Coordinating Committee, (SNCC), a black activist movement, as possible models for Mexican Americans to emulate."[149] Additional issues arousing mass political action on the part of MAYO included racial discrimination, police brutality, and labor organizing.[150] Furthermore, MAYO's rhetoric and ideology emphasized devotion to *la raza* (Chicano people) and Chicano cultural nationalism and underscored the importance of incorporating the techniques of mass demonstration to achieve its goals.[151] MAYO had thirty chapters at universities and colleges throughout Texas, with a total membership reaching over one thousand.[152]

The organization expanded across Texas in large part because of its active role in training Chicano students to organize collectively, draft grievances, negotiate with school officials, and promote a confrontational style of politics by encouraging Chicano students to boycott classes. MAYO further motivated Chicano students to express pride in their ethnic Mexican culture and Spanish language throughout their protest movement. In one of his memoirs, José Angel Gutiérrez describes his and his cofounders' vision and purpose in establishing the group: "We saw MAYO as an organization of organizers. . . . We were going to challenge the gringo [Anglo] power structure, once and for all. Our generation was going to change politics forever and take back political control in those areas where we [Chicanos] were the majority of voters."[153] New recruits inducted into MAYO adhered to twelve membership requirements. The main ones included (1) a sincere desire to help La Raza as well as oneself, (2) a basic knowledge of what the movement was about, (3) a desire to put La Raza first and foremost, (4) a belief in the unity of Chicanos, (5) a belief that all Chicanos had every right as human beings and that they were not inferior to any race or nationality, and (6) support for all fellow MAYO members in times of crisis.[154] Former MAYO activist Carlos Guerra recalls that group members initially became active in the National Farm Workers Association in Texas and were politicized by the farmworkers' cause under César Chávez before focusing their attention on educational issues concerning Chicano students.[155] Mexican American college students in San Antonio were among the main catalysts of MAYO, "assisting Chicano high school students with voicing their problems and helping them stay in school" and "developing a state-wide MAYO organization and a system of communications."[156]

In his book *Mexican American Youth Organization: Avant-Garde of the Chicano Movement in Texas*, California activist-scholar Armando Navarro offers a detailed analysis of the factors that led to the formation and demise of MAYO. He acknowledges the influence of national Chicano leaders, including Reies López Tijerina, César Chávez, and Rodolfo "Corky" Gonzales, thereby connecting Texas to the larger Chicano Movement.[157] Navarro introduces the reader to José Angel Gutiérrez and the four other Chicano activists who founded and organized MAYO at St. Mary's University in San Antonio in 1967. He also details and evaluates MAYO's history, political influence, community leadership, strategies and tactics, and ideology throughout the student movement. MAYO emerged as one of the foremost Chicano student groups because of its participation in numerous student walkouts, anti–Vietnam War demonstrations, and other such protests that led to the creation of the Raza Unida Party in Texas in 1972. Navarro's book offers a unique glimpse into his observations as a Chicano Movement participant and includes information from oral interviews with numerous other movement activists in Texas. Thus, he provides an insightful analysis into the dynamics, formation, and function of MAYO as a prominent organization in Chicano and Civil Rights Movement history during the 1960s. His work specifically examines the Chicano student movement's historical roots throughout the early to mid-twentieth century. His discussion of three important mini case studies of South Texas high school walkouts involving MAYO—in Edcouch-Elsa (1968), Kingsville (1969), and Crystal City (1969–70)—provided the framework for *"We Want Better Education!"*[158] However, Navarro devotes only one chapter to MAYO's role in these walkouts, based primarily on data from newspaper accounts.

In assessing MAYO's involvement, he only hints that various students from universities in South Texas, such as Pan American College (now the University of Texas Rio Grande Valley in Edinburg) and Texas A&I University (present-day Texas A&M University–Kingsville), were called "outside agitators" by their critics. Navarro makes almost no mention of the specific MAYO members who were involved, where they conducted their meetings, or how they met with Chicano students throughout South Texas. Another major flaw of Navarro's study is that he gives MAYO too much recognition for planning each walkout and attributes the organization of the protests to this group's members without discussing or even mentioning the names of the key local student activists involved. Except for the Crystal City walkout, Navarro views the school protests as unsuccessful since the local school boards did not endorse all the student demands that he claims MAYO wrote. His work does not elaborate on whether local Chicano students had any input or suggestions for drafting the demands, and he fails to detail the experiences of women activists. *"We Want Better Education!"* attempts to fill in the gaps of Navarro's study by discussing the extent of local student involvement in the walkouts.

According to Navarro, MAYO's "record of instigating thirty-nine [student] walkouts between 1968 and 1970 plus other mass confrontations demonstrates the power and mobilization capability it developed during those years."[159] MAYO helped engender a political/militant consciousness among local Chicano students by teaching them a Saul Alinsky component of direct-action strategies, tactics, and organizing methods.[160] In South Texas, as in most other places throughout the state where walkouts occurred during the late 1960s and early 1970s, "MAYO was at the forefront, directing and mobilizing . . . youth and [their] parents into action."[161] MAYO cofounder José Angel Gutiérrez argued, "MAYO required the inclusion of parents and the formation of support organizations before engaging in the school walkouts."[162] Nevertheless, Navarro asserts that MAYO "was eager to use the boycott to flex [the organization's] developing mobilization muscle."[163]

In the late 1960s, MAYO emerged as the foremost social and political action group supporting Chicano students throughout South Texas. This loosely organized, grassroots student group influenced and encouraged ethnic Mexicans to protest their schools.[164] During the years of its existence, MAYO's organizing efforts culminated in the implementation of three major objectives: economic independence, local control of education, and political strength and unity through the establishment of a third party.[165] Those instrumental in establishing contacts between MAYO and Chicano students included José Angel Gutiérrez, Willie Velásquez, and Mario Compean. As one of MAYO's primary leaders, Gutiérrez asserted that this transformation involved removing Anglos from the economic, political, and social base of support from which they operated.[166] He and others in MAYO first intended to bring about this transformation in the public school system of Texas. This book underscores how MAYO facilitated student protests when school officials failed to meet their demands. Even though Gutiérrez shared his advice, knowledge, and expertise with those who participated in the walkouts, he achieved his greatest success in political change in Crystal City. Gutiérrez achieved this success when he moved back to Crystal City in 1969 and renewed friendships with numerous people in the community, relying on his personal knowledge of the local school system, and he likely felt loyal toward his hometown. This work further examines his role as a charismatic, militant leader of the Chicano student movement of South Texas.

The Civil Rights and Anti–Vietnam War Movements that engendered the larger societal and political forces of the 1960s provided the impetus for the rise of the Chicano student movement specifically oriented toward change in the American educational system. The Chicano Movement was in full swing, with broad-based organizing and protest movements that included young student activists who supported such issues as the restoration of land grants, farmworkers' rights, economic development, cultural autonomy, voting rights, political representation, and an end to job discrimination and police brutality. The rumblings of Chicano student activism suddenly gained national attention in March 1968 when approximately ten thousand Chicano students walked out of five East Los Angeles high schools—Lincoln, Roosevelt, Garfield, Wilson, and Belmont. Local adult community organizers made students aware of the educational inadequacies in the local school system and initially conceived the student strike. Such people included Sal Castro, a teacher at Lincoln High School; David Sánchez and Carlos Montes of the Brown Berets; and college students Vicki Castro, Carlos Muñoz Jr., and Montezuma Esparza.[167]

Relevant Studies on Chicano Activism in Education in California

Activist-scholar Juan Gómez-Quiñones, an influential figure in the creation of Chicano studies in California, wrote the first major analytical study on student activism, *Mexican Students Por La Raza: The Chicano Student Movement in Southern California, 1967–1977*. His work defines the "student movement" as the activities and beliefs of on-campus student organizations whose members had a common political consciousness and purpose.[168] The book further assesses the proliferation of Chicano manifestos such as El Plan Espiritual de Aztlán and El Plan de Santa Barbara, concluding with the 1970 National Chicano Moratorium protest opposing Mexican American participation in the Vietnam War. His overall conclusion is that "the student movement developed as a part of the broad social and political movement of the Mexican people in the United States," and he describes the history of this movement as a "piston" firing along with other "pistons" in order to move the so-called vehicle of resistance.[169]

Chicano activist-scholar Carlos Muñoz Jr.'s *Youth, Identity, Power: The Chicano Movement* (1989) was hailed as the first major book-length study on Chicano political activism and new social movements during the civil rights era in California. Muñoz, a political scientist and participant in the 1968 East Los Angeles school walkouts, offers his personal insights, perspectives, and recollections of Chicano student activism in Southern California. He defines the Chicano student movement along with the larger Chicano Movement as "a quest for a new identity and for political power . . . [it] . . . represented a new and radical departure from the politics of past generations of Mexican American activists."[170] Thus, the movement introduced a different brand of the political activism from past Mexican American generations. In agreeing with historian Juan Gómez-Quiñones, he believes that ethnic Mexican students were major contributors to the drive for social change among Chicanos in shaping larger struggles for racial and political equality in American society. Muñoz also agrees with historian Rodolfo Acuña in maintaining that the movement led to the establishment of Chicano studies and other programs that gave Mexican American students access to institutions of higher learning, such as the Educational Opportunity Program (EOP). Most scholars generally agree that Chicano student activists on high school and college campuses began to develop their own political consciousness and form their own social protest movement because of their working-class background and support of the farmworkers' movement led by César Chávez and Dolores Huerta.

Although much of Muñoz's work focuses on explaining the political ramifications of the Chicano student movement in Southern California, he does give a sense of the regional breadth of Chicano activism from La Raza Unida in Texas to the Crusade for Social Justice in Denver, Colorado. In referencing events in Texas, Muñoz briefly mentions the Crystal City walkout, but he does not elaborate on how it involved the politicization of Chicano students outside California.[171] Nevertheless, the themes of student empowerment and ethnic consciousness run throughout the narrative while recalling the integral roles Chicanos played in the antiwar and free speech movements.

One major work that examines the historical evolution of the Chicano Movement in Los Angeles is Ernesto Chávez's *"¡Mi Raza Primero!"* [My People First]: *Nationalism, Identity, and Insurgency in the Chicano Movement in Los Angeles, 1966–1978* (2002). A key part of his study gives background information concerning Chicano youth insurgency in Los Angeles. In 1968, the Brown Berets organization gained much notoriety by encouraging thousands of Chicano students from five East Los Angeles high schools to walk out and boycott classes. Chávez details social and educational conditions in Los Angeles that were similar to those in South Texas, including racial discrimination against students of Mexican origin, the small number of ethnic Mexican faculty and administrators in the school district, the deplorable condition of the school buildings near Mexican American neighborhoods, and Chicanos' high failure rate in school.[172] Although he does not focus on the emergence of Chicano student walkouts outside California, Chávez reveals that young people played a key role in the development of the Chicano Movement in one of America's largest cities, which inspired student-led protests elsewhere in the US Southwest.

One insightful autobiographical text, *Blowout! Sal Castro and the Chicano Struggle for Educational Justice* (2011), based on the life of Chicano educator and activist Sal Castro, contextualizes the political and social climate of the 1960s Chicano Movement, including the roles of high school and college student activists.[173] Author and historian Mario T. García offers a vivid account of Castro's recollections that integrates Castro's story within the larger Chicano Movement. García incorporates almost ten years of interviews to recap the story of the walkouts, primarily from the perspective of the man who served as an adult organizer and mentor to the student leaders in East Los Angeles. In first narrating Castro's life experiences, including his childhood and early teaching career at Lincoln High School, García helps the reader understand the educational inequities of eastside schools in Los Angeles such as underfunding, inadequate staffing, and lack of student leadership, in addition to illustrating why this charismatic teacher motivated his students to fight for educational justice. García provides a captivating and engaging life story, or *testimonio*, of Sal Castro, one of the most important leaders of the Chicano student movement, and credits Castro for inspiring countless Chicano students to succeed in their academics and in their lives, take pride in their Chicano culture, and become leaders in their schools. Castro's *testimonio* further recalls how he and students of Mexican origin were ridiculed for speaking

Spanish and tracked into vocational courses, which for most meant being pushed to pursue low-wage menial labor or the Vietnam War draft. Another significant part of *Blowout!* details Castro's role as an activist and mentor to students who participated in the first mass movement of "blowouts" or walkouts that marked the beginning of the Chicano Movement in California. Although *Blowout!* fills a major void in the history of the Civil Rights and Chicano Movements, the book devotes just two chapters to the major events of one particular case study, the East Los Angeles High School blowouts in 1968. Unlike previous scholars' works, my narrative includes multiple case studies that shift the spotlight onto Chicano students' collective experiences and background as principal actors in the Chicano Movement.

In reminiscing about the sense of ethnic pride students felt while participating in the walkouts, Castro recalled: "Kids out in the streets with their heads held high. With dignity! It was beautiful to be a Chicano on that day."[174] Thus, the East Los Angeles walkouts were the first major student protest of the Chicano Movement, and the repercussions were felt by other ethnic Mexican students throughout the US Southwest. In response to this type of student activism, Chicano students in South Texas began organizing their own movement for educational reform and political empowerment in San Antonio's West Side a month after the East Los Angeles walkouts.

3

The Chicano Student Movement in South Texas Begins in San Antonio's West Side

The first reported Chicano student demonstration in Texas occurred at Sidney Lanier High School, one of the oldest schools in San Antonio, in April 1968.[1] The school was, and remains, situated in a historic and traditional ethnic Mexican barrio, a low-income neighborhood in San Antonio's West Side. This part of the city is also the oldest urban Mexican American neighborhood in Texas.[2] According to former students Edgar Lozano and Ignacio M. García, Lanier High School had a predominantly ethnic Mexican student population of just over 97 percent at the time. Working-class Mexican immigrants and native-born Mexican Americans have resided in this area for many years, and people refer to it as the Mexican "world" of San Antonio.[3] In examining their historical origins in the twentieth century, historian Ricardo Romo notes, "The majority . . . living in San Antonio during the 'Roaring Twenties' and the Great Depression years were initially Mexican immigrants."[4] This part of San Antonio has historically been the poorest part of the city as well. Most local residents were segregated from the Anglo residents and often shied away from challenging or questioning the status quo regarding their second-class status in society.[5] Although San Antonio did not have a system of segregation quite as stringent or apparent as in the small farming towns of Texas, similar conditions largely mirrored what was happening in the remote rural communities of Edcouch-Elsa, Kingsville, and Crystal City.[6] Thus, residential segregation and social separation between Anglos and ethnic Mexicans in San Antonio allowed city leaders to establish school district lines that created school segregation.[7] Ironically, San Antonio remained one of the most economically segregated cities in the nation despite being the first major city in the South to desegregate its public school system following the Supreme Court's 1954 *Brown v. Board of Education* ruling that outlawed segregation in public schools.[8]

Poverty-stricken conditions in San Antonio's West Side included poor health, high unemployment, substandard housing, inadequate sanitation, flooding, lack of drainage and sewage systems, and low educational achievement.[9] Chicano scholar-activist David Montejano discusses the segregation and discriminatory treatment that was evident in the barrios of this part of the city during the early to mid-century: "The public schools in these cities [in Texas] were segregated, businesses refused to serve Mexicans in places patronized by Anglos, and the Catholic churches conducted special services to prevent contact between Mexicans and Anglos . . . as the 'Mexican town' of San Antonio grew in the 1930s, new subdivisions on the Anglo side (such as the Jefferson and Harlandale areas) began to adopt restrictive covenants prohibiting the sale or rental of properties to persons other than of the Caucasian race—'implicitly excluding the Mexicans'"[10] Historian Richard García also comments on the influx of Mexican immigrant labor at the outset of San Antonio's industrial development: "Without question, the San Antonio trade and farming area served as a magnet for Mexican immigrants, as a base of population growth for the San Antonio Mexican community, and as a cultural support area for the urban Mexicans in San Antonio who were being acculturated. . . . The city was worker-intensive, since it had never developed a heavy industrial base. Mexicans were needed as a source of cheap labor to work in the city's multiplicity of light industries: railroad yards, packing plants, military bases, garment factories, service establishments, and the retail trade."[11] Ignacio M. García also remembers: "The part of San Antonio that my family moved to in the mid-1950s was a big gathering pool of poor, long-term residents as well as recently arrived undocumented and unskilled Mexican workers . . . [when] San Antonio was as Mexican a town as any could be on this side of the border . . . [and] being Mexicano affirmed one's humanity and the dignity that came with being a person."[12] Regarding the high school's role in the local community, García asserts: "Lanier had become as much a part of the central west side of San Antonio as had the parks, restaurants and churches. It played a big part in the young people's lives and in the economics of the barrio."[13] However, he dispels the notion of Lanier as the typical inner-city school plagued by crime and apathy: "Violence, vandalism, and absenteeism, so often associated with urban, inner-city schools, were not major problems at Lanier."[14] Homer D. García, no relation to Ignacio, and also a 1969 Lanier alumnus, still remembers the rigid social class structure, race relations, and inequality in the mid-twentieth century: "In my childhood, ethnic racial communities lived in separate and unequal communities because of Jim Crow laws and especially because of the class structure that put whites on top and minorities at the bottom. In comparison to whites, people of color had schools that were less well financed, staffed, and equipped. Minorities faced covert and overt discrimination in the job market, justice system, and government. They also had greater rates of substandard housing, disease, death rates, poverty, and imprisonment."[15] Such conditions contributed to the poor-quality education that students received at Lanier High School for many years. Nearly 60 percent of all ethnic Mexican residents lived in twelve housing projects for low-income families, and almost half (49.7 percent) lived in homes with plumbing, compared to 94 percent of Anglos.[16] Most young people who experienced these conditions in the barrios around Lanier were either first- or second-generation Mexican Americans born and raised in San Antonio during the early to mid-twentieth century.[17]

Another insightful source that verifies the real-life accounts of abject poverty in San Antonio's West Side is a 1968 CBS News documentary, "Hunger in America."[18] The first segment included footage of HemisFair '68, a six-month World's Fair that marked the 250th anniversary of San Antonio's founding in the downtown area. This glamorous exposition showcased how San Antonio's downtown was miraculously transformed "from a slum to jewel box," in the words of then–Texas governor John Connally. The CBS report then shifted to the city's West Side, where "the jewels don't glitter so brightly" because of substandard conditions that impacted approximately one hundred thousand residents—a quarter of the city's Mexican American population—who were "hungry all the time."[19] Ralph Ruiz, a local priest, narrated much of the broadcast and visited the homes of various ethnic Mexican families to assess the number of missed meals and lack of basic nutrition. A grim part of the documentary showed an eleven-year-old girl, covering her face with her hands, involved in solicitation for prostitution because of a lack of food, and malnourished babies dying in the pediatric ward of a San Antonio charity hospital. The next shocking part showed an interview with A. J. Ploch, a Bexar County commissioner for eighteen years. The news reporter first asked Ploch, "Why aren't they [San Antonio schoolchildren] getting enough food?" He bluntly assumed, "Because the father won't work and I mean won't [do any] work." The reporter next inquired about the adverse effect of a child's hunger on his or her ability to complete school. "Do you really need school other than an eighth-grade education?" Ploch replied. "That's another thing people keep talking about is education, this college education, it's not necessary." He further asserted, "You'll always have that [hunger] condition. If you don't have that condition, then you'll never have Indians and chiefs. And you've got to have Indians and chiefs . . . you'll always have it [hunger] because some men just ain't worth a dime."[20] Such condescending remarks reflect the apathy and racial attitudes of certain county officials at the time. Upon remembering Ploch's televised interview fifty years later, Ralph Ruiz maintains: "He [Ploch] was a mirror of so many in San Antonio who thought the same way he did [in 1968]. And acted the same way and didn't give a damn the same way he did."[21] Thus, he expressed his frustration on behalf of those who lived in the most destitute situations in San Antonio's West Side over the years.

Prior to the 1960s, one grassroots organization that first sought redress of the educational inadequacies in San Antonio's West Side was the Liga Pro-Defensa Escolar (School Defense League, or School Improvement League), which emerged from LULAC. Local businessman and community leader Eleuterio Escobar Jr. founded the Liga at the International Institute in San Antonio, representing over forty civic organizations, on December 14, 1934.[22] Escobar understood firsthand the adverse effects of segregation as a young boy when he attended a segregated elementary school along with other Spanish-surnamed children in Pearsall, Texas.[23] After serving in the US Army in World War I, Escobar became a self-made businessman and established the Escobar Furniture Company. Most of his customers were Mexican American "since this was the only furniture store owned by a Mexican American" in San Antonio in 1924.[24] At the height of the Great Depression in the early 1930s, Escobar as well as other local community activists, including prominent civil rights lawyer Alonso S. Perales, began to promote educational reform and greater participation in electoral politics among Mexican Americans.[25] Escobar commented on the lack of Mexican American representation within the city, and the need for more community-wide participation in electoral politics: "At that time, Mexican-Americans did not have a voice in the city, county or state governments, and the only representatives that we had were a few policemen, street sweepers, and garbage collectors."[26] The conditions of the Depression, segregation, and racial discrimination mobilized Mexican American voters of the middle class, most of whom were business and professional men.

By 1934, Escobar was instrumental in organizing LULAC Council #16 and became chair of the council's Committee for Playground and School Facilities. The committee emphasized community participation and engaged in "action research" by documenting the substandard conditions that plagued Mexican American students with the intent of addressing all relevant issues and problems.[27] According to the committee's records, Mexican American students were crowded into eleven schools in the West Side, while the rest of the city had a total of twenty-eight schools. The school district spent exactly $422,203.48 on the eleven schools yet retained a surplus of $376,948.52, which the school board chose not to allocate for the renovation of schools. Only 259 teachers had the credentials to teach in West Side schools, while 330 taught students in predominantly Anglo schools. The school board spent an average of $24.50 per student in the West Side but $35.96 elsewhere. Forty-eight Mexican American students were crammed into one classroom, and over one thousand first graders attended half-day classes in two shifts because of overcrowding in the West Side.[28] Finally, Escobar noted that thirty-four temporary frame rooms existed on West Side school campuses, while schools in other parts of the city used just ten such rooms. At Lanier High School, administrators assigned classes in the cafeteria, auditorium, library, dining rooms, and cooking and sewing rooms.[29] Another committee report indicates: "Occasional inquiries have been made of children on the streets and they [West Side school administrators] say they [Mexican American children] are not in school because there is no room for them."[30] Thus, Escobar and the committee concluded that overcrowded conditions and the drastic shortage of adequate and functional facilities posed the biggest problem for the West Side school system.[31]

The committee continued to gain public support throughout the Mexican American community and appealed for endorsements from other civic and community action groups. "Within a few months of its formation the committee had developed a coalition for school reform from seventy-three civic, social, labor, and religious groups representing 75,000 persons, and on October 24 sponsored a rally that drew 10,000, mostly women and children."[32] The committee's objective centered on promoting equitable spending for West Side schools to upgrade and expand educational facilities such as classrooms, cafeterias, auditoriums, and playgrounds to alleviate overcrowding in dilapidated buildings.[33] The LULAC committee headed by Escobar chose to host the rally outside Lanier High School to greet L. A. Woods, superintendent of schools for the State Board of Education, and inform him of the West Side community's support for educational reform.[34] Those who spoke at the event included Father Carmelo A. Tranchese, pastor of Our Lady of Guadalupe Catholic Church; LULAC leaders James Tafolla, Orlando F. Gerodetti, and Ermilio R. Lozano; Alonso Perales; Mrs. María Hernández, secretary of the Orden Caballeros de América; Carlos E. Castañeda, librarian-historian at the University of Texas; state representatives P. H. Dickson and Franklin Spears; and Superintendent Woods.[35] Escobar, of course, spoke as well and later regarded this momentous occasion as the most "impressive and emotional scene that I have ever seen."[36]

LULAC sponsored this historic rally, which allowed community activists to present their list of grievances to Superintendent Woods outlining the educational needs of Mexican American students. Their needs were as follows: additional classroom space, school heating, window shades and drapes, better student/teacher ratios (currently 130 students per teacher), and better conditions in schools in the West Side. Maria Hernández, the only Spanish speaker, directed her complaints to Superintendent Woods: "Los hijos de ellos no tuvieron culpa de nacer con ojos negros, pelo café y no con ojos azules. Todos somos apoyados por el pabellón de las barras y estrellas. Yo quiero que usted tome esta gestión del pueblo como protesta y disgusto de las condiciones pesimas." (Their [Mexican Americans'] children were not at fault for being born with black eyes and brown hair and not with blue eyes. We are all supported by the stripes and stars of the [US] flag. I want you to take this gesture of this community as a protest and disgust over the terrible conditions.)[37] After hearing Hernández's impassioned remarks, Superintendent Woods promised to appoint a commission to investigate the complaints and resolve any problems concerning inequities. In a letter to Escobar, Woods vowed that he was "not going to be a party in hurting the Latin-American children in San Antonio."[38] He further believed that "the first step the School Board should take is to remedy the dismal conditions of west side schools," and "if you [LULAC] continue working as you have been up until now, the Board will accede to your just demands."[39] However, despite continued support from Woods via written correspondence, San Antonio School Board president R. S. Menefee refused to negotiate a solution with LULAC because of Escobar's involvement. On November 22, 1934, the school board issued an official statement that read: "We do not see the necessity for meeting with LULAC. Since January I called to the Board's attention the conditions [regarding the West Side schools] and since then we have tried everything possible to provide these people more facilities. We have constructed a new school with 16 rooms. . . . If we were free from outside interference, the Board could go about its business in a much better way."[40] This rather contentious situation eventually led to Escobar's resignation from the education committee of LULAC Council #16. Other organizations that supported this LULAC council expressed their dissatisfaction over the situation and agreed to form a new alternative committee, with Escobar as its new president, known as the Liga Pro-Defensa Escolar.[41]

One of the organization's official letters denounced the local school board for the lack of new infrastructure during one ten-year period: "From 1937 to 1947 the San Antonio School Board of Education did not even approve the construction of a single school for the West Side."[42] Additional documentation from the Liga claims that over two thousand students used temporary frame rooms, more than fifty students occupied each classroom, and approximately six thousand children did not attend school because of inadequate facilities.[43] The Liga disbanded in 1935 but reorganized in 1947, when it became more popularly known as the School Improvement League. Thirty-seven Mexican-descent organizations reorganized the league before eighty-six such groups, both male and female, supported the newly reformed organization, including such notable participants as the Catholic Archdiocesan Office for the Spanish Speaking, the Latin American Ministerial Association, and the Wesley Community House.[44]

86 ~ CHAPTER 3

The School Improvement League promoted its message of education reform using English- and Spanish-language media by speaking out against the use of wooden buildings as schools, and it petitioned the school board to build six to eight new elementary schools, one junior high, one senior high, and one vocational school in November 1947.[45] The league organized a mass rally that attracted approximately three thousand people for greater public exposure of its campaign at Lanier High School, featuring scholar Dr. Carlos E. Castañeda from the University of Texas at Austin.[46] The organization ran a successful campaign in support of a $9.3 million bond issue for school construction in 1950 before disbanding once again around 1956.[47] Despite the Liga's call for support of the educational cause among community members, the conditions of the schools changed little over the year. Thus, the work of the School Improvement League attests to earlier efforts toward educational reform that first called attention to the substandard conditions and insufficient funding of West Side schools that had existed for decades prior to the local student movement in 1968. The ability of this organization to engage in collective action and pursue expanding political opportunities became apparent given the substandard conditions of schools for ethnic Mexican students. This pre-1960s movement for public school reform strived to work toward a common goal, thus laying the groundwork for Chicano activists to work toward improving the quality of education and treatment of Mexican American students. Chicano activists in San Antonio's West Side would later utilize the organizing strategies of the School Improvement League to suit their needs, albeit in a different manner, by engaging in community-wide activism.

Former Lanier student Julio Noboa claimed that educational deficiencies existed at his school during World War II. He recalled how Mexican American students at Lanier made important contributions to support the war effort: "During the war years, Lanier transcended social constraints, including low expectations of its student body, and fostered a patriotism that would lead to 550 of its young men serving in the military, scrap-metal drives that collected 123,000 pounds, a vigorous ROTC program, and a deep pride in its contributions."[48] Noboa underscored that the instructional purposes of Lanier High School since its founding reflected the poor socioeconomic conditions of the school's community. In describing his school experiences during World War II, Noboa underscored the racism inherent in the school's vocational curriculum, which channeled Mexican American students into low-income trades, and the attempts of local school administrators to "Americanize" Mexican American students, whom they regarded as culturally and racially inferior. His recollections of Lanier High School indicate that Mexican Americans did not receive the same educational opportunities afforded to white students.[49]

Beginning in 1914, the progressive educational theories of John Dewey greatly influenced the instructional methods and curricula of school districts in major US Southwest cities such as Los Angeles and San Antonio, including the implementation of vocational training and Americanization programs for ethnic Mexican students.[50] Lanier and Edgewood High Schools in San Antonio's West Side offered various courses that prepared Mexican American students for vocationally oriented work to meet the city's growing demand for labor pertaining to urbanization and industrialization. Therefore, as indicated by Richard García, "Many of San Antonio's schools, consequently, offered commercial training, shop, carpentry, furniture making, woodworking, pattern making, mechanical drawing, and other vocational courses."[51] Lanier offered twelve vocational courses ranging from such male-dominated classes as auto mechanics to home economics for females, which were "busy all year around" by 1968.[52] School officials implemented a different type of curriculum based on various educational studies that supported the teaching and vocational training of ethnic Mexican students in segregated schools. They also established new methods of record keeping that considered a student's race, nationality, and mental condition. These changes in educational pedagogy, ethnic isolation, and record keeping meant that "a vocational orientation, not a professional orientation, segregation, not integration, and a retardation category, not a progressive one was established as the philosophical cornerstones for the Mexican student population."[53]

Government records detail the educational inadequacies that plagued Chicano students at Lanier High School and other predominantly Mexican American schools. Such problems became the subject of investigation by the US Commission on Civil Rights during one scheduled meeting with Mexican American students at Our Lady of the Lake University in San Antonio. The commission held a six-day hearing from December 9 to 14, 1968, to examine civil rights issues facing Mexican Americans in the US Southwest such as education, employment, administration of justice, and economic issues. After facing a public backlash from the local political establishment, Rev. Theodore Hesburgh, president of Notre Dame University and vice chair of the commission, replied: "We are not an enforcement agency. We make reports to the President and to Congress. All we do is hold up a mirror to the community and let them tell us if there are any problems, and that's what we're doing here."[54] This historic hearing was the first time any federal agency had gathered information to investigate such problems affecting Mexican Americans in the United States. Dr. Hector P. García, the first Mexican American appointed to the commission, made known the significance of the hearings on behalf of Mexican Americans seeking "to fully realize their personal and group identity and at the same time . . . strive to obtain

88 ～ CHAPTER 3

full equality and treatment as first class citizens of the United States."[55] While the hearing examined issues in a five-state area of the US Southwest, much of the investigation concentrated on South Texas and San Antonio.

The commission's hearing shows that numerous scholars, researchers, public officials, business and industrial leaders, educators, and students attended from throughout the country. However, María Hernández, a female activist from the School Improvement League, and her husband testified against "the embarrassing problem of racial discrimination" against Mexican Americans and African Americans.[56] Participants contributed significant information on the learning experiences and educational needs of Mexican Americans in US public schools. Upon reflecting on the significance of this historic hearing many years later, former student Ignacio M. García contends: "The commission's report served as another spark in the flames of activism that were sweeping the Chicano barrios of the Southwest."[57] Students from Lanier High School included Homer D. García, José Vásquez, Edgar Lozano, and Irene Ramírez.

Figure 1. Five San Antonio teenagers give testimony at US Commission on Civil Rights hearing on Mexican American problems in the Chapel Auditorium of Our Lady of the Lake College. *Left to right*: José Vásquez, 1968 graduate of Lanier High School; Edgar Lozano, senior at Lanier; Martín Cantú, 1968 graduate of Edgewood High School; Homer D. García, senior at Lanier; and Irene Ramírez, senior at Lanier. December 9, 1968. *San Antonio Express-News* Photograph Collection / UTSA Special Collections.

The first grievance expressed by the five students was the punishment or unjust treatment ethnic Mexican students received for speaking Spanish at school. Irene Ramírez, a senior at Lanier High School, recalled how school administrators reprimanded her for conversing in Spanish in the classroom.

MR. GLICKSTEIN: (acting staff director for the US Commission on Civil Rights): And how were you punished? What sort of punishment was it?

MISS RAMÍREZ: The dean of girls, she paddled us.

MR. GLICKSTEIN: Paddled you?

MISS RAMÍREZ: Yes, sir.

MR. GLICKSTEIN: What was your reaction to—I'm sure the paddling hurt, but aside from the physical discomfort, how did you feel about being punished for speaking Spanish?

MISS RAMÍREZ: Well, I didn't like it. I didn't like the idea of being punished because I was speaking Spanish.... To me it is a way to identify myself. I mean I feel that it is my language and I don't see why I shouldn't speak [Spanish in school]. But... since [the time] you enter elementary school you are taught that it is bad. And I just didn't feel this way, but I was punished anyway. And I couldn't really say anything because I didn't know how the other students felt. And, well, I just didn't like it at all.

MR. GLICKSTEIN: Did you feel embarrassed or ashamed?

MISS RAMÍREZ: I was very embarrassed. I didn't like it [receiving punishment for speaking Spanish at school].[58]

This type of incident was common among Mexican American students at this time and became a key grievance among Chicano students in South Texas. Education historian Gilbert G. González suggests that incidents like those that Irene Ramírez experienced revealed how public school officials identified "the Spanish language and Mexican culture as contradictory to educational success."[59] During and prior to the 1960s, most public schools across South Texas had an unofficial, de facto no-Spanish rule.[60] Former student Ignacio M. García describes the school administration's method of identifying and admonishing those who spoke Spanish at Lanier: "Student monitors were assigned to walk around in the hallways and the schoolyard to catch other students speaking Spanish. When they did, they gave the Spanish speaker a violation slip... at Lanier it meant having your parents come to school to be lectured about teaching their children English."[61] According to one educational study by the US Commission on Civil Rights, approximately 66.7 percent of all Texas schools discouraged the use of

90 ∾ CHAPTER 3

Spanish in classrooms.[62] Edgar Lozano, a senior at Lanier High School, further elaborated on the stigma associated with speaking Spanish at school in his comments to Glickstein:

> MR. LOZANO: How would you like for somebody to come up to you and tell you what you speak is a dirty language. You know, what your mother speaks is a dirty language . . . that is the only thing [language] that I ever heard at home. A teacher comes up to you and tells you: "No, no, you know, that is a filthy language, nothing but bad words and bad thoughts in that language." I mean they are telling you that your language is bad. You hear it [Spanish spoken] at home. Your mother and father speak a bad language, and you speak a bad language. I mean [teachers say] you communicate with dirty words, and nasty ideas. I always thought when I was in elementary [school] that [stigma] really stuck in my mind.[63]

Both Ramírez's and Lozano's statements reaffirm why Chicano students demanded social acceptance and free expression of Spanish at school. Mexican American students at Lanier High School had longed for this type of social change well before the 1960s.

One prominent political figure and community activist who was born and raised in the same barrio around Lanier High School was then–state senator Joe J. Bernal, who offered sympathy and support for Chicano students. Bernal, a 1944 Lanier graduate, recalled school administrators restricting him and his fellow classmates from speaking Spanish at the school during the early 1940s. During one interview, he remembered seeing the school's student council distributing ribbons stating "I'm an American, I speak English" at the beginning of every school week.[64] However, members of the student council were quick to take away the ribbons of Mexican American students who uttered words or phrases in Spanish.[65] In addition, hall monitors usually patrolled the school to report other students who spoke Spanish.[66] The ribbons likely served as one way to reinforce the notion that Spanish was somehow "un-American" and intolerable. In the late 1960s, schoolteachers, including a few who were Hispanic, continued to coerce Chicano students into following this unofficial school mandate by asking them, "Why can't you be a good Mexican?"[67] Mexican American students were further subjected to intimidation for speaking Spanish in school, according to one observer: "I recall the algebra teacher who threatened to slap any student in the mouth if caught speaking Spanish, even if out in the playground. Suspensions were common if you did not speak English."[68] Thus, student activists at Lanier High School took drastic action in April 1968 to end the humiliation that ethnic Mexican students had endured for many years.

Homer D. García, one of the key student activists at Lanier, described Chicanos' need for better counseling at his school. He argued that school counselors did not encourage students to enroll in college and pursue professional career opportunities after high school. García offered his explanation for this inadequacy during the commission hearing:

MR. GLICKSTEIN: At Lanier do the teachers encourage students to think in terms of going to college?

MR. GARCÍA: Well, some of them.

MR. GLICKSTEIN: Do you ever have representatives of colleges in the area come to school?

MR. GARCÍA: Well, just until recently, you know, we have a new principal, and he has provided us with representatives from SAC.

MR. GLICKSTEIN: SAC is San Antonio College?

MR. GARCÍA: Yes, sir. It is San Antonio College. But before we didn't have any of this. It has just begun just recently.

MR. GLICKSTEIN: Are persons brought to school to discuss career possibilities with students? For example, do they ever bring in a prominent businessman or a lawyer or an educator to urge you to enter those professions?

MR. GARCÍA: No, sir. Before this year all we had was—Well, criminals were brought in from the penitentiaries to encourage us not to go into the life of crime. This is the only interest they have shown as of yet to not go into any special career, and that is a life of crime, that is the only one, so far.[69]

This part of García's testimony indicates that educators at his school failed to advise Mexican American students and relied on prison inmates as invited speakers to dissuade students from becoming criminals. In one recent memoir, García maintains: "The focus of the institution was on preparing Hispanic students for vocational jobs because the Anglo establishment had no faith that we [Chicano students] could intellectually handle anything beyond lower-paid occupations . . . the school system resisted offering college preparatory classes in my high school because it did not feel that Hispanic students could handle them."[70] Former student Stephen Castro criticized school counselors for bringing in only "ex-convicts to our school to scare us away from jail. Those are not role models."[71] Fellow classmate Rafael Castillo recalls seeing military recruiters and officers informing male students about the enlistment process on other occasions at student assemblies.[72] However, other local high schools invited astronauts, engineers, and well-known politicians to speak to their students about seeking promising career choices.[73] School officials at Lanier never requested that such people speak to their students. Richard Teniente, a 1946 Lanier graduate and trustee on the San Antonio School Board, explained his reason for this disparity: "We have had situations where the ninth grade counselors have told the youngsters not to prepare for college because there are not enough scholarships available for them to make it through college. We have had the same counselor tell youngsters that it takes money, clothes, and things that you cannot afford, so you better prepare for something else. This is the [biased] attitude we [Mexican Americans] have had [to endure at Lanier]."[74] This part of Teniente's testimony further attests to the lack of equitable counseling services in predominantly Mexican American schools such as Lanier.

José Vásquez, a 1968 Lanier graduate, alleged that his school did not adequately prepare him for more rigorous studies in college. Vásquez managed to enroll as a freshman at St. Mary's University in San Antonio during the time of the commission hearing. While speaking at the hearing, Vásquez admitted that he struggled to master and communicate proficiently in English while a student at Lanier and that this hindered his ability to succeed academically in college. Moreover, Vásquez attributed his deficiency to poor instruction in English grammar at the school. He explained: "One of my biggest problems right now is English, which I still have many difficulties in, especially sentence structure, communicating, written communication in English." Vásquez also argued that school counselors purposely tracked Mexican American students at Lanier into vocational education, and one counselor tried to convince him that pursuing a vocational trade "would be the best thing [he] could do" since he presumably "would not finish high school."[75] One official government study further validates Vásquez's argument: "School officials admit that there are junior high school counselors, especially in almost exclusively Mexican American schools, who guide the Mexican American students toward the predominantly Mexican American vocational high schools because they believe this type of school to be most appropriate for the Mexican American student."[76] Education scholar Rubén Donato confirms that students of Mexican origin during this era were often tracked into vocational education programs and low-level curricula. This "dual system of education" meant that "working-class and minority youth were given the skills necessary for the lower echelons of the labor market while middle-class youth received an academic education that coincided with the social and cultural hegemony they already possessed."[77]

In answering one final question about whether the curriculum in the San Antonio school system satisfied Mexican American students in the late 1960s, Vásquez replied, "No, I don't think so."[78] Vásquez and other Mexican American students had trouble mastering English grammar skills at least in part because of the poor quality of instruction in the public school system. College preparatory instruction had not been a priority for educators at the school for many years; the founders of Lanier decided to name the school's mascot "Voks" to underscore the preparation of students for vocational trades.[79] Ignacio M. García further acknowledges the mascot's true meaning and significance in his own memoir: "Shortly after it opened its doors Lanier had settled on vocational education as best for us Mexican kids . . . our mascot was the Vok, . . . a screw [actually a gear] because that seemed to appear periodically in our yearbooks and in the large banners for football games."[80] In an effort to steer away from being tracked into a vocational trade such as body and fender repair, former student Rafael Castillo pleaded with school counselor Nancy Templeton to assign him a course providing academic training.[81] "Look, it's all we have [vocational courses]. And, besides, we don't have anything else," she replied. "Well, how about art?" Castillo asked. After her initial objection, Templeton relented and told him, "OK, we'll place you in commercial art."[82] He remained in the art class for one year before transferring to a journalism course. Thus, the school initially tracked Mexican American students into a vocational curriculum preparing them for low-wage trades. According to Castillo, school counselor Templeton often enrolled Mexican American students in vocational courses rather than considering the students' interest in pursuing professional fields.

At another point during his hearing with commission officials, Vásquez discussed student grievances pertaining to the lack of cultural content on Mexican Americans in Texas history textbooks. When commission member Dr. Hector P. García asked Vásquez whether the Texas school curriculum on the state's history was accurate and truthful, Vásquez responded, "I am given the impression that the Texas history that is being shown to me is the Texas history of the Anglo here in Texas, not the Texas history of the Mexican American or Mexicano. It is to show that the Anglo is superior." Additionally, Vázquez's claims received support from at least one professional educator who evaluated such textbooks and claimed that they "reinforced a sense of Anglo superiority and degraded the image of Mexican Americans and other ethnic minorities."[83] Historian Arnoldo De León asserts that Anglo stereotypes of people of Mexican origin in Texas have often permeated traditional historical writing, underscoring ethnocentric folklore and racial bias. Such stereotypes were visible in many history books in Texas, often portraying Mexican Americans as indolent, uncivilized, reprobate, sexually promiscuous, and culturally inferior.[84] Ignacio M. García believes these stereotypes only served to characterize ethnic Mexican people as subordinate because of romanticized interpretations of past conflicts: "Whether it was the Battle of San Jacinto, the US-Mexico War, or even the Alamo, where Anglo Texans had managed to turn a rout into a moral victory, we were always losing, and they were always winning. . . . We were separate but unequal and always uninvited."[85] He also adds: "Speaking to our [Mexican American] history meant revealing what mexicanos had always known: the state of Texas had been founded on anti-Mexican sentiments; violence had been directed against the people who had invited American settlers in, and by all kinds of laws and practices whites had segregated, exploited, and diminished the social value of the Mexican and Mexican American population."[86]

Former Lanier students Rosie Peña and Irene Yañez confirmed that many young Mexican American students felt a strong sense of shame upon learning the most prevalent historical interpretation of the Texas Revolution in school during the 1960s: a revolt by liberty-loving Anglo-American newcomers against Mexican cruelty and intolerance.[87] The testimony of James Sutton, a history teacher at Lanier High School, further validates Chicano students' claims: "The trouble with the Texas Revolution is like anything else in Texas history, it is Anglo orientated. We look at the Texas Revolution from one side only, the [Anglo] colonist viewpoint."[88] Chicano student activists such as Vásquez refused to accept the credibility of such historical writing in high school textbooks. In short, Vásquez and other Chicano students contended that their school's curriculum reinforced negative stereotypes and historical myths about Mexican Americans.

Mexican American students such as Daniel Hernández felt stereotyped in public while working in San Antonio's annual Fiesta Parade downtown in the 1960s.[89] Throughout their adolescent years, he and some of his friends from Lanier sold homemade food and beverages at the parade in order to raise money to help support their families, who were living in low-income neighborhoods throughout San Antonio's West Side. This experience made him more conscious of Mexican Americans' subservient role in society as those who served and catered to mostly white American patrons at the parade. Most Mexican American high school students in San Antonio never went to enjoy the festivities and celebration because they usually worked as food vendors throughout the event. Thus, issues of wealth inequality and economic dependence became inextricably linked to racial and social class status within the city. Such circumstances in the city further motivated students to walk out of their school to oppose their subservient position in the educational system as those suitable only for low-wage manual labor or domestic work.[90]

During the hearing before the Civil Rights Commission, local priest Ralph Ruiz commented on the decline in government welfare funding that also contributed to the income inequality, food inadequacy, and need for community-based charity of those plagued by poverty in the West Side. He stated: "Economically they are poor, so much so that it is even difficult for them to buy enough food to eat. . . . Prior to the TV documentary, Hunger in America, the maximum was

$135 per month for a family of four and more. And after that, now at present [December 1968], I think it is $123, maximum.... I invite any one of you or all of you to come to my place for one day and see how much food is given away to these people. It is inhuman that we should be pushing our [low-income] people to beg for food. I wouldn't even say un-Christian, I mean inhuman."[91] He further accused both local and federal government welfare agencies of intimidation and harassment, and the FBI of bullying and violating the privacy rights of families living in the West Side while attempting to prove false the claims of poverty that left an estimated 62,000 to 114,000 people with inadequate diets. Another of his arguments painted a stark contrast between the haves and have-nots (high- and low-income neighborhoods) in San Antonio: "We have before us then two San Antonios, one a city, a San Antonio growing with prosperity and economic liability, the other a San Antonio [in the West Side] which has grown only in its intensity of its problems [because of poverty and neglect]."[92] Education that would prepare students for higher-skilled, higher-paying jobs, the one medium that most reformers and community activists believed could solve such problems, loomed only as a luxury for most West Side residents. Thus, social marginalization and economic poverty were among the key factors that led to a rise in students' collective consciousness during the Chicano Movement.

Homer D. García's Premonition concerning His Role as a Catalyst of the Chicano Student Movement

One student activist who became a target of intense scrutiny and antagonism for refusing to accept the traditional subordinate role of Mexican American students at Lanier High School was Homer D. García. Born in 1951, García was the eldest son of Alice Calderon García and Ireneo Villegas García, of Mexican and Native American origin (Tap Pilam Coahuiltecan).[93] His mother was a former migrant worker who left school to assist her family after the death of her father. After serving in World War II, his father returned home and began working as an upholsterer at Kelly Air Force Base.[94] Prior to attending Lanier in the mid-1960s, García often had recurring nightmares of standing in front of a school as lightning struck across the sky. García believes that one of his most important spiritual missions in life was to challenge the school to raise its expectations regarding Mexican American academic achievement, and to encourage the implementation of a college preparatory curriculum.[95] Such a mission was prophetic for García as he embarked on a spiritual quest to serve others and promote social justice issues through political activism in 1968.[96]

Two major events sparked Mexican American students' political activism prior to the 1968 student movement at Lanier. The first phase of student activism began in their junior high years during a series of meetings of the Young Leaders Club sponsored by the Inman Christian Center in San Antonio, a religious-based community center in underserved, low-income neighborhoods.[97] The after-school programs and public sessions sponsored by the community center offered Edgar Lozano and other young students the opportunity to learn how to evaluate the significance of educational issues and community activism prior to attending Lanier.[98] The second phase of the students' political awakening occurred in the fall of 1967 when Dan Salcedo and Joe Bernal, sponsors of the Inman Christian Center, organized a field trip to Center Point, Texas, where a small group of male Lanier students received information on political issues, organizing strategies, and leadership training.[99] The organizers of the retreat chose not to invite Homer D. García because of his low score on a questionnaire given at the school assessing students' liberal political views and cultural values.[100] Female students including Irene Yañez first met Senator Bernal at Cooper Junior High, where he began grooming and teaching students about the American form of democracy and the importance of parliamentary decision-making according to *Robert's Rules of Order*.[101] By the spring of 1968, local Chicano students began organizing and conducting their own meetings to identify their educational needs by evaluating the conditions of the school. They soon formed a student "steering committee" led by Edgar Lozano to draft their list of grievances. The committee members included Stephen Castro, Pablo Ortiz, Homer D. García, José Vasquez, Daniel Hernández, Elida Aguilar, and Irene García.[102]

In the first week of April 1968, the committee agreed to draft and disseminate protest leaflets on campus despite the risk; the penalty for distributing such flyers on campus was permanent suspension.[103] On one occasion, García was immediately summoned to the office of principal Fidel L. Tafolla for leafleting. Tafolla, who had become the first Mexican American principal of the school in 1963, rebuked García for giving out the leaflets. Former student activists at Lanier regarded Tafolla as a "Tío Taco" (Mexican American equivalent of an Uncle Tom), or one who believed that Mexican Americans had to do everything possible to appease the dominant Anglo society and disavow their ethnic Mexican identity in order to succeed in life. After giving García a verbal reprimand, Tafolla quickly demanded to know the names of the students and community members responsible for the production and distribution of the leaflets. When García refused to answer, the principal then decided to have one of the PE coaches frisk him before searching his personal briefcase for the leaflets.[104] Tafolla sought to quell the student movement by identifying the names of its leaders. As soon as the principal left the room to find the coach, García frantically hid the leaflets in the bottom drawer of the office desk. The frisking and search of García's briefcase proved unsuccessful, and the principal finally dismissed

García.[105] García resolved to question the principal's order for an intrusive search without presenting evidence of clear danger to the school. This type of incident eventually led to the involvement of the Mexican American Legal Defense and Educational Fund (MALDEF), a legal rights advocacy group that organized in 1968 to assist Mexican Americans seeking litigation in education, employment, and police-brutality cases.[106] In early April 1968, García and the steering committee suddenly emerged as the protagonists of the Chicano student movement at Lanier with demands for educational reform at the school.

The Lanier High School Student Action and Its Aftermath

Student political activism at Lanier High School occurred not long after the more famous East Los Angeles blowouts. Although local residents and former students continue to dispute the occurrence of an actual school-wide walkout, the *San Antonio Express* claimed that approximately seven hundred students, most of them Mexican American, demanded a better curriculum and more "democracy" or decision-making in extracurricular activities.[107] This newspaper account further reported that "triggering the student unrest was the method of selection of candidates for the student council and the manner in which officers of the council are selected by faculty members and the principal."[108] On April 9, 1968, Chicano students' frustrations became apparent after the faculty sponsor of the student council, Alicia Dominguez, prohibited them from engaging in a debate concerning the school's curriculum during a student council meeting in the school auditorium, with an estimated fifty students in attendance.[109] Student council members including Homer D. García and Elida Aguilar discussed the lack of quality education at Lanier and questioned why the school had almost no college preparatory courses like those in predominantly white schools in the northern part of the city.[110] One official record also confirms the reason García and the other students gave for their protest in support of "democratic elections in which the student council officers would be elected by the students and not the faculty" and the right to speak Spanish on school grounds.[111] However, they first sought to propose an amendment to the student council constitution that would grant students the opportunity to select their own leaders.[112] Both García and Aguilar were following the proper procedures for conducting an orderly dialogue during their presentation according to *Robert's Rules of Order*, the standard handbook for parliamentary procedures and the facilitation of discussions during business meetings. Without warning, an altercation ensued when the sponsor became belligerent toward the students and told them to "shut up" and sit down in order to stop further discussion.[113] Her verbal reprimand was a stern warning against student dissent. Aguilar ignored the sponsor's demand for silence, stood next to her seat, and asked why students could not freely exercise their right to free speech and other such constitutional rights, while expressing her shame over the denial of such rights.[114] One news account states that Aguilar had been reprimanded because she was not allowed to see the student council's constitution during the meeting, and that "triggering the student unrest was the method of selection of candidates for the student council and the manner in which officers of the council are selected by faculty members and the principal."[115] A few other students in attendance also told Dominguez, "You're not our dictator, you're [just] our sponsor," believing that she had no authority to disrupt or stop the orderly conduct of the meeting.[116] Former student Irene Yañez further believed that Dominguez infringed on the students' right to free speech at the school by refusing to acknowledge student feedback or show respect for their thoughts and opinions.

Quarreling ensued, whereupon twelve to fifteen Chicano students suddenly chose to walk out in protest in what became known as the Lanier student action of 1968.[117] In anticipation of the faculty sponsor's reaction, García reveals that he and the other student activists had previously planned to walk out of the meeting: "Because we expected the faculty sponsor of the student government group to object to our discussion, a walk-out of the meeting was organized prior to the meeting."[118] Shortly after the student council walkout, García went to the principal's office to voice his disapproval, much to the chagrin of the principal, who claimed that students had no human or civil rights in school.[119] García maintains that the walkout failed to spark a school-wide protest: "Although there was never a mass school walkout, the one that took place at the student council meeting was as close to a walkout if there ever was one."[120] Fellow classmate Ignacio M. García further confirms Homer D. García's account that the walkout was uneventful and inconspicuous at the time: "The walkout at the school . . . never materialized, although a few students did march out of school."[121] Ignacio M. García did not recall the names of the students who participated in the march.

Over the next few days, Homer D. García was subjected to numerous interrogations by administrators and certain teachers regarding his opinion about the school's inequities. This questioning escalated into verbal tirades at times when administrators made degrading insults and threats toward García. Lanier student leaders (the president of the student council, the editor of the yearbook, the highest-ranked student officer of the ROTC, etc.) were allowed to witness García's interrogations but remained silent and showed no sympathy or concern. García does not fully understand why he had to face such intense scrutiny in private and still recalls how unnerving his mistreatment felt: "I was made to stand for days and not allowed to go to the restroom, drink water, or eat so that I could respond to rapid fire questions for many hours at a time. . . . They tried so hard to make me break so that I would give them the information which they sought. Questioners pounded on desks, slammed doors, and yelled at me. I was threatened with arrest, handcuffing, beatings, and placement in a juvenile detention facility for disturbing the peace, inciting a riot, and making false accusations about inequities.... I was labeled a 'militant,' 'radical,' 'anarchist,' and worst of all...a 'communist.'"[122] Shortly after the Lanier High School walkout, García's teachers also began expressing their aggravation and outrage toward him because of the protest:

> One teacher threatened to slap me if I ever said anything to her. A former homeroom advisor said that I was one of the biggest disappointments of his professional life because I had misused the leadership mentorship he had provided by my doing evil things with it. My band director topped them all by saying that "I'd better not pull that s*** [protest activity] in his band or he'd get me suspended for keeps," unlike the last failed attempts which he had masterminded. He threatened to make my life miserable the following year if I stayed in the band. His warning caused me much pain because I loved music and had excelled somewhat as a trumpeter.[123]

At one point during his interrogations, García became furious when his interrogators did not allow him to use the restroom, further accusing them of child abuse.[124] One local underground news account indicates that he was "interrogated from five to eight hours" and "was standing, trying to answer questions, clarify statements, and deny accusations."[125] In response to his bold and audacious remarks, the school administration agreed to indefinitely suspend Homer D. García for supposedly "having a bad attitude," which attracted the attention of other Chicano students at Lanier.[126] He could not comprehend why school officials and certain classmates continued to express such disdain toward him. Administrators also subsequently suspended six to twelve other students who walked out of the student council meeting on April 9.[127]

After hearing about the administration's reprimand, Chicano students soon began holding informal meetings at Voks Corner, a small hamburger restaurant outside the school, to discuss their dissatisfaction over García's suspension and to assess the conditions of the school. Eventually they drafted a list of demands for reform.[128] Moreover, this popular student hangout became a Chicano social space that engendered the rise of collective and ethnic consciousness: "For the first time, the Voks Corner ceased to be a place only for discussing the upcoming football game or Friday gym dance, and became a place where we, as Mexican Americans, began to talk about what lay beyond the borders of the barrio, and how we related to that other [Anglo] world."[129] MAYO cofounder Willie Velásquez advised the students to form a coordinating committee and to formulate demands according to their concerns.[130] The Chicano student movement at Lanier included a talented cohort of student council leaders, athletes, and members of the school's debate team and drama club.[131]

During their discussions, fifteen to twenty local Chicano students began organizing themselves to discuss the conditions of the school before drafting thirteen demands and grievances alleging that their school had not adequately prepared them for college.[132] MAYO members served only as outside advisers since they were mostly college-age activists and did not draft the entire list of demands.[133] Although the organization was still in its early stages of development, it offered supportive organizational resources to further mobilize student activists at Lanier such as moral support, encouragement, advising, and protest tactics. The main demands were that

- more assemblies on various careers be offered;
- student complaints be investigated by faculty members;
- students be allowed to comment about school policy without being subject to punishment;
- copies of constitutions from every on-campus club be made available to all students;
- a moment of silent prayer be observed before all student council meetings;
- more information be made available pertaining to scholarships and other financial assistance programs;
- Mexican American students be allowed to speak Spanish at school;
- no action be taken against any teacher or student who had taken part in the movement and that all suspended students be reinstated and their names cleared.[134]

Another demand student protesters at Lanier were adamant about was "having their history and culture taught in school."[135] Key leaders responsible for drafting the demands included Homer D. García, Daniel Hernández, Edgar Lozano, Pablo Ortiz, and Stephen Castro.[136] Student leader and spokesperson Homer D. García summed up the concerns many Chicano students had regarding their inability to succeed in school. He commented, "We at Lanier are not ready for college. We don't even have calculus and algebra. If Anglo-Americans can handle calculus, so can we. We Mexican-Americans are just as good. But if they offered these things to us now, we couldn't pass them—we're not prepared."[137] García alleged that the San Antonio school system refused to offer college preparatory courses at his school because Mexican Americans were not considered "accelerated students." Thus, García explained the reason for his participation in the school boycott: "People say Mexican Americans don't want an education. All we want is a better education."[138] One representative (name unknown) of the Lanier Alumni Association pledged his support to the protesting students who were seeking enrollment in advanced courses: "The association is behind you. You need to be prepared for college." García expressed his desire for school officials to implement the demands but also suggested the Chicano students' next course of action if the demands were not met: "I guess we'll have to take to the streets [to continue the protest]."[139] Relevant statistical data suggest the need for "better education" at Lanier.

A 1968 report by the US Commission on Civil Rights indicates that more Mexican American students enrolled in more rigorous courses at Jefferson High School than at Lanier. Exactly 255 Mexican Americans registered for geometry, 163 for algebra II, 49 for trigonometry, 21 for physics, and 108 for chemistry at Jefferson compared to 103, 51, 7, 9, and 41 in the same courses, respectively, at Lanier.[140] Mexican Americans accounted for approximately 57.9 percent of the total high school enrollment in the San Antonio school system but represented 82 percent of those taking vocational classes.[141] The data do not indicate why such a large percentage of ethnic Mexican students enrolled in vocational classes— that is, whether it was by choice or because of counselor advice.

Julio Noboa asserted that the low-level curriculum of Lanier reflected the underprivileged socioeconomic environment of the school community. He further maintained that school officials promoted the abundance of vocational courses at Lanier High School to prepare students for blue-collar, entry-level positions. In commenting about Lanier's course offerings, Noboa stated: "Clearly, Lanier's curriculum was more oriented toward preparing skilled tradesmen and women for the working class. The very abundance of shops and the absence of advanced math and science courses was a marked characteristic of Lanier recognized even decades later by its former students."[142] Mexican American students faced significant disadvantages at Lanier, unlike those attending affluent schools. Former Mexican American students contend that other local high schools always had newer facilities, more financial resources, and a predominantly Anglo-American student population.[143] Noboa further indicated that there was a weak curriculum prior to the Lanier student protest of 1968. The urgent need for curricular reform served as a key grievance for student protesters who demanded that their school offer college preparatory classes.

The Lanier student action also attracted the attention of the Mexican American community throughout San Antonio's West Side during three public meetings at the Guadalupe Catholic Church from April 9 to 11, 1968. Romigio Valdez, counselor for the San Antonio Neighborhood Youth Organization, and

Father Miguel Barrigan of the Bishop's Committee for the Spanish-Speaking emerged as major proponents of student demands. Both claimed that Lanier High School had a "kick-out problem" affecting Mexican Americans.[144] They claimed that Lanier principal Fidel Tafolla "kicked" Chicano students out of school to punish them for expressing dissent. Moreover, they accused Tafolla of discouraging Mexican American students from participating in student council activities and speaking Spanish at school. Explaining why only a few Mexican American students graduated from Lanier, Barrigan and Valdez said that the school had a "drop-out problem." These accusations against the principal, along with the ongoing walkout, led to the expulsion of nine students.[145]

State senator Joe Bernal decided to meet twice with a total of 130 Chicano students after the protest began, praising them for voicing their grievances. He further commended them for demanding the revision of textbooks and the school curriculum regarding the culture and history of ethnic Mexican people.[146] While attending a public meeting with school administrators, Bexar county commissioner Albert Peña received a standing ovation from Chicano students and their supporters for expressing his opinion on the school controversy. He commented: "We don't have handicapped children, we have a handicapped educational system. We're not handicapped because we're bilingual—we're handicapped because we have an educational system that doesn't understand bilingual students."[147] Thus, Chicano students and supporters urged their school to incorporate Mexican American cultural distinctiveness as a significant part of the school's curriculum. The student movement began to attract community-wide support during a series of meetings at the nearby Guadalupe Catholic Church.

The climax of the Lanier student movement occurred during a meeting with parents and the student leaders in the Guadalupe Catholic Church parish hall near the school on April 10, 1968. Approximately seven hundred people attended.[148] The meeting included student leaders José Vásquez and Homer D. García, school officials, parents, and community members. School officials recruited a few of their own "model" students from Lanier to defend the legitimacy of the school's rules. Chicano students rebutted such testimony by underscoring the school's academic flaws, such as low-quality instruction. According to one eyewitness account from former student Ignacio M. García: "The student leaders continually pointed out rules and practices they described as humiliating and degrading to the Mexican American community ... [and] they repeatedly demanded respect for the culture and traditions they brought from home."[149] He further expressed his perspective regarding school officials' low expectations for learning in contrast to the Chicano students' desire for a better future beyond educators' mediocre expectations of them: "The school was supposed to be the beacon of light that would lead us to a better life, but all that came from the school officials' defense was the offer of a stable life of hard work, limited mobility, and a traditionally well-played football schedule. . . . What I was hearing from the student protesters were new challenges, new horizons, all these things that my parents and an occasional good teacher had taught me to believe in."[150] Parents such as Agustin Aguilar, whose daughter Elida had been expelled after the April 9 student council meeting, voiced his dismay regarding the treatment of students at the next community-wide meeting.

Aguilar made known his disappointment concerning the administration's decision to arbitrarily expel his daughter at the meeting on April 11. He further claimed that Principal Tafolla had discouraged him from defending his daughter by saying that he could opt to keep her out of school indefinitely rather than seek reinstatement.[151] One news account estimates that as many as 1,100 students and their parents, and residents from the surrounding community easily exceeded the capacity of the Guadalupe Catholic Church parish hall, including those standing outside the building.[152] Members of the Community Relations Commission, a local citizens' advisory group offering assistance to school officials, were present to listen to the student demands. One written account of Aguilar's perspective on the controversy of his daughter's expulsion reads: "My daughter was expelled from Sidney Lanier High School and the reasons were insubordination. It appears this accusation is without foundation. I wasn't even allowed to hear her side of it . . . I was accused of being a careless father by the principal when I was called to his office. Then he told me to take her to another school and to go to the school board or the Supreme Court if I didn't like it—he just didn't want her in his school."[153]

Local lawyer Pete Tijerina offered legal assistance to expelled students. Their parents argued, "They [the expelled students] were arbitrarily expelled on no legal grounds." Upon discussing Principal Tafolla's willingness to hear feedback from students prior to their expulsion, Homer D. García claimed that the principal failed to meet with them and carefully listen to their reasons for the protest. Furthermore, other Lanier students who were not expelled remember one administrator using the school's intercom system earlier in the day to announce that any student attending the meeting would "face serious consequences."[154] Elida Aguilar further contended that school officials purposely planned to restrict the participation of students and their parents when they attempted to call a secret meeting with just fifteen students, including three from the student steering committee, on the afternoon of Monday, April 8.[155] The twelve other students invited to attend were proadministration and had opposed the Lanier student protest movement, according to Homer D. García, who also believed the meeting had been a ploy for school officials to avoid negotiations with the entire steering committee.[156] Chicano students' accusations against school officials,

Principal Tafolla in particular, began to win over the loyalty and sympathy of community members who were becoming more aware of the school's inequities.

The reaction to school officials' decision to expel key student activists such as Homer D. García and Elida Aguilar was reminiscent of Senator Robert Kennedy's investigation during formal hearings of the US Senate Migratory Subcommittee regarding growers' treatment of farmworkers on strike in Delano, California, in 1966.[157] Throughout these hearings, approximately one thousand people crowded into the Delano High School auditorium. At 11:00 a.m., Senator Kennedy demanded reserved seating for farmworkers and their families throughout the rest of the proceedings after he noticed that the growers and their supporters occupied nearly all the seats.[158] Chávez soon testified that police had kept photographs and dossiers of farmworkers, deliberately intimidated and arrested those on strike, and sought to disband their nonviolent protest in support of the growers.[159] Kennedy's cross-examination of Kern County sheriff Leroy Gaylen remains the most enduring moment in the confrontation over the validity of the protesters' arrests:

KENNEDY: Why are the picketers arrested as a preventive measure?

GAYLEN: Well, if I have reason to believe that there's going to be a riot started, and somebody tells me that there's going to be trouble if you don't stop them, then it's my duty to stop them.

KENNEDY: And then you go out there and arrest them [strikers in the farmworkers' movement]?

GAYLEN: Absolutely.

KENNEDY: And charge them?

GAYLEN: Charge them.

KENNEDY: What do you charge them with?

GAYLEN: Violating unlawful assembly.

KENNEDY: I think that that is a most interesting move. Who told you that they were going to riot?

GAYLEN: The men right out in the field that they were talking to said if you don't get them out of here we're going to cut their hearts out. So rather than let them get cut, you remove the cause.

KENNEDY: This is the most interesting concept, I think, that you suddenly hear talk . . . about somebody's going to get out of order, perhaps violate the law, and you go in and arrest them, and they haven't done anything wrong. How do you go arrest somebody if they haven't violated the law?

GAYLEN: They are ready to violate the law, in other words . . .

Suddenly the crowd roared in bewilderment as Kennedy struck his fist on the table and leaned back in disbelief at the sheriff's reply.

KENNEDY: Could I suggest that in the interim period of time, in the luncheon period of time, that the sheriff and the district attorney read the Constitution of the United States?

The room erupted in laughter and applause from farmworkers in the audience.[160]

Those at Lanier who faced expulsion from school because of their involvement in the student council meeting "strike" endured the same type of treatment as those arrested during the farmworkers' strike in Delano.

School administrators favored expulsion for the outspoken activists in the student strike even though the students aired their grievances in a peaceful manner and did not deliberately violate school rules. The administrators likely believed that the expulsions would bring the student strike to an abrupt end and would prevent students from assembling en masse and engaging in a school-wide protest. School officials in Edcouch-Elsa, Kingsville, and Crystal City later employed this tactic during the walkouts at their schools despite the lack of due process and fair procedures. School boards also approved new policies that infringed on students' rights to peaceful assembly and free speech. The series of community-wide meetings at the Guadalupe Catholic Church demonstrates Chicano students' efforts to explore their expanding political opportunity to advance their interests while leveling their bargaining position to negotiate on par with school officials. Negotiations between student protesters and school officials deteriorated when the two sides failed to reach a mutual resolution after the last meeting at the church. However, Chicano students continued to press for their demands.

As the students continued to publicize their desire for educational reform at their school, San Antonio School District superintendent Oscar Miller felt compelled to seriously consider implementing their demands. He arranged a meeting with the teachers, Chicano students, and their parents at the San Antonio Independent School District board auditorium in an attempt to meet their demands, thus offering a resolution to the dispute.[161] On the day of the meeting, student activists had given out a protest leaflet expressing disdain toward the school board and Principal Tafolla as a way to galvanize support among the parents in attendance. The leaflet read as follows:

> ¡LANIER PARENTS! Stand up and protest the abuses by the school board and principal Fidel Tafolla against your sons and daughters. The schools are owned and kept by the citizens and taxpayers. The members of the School Board and the school principals are only employees of the public just like the garbage collectors and have no more right to dictate to

you than a mail carrier. Many garbage collectors could give lessons in respect, dignity, and common courtesy to Superintendent Miller—this man is paid a salary of $25,000 a year he does not deserve or earn.[162]

Shortly after the start of the meeting, Miller said he believed that most of the students' demands were "reasonable" and that the demand for more advanced courses was "encouraging and gratifying."[163] However, Miller could not reassure student protesters and their supporters that all their demands would be met, and he appealed for unity at Lanier High School, encouraging parents to take a more active role in school affairs. Former student activist Ignacio M. García reported: "Nine of the demands were granted as they were proposed. The one most popularly received was the one dealing with speaking Spanish at school."[164] Community Relations Committee executive director Dr. Sterling Wheeler declared, "This [granting of the nine demands] is a victory for persons; students, parents, teachers, principals and administrators. Everyone is going to benefit."[165] The loudest applause was heard when it was announced that students should not be punished for speaking Spanish on school grounds. However, student leader Edgar Lozano summed up his elation with Miller's announcement by saying, "We know what we won . . . but the fight ain't over yet because we're not going to quit until we get what we want [including better-quality education]."[166] By the end of the meeting, the students had decided to end their protest, return to classes, and cooperate with school officials. Despite this mutual agreement between the student steering committee and the Lanier administration, the arrangements for readmitting Homer D. García took longer to resolve.

Two significant meetings took place to decide the terms for readmitting García in mid-April 1968, more than one week after the series of community-wide meetings at the Guadalupe Catholic Church. The first meeting was between García, attorney Pete Tijerina, community activists, and school district officials.[167] These officials included superintendent Oscar Miller, principal Fidel Tafolla, vice principal Carl Lieb, and assistant principal J. D. Brown. García received assistance from Tijerina, an attorney from San Antonio, after his uncle, Manuel Calderon, requested legal advice. According to García, news and television reporters were present as well.[168] The two groups met in front of the school, where Tijerina was negotiating with school administrators to ensure García's return to school without restriction or condition. During this informal gathering, students inside the school crowded behind the windows of their classrooms to watch this rare confrontation with much intrigue and curiosity.[169] After the seemingly endless exchange of arguments regarding García's reinstatement, administrators finally agreed to let García return to school after his attorney threatened to bring a class action and file suit against each of them.[170] They also promised not to subject

García to any further interrogation without his parents' permission. However, school officials soon reneged on their promise by secretly attempting to coerce García into signing an admission of guilt for allegedly violating school rules.[171]

The second meeting took place at the school district central office early the next day when García came back to school. In a last-ditch effort to subdue García, Lanier administrators secretly arranged for García to undergo one more private interrogation by the superintendent and his staff. Before leaving campus, García used a phone in the school's main office to inform his attorney of the situation and his impending abduction from school.[172] According to García, he "went along with their [school officials'] smuggling me out of school because I knew that school officials would be caught red-handed violating my civil rights."[173] When the principal and his staff arrived at the school district office escorting García later in the day, Tijerina, activist priests Ralph Ruiz and Henry Casso, and the media were already on the scene.[174] While attempting to enter the central office building, Superintendent Miller prohibited Tijerina from entering. Turning to face a few members of the press at the front entrance, Tijerina said, "Did you all hear that [Superintendent Miller's comments]? We're taxpayers and I am his [Homer D. García's] attorney and I am not being allowed in to be with my client? C'mon, Homer, we are pulling you out of school . . . and we are going to sue you [the San Antonio school district] for ten million dollars!"[175] As Tijerina and García began to walk away, Miller relented and pleaded with them to negotiate once more, saying, "Okay, okay, okay, come on in [to the central office building]!" During this second impromptu meeting with the administrators, Tijerina announced that he would seriously consider filing criminal charges against them for kidnapping and for violating his client's civil rights during the first unwarranted interrogation at the school.[176] He further warned school officials of his intention to sue the district unless they agreed to reinstate García in school and not reprimand him for taking part in the protest. Father Ralph Ruiz criticized the school administrators' unchecked use of authority in interrogating García.

During the negotiations, Ruiz further warned school officials that members of his church congregation and parents in the Lanier community would burn down the school should word of García's interrogations and kidnapping go public.[177] García summed up the rest of the situation, and finally the school officials capitulated to the student demands:

> It was at that point that my attorney and community leaders were so infuriated with school officials that they began to walk out of the meeting. The superintendent begged us not to leave and to negotiate with him in good faith. As we went down the list of demands, he instructed my school principal and vice principal to follow his instructions to

implement the necessary changes. In some cases, the superintendent had to order submission when my high school administrators seemed hesitant to follow instructions.

Community protests, press coverage, and legal representation, as well as threats of a class and criminal actions were needed to reinstate me in good standing in school, but more importantly, it resulted in reforms being put in place. We were promised college-preparatory classes, a stop to no-Spanish rules, no retaliation against student leaders, and other policy changes.[178]

García graduated from Lanier High School the following school year but was treated as an outcast at school by certain administrators, teachers, and students. He also felt shunned by various former teachers and classmates who lost respect for him because of his involvement in the student movement. Commenting on her decision to risk permanent expulsion for protesting, Elida Aguilar told one news reporter, "When my little sister goes to Lanier I know she will receive a quality education and be prepared to compete for jobs. With the education I am receiving, I know I am not prepared to compete. To me, this is worth it."[179] Thus, the Lanier student protest movement led to the start of educational reform in San Antonio's West Side at almost the same time that those at nearby Edgewood High School began voicing their desire to improve the conditions at their school.

Origins of Chicano Student Activism during the Edgewood High School Walkout

Shortly after the Lanier student action, another student protest occurred, this time at Edgewood High School. Edgewood occupies the central West Side of San Antonio and is part of a separate school system from the San Antonio ISD. Most former students refer to Edgewood High School as the "school at the edge of the woods" because it was once located on the outskirts of the city, surrounded by a thick forest.[180] Local resident and former student Diana Briseño Herrera remembers when Edgewood had "no paved streets, it was all gravel streets."[181] Edgewood was first established over one hundred years ago in a small remote farming community just outside the San Antonio city limit. On May 8, 1905, Bexar County judge Robert B. Green bought a tract of land for one dollar from Carl and Friederike Frey "for the purpose of a school sight [sic], and to be used for school purposes only."[182] Many families began relocating to the area for its fertile soil and supply of artesian water for irrigation, and the name "Edgewood" soon became popular. Its population increased after Kelly Field was built. The city was given a deed to land around Elmendorf Lake to construct a new park in 1917. Edgewood established its own independent school district upon receiving approval from the Bexar County Commission in 1922.[183] Edgewood's first graduating class included just twelve students, in 1937.[184] Student enrollment more than doubled throughout the 1950s—from 5,140 in 1950 to 13,416 by 1959.[185] A new Edgewood High School was built in 1954. By the 1960s, the Edgewood School District had added eight new schools, including Kennedy High School, named for President John F. Kennedy, in 1963, and Memorial High School in 1968.[186]

While vice principal at Edgewood High School during the late 1950s, José Cárdenas received a request from an anonymous female student that she be allowed to drop her English course during the last semester of her senior year. Dropping the required course would mean that she would not be able to graduate with her class. After extensive discussion, Cárdenas eventually admitted that the real reason for dropping the course was that her family could not afford a dress for the senior prom, nor could they afford the school yearbook, graduation pictures, senior ring, invitations to the graduation ceremony, cap and gown, and other such expenses. Peer pressure was such that she found it more convenient and less expensive to finish school during the summer. Although we do not know the exact circumstances of the student's family situation, her decision to postpone her graduation suggests that certain economically disadvantaged students felt stigmatized by their peers who came from affluent neighborhoods in the city.[187]

Former students and a former teacher have given their own accounts describing the inequities and substandard conditions evident at Edgewood during the 1960s. Richard and Diana Herrera remember noticing the lack of air conditioning at the school, using textbooks more than ten years old, seeing other students standing against the cafeteria wall waiting for a place to sit, looking out of broken windows, and hearing others complain about the lack of college preparatory courses such as advanced math.[188] Diana Briseño Herrera, Richard's high school sweetheart, was told by the school counselor not to enroll in college because "you're going to marry Richard and have babies."[189] Other Mexican American female students faced this same treatment by the counselor, who believed that they were bound to become pregnant housewives immediately after completing high school. Senior Louis Martínez expressed his discontent regarding the lack of supportive counseling at the school: "A lot of us [Mexican American students] didn't want to go into vocational fields, a lot of us wanted to go into professional fields and we weren't given that [type of] guidance."[190] Martínez believed that he and other Mexican American students did not receive adequate counseling to pursue professional career fields. In reminiscing about the protest thirty years later, walkout participant and 1967 Edgewood graduate Linda Bononcini spoke out on the deplorable conditions. She stated, "We had to wear our coats during the winter; windows and doors were broken; the restrooms were never working;

110 ∼ CHAPTER 3

there was no toilet paper."[191] Senior Rebecca Campos Ramírez expressed her concern regarding toilet paper: "I now remember that we [students] did run out of toilet paper and paper towels. I remember telling my parents about it and my father buying a four-pack just so that I could take some to the school."[192] She also recalls seeing most classrooms deteriorating, and watching birds flying through the broken school windows.[193] Band member Elva A. Garza wore old tattered uniforms because the school did not buy new ones.[194] Junior class president Rosendo Gutiérrez further commented on this neglect of student needs: "We're talking about a basic environment, but aside from that, our gymnasium. No shower stalls, and dirty showers giving students zero privacy and athlete's foot. Facilities were in rundown conditions. Many were missing windowpanes. Replacement of faulty tools in school shops, installation of stair rails and fire extinguishers and extermination of rodents and insects . . . and we want a gym, not a barn."[195] Students attested to the low-quality education at Edgewood, the poorest school district in the San Antonio area. Edgewood school alumnus (class of 1960) and MAYO member Mario C. Compean, who served as the unofficial liaison between Chicano students and MAYO, was disappointed. He and other activists believed that local school officials did little to remedy these conditions.[196] Furthermore, he had been discouraged from attending college during his high school years at Edgewood and still remembers the advice he was given by the school counselor:

> I was a good student academically but had no options. I was not aware of any scholarship money. The counselors were no help . . . when I found out about it, the next day I was at St. Mary's [University] campus [in San Antonio]. (But) when I first met the counselor that's what he told me: your best option is the military. Sign up for the army. [The counselor] nearly fell out of his chair and told me, "you don't have what it takes to go to college" . . . "the best thing for you to do is to join the army." That's exactly what he told me.[197]

Thus, he could relate his experience of educational neglect and was among those who advocated for equity and the hiring of educators who could properly advise students at the school without judgment or bias.

Such conditions adversely affected others at the school, including English teacher Ben Gutiérrez. He remembers feeling disconcerted by the principal's sudden directive to remove his jacket on a cold winter day: "It was freezing. I had my jacket and my gloves, and the principal said, 'Gutierrez, take your jacket off, and take your gloves off, and pretend that you're warm.' So, the students can take off their jackets also and don't complain that it's below 32 [degrees Fahrenheit]."[198]

Schoolteacher Martha Jane Trudo also commented: "It would have been nice to have good books and chairs that weren't broken. The classrooms weren't painted. If they were, the paint was peeling. There were not enough books and supplies to go around. The hallways were dark. And none of it seemed to merit the attention of the superintendent and staff."[199] Edgewood student protesters created a movement to gain political empowerment and seek the necessary improvements in educational financing. In the spring of 1968, Chicano students refused to tolerate these conditions any longer—conditions that reflected the educational neglect they felt—resulting in the rise of their collective consciousness to address their marginalized status.

During the early stage of the local student movement, Martín Cantú, a 1968 Edgewood graduate, explained that he and other Chicano students drafted and presented a list of nine demands with the title "Edgewood High School Student Body Grievances."[200] Cantú highlighted the major demands, including "better discipline, a grievance board, and better restrooms and general improvements in the school... better qualified teachers as well as counseling."[201] None of the demands expressed Chicano students' desire to speak Spanish freely at school. One of Cantú's classmates and a student activist, Rosendo Gutiérrez, saw local Chicano students drafting and revising student demands during the Edgewood Student Council Convention and at informal meetings at students' homes in April 1968.[202] MAYO members did not draft the entire list of demands but likely knew of the student movement at Edgewood since they had younger relatives or neighbors attending. Albert Sabater was one of the few schoolteachers who supported the walkout, and he may have been one of the key people responsible for informing MAYO of the movement, since he was a graduate of St. Mary's University where MAYO was active.[203] The Civil Rights Commission's investigation of Edgewood High School documents major problems and inadequacies affecting Chicano students prior to the walkout.

Cantú's testimony before the commission meeting in San Antonio highlights an important student demand that reveals the kind of educational deficiencies that plagued the school:

> MR. CANTÚ: One of the reasons we asked for better qualified teachers was because Edgewood had the highest number of non-degree teachers, and, of course, we did not feel that we had the best qualified teachers in the world.
>
> Because usually you might find some of the teachers asking you to type their exam papers for their college term paper.... And so this year I was told by one of the school board members that we had more non-degree teachers than ever before.[204]

One government source substantiates this contention. Exactly 591 (57 percent) of the 1,024 faculty members employed by the Edgewood school system in the mid-1960s did not have college degrees and were hired as emergency-permit teachers.[205] According to another study by historian Ignacio M. García, 98 percent of teachers without a college degree were assigned to teach in schools in economically poor communities with a predominantly ethnic Mexican population throughout San Antonio.[206] Additionally, approximately 76 percent of all non-degree-holding, emergency-permit faculty were Mexican American, and Edgewood teachers earned an average of $4,104 during the 1966–67 school year, the lowest teacher salary in the state.[207] Another grim statistic reveals the consequences the Edgewood school system suffered by employing underqualified teachers. Exactly 516 Mexican American students dropped out of school during the 1967–68 school year, accounting for 95.2 percent of all dropouts in the school district.[208] Thus, Cantú attributed the educational deficiencies at his school to the significant number of poorly paid teachers lacking the proper credentials to teach.

Community activist and MAYO leader Mario Compean recalls that such educational inequities bothered him and others. He agreed with former student Martín Cantú's contention that the Edgewood School District's inability to hire qualified teachers severely hampered ethnic Mexican students' progress in school. In addition, Compean mentioned other key problems that undermined Chicano student morale, such as the dilapidated condition of school buildings, and the Edgewood school system's lack of a suitable financial base or revenue with which to fund improvements.[209] These deficiencies motivated students to walk out and use collective action to eventually challenge their school system to consider their demands, expanding political opportunity for educational reform.

One study of nine San Antonio–area school systems substantiates Compean's argument about the disparities in educational finance. In the 1967–68 school year, the Edgewood School District spent a total of $356 per student and had a Mexican American student enrollment of nearly 90 percent.[210] In contrast, one of San Antonio's predominantly Anglo-American school systems, Alamo Heights ISD, spent $594, exactly $238 more than Edgewood's total per student. As members of one of the city's most affluent school districts, Alamo Heights schools had a Mexican American student enrollment of only 18 percent.[211] Such conditions contributed to the educational deficiencies in the Edgewood school system because it was the most poorly funded school district in the San Antonio area during the late 1960s.

Compean stated that this disparity in school finances existed in the San Antonio area because Edgewood's school community had been predominantly low-income, working-class families residing near Kelly Air Force Base. The base had once served as the largest employer of Mexican Americans, offering them low-skilled, entry-level jobs.[212] Other factors that contributed to the Edgewood school system's meager amount spent per student included low-valued residential properties, the presence of nontaxable federal and/or public land, and the lack of industrial development in the school district's community.[213] These factors led to Edgewood's mediocre financial capacity and affected the hiring of qualified teachers and the allocation of funds to refurbish school buildings.[214]

Another key student demand suggests another concern organizers had about student academic performance. They asked school administrators to implement college preparatory classes such as chemistry, physics, algebra, and computer programming.[215] Chicano students met at homes to draft demands while parents formed the Edgewood Concerned Parents Organization prior to the walkout.[216] Parents playing key roles in this group included Demetrio P. Rodríguez, Martín Cantú, Reynaldo Castaño, and Alberta Snid.[217] Such parental support and the involvement of MAYO further mobilized students by offering organizational resources such as moral support, trust, encouragement, advising, and knowledge toward the pursuit of movement goals. In April 1968, Edgewood principal C. H. Mangum agreed to meet local student activists at the home of Robert Klebhan, colonel of the high school's ROTC program. According to former student Rosendo Gutiérrez, several meetings were held at his house, located across the street from the Edgewood gym, to discuss demands, but Mangum did not acknowledge them as a legitimate proposal for improving conditions at the school.[218] School superintendent Bennie Steinhauser expressed his skepticism regarding the student movement: "Most of these boys and girls are fine students who have been misled and are being used by a few adults. Parents should become very aware of what their students are doing."[219] MAYO leader Willie Velásquez encouraged the students to continue their movement, urging them to assess the quality of education at the school: "With the education you get at Edgewood, most of you are going to wind up either in Vietnam or as a ditchdigger. At [affluent schools in San Antonio such as] Jefferson, Alamo Heights or Lee, there is a chance that you'll go to college. But 85 percent of you [at Edgewood] will not go—$80 a week is the most you will earn the rest of your life. Tell Steinhauser this is the problem."[220] After school officials refused to consider the grievances, some three hundred to four hundred Chicano students at Edgewood agreed to walk out on May 16, 1968. Walkout participant Manuel Garza believes the school district failed to seriously address student demands before the protest: "If anything, it [the reason for the walkout] was the denial to hear us [students] out. That's what sparked it [the walkout]."[221] Another former student protester, Louis Martínez, explained his perspective: "There was tension in the air, [and] there were undercurrents flowing through the student body so the walkout was not unexpected."[222]

Student dissent toward the school system suddenly became evident as the student movement gained momentum.

Students had already planned to walk out of school on the morning of May 16 after the school district failed to seriously consider their demands. As soon as the walkout began, Richard Herrera, a junior at the school, remembers seeing students filing into the hallway chanting "walkout" during his English class at 10:20 a.m. However, just as he and his classmates stood up from their desks to join them, Herrera's teacher, Mrs. Mooney, stood in front of the classroom door and threatened to fail anyone who left the school.[223] A few minutes after giving her a stern warning, Herrera's brother suddenly thrust the door open and pushed Mooney out of the way, allowing students to join the protest. Other teachers tried to stop students from walking out as well, but to no avail. Some protesters sang "Amen," a gospel song popularized by the 1963 movie *Lilies of the Field* starring Sidney Poitier, as they left the school.[224] Meanwhile, Edgewood principal C. H. Mangum issued his own ultimatum and told various members of the senior class that he was not going to allow them to graduate, and he further threatened to revoke their academic scholarships if they protested outside the school.[225] Undaunted by this ultimatum, senior Herlinda Sifuentes still decided to join the walkout and risk the loss of her scholarship with the federally funded precollege program Upward Bound "because the [educational] needs [at Edgewood High School] were so great."[226] Junior Diana Briseño refused to walk out and remained in school but eventually came to understand the significance of such action: "I believed in the [public school] system. I truly believed it [the system] would take care of its children, I always believed the adults [educators] would protect the education and take care of the inequities, and the system did not," and "I [initially] thought it [the walkout] was wrong."[227] James Castano, junior class president, explained his decision to walk out after the protest began: "I did not leave the school because I was running away from my studies. I want a good education. That is why I am here [participating in the walkout]."[228] As student protesters continued to leave classrooms, they began assembling off Thirty-Fourth Street near the school and were given picket signs, most likely from members of MAYO and other outside supporters. Walkout participant Rebecca P. Ortiz felt she and other protesters were in "rally mode" as soon as the walkout began.[229] The yelling, clapping, and chanting soon echoed throughout the entire campus, attracting the attention of the media and the larger Edgewood community.

Within an hour of walking out, the protesters marched from the school to the district's administration offices.[230] En route to the central office, they were escorted by local police across Highway 90 and demanded a meeting with superintendent Bennie Steinhauser.[231] Walkout leader James Castano led the

Figure 2. Edgewood High School protest march, San Antonio, Texas. *San Antonio Express*, May 17, 1968.

demonstration outside the administration building where numerous students carried picket signs that read "Everyone in America Deserves a Good Education," "We Want a Better Education," "We Want a Gym, Not a Barn," and "Better Library, Better Teachers, Better Schools."[232] After an anxious wait to speak with Steinhauser, someone appeared from the school district office building to announce that the superintendent was away from his office and out to lunch.[233] In response to the student insurgency, Steinhauser later remarked, "This is so clearly a Willie Velasquez and Father Henry Casso inspired activity. Most of the students don't even know what they are supposedly unhappy about.... Velasquez is a professional agitator. He gets paid for it."[234] Steinhauser further believed the walkout occurred after one school board member stated that some Edgewood students felt marginalized at the school because they came from low-income families.[235]

Meanwhile, the school district's suspension of teachers Janie Hilgen and Albert Sabater stoked further controversy. School administrators suspended Sabater and Hilgen for leaving their assigned posts during the walkout. Sabater reportedly spoke at a student rally and Hilgen held an informal English class for an estimated 150 protesters just outside the school.[236] Both events occurred shortly after the walkout. Some students chose to go home rather than join Hilgen's class outside, according to senior George Torres. He further reiterated on behalf of Chicano students, "We want a better education."[237] Later in the day, administrators obtained a court order mandating that the two teachers stay off school grounds.[238] Teachers such as Hilgen believed they understood why the protest took place: "We want guarantees that conditions will improve. Their [the students'] demands [were] not excessive."[239] Hilgen was also willing to "teach them [students] in a barn" if necessary.[240] Nevertheless, school officials reprimanded teachers who accompanied students during the walkout. Superintendent Steinhauser took decisive action by immediately suspending both Sabater and

Figure 3. Miss Jane Hilgen teaching an English class on the curb in front of Edgewood High School. She was suspended from her job as a result of her activities during the walkout. Courtesy of Ford Foundation Photographs, series 3.9, box 91, folder 1555, Rockefeller Archive Center, Sleepy Hollow, New York.

Hilgen pending an investigation of their role in the student protest and requested a temporary restraining order prohibiting them from returning to school.[241]

Despite their pleas for social and political change, Edgewood protesters negotiated with school officials and agreed to return to school on May 20. Student leader James Castano told one local reporter that student protesters decided to resume their classes after the walkout "just to show that we're not rabble-rousers.... We walked out for a good cause, but we're going back in to show that we didn't walk out from an education."[242] On the evening before they returned to school, walkout participants added a new item to their list of demands, requesting the reinstatement of teachers Sabater and Hilgen for their support of the walkout.[243] The next day, approximately five hundred Chicano students and their parents held a meeting at Holy Cross High School in San Antonio to discuss a campaign for remedying deficiencies at Edgewood.[244] During the meeting, Ray Montalvo and Martín Cantú, the only students who were suspended for participating in the walkout, were allowed to return to school after receiving instruction from their attorneys.[245] After the Edgewood school boycott, school authorities granted certain concessions regarding the upgrade of school facilities and the hiring of qualified teachers. During an interview with public radio show host Dick Gordon in 2008, Richard and Diana Herrera discussed the improvements to the school. Such obvious changes included the revamping of floors, refurbishing of the gym, remodeling of the cafeteria, addition of circulating fans, restoration of lockers and windows, repainting of walls, supply of additional textbooks, and the cleaning of restrooms, and they "even allowed us [students] to have a smoking area."[246] Vice principal José Cárdenas would soon be named superintendent of Edgewood, and in the early 1970s he founded the Intercultural Development Research Association (IDRA). IDRA generates research and provides training and curricular support to low-income and Latino schools, teachers, and students. Clemente Sáenz, president of the board of trustees, recruited Cárdenas for the position after the entire board offered him the job.[247] Thus, the outcome of the walkout demonstrates that the political transformation of the students led to significant enhancement of facilities and greater institutional support. Another major event that moved officials to promise reform occurred when the parents of four student protesters filed a civil suit in federal court a few months after the walkout began.

The Edgewood School Case

On June 30, 1968, parents Demetrio Rodríguez, Martín Cantú, Reynaldo Castaño, and Alberta Snid filed a civil lawsuit in the federal district court for the Western District of Texas. Their case against the San Antonio school system directly challenged the inequality of educational funding in public schools in Texas.[248] The plaintiffs argued that Mexican American students' right to a quality education was a constitutional right that San Antonio–area schools denied them. Parents such as Rodríguez expressed concern about the glaring inequities at Edgewood High School, from the lack of "Bunsen burners [in science rooms] to broken windows [in classrooms]" as well as inadequate supplies, the hiring of uncertified teachers, the lack of air conditioning, and the overall decrepit condition of the school.[249] This landmark case specifically addressed Texas' method of allocating funds to public school districts by property tax assessments and real estate formulas.

San Antonio civil rights attorney Arthur Gochman, referred by MAYO activist Willie Velásquez, represented the group of parents in the case.[250] The Edgewood walkout was an important factor in the parents' decision to file the case. They believed the case would help solve the problems that plagued their children in the school. Prior to the case, the parents discussed educational issues and the contemplated court proceedings after forming a grassroots community action group known as the Edgewood District Concerned Parents Association.

This group included parent leaders such as Demetrio Rodríguez, Alberta Snid, and other Mexican American parents, mostly mothers.[251] Rodríguez was a navy and air force veteran who served in both World War II and the Korean War and was a sheet-metal worker at San Antonio's Kelly Air Force Base.[252] Prior to joining the Edgewood parents' association, Rodríguez participated in Mexican American civil rights organizations, including the American GI Forum, LULAC, and the Mexican-American Betterment Organization in San Antonio, and traveled throughout Texas in support of school desegregation in the aftermath of *Brown v. Board of Education* (1954).[253] He sued Edgewood ISD because two of his children attended a poorly equipped, dilapidated elementary school unlike the facilities in nearby Alamo Heights, an affluent school district within the San Antonio metropolitan area.[254] Another key organizer and the only single parent of the group, Alberta Snid, and her four children were plaintiffs in the case as well.[255] Acting chair E. R. Pruñeda further announced the group's intention of taking legal action, alleging the school district's violation of Mexican American students' civil rights and the right to an education under the Fourteenth Amendment to the Constitution guaranteeing equal protection under the law.[256] An additional allegation listed by the plaintiffs included the creation of a suspect class of people based on wealth or infringing on poor students' rights to public education.[257]

Statistics contrasting the Edgewood and Alamo Heights school districts demonstrated financial disparities. The average assessed taxable property value per student for Edgewood during 1967–68 was $5,960, compared to over $49,000 for Alamo Heights.[258] The median family income for the Edgewood school community at the time was $4,686, versus $8,001 for Alamo Heights. Dr. José Cárdenas, superintendent of Edgewood schools, provided Gochman with data demonstrating the lack of funding for property-poor school districts.[259] Such data showed how financial disparities led to inferior schools. According to information supplied by Cárdenas, nearly 32 percent of Edgewood students dropped out between grades seven and twelve.[260] According to co-counsels for the plaintiffs Mark G. Yudof and Daniel C. Morgan, Dr. José Cárdenas testified as to the educational dreams of students and parents in his school system prior to the trial. He also assessed the impact of the district's financial struggle to maintain its educational programs and began to suggest the implementation of a more equitable model for school financing before the assistant attorney general for the state abruptly ended the deposition. Regarding the quality of teaching in both school districts, nearly half (47 percent) of Edgewood's faculty lacked the credentials to teach, while almost 90 percent of Alamo Heights' teachers were fully certified.[261]

Chicano education scholar Richard Valencia cites additional selected indicators of educational quality based on court data to further illustrate the vast inequality of wealth between the Edgewood and Alamo Heights School

Districts. These include professional salaries per pupil ($372 for Alamo Heights and $209 for Edgewood), percentage of teachers with master's degrees (40 for Alamo Heights and 15 for Edgewood), percentage of staff with emergency teaching credentials (11 for Alamo Heights and 47 for Edgewood), and the student-to-counselor ratio (645 for Alamo Heights and 3,098 for Edgewood).[262] During the 1967–68 school year, the Edgewood school district enrolled approximately twenty-two thousand students in its twenty-five elementary schools and twelve secondary schools, including 90 percent who identified as Mexican American, 6 percent as African American, and 4 percent as white.[263] In Alamo Heights, the enrollment was approximately five thousand students in six schools throughout the district and included 81 percent white (non-Hispanic), 18 percent Mexican American, and less than 1 percent African American for the same school year.[264]

In the late 1960s, the allocation of funding remained racialized because of financial disparities across school districts in Texas. For example, the average income for each student in predominantly Mexican American school districts (80 percent or more) was less than half that in districts that were less than 20 percent Mexican American.[265] During the 1967–68 school year, the amount of funding spent for education in Mexican American school districts was three-fifths (60 percent) of the total spent in predominantly Anglo schools.[266] By the 1969–70 academic year, Texas ranked near the bottom (forty-ninth out of fifty states) in high and low expenditures per student, $5,334 and $264, respectively.[267] School finance reform had not been a major issue in the Texas legislature since the formation of the Gilmer-Aikin Committee in 1949, which had established a new public school finance system for the second half of the twentieth century.[268] An important part of the new system included the Minimum Foundation Program, which set formulas for distributing funds for personnel and operations in an effort to promote a state-supported educational minimum and equalized tax burden.[269] The Edgewood walkout had fueled the passion of students and their supporters for seeking a feasible solution to a more egalitarian method of school financing by the early 1970s.

The defendants included the State Board of Education, the commissioner of education, the state attorney general, and the Bexar County Board of Trustees. The case, *Rodriguez v. San Antonio Independent School District*, was named after Demetrio Rodríguez, chief plaintiff. Although Superintendent Cárdenas wanted to testify as an expert witness on behalf of the plaintiffs, school district attorney Gregory Luna advised him not to do so because he represented the district, one of the defendants in the case.[270] The original complaint listed the seven school districts in the San Antonio area and the attorney general of Texas as the defendants in the original complaint, and a three-judge panel was chosen to hear the case.[271] Both the litigants and the three-judge panel understood that the case held consequences not only for San Antonio, but for the entire nation because "in reality, the whole statewide system of financing education was under attack."[272] The case switched to a class action suit because of its statewide repercussions "on behalf of school children throughout the State who are members of minority groups or who are poor and reside in school districts having a low property tax base."[273] By assessing unequal disparities in per pupil expenditures, the case meant "to illustrate the manner in which the dual system of finance operates and to indicate the extent to which substantial disparities exist despite the State's impressive progress in recent years."[274]

Syracuse professor of political science Joel Burke, who served as an expert witness for the plaintiffs, provided additional information based on his research, which examined school funding on the state and national level. State and federal funding did not equalize per-student spending in San Antonio. School districts with a market value of taxable property per student above $100,000 had $856 in total revenue per student, including local, state, and federal funding. Poor school districts with a taxable property per student value below $10,000 generated a mere $441 in total revenue per student.[275] Burke's testimony further revealed that the ten wealthiest school districts had an equalized tax rate of 31 cents per $100, while the four poorest school districts had a higher equalized tax rate of 70 cents per $100 of assessed valuation.[276] The most affluent school systems' low tax rate yielded an expenditure of $585 for each student, whereas underprivileged schools were able to raise a mere $60 per-student expenditure with their higher tax rate.[277] Consequently, Gochman argued that financial disparities in Texas public schools, including such factors as the lowest median family income in property-poor school districts, resulted in poor student performance. He further emphasized the state's inability to adhere to the principle of equal educational opportunity in the distribution of state resources.[278]

As in the famous *Brown v. Board of Education* case, social science data played an important role in Gochman's argument. It helped prove the effect of inferior schools on ethnic-minority students, illustrating the correlation between race and per-student spending. More to the point, Gochman claimed that Texas' method of allocating funding to public schools did nothing to alleviate the conditions of property-poor schools with predominantly ethnic-minority student populations. Overall, he argued that the unequal dispersal of educational funding in the Texas school finance system violated the Equal Protection Clause of the Fourteenth Amendment.[279]

This argument resulted in the three-judge panel of the federal court ruling in favor of the plaintiffs on December 23, 1971. According to Carlos R. Soltero, a leading Latino civil rights lawyer based in Austin, "At the heart of Rodríguez was the question of how public schools could be financed consistent with the Equal Protection Clause as applied to funding of public schools by states or state agencies."[280] The ruling required the Texas legislature to reestablish the state school finance system in compliance with the equal protection provisions of the US and Texas Constitutions.[281]

The three-judge court also did not deem the state's charge of communism and socialism against the plaintiffs to be a basis for seeking equalized school funding.[282] This heightened interest in communism on the part of state assistant attorney general Pat Bailey reflected a deep concern with the rampant Cold War hysteria or Red Scare of the time. He made this concern especially apparent in his response to Superintendent Cárdenas's call for equalized school funding, in which he stated somewhat emphatically in a court deposition before the trial, "There is a name for that [communism]. I have no further questions."[283] The state had two years to make the appropriate adjustments and correct the defects in its education finance system.[284] In the meantime, the court stood by to render its own remedy in the event the state failed to provide an acceptable plan, thus retaining jurisdiction over the case. The verdict, however, represented a short-lived victory for Texas' low-income school districts with predominantly ethnic-minority student populations like Edgewood. Within a few months, the defendants appealed to the Supreme Court in an attempt to reverse the lower court's decision.

The case went to the US Supreme Court as *San Antonio ISD v. Rodriguez* on October 12, 1972. During the trial, the state of Texas enlisted the services of Charles Alan Wright, a distinguished constitutional scholar and professor of law at the University of Texas, while Arthur Gochman again represented the plaintiffs.[285] The main strategy of the state in the second case was to show that the Constitution did not support the proposition that education was a fundamental interest and poverty a suspect classification.[286] Gochman emphasized the importance of education as a means of socioeconomic advancement and good citizenry, further arguing that Texas' finance system had failed to provide adequate resources to meet Edgewood students' educational needs. Upon reaching its decision on March 21, 1973, the Supreme Court did in fact overrule the initial federal district court ruling by a five-to-four decision. In making the ruling, the court declared that education is not a constitutional right and that each state government is responsible for the affairs of its school systems.[287] Furthermore, the court rejected Gochman's charge of discrimination based on wealth.

Justice Lewis F. Powell Jr. announced the majority's opinion in the decision. His judgment consisted of the following main points: the "historically rooted dual system of financing education could not withstand the strict judicial scrutiny" that applied to examining "legislative judgments that interfere with fundamental constitutional rights or that involve suspect classifications"; equal protection for education under the Constitution did not exist; discrimination on the basis of wealth was ambiguous; and the Texas system did not disadvantage any suspect class.[288]

Furthermore, the plaintiffs' arguments did not convince Powell that a direct correlation existed between equalized funding and the quality of education.[289] Justice Thurgood Marshall, who voted in favor of the original decision (1971), called the high court's majority ruling "a retreat from our historic commitment to equality of educational opportunity and as an unsupportable acquiescence in a system which deprives children in their earliest years of the chance to reach their full potential as citizens."[290] In comparing the situation of Mexican American schoolchildren to one of Texas' most famous school desegregation cases, *Sweatt v. Painter* (1950), he further stated, "It is difficult to believe that if the children of Texas had a free choice, they would choose to be educated in districts with fewer resources, and hence with more antiquated plants [facilities], less experienced teachers, and a less diversified curriculum."[291] US circuit judge Jeffrey S. Sutton commented on Justice Marshall's opinion regarding the purging of all forms of school segregation vis-à-vis Mexican Americans in 2008: "As one of the winning lawyers in Brown [v. Board of Education], Justice Marshall surely appreciated the significance of the case, including the possibility that the promises of Brown would never be fulfilled unless the courts not only eliminated de jure segregation by race but also curbed the effects of de facto segregation by wealth."[292] The Supreme Court's decision represented a devastating defeat to the supporters of school finance reform. Nevertheless, the Rodríguez lawsuit highlighted the heart of the controversy regarding how property-poor school systems such as Edgewood failed to receive adequate funding and resources, and how this negatively impacted students' education.

The case marked the beginning of a prolonged struggle to find a more even-handed method of funding public schools to provide quality education for all schoolchildren. However, the state's public school funding system remains at the center of controversy. The state legislature continues to debate this issue today despite ongoing political discourse and litigation in the courts. Carlos Soltero argues: "The basic claim of those opposing the plaintiffs was that Rodríguez had decided the issue, that school funding was a political question not to be considered by the courts, and that judicial interference would conflict with the value of control over local schools."[293] Various educational disparities in the allocation of school funding and per-student expenditures continue to exist based on race, class, and property values. The quality of education for Mexican Americans attending property-poor school systems hangs in the balance. Although this ruling did not favor equalizing school funding throughout San Antonio or across Texas, it confirms the attempt by Edgewood students and their supporters to achieve greater political leverage and their desire for inclusion in the school's power structure. Nonetheless, the student movements at Lanier and Edgewood High Schools sparked the beginning of a call for drastic educational reform and political empowerment for Mexican Americans in South Texas. Such student insurgency was replicated across rural South Texas in other predominantly Mexican American communities.

Summary and Conclusion

The Edgewood and Lanier High School walkouts emerged as the first major Chicano student protests in South Texas. Recollections by former Lanier High School students indicate that racism had been inherent in the school's vocational curriculum, which tracked Mexican American students into low-paying trades. They further contended that local school administrators attempted to "Americanize" Mexican American students since they were regarded as culturally and racially inferior. An investigation into conditions at Lanier by the US Commission on Civil Rights revealed the educational deficiencies that affected Mexican American students. The commission's record underscored the perspectives and viewpoints of Mexican Americans students. It indicated that many ethnic Mexican students received poor instruction in English grammar at the school and were belittled for speaking Spanish on school grounds, and that educators purposely tracked them into vocational education and trade courses rather than college preparatory classes. The low-level curriculum of Lanier reflected the poor socioeconomic environment of the school's surrounding community.

The La Raza Unida Conference held at John F. Kennedy High School in San Antonio several weeks prior to the walkout provided an initial gathering point for local Mexican Americans to discuss educational issues. Those in attendance included student movement organizers José Angel Gutiérrez, Willie Velásquez, and Mario Compean. They and other student activists became instrumental in establishing contacts between MAYO and local high school students at Lanier and Edgewood. Meetings between MAYO and local Mexican American youth marked the birth of the Chicano student movement in South Texas.

The landmark case *Rodriguez v. San Antonio Independent School District* challenged Texas' method of allocating funds to public school districts according to their property-tax bases, thereby violating the Equal Protection Clause of the Fourteenth Amendment. *Rodriguez v. San Antonio Independent School District* represents Chicano student movement activists' attempt to remedy educational deficiencies at their school through litigation. Although the Supreme Court ruled against the plaintiffs, the case represented Mexican Americans' desire to gain the power to carry out public school reform via the federal legal system. A favorable decision on the part of the Supreme Court would have had national consequences that could have positively impacted similar poor minority communities across the country. The call for this type of community activism later resurfaced during the Edcouch-Elsa school walkout and subsequent school court case.

4

The 1968 Edcouch-Elsa High School Walkout
Chicano Student Activism in Deep South Texas

The Edcouch-Elsa school walkout of November 1968 was the first major Chicano student protest in the Rio Grande Valley of Deep South Texas. Particular attention here will focus on the key issues and school grievances reflecting the collective consciousness and shared beliefs of Chicano students at Edcouch-Elsa Junior and Senior High School. This chapter will further reveal the major actors and supporters of the Edcouch-Elsa walkout. Movement activists from MAYO helped mobilize Chicano students and replicate student insurgency in Edcouch-Elsa. Moreover, MAYO, building on its previous participation in the organization of the Lanier walkout and subsequent court case, sought to carry out its educational reform agenda in Edcouch-Elsa and promote political empowerment of Chicanos.

The post–World War II era marked a period of unprecedented resistance against racial segregation and discrimination. The outcome of the African American–inspired *Brown v. Board of Education* case and the famous Montgomery bus boycott initiated the beginning of the modern Black Freedom Movement of the 1950s and 1960s. National attention from newspaper, radio, and television reporters and cameras documented the struggle to end racial inequality. Activists in the African American Civil Rights Movement negotiated with politicians, business executives, union leaders, and public administrators to break down barriers against equal opportunity with varying degrees of success. Prominent movement icons such as Martin Luther King Jr. and Rosa Parks became legendary after the Montgomery bus boycott. Much of the nation learned of the boycott and other movement events via television or newspaper, captivating and inspiring many people to stage their own protests, including young people in Edcouch-Elsa. Edcouch-Elsa experienced virtually no social protest from the early to mid-twentieth century until the student walkout in 1968. In-depth interviews with various Chicano students and community members in Edcouch-Elsa indicate that the longstanding practice of de facto segregation, discrimination, and unequal facilities in their school system precipitated the local walkout.

Carlos Calderón, a former North Edcouch Elementary teacher from 1949 to 1950, wrote a master's thesis comparing the two racially segregated elementary schools in Edcouch-Elsa. He looked at the two school buildings, examining such facilities as classrooms, restrooms, and drinking fountains. He also investigated other significant differences such as medical services, intramural sports, music instruction, and busing.[1] In assessing the conditions at the "Mexican" school, Calderón argued that the physical appearance and condition of North Elementary were clearly substandard and created a poorer learning environment. He concluded that Mexican schools "were inferior in every respect" when compared to predominantly white schools.[2] Anglo teachers at North Elementary also contributed to the educational inequality. Many imposed separate standards of grade promotion for Mexican American students and Anglo students, especially regarding advancement from first to second grade.[3] Eloisa Carillo, another local resident, asserted that Mexican Americans had "a wooden school with outhouses and wood-burning stoves . . . [while] Anglos had a brick school with gas heaters and inside plumbing."[4] Similar practices and conditions were also evident in other Texas schools.

In November 1968 over 190 Chicano students walked out of Edcouch-Elsa Junior and Senior High School demanding social justice and alleging educational failure. They boycotted classes shortly after the first class on the first day, participating in the community's first major youth protest. Located between Edcouch and Elsa, the high school enrolled nearly 940 students, over 90 percent of whom were Mexican American.[5] The walkout was both a product of and a contributor to 1960s Chicano militancy. To understand why the walkout occurred, we must first examine Edcouch-Elsa.

The town of Edcouch was named for Edward Couch, local landowner and banker, and its sister city Elsa was named for Elsa George, wife of a resident landowner. Both towns were developed in the late 1920s and were incorporated by 1940.[6] Mexican Americans living in Edcouch-Elsa in the mid-twentieth century began to voice their dissatisfaction with the educational facilities and conditions of the schools. Jacinto González, the first Mexican American to serve on the Edcouch-Elsa School Board in the mid-1930s, frequently requested additional resources to address the deficiencies at North Edcouch Elementary. He asked that school administrators hire more qualified staff.[7] González's appeals were ignored. After the end of his term as trustee, the next Mexican American to win a seat on the Edcouch-Elsa School Board was former protest leader Eddy

González (no relation to Jacinto), in the early 1970s. Thus, the adverse conditions of racial and class subjugation impacting Mexican Americans in Edcouch-Elsa continued throughout most of the twentieth century.

Maricela Rodríguez,[8] who was in eighth grade at the time of the 1968 walkout and was one of its youngest participants, said she was treated differently from Anglo-American students. On numerous occasions, school counselor Gretchen Sorensen detained her and other Mexican American female students to measure their skirt length, supposedly to enforce the dress code. However, Rodríguez said that Sorensen did not stop any white female students. Sorensen frequently sent Mexican American students home if she considered their skirts too short. Mexican American male students' appearance was also regulated, and Sorensen measured their hair and shirtsleeves. This situation led Rodríguez to consider walking out.[9] Rodríguez also lamented, "It was the Mexican Cheerleaders who did all the cleaning and all the work." After she walked out, the school stripped Rodríguez of her awards in school. She quit the protest after one day and then took her mother to the school to apologize for walking out.[10] School officials did not address this type of differential treatment of Mexican American students.

Uvaldo Vásquez was another eighth-grade student who experienced discrimination. School coach Kenneth Kachtik reprimanded him for speaking Spanish during a physical education class. Vásquez told a friend to throw him the ball in Spanish, saying, "Dame la pelota," and upon hearing this phrase, Kachtik scolded Vásquez in front of the other students and instructed him not to speak Spanish at school.[11] Vásquez felt embarrassed and afraid to utter a word in Spanish. As a result, one demand of the walkout was that Chicano students have the right to speak their "mother tongue" on school grounds. Education historian Gilbert G. González suggests that such restrictions were widespread across the Southwest and indicate that US public school officials identified "the Spanish language and Mexican culture as contradictory to educational success."[12] Local resident Eloisa Carillo confirms that most schools across the Rio Grande Valley had an unofficial, de facto no-Spanish rule.[13] Thus, Chicano students at Edcouch-Elsa began to see their Spanish language and cultural traditions come under fire, giving rise to their collective consciousness of feeling socially marginalized.

Sophomore Frank Vallejo felt resentment because of another incident. His friend's girlfriend, also Mexican American, was pregnant, and counselor Sorensen had advised her to drop out. Vallejo confronted Sorensen and pleaded with her to let the female student remain in school. Sorensen placed him on a three-day suspension for disagreeing. This incident led him to doubt the counselor's ability to properly advise the pregnant student and motivated him to later walk out.[14] The school had no alternative educational program for pregnant students at the time.

Eddy González, an eleventh grader, was also impacted by a similar affront. Assistant principal Juan Gorostiza, a Mexican American, told González to cut off his long sideburns to comply with the dress code. After cutting off one of his sideburns, González saw classmate Will Carter, a white student, walk into the restroom with long sideburns. When González asked Gorostiza whether Carter should cut his sideburns as well, the assistant principal replied that only González had to do so. González then refused to cut his other sideburn, and Gorostiza suspended him for three days. González's mother approached school officials the next day. After his mother's intervention, administrators let González return after missing one school day. But Gorostiza's unwillingness to enforce the school dress code equally heightened González's defiance. González was also mistreated on numerous occasions by principal Marvin Pipkin, who struck him with a large wooden paddle for speaking Spanish.[15] Such mistreatment led him to question why school administrators rendered such punishments to students whose first language was Spanish.

Rodríguez, Vallejo, González, and other Chicano students were upset and angered by the unequal treatment of Anglos and Mexican Americans. Many criticisms focused on counselor Gretchen Sorensen, who purposely dissuaded Mexican Americans from attending college, suggesting instead that they pursue manual labor, learn a trade, or join the military. Sorensen told walkout leader Freddy Sáenz that he had "a good arm and would be good for [serving in] the army."[16] Likewise, Sorensen did not inform protest leader Raúl Arispe and other Mexican American male students about college so they could avoid the Vietnam War draft. Arispe admitted that he did not know Sorensen was there until he was a junior. He believed she favored Anglo-American students and acted as a "special teacher" while encouraging Mexican American male students to "join the army."[17] Bene Layton, a Mexican American senior, recalled Sorensen telling him that he would be a good army recruit. He described Sorensen's office as a favorite "hang-out" spot for white students, where she reserved college preparatory classes for them.[18] He did not walk out. Junior Felix Rodríguez expressed interest in going to college for electrical engineering but remembered Sorensen telling him to pick a vocational trade or join the army.[19] Sorensen's instruction was typical of the advice she gave to Mexican American male students.

Sorensen offered Mexican American female students racialized and gendered advice. She discouraged them from attending college and pursuing skilled labor jobs since she believed that they would make their living as secretaries, homemakers, or domestic servants. They were often oriented toward migrant agricultural labor like that of their parents. According to scholar Thomas P. Carter in his classic 1970 book, *Mexican Americans in School*, "The academic success of a Mexican American child depends on the degree to which his home has been oriented to Anglo middle-class culture."[20] Thus, Mexican American students in Edcouch-Elsa were poorly served by the school system, which had traditionally accommodated white, middle-class, college-bound students.

Former protest leader Mirtala Villareal, a junior, pointed to another difference in treatment: new and up-to-date school equipment reserved for white students. The school bought new electric typewriters for white students in typing class. The Mexican American students had to use old manual typewriters that often broke down. According to Villareal, these typewriters made it difficult for Mexican American students to master typing.[21] The unequal allocation of equipment underscored the fact that Mexican American students were viewed as subordinate.

Porfirio González, whose daughter Herlinda was in eighth grade at the time of the walkout, also recalled the poor conditions. When González visited one of his daughter's teachers, he noticed that the classroom was divided into two sections, one side for whites and the other side for Mexican Americans. He further observed that the Mexican American side did not have a fan and had broken windows, while the white side had a big fan and all the windows were intact. When asked why Mexican American students had to endure these unpleasant conditions, the teacher told González to speak to superintendent A. W. Bell. Dissatisfied with the teacher's response, he left the school in dismay. Unequal classroom conditions were prevalent in southwestern schools. School districts such as Edcouch-Elsa did not have official written policies mandating segregation. Later, daughter Herlinda asked for permission to participate in the walkout, and González responded, "¡Seguro que sí, tienes mi permiso!" (Yes, of course you have my permission.)[22]

Mexican American teachers at the school were divided on the walkout: some understood, while others did not. Eugene Gutiérrez, then a biology teacher, recalls Sorensen belittling a Mexican American student for seeking his assistance in filling out college application forms. Gutiérrez observed Sorensen asking the student, "How do you expect to go to college when you can't even fill out the form?" Although Gutiérrez acknowledged that Sorensen made an inappropriate comment, he believed that Chicano students at Edcouch-Elsa did not need to walk out.[23] Schoolteacher Geneva García believed that the Chicano student protesters became rebels as a result of being misled and falling under the negative influence of outside agitators.[24] Art teacher Homero Díaz, on the other hand, sympathized with the rebels. He agreed that some Anglo-American teachers were "very hard on the kids [Mexican American students]," and the students resented the harsh treatment. Díaz further said that many white teachers at the high school in the 1960s did not tolerate Mexican American cultural differences or Spanish.[25] However, the main reason for his refusal to support the student movement was his commitment to teach rather than participate in students' rights issues. In any case, even Mexican American teachers who sympathized with the Chicano students made almost no effort to support the protesters. Comments by former teachers suggest that in general they did not identify themselves as Chicano, nor did they approve of Chicano protest.

Although commentary from Anglo-American teachers and administrators reveals their disapproval of the student protest, they further indicate how the protest significantly affected the school and larger community. Longtime educator Francis Anderson believed the walkout was one of the most polarizing experiences in community history. "We lost some very good people because of that boycott," she said, referring to the mass departure of Anglo residents as a result of the growing political clout of the local Mexican American community.[26] Although faculty member Willie Ruth Foerster opposed "discriminating against the Latins," she further argued that "it wasn't bad enough" for students to conduct a massive and "unnecessary" walkout.[27] School administrators such as Principal Pipkin and Superintendent Bell did not express any willingness to meet the demands of the student protesters and viewed the walkout as a serious act of insubordination. School trustee Billie Cellum underestimated the students' resolve and ability to organize a school-wide walkout but eventually admitted that he "learned a lot" and better understood the student protesters' perspective and reasons for walking out in the aftermath of the protest.[28]

Origins of Student Activism in Edcouch-Elsa

In mid-October 1968, various Chicano students, their parents, and interested community members began meeting to address certain educational issues to make known their desire for greater political autonomy in their school system. Most meetings were held at the homes of student leaders in Elsa, such as Javier Ramírez (senior), Raúl Arispe (senior), José Luis Chávez (junior), and Mirtala Villareal (junior). An estimated forty to fifty people attended.[29] These former students were unable to confirm the exact numbers of attendees, most likely because there were no attendance records since such meetings were often informal and arranged on short notice.

Among those presiding were Jesús Ramírez, a MAYO leader from nearby San Juan, and Javier Ramírez (no relation to Jesús), who served as the main spokesperson and student leader. Regulars included Arispe, Villareal, Artemio Salinas (senior), Arnulfo Sustaita (senior), Homero Treviño (senior), Eddy González (junior), and Freddy Sáenz (sophomore). These students eventually emerged as leaders because of their outspokenness, strong character, and leadership abilities. Lali Sáenz, Freddy's older sister and a 1965 graduate of Edcouch-Elsa High School, helped students connect to MAYO. She also became more politically active because of her experience as a migrant education aide in Michigan, assisting migrant farmworker students in the summer. Freddy remembered MAYO's help in training students: "And those guys [MAYO members] really taught us how to organize . . . we had structured meetings, wrote goals and objectives . . . that kind of stuff."[30] Thus, Lali served as a facilitator between the students and "outside resources." She contacted Raúl Yzaguirre of the new Colonias del Valle organization, who advised her to "organize the parents."[31] This "outside resource" assisted Chicano students in building their base of support during the initial stages of the protest. According to Juan Gómez-Quiñones, one of the foremost scholars in Chicano studies, "A [local] student movement is often the training and experimental ground for leadership, membership, concepts, tactics, and goals."[32] The development of the Chicano student movement in Edcouch-Elsa is a case in point.

In addition to local Chicano youth, also present at these meetings were a few members of the Political Association of Spanish-Speaking Organizations (PASSO), and Volunteers in Service to America (VISTA). PASSO was a conglomeration of politically active Mexican American organizations based throughout much of the Southwest. VISTA served as a domestic Peace Corps–type operation intended to help low-income communities.[33] However, Chicano students in Edcouch-Elsa attributed much of their grassroots leadership training to MAYO.

PASSO and VISTA members played more limited roles during the emerging movement in Edcouch-Elsa. They offered moral support and encouragement before and during the walkout. Former VISTA member Arturo Salinas urged his brother and walkout participant Artemio to remain involved.[34] Members of all three organizations made protest signs and provided food and moral support.

Student protesters and their supporters drafted a list of fifteen demands and two recommendations. The regional press credited MAYO for its prominent role in drafting and promoting the demands.[35] The petition stated, "We the student body of Edcouch-Elsa Junior and Senior High School, demand of the officials and administrators" the following. Among the most important demands were that

- no disciplinary action be taken against any student or teacher involved in the local movement;
- students select their own candidates for student council;
- Chicano students have the right to speak their mother tongue, Spanish, freely on school grounds;
- blatant discrimination against Mexican American students at school cease immediately;
- new courses be introduced as a regular part of the curriculum to reflect the contributions of people of Mexican origin to the state and region.[36]

The two recommendations were that community members should drive school buses instead of teachers, and that the time between class periods should be five minutes instead of three.

The demands emphasized the students' longing for respect and dignity as people of Mexican descent. They regarded Spanish usage and ethnic Mexican cultural awareness as an integral part of education. The grievances further expressed Chicano exclusion, citing the school's failure to value ethnic Mexican cultural background, implement a curriculum reflecting their cultural heritage, and promote Mexican American academic progress.

Javier Ramírez first gained awareness of how to formulate demands and organize collectively after his junior year at Edcouch-Elsa. In the summer of 1968, Ramírez traveled to Michigan with migrant farmworkers. He rode with a family to Detroit to find a job on an automobile assembly line. While working in an auto factory there, Ramírez met labor unionists and heard them discuss their dissatisfaction with workplace conditions. His conversations with workers taught him valuable lessons in organizing. By the end of the summer, Ramírez had gained a newfound political consciousness.[37] His experience provided insights that helped direct the Edcouch-Elsa student protest movement shortly after the start of his senior year.

Notes taken by student leader Javier Ramírez during Chicano students' meetings reveal how school officials reacted to the demands.[38] According to the notes, school coach Tom Hardy said the list of demands was "funnier than the Sunday news comics," and teacher's aide Javier Gutiérrez sarcastically remarked, "You know what you people can do with this paper?"[39] Ramírez's notes added that teacher Gilbert Castañeda attempted to discourage students from participating, saying, "I haven't read this thing [list of demands] yet, but I am not willing to do anything. I advise you people to forget about this movement." Another school official, federal program director Martin Peña, tried to convince student leader Raúl Arispe and other protesters to quit. Both Mexican American and white educators opposed the local student movement.

Opposition to the student movement also came from outside the school. The *McAllen Monitor* newspaper received word from an anonymous source that a protest was forthcoming, and rumors of a walkout spread quickly. The Edcouch-Elsa School Board and regional press often referred to MAYO, PASSO, and VISTA members as "outside agitators." These groups mobilized students to collective action by networking with adult activists, offering moral support and advice, and making protest signs. Many in the community, including Elsa mayor Neal Galloway, believed that such "outside agitators" had planned the walkout.[40] Edcouch-Elsa school superintendent A. W. Bell believed that MAYO had already secretly met with local students a few weeks prior to the walkout.

An incident in late October brought MAYO's role to the attention of school officials. Two unidentified Chicano high school students were expelled for refusing haircuts. Two unidentified MAYO members ignited a dispute at the school when they accompanied local students protesting the expulsions and claimed that certain educators had deliberately mistreated Mexican American students. The *McAllen Monitor* reported that the school board regarded these individuals (who lived in Edcouch-Elsa and attended Pan American College in nearby Edinburg) as the first "outside agitators."[41] As a result of this incident, the school board sought to prevent similar confrontations with outside agitators. Fearing that a walkout or other protest was pending, the school board took immediate action and called an emergency meeting on November 4, 1968.

Superintendent Bell claimed that the meeting's purpose was to ban the use of illegal drugs on school grounds, even though no major instances of drug abuse by students had occurred. The reason for the meeting was actually to pass a new rule that banned students from initiating a protest or demonstration. The policy approved at the November 4 special meeting stated that "any student who participates in a demonstration or walk-out not previously approved by the office of the principal, shall be expelled from school for the remainder of the semester and no credit may be earned during that semester." Board members also approved another policy intended to hinder the influence of outside agitators. It stipulated: "No student shall be permitted to attempt to recruit or solicit, on campus, members for any organization which tends to disrupt, interfere with, or create unrest or dissension among students in the educational program."[42] These new policies became a source of intense controversy and dispute among students, their parents, and school officials in Edcouch-Elsa. Officials approved the November 4 school policy to prevent student activists from initiating a school-wide protest, thereby circumventing students' right to assemble peacefully and exercise their right to free speech.

Chicano students and their supporters asked the board to hold an emergency meeting on November 13 to address their demands. The newly approved school board policy explained the proper channels for complaints: "It is not the intention of the board to discourage legitimate complaints. Proper channels for complaint by a student or parent is from teacher to principal to superintendent to the school board. Any parent or student who believes he has received unfair treatment should complain through the proper channels."[43] Javier Ramírez states that he, other student leaders, and parents did attempt to adhere to the proper channels at least twice, meeting with Superintendent Bell and school board president Billie Cellum.[44] But the officials would not agree to call an emergency meeting. Cellum told student leaders that the board could not meet with them until Monday, November 18, the date of the next regularly scheduled board meeting.[45]

The school board was willing to call an emergency meeting on November 4 upon hearing rumors that a walkout or other protest was pending, which suggests that working-class Mexican Americans had little political clout in the school district's decision-making structure. Ramírez's notes reveal part of a written public announcement that student leaders released to express their discontent with the board's response:

> We [student leaders] have been to speak with the superintendent [A. W. Bell] to discuss the possibility of having a special meeting with the school board, but he had told us that it could not [meet], . . . We [student leaders] have spoken to School Board President Billy Cellum and also had told him that we wanted to have a special meeting, but he told us that it would be impossible since various school board members went out of town. We told him that if this action is not taken seriously, that students will have to take action with a boycott of classes and will not attend (or return to classes) until the proper action is taken by the school board.[46]

The refusal to call an emergency meeting suggested that school officials did not consider student demands serious or urgent and were hesitant to acknowledge the students' interest in attaining negotiating power within the school system. Disappointed and frustrated, students refused to wait any longer and began considering a boycott of classes.

On November 11, Chicano students and their supporters held a public meeting at the Elsa Community Center. Approximately two hundred people attended and discussed the list of demands. This open forum brought greater attention and awareness to student issues. Among the most distinguished civic leaders in attendance were state senator Joe Bernal and Richard Avena of the US Commission on Civil Rights, both from San Antonio, and American GI Forum founder Hector P. García of Corpus Christi. Javier Ramírez presided over the meeting, where he and a committee of five other students formally announced their demands.[47] Senator Bernal acknowledged Chicano students' longing for social change and racial equality at their school, stating: "These students are saying what we [the older generation of Mexican Americans] didn't say when we were young or students. They are asking for dignity and self-respect. . . . This feeling that we [Mexican Americans] are different or inferior because we speak Spanish should not exist."[48] Bernal's statement suggests how he and other sympathizers of the Mexican American Generation tried to connect with the Chicano Movement and its young activists despite advocating older ideas and insisting on working within the system.

Martin Peña, federal programs director for the Edcouch-Elsa School District, also attended and refuted Chicano students' charge that the district lacked sufficient funds for their educational needs. When allowed to speak at the meeting, Peña reported on school funding. He stated: "This year we [school system] will spend $35,000 on free food for students, $10,000 on clothes and $10,000 on medical aid for students that need it. I am trying to tell you that the [school] district isn't all bad."[49] Before the end of the meeting, parent Luis Chávez spoke before the audience to encourage others to support student efforts:

> I will be at the front of the parent delegation when the students present their demands. And I, as a father of three students in high school, urge you parents to join these students. I saw them huddling around in a group, and since I think we parents must watch the thoughts and actions of our children, I stopped to see what they were doing. I can tell you these youth don't speak of anything wrong. We parents lack understanding and sometimes lack interest and we need to lend them moral support. We need unity between students and parents."[50]

The meeting fostered cooperation, candidness, and harmony among students and their adult supporters, adding momentum to the Chicano student movement in Edcouch-Elsa.

Another gathering that greatly advanced the unity and solidarity of the student movement occurred on the evening of November 13. Around five hundred to six hundred Chicano students, their parents, and community members attended a rally in a parking lot near the school auditorium. Like many Chicano students in attendance, Mirtala Villareal and her sister Nelda Villarreal Treviño recall the intense sense of restlessness and dissatisfaction.[51] Former student Felix Rodríguez also remembered the passionate, emotional outcries favoring the walkout.[52] Sympathetic yet cautious of the protest's timing, Rodríguez stood out as one of the few who tried to convince others not to act on impulse. He argued for continued negotiation with the school board and believed that Chicano students did not need to protest.[53] Most others disagreed. During the rally, the students were convinced that they had no alternative but to boycott classes and announced their decision to walk out the next day.[54]

The Walkout and Its Aftermath

It was a cold, windy, and cloudy Thursday morning at the Edcouch-Elsa High School campus on November 14, 1968. It seemed like another typical day at school until classes began. Suddenly 192 Chicano students rose from their desks

Figure 4. Students boycotting classes at Edcouch-Elsa High School. *McAllen Monitor*, November 14, 1968. Courtesy of Margaret H. McAllen Memorial Archives, Museum of South Texas History.

and walked out of their classrooms almost simultaneously.[55] After walking out, the student protesters assembled in front of the school and off campus across an unpaved dusty road, US Highway 107, and engaged in a peaceful protest, exclaiming, "Boycott classes!" They carried picket signs with slogans such as "We want better education," "Viva la Revolución," "Let's put the school board gestapo down," "Viva la raza," and "We will overcome," the last sign reminiscent of African American freedom struggles.[56] Moments after the protest began, the students gathered around the school's flagpole, recited the Pledge of Allegiance, and sang "The Star Spangled Banner."[57] Chicano activist-scholar Armando Navarro indicates that assembling around the flagpole was a popular protest tactic utilized by MAYO to refute allegations of its association with communists.[58] Parents and law enforcement officials rushed to the scene. Many were shocked and bewildered, asking how such an incident could have occurred in this small, quiet community.

Most deeply distressed were the parents of students in the walkout. Some parents remained supportive of their children, while others reacted with outrage. Numerous parents took their children out of the protest and urged school officials to reinstate them in school. Maricela Rodríguez recalls that her mother, an employee of Vahl'sing Packing Shed, arrived at the school shortly after the walkout. She scolded Maricela and pleaded with assistant principal Juan Gorostiza to allow her return.[59] Other parents such as Rebecca González spoke out against the walkout and insisted that Chicano students end their protest.[60] Police chief Eloy Zavala feared parents would become angry and incite an altercation with school administrators, blaming them for not preventing the walkout.[61] As students picketed a few yards from the school's entrance, principal Marvin Pipkin, assistant principal Bill Thompson, teachers Daniel Martínez and Fran Galloway, and an unidentified teacher stood in front of the school, urging students to return to classes but also writing down the names of student protesters.[62]

As the protest continued, walkout leaders and their parents met with Principal Pipkin and Spanish teacher Juan Tomassini, who served as translator. The student leaders included Javier Ramírez and Raúl Arispe, while Luis Chávez, a parent of three students who walked out, spoke on behalf of the protesters' parents. They met outside the school and in the principal's office throughout most of the day but could not reach an agreement to end the protest. Pipkin was unwilling to compromise or acknowledge the students' demands, declaring, "We [the school system] will not yield one iota as long as I am principal. The students will not dictate the policy."[63] Pipkin sternly warned that any student who participated in the walkout would receive a three-day suspension and be subject to action by the school board. School officials such as Pipkin sought to maintain

Figure 5. Luis Chávez (*center*), leading the committee of parents supporting student demands, speaks with Edcouch-Elsa High School principal Marvin Pipkin (*right*) as about one hundred protesting students stage a boycott. Student leaders standing with Chávez are Javier Ramírez (*right of Chávez*) a senior at Edcouch-Elsa High School, and Raúl Arispe (*left of Chávez*) also a senior at Edcouch-Elsa High. Pipkin held a meeting with parents and student leaders in his office soon after his statement on the back doorstep. *Edinburg Daily Review*, November 14, 1968. Courtesy of Margaret H. McAllen Memorial Archives, Museum of South Texas History.

influence and control the decision-making process of the school system, which excluded the concerns and representation of Mexican Americans as a marginalized group.

The student protesters were suspended for three days. Before serving their suspension, students announced that they would not return to school until the school board agreed to consider their demands. They believed their absence would, as student leader Javier Ramírez proclaimed, "hit the school where it hurts" by reducing the school's average daily attendance and thus its allocation of state educational funds.[64] This was another popular protest tactic of MAYO— drastically lower a school's average daily attendance and thereby reduce its funding.[65] By using this method, students intended to pressure school officials to seriously consider their demands.

Six hours after the walkout began, classes were dismissed early because of an alleged bomb threat. According to one source, Principal Pipkin claimed that an anonymous person called the superintendent's office to say that a bomb had been planted in the high school.[66] Walkout supporter Arturo Salinas contends that school administrators may have falsely reported the bomb threat in an attempt to disrupt and stop the protest.[67] Whether a threat was actually received is unclear, but no bomb was discovered on campus.

The protest resumed early the next day, November 15. Claiming noisy demonstrations were disrupting classes, school officials tried to stop the protest by filing charges against student leaders. Principal Pipkin and Assistant Principal Thompson filed misdemeanor charges of loitering on school grounds with the Hidalgo County Sheriff's Department in nearby Edinburg.[68] However, police chief Eloy Zavala recalled that school administrators did not notify him or other local law enforcement officials that they were seeking the arrest of student leaders, and he believed that the administrators "bypassed" the Edcouch and Elsa city police in favor of the county sheriff's department.[69] It is unclear why school administrators contacted the sheriff's department rather than local law enforcement officers to make the arrests.

To proceed with the arrests through the sheriff, Pipkin met with district attorney Oscar McInnis and sheriff E. E. Vickers. The *McAllen Monitor* reported that Vickers would "serve the papers" or warrants for arrest when obtained.[70] He and deputies Pat Ramsey and W. T. Freeman arrested the following student leaders at 2:30 p.m.: Mirtala Villareal, the only female, seventeen; Freddy Sáenz, the only juvenile, sixteen; Homero Treviño, nineteen; Arnulfo Sustaita, nineteen; Artemio Salinas, eighteen; and Javier Ramírez, seventeen. Sáenz recalled the exact moment of his sudden arrest: "I remember I was getting ready to eat [outside the school during the protest] when all of a sudden a cop came from behind and said, 'You're under arrest.'"[71] Sheriff's officers took Ramírez into

Figure 6. Supporters from Edcouch-Elsa and other surrounding communities held a candlelight vigil for four incarcerated student protestors outside the Hidalgo County Jail until the early morning of November 16, 1968. *Edinburg Daily Review*, November 17, 1968.

custody outside the office of justice of the peace Uvaldo López in Edcouch, and Salinas was apprehended later in the day at his home in Elsa.[72] Vickers released Villareal on her own recognizance shortly after arraignment, perhaps because of her gender. School officials assumed that the arrests would end the protest and that student protesters would return to classes. However, the arrests only added fuel to an already raging fire of movement activism, as the student protest leaders became martyrs for their cause.

On the evening of November 15, Salinas, the last of the six protest leaders taken into custody, was placed in the county jail in Edinburg. Shortly after his arrival, an estimated 200 to 250 students, parents, and community members from Edcouch-Elsa and surrounding areas began a candlelight vigil outside the jail to reaffirm their support for the incarcerated protest leaders. The vigil, according to walkout leader Artemio Salinas, boosted their self-confidence and lifted their spirits.[73] Many participating in the vigil lit and held candles, and a few held protest signs stating "Free the Students." The *Edinburg Daily Review* reported that during the vigil, protest leaders responded to supporters by turning on cigarette lighters that lit up their dark jail cell.[74] The incarceration of students further united those who supported the student movement and viewed the arrests as unjust. Like Mahatma Gandhi and Martin Luther King Jr., Chicano students engaged in civil disobedience as a means of effecting social change.

Throughout much of the night, supporters anxiously awaited the release of Artemio Salinas, Freddy Sáenz, Homero Treviño, and Javier Ramírez. Protest leader Arnulfo Sustaita had been released earlier in the afternoon when two Edcouch residents signed a surety bond on his behalf.[75] Justice of the peace Uvaldo López of Edcouch indicted all five male protest leaders, setting their bonds at $500 each, and imposed a $25 fine on the loitering charges. Edinburg attorney Ralph Vidaurri filled out the bond forms for the four remaining students after midnight upon the request of city manager Gary Gwen and police chief A. C. González.[76] The Hidalgo County Sheriff's Department finally released the four students early on Saturday morning, November 16.

No protest took place on the Edcouch-Elsa High School campus during November 16–17, and the weekend was free of the shouting, chanting, clapping, and cheering that had filled the air the previous two days. But Pipkin feared that the weekend quiet was just "the lull before the real storm." He reiterated his stern position that student protesters would not influence how the school system would handle further demonstrations. Speaking on behalf of the school board, Pipkin stated, "We plan to take every possible legal action against all students and outsiders who are loitering on the campus Monday."[77] In assessing the walkout's impact, Pipkin claimed that his faculty of forty-five teachers, which included twenty-two Mexican Americans, was united in an effort to deal with the situation.[78] He also reminded reporters that student protesters would have the opportunity to present their demands and complaints at the regularly scheduled school board meeting on Monday, November 18.

On Monday morning, Chicano students staged a brief protest in front of the school without incident. No further protest activity occurred at the school afterward. During the evening, an estimated 450 people attended the school board meeting in the high school's library. Among those present were school board members including school federal programs director Martin Peña, as well as Principal Pipkin, Superintendent Bell, and a few faculty members.[79] At the meeting, the board discussed the validity and legitimacy of the protesters' demands. R. P. "Bob" Sánchez, an attorney from nearby McAllen, spoke on behalf of the protesters and read their demands to the board. He urged the board to conduct individual hearings for protesters suspended from school and to permit them to resume classes.

Sánchez argued that the school board's reaction to the protest had infringed on the students' constitutional rights to free speech and assembly. He declared, "Our forefathers gave us some civil rights which the poor, down-trodden

Figure 7. McAllen attorney Bob Sánchez read the fifteen demands of the protesting students who staged a class boycott on November 14, 15, and 18, 1968. Sánchez pleaded that the students be allowed to return to classes on November 18 and be called in for punitive action later. But the school board refused to allow the students back into classes until each appeared for individual hearings before the board. The board took no action on a student recommendation that an eighteen-member committee be appointed to study the student complaints. Photo by Robert Meckel, *Edinburg Daily Review*, November 19, 1968. Courtesy of Margaret H. McAllen Memorial Archives, Museum of South Texas History.

Mexican-American students are just now waking up to and thank God they are."[80] In discussing student demands, he alleged that the Edcouch-Elsa school system discouraged its Mexican American students from speaking Spanish and failed to provide adequate counseling and preparation for college. The school system also needed to adopt textbooks that included Mexican American contributions. Sánchez pleaded with school officials to consider the students' complaints, saying, "Believe me, they didn't enjoy this boycott. I am serious when I tell you these students want to come back to school. We are not here in arrogance... we will meet you halfway."[81] He proposed an eighteen-member board to investigate complaints, consisting of six students, six parents, and six school board members. To the dismay of Sánchez and protesters, school officials took no action.

Superintendent Bell recommended that the school board take up the students' cases individually while continuing their suspensions. According to one record, he called for the suspensions to remain in force "until the Board can give each student, with his parents and attorney, an opportunity to appear before the Board to show reason why he or she should not be expelled for the remainder of the semester." Bell also suggested that the school board begin conducting meetings the following night. Board member Gilbert G. González moved to continue the suspensions because he was prodded to do so by the Anglo board members.[82] Calvin Smith seconded the motion, while the rest of the board approved it except for fellow trustee Israel Montoya, who abstained. Former Edcouch-Elsa student Nelda Villarreal Treviño suggests that Montoya most likely chose to abstain because he feared that voting against the motion might arouse suspicion against him on the part of Anglo school officials.[83] Board president Cellum announced that the students, parents, and attorneys should arrive at school starting the next day, November 19, in order to appear before the board about expulsion. Bob Sánchez summed up his disappointment with the board's decision, stating, "We don't think they treated us fairly. We want them to take the kids back to school. They are presuming them to be guilty."[84] He thought the expulsions were already predetermined, unjust, and lacking in due process and impartial procedures.

School board hearings with students and parents took place over the next three days, November 19–21. The controversial November 4 board policy, which called for expulsion of unruly demonstrators, was used as the basis of the proceedings. School board meeting minutes indicate that those expelled had "an adverse effect upon the welfare of the school and the best interests of other students."[85] All readmitted students were "under probation requiring good behavior."[86] According to Cellum, the criteria used to recommend expulsion or readmission included the student's contrition and the principal's assessment of his or her involvement in the walkout.[87] None of the students arrived with an attorney, but relatives such as parents, siblings, and grandparents were present. Most were skeptical about the fairness of the process. Parents employed by the Vahl'sing Packing Shed or other businesses with many Mexican American laborers urged their children to go back to school, fearing that their Anglo employers would fire them.[88]

At a special meeting on November 29, the school board expelled the walkout's key participants. Among them were student protest leaders Ramírez, Arispe, Sáenz, Treviño, Sustaita, Villareal, and Salinas. This record also reveals that school officials expelled Arnulfo Garza for violating his terms of probation after returning to classes on November 21, readmitted Leonel Garza under probation after expelling him at his hearing on November 19, and allowed eighty-seven students to return to classes under probation without a hearing. An estimated 192 students took part in the walkout according to school board records.[89] After the hearings, the board readmitted students based on their pledge to repent after they renounced their involvement in the picket-sign protest that took place after the walkout. The school board most likely expelled certain students during the November 19–21 hearings after teachers and principals identified them on the day of the walkout.

Other students returned to classes on probation because the hearings of the school board viewed their involvement in the walkout as inconspicuous and brief. Nevertheless, school officials managed to identify and expel many of the walkout's key instigators or leaders on this same date. The board meeting record for this day reveals only that they received immediate expulsion for the remainder of the semester, and it fails to indicate whether the students were expelled upon attending hearings by the board. By conducting hearings, the school board sought to determine whether to expel certain students based on the extent of their involvement in the walkout. Thus, the hearings lacked proper mediation and impartiality since school board officials and administrators had already accused certain students of inciting the walkout, especially those expelled on November 29.

The expelled students then faced the dilemma of how to continue their education. Some sought to enroll in classes in the neighboring school districts of Edinburg, Weslaco, Donna, Pharr–San Juan–Alamo, and McAllen, but these districts refused to admit them, fearing that a walkout or protest might take place on their campuses. The only exception was Eddy González, who enrolled in nearby Edinburg after he and his family moved and rented a home there.[90] Despite security concerns, Leo J. Leo, mayor of La Joya, Texas, provided the expelled students an opportunity to remain in school by helping to admit them to his city's school district. Leo argued that they should not be left to "roam the streets" even though they had been expelled.[91] Given this opportunity, the expelled students sought transportation to La Joya.

To attend school in La Joya, sixty miles southwest of Edcouch-Elsa, about thirty students rode in an old school bus that had transported local bracero workers to their jobs a few years earlier. Alonzo López and Carlos Arispe, parents of student protesters, bought the bus from Raúl Garza of Elsa for $500, and students and their relatives contributed five to fifteen cents for gasoline every day.[92] Protest leader Raúl Arispe drove the bus, which students boarded every morning at 5:00 a.m. so they could arrive on time for school by 7:00 a.m. Police escorted the bus to its destination to prevent the students from stopping at cities along the way and to prevent further protest activity.[93] They traveled back to Edcouch-Elsa once classes ended, normally arriving home at 7:00 p.m. However, bad weather and mechanical problems with the bus frequently delayed their arrival at school and home.

The students were well received by the La Joya School District, and there were no major complications. Former students Nelda Villarreal Treviño and Freddy Sáenz described their educational experiences at La Joya High School as memorable and pleasant: they were allowed to speak Spanish freely, ate Mexican food in the cafeteria, and were greeted with "buenos días" by Mexican American teachers in the classroom.[94] Student recollections of the La Joya School District also reveal this community's public acceptance of Spanish and recognition of ethnic Mexican culture, which were lacking in Edcouch-Elsa. The expelled Edcouch-Elsa students attended school in La Joya for the remainder of the fall semester. Enrolling at La Joya allowed the students to make up missed schoolwork throughout the course of their expulsion.[95]

The students' plight became widely known throughout the state and nation. After the walkout, they received expressions of support from many well-wishers, including telegrams from members of prominent Chicano organizations such as MAYO, La Raza Unida, and the Brown Berets. One telegram from the MAYO chapter in San Antonio stated, "Los MAYO's de San Antonio are with you all the way for better education for la raza [the Mexican American people]. Viva [long live] Edcouch-Elsa."[96] Miguel Barragán, then-consultant of the Southwest Council of La Raza in Phoenix, Arizona, praised the Edcouch-Elsa Chicano student movement. He wrote, "We are proud of young Mexican Americans like you [who] are willing to make the sacrifice to organize and lead the community in its efforts to rectify the educational policy that hurt la raza in Texas. We commend you for your courage and fully endorse your list of demands to the Edcouch-Elsa Independent School District officials. Viva la causa [long live the cause]."[97] The chair of the Brown Berets chapter in San Francisco, California, Tony Medina, noted in his telegram, "Congratulations for your most courageous attitude on the blow-out [walkout] for it takes heroic carnales [brothers or members of ethnic Mexican background] like you to ascend up for la causa.[98] These telegrams not only conveyed best wishes for the Edcouch-Elsa student protesters but identified Edcouch-Elsa as one of the numerous stages of student insurgency that were part of the Chicano Movement. Community activist Adela Sloss Vento of nearby Edinburg also expressed her support of the walkout: "Give justice, and do not discriminate against Mexican-American students for their knowledge of the Spanish language and culture. You [Texans] will be doing a great service to our country, for they will be useful American citizens of the future. We know that we live in a democracy and that we have responsibilities under a democracy, but no state [Texas] has the right to deny our rights [to speak Spanish and enroll in Mexican American studies courses] under a democracy."[99]

These documents reveal the growing national network of support that was one key building block of the social movement calling for educational reform in Edcouch-Elsa, thus reaffirming the collective action, political consciousness, and mobilization of local Chicano activists. In December 1968, five Edcouch-Elsa students and their parents continued their fight for educational equity by filing a civil suit in federal court in Brownsville, Texas.

Legal Repercussions: The Edcouch-Elsa School Case

Protest leaders Ramírez, Arispe, Villareal, Chávez, and Salinas and their parents challenged the validity of the school board's punishment of the protesters by suing the Edcouch-Elsa School District. On November 22, 1968, these five expelled students and their parents filed a civil suit in US federal district court in Brownsville, Texas.[100] It is likely that MAYO encouraged the students and their parents to take legal action. MAYO had formed a close working relationship with, and received legal aid from, the Mexican American Legal Defense and Educational Fund (MALDEF), a Chicano legal rights advocacy group based in San Antonio.[101] Historian Guadalupe San Miguel notes that "MALDEF's initial efforts in educational litigation focused on defending Mexican American individuals punished by school officials for engaging in civil rights or political activities."[102] Civil rights pioneer and educator George I. Sánchez "was involved in the brainstorming that resulted in the Mexican American Legal Defense and Educational Fund (MALDEF) in 1968 with a $2,200,000 start-up grant from the Ford Foundation," along with attorney Pete Tijerina, who was in contact with Jack Greenberg, Director-Counsel of the Legal Defense Fund of the National Association for the Advancement of Colored People (NAACP).[103] The collaboration between MAYO and MALDEF was instrumental in assisting the Edcouch students when they filed and presented their case.

Chicano students attempted to pressure their school system to initiate educational reform through this historic court case. The basis of the case was "to enjoin the school board of Edcouch-Elsa High School from depriving students of their right to education without due process."[104] The plaintiffs' complaint cited the right of students in a public school not to be suspended from that school (A) because of their participation in student activities meant to bring valid complaints to the attention of the school board of trustees, and (B) without a prior hearing, in violation of their rights under the First and Fourteenth Amendments of the US Constitution.[105] The plaintiffs sought a temporary, and eventually a permanent, restraining order that would allow them to resume classes at their school.

The plaintiffs included three arrested on November 15, protest leaders Javier Ramírez, Artemio Salinas, and Mirtala Villareal. Since the court considered the five students minors, their parents filed suit on their behalf. The students were advised by their attorneys, including R. P. "Bob" Sánchez, and by MALDEF attorneys Pete Tijerina, Mario Obledo, and Alan Axelrod. Additional plaintiff attorneys included James De Anda, a civil rights attorney from Corpus Christi dating back to the 1950s, and Jack Greenberg, Norman Amaker, and Vilma Martínez, affiliated with the NAACP LDF. The defendants in the case were the Edcouch-Elsa School District, Superintendent Bell, Principal Pipkin, and school trustees Israel Montoya, Gilbert G. González, Eddie Thomas, H. D. Skinner, Calvin Smith, and Billie Cellum. James S. Bates and Eddie Henrichson from nearby Edinburg, who were already under contract to represent the school district, served as the defendants' attorneys. US federal district judge Reynaldo G. Garza, a 1961 judicial appointee of President John F. Kennedy, presided over the case. He was also the first Mexican American federal judge in US history.[106]

The plaintiffs alleged that the defendants had violated the US Constitution by prohibiting student protesters from obtaining their public education without due process. They further accused school officials of mistreating them by engaging in racially discriminatory practices. In addition to seeking a temporary restraining order and then a permanent one, the plaintiffs urged that upon the final hearing of the case, the "defendants be enjoined from taking any punitive measures against plaintiffs and the class they represent arising from plaintiffs' actions."[107] The plaintiffs' attorneys requested that the students named in the case be allowed to return to school, that the defendants pay $50,000 in damages to all Edcouch-Elsa High School student protesters as well as cover the court fees, and that school officials be prevented from taking any punitive measures against the plaintiffs.

On December 18, the court filed the pretrial order, and the defendants and their attorneys made a motion to contest the plaintiffs' accusations against them. This motion stated that the defendants requested a trial by jury.[108] Expecting a jury trial, attorneys for both sides had conferred the previous day to work out stipulations for the trial, such as the number of witnesses to be called.[109] Elsa police officer Jake Foley, Elsa police chief Eloy Zavala, Luis Chávez (father of protest leader José Luis Chávez), and protest leader Raúl Arispe were sworn in as plaintiffs' witnesses. Edcouch-Elsa schoolteachers Raúl Champion, Javier Gutiérrez, and Robert Cunningham as well as school superintendent A. W. Bell were sworn in as witnesses for the defense. Court proceedings indicate that evidence had been presented to the court on the merits of the case. All defendants' motions to dismiss were carried along with the case as well. The court granted the defendants' "motion to sever issue of damages" and could have called for a trial by jury if the plaintiffs had contested the motion.

The trial began the same day, when Principal Pipkin was sworn in and testified as the first witness. Judge Garza questioned Pipkin about the criteria used

146 ∼ CHAPTER 4

to determine how students were expelled. The judge argued that the way students "kowtowed" to the principal was an example of selective enforcement of the school board's November 4 policy, which held that any student taking part in a demonstration was subject to immediate expulsion.[110] Judge Garza denounced this policy, stating that it was unconstitutional because it violated the students' rights to free speech and peaceful assembly.[111] Attorney Bob Sánchez argued that the students' protest was "a legitimate civil rights expression of their First Amendment free speech rights."[112] After Pipkin testified, attorneys for the defense requested a fifteen-minute recess.

When the court reconvened, the trial came to a surprising end as attorneys from both sides announced a settlement. The *McAllen Monitor* reported: "In a dramatic turn of courtroom events, the old order of hickory stick discipline in the classroom was shattered Wednesday in US District Court in Brownsville."[113] The attorneys agreed that the Edcouch-Elsa School Board rule against student walkouts was unconstitutional because it violated the students' civil rights. Under the settlement, all student protesters would be allowed to return to classes at the beginning of the 1969 spring semester. The final ruling stipulated that the plaintiffs and all other expelled students could return to school on January 6, 1969, and could make up the schoolwork they had missed. Plaintiffs were awarded nominal and actual damages of $240 for school transportation expenses and tuition costs to attend classes outside the defendants' school district, to be paid to attorney Bob Sánchez as trustee for the plaintiffs. The defendants also had to notify all plaintiffs and other expelled students of their reinstatement in school and pay all taxable court costs of the plaintiffs.[114]

By agreeing to these provisions, the plaintiffs waived their claim to $50,000 in damages from the school board. Instead, they agreed to defer this charge to a later date for a trial by jury. Superintendent Bell admitted that he and the other defendants had difficulty fighting this legal battle because his school district could no longer afford to pay the court costs. The *McAllen Monitor* concluded: "With a legal order that could be reverberating for some time in the age of student dissent, the Edcouch-Elsa school board made what amounted to an unconditional surrender in its month-long battle with 192 rebellious students, either suspended or expelled from the school as a result of a Nov. 14 walkout and demonstration."[115]

As people filed into the hallway just outside the courtroom, the plaintiffs and their supporters rejoiced over the decision. Protest leader Raúl Arispe excitedly screamed, "We won, we won, it's going to be great to get back into school!" Fellow leader Javier Ramírez summed up his elation by simply saying "Viva la raza!" to news reporters.[116] The ruling was an astonishing outcome not only for the students, but also for MALDEF, which had achieved its first major Chicano civil rights victory in court. Commenting on this milestone, Sánchez later wrote in a letter to MALDEF general counsel Mario Obledo: "This case has been a tremendous victory for the Fund [MALDEF] itself. The case has been undoubtedly a trailblazer for La Raza as heretofore our poor people had only either read or been told about such things as the Bill of Rights, and for the most part had thought that these things were merely history. Now they know that they are actually a reality and that their constitutional rights can be enforced today."[117] The ruling set a legal precedent for Chicano students and upheld their right to protest peacefully as part of their constitutional rights. The decision further represented a victory that legally protected ethnic-minority students' right to voice grievances against their school system.

The ruling in the case was an important victory that gave legitimacy to the students' struggle. The walkout enabled local Chicano students to emerge as the principal actors seeking institutional reform. Many noticeable changes occurred during the years following the walkout. In particular, the number of Mexican Americans hired as teachers and administrators increased substantially. In 1970, Eleazar Villanueva was hired as an assistant principal, joining Juan Gorostiza. Eugene Gutiérrez, who had been a biology teacher at the school, became its first Mexican American counselor in 1970, and educators Elvira López and Frank Saldivar joined him as additional counselors in 1974.

Educational reform and expanding political opportunities resulting from the student movement were also pursued through the election of Mexican Americans as school board members. Even former protest leader Eddy González served as a one-time board trustee in the early 1970s. People of Mexican origin had previously had minimal representation on the school board and rarely held positions of authority in the school district's central administration. By 1974–75, Mexican Americans dominated the school board and created twelve new administrative and staff positions at the high school. These included a curriculum director, a Title I migrant counselor, an athletic director, an evaluation planner, an attendance secretary, three community aides, a parent involvement committee, and a bilingual education director.

By 1975, Mexican Americans filled nearly every prominent position within the school system. In explaining the most important ramifications of the walkout, longtime Edcouch-Elsa school trustee Rubén Rodríguez noted that the school board had "opened doors" by hiring more Mexican American teachers and administrators.[118] This hiring of twelve Mexican American administrators and faculty led to structural changes in the school system as Chicanos increasingly took part in the district's decision-making. It is difficult to determine to what extent the walkout prompted these changes. Former student activist Felix Rodríguez asserts that the local student movement ushered in strong winds of political and social change with the force of a runaway train.[119] Clearly, however, the educational power structure in Edcouch-Elsa had been challenged by Chicano students, their parents, and concerned members of the Mexican American community who had traditionally been marginalized and deprived of influence over school policy decisions.

Summary and Conclusion

The Edcouch-Elsa student walkout was the first such action taken by students protesting conditions in the Rio Grande Valley of Deep South Texas. This protest was significant in that it led to Chicano students availing themselves of their constitutional rights to effect change in the region. In addition, it resulted in MAYO's continued development as an organization skilled in the defense of educational reform, and it also led to MALDEF's first successful court case. By the fall of 1968, MAYO had established numerous chapters throughout various cities in Texas, including Edcouch-Elsa. Various Chicano students, their parents, and local MAYO members such as Jesús Ramírez began holding a series of informal meetings. A few members of the Political Association of Spanish-Speaking Organizations (PASSO) and Volunteers in Service to America (VISTA) also attended the meetings and further mobilized students to engage in collective action to overcome their status as a socially marginalized and politically powerless group.

In December 1968, MAYO encouraged students and their parents to take legal action and helped local parents receive legal aid from MALDEF. The plaintiffs' complaint alleged that the defendants had violated the US Constitution by prohibiting student protesters from obtaining their public education without due process. Plaintiffs further alleged that school officials had treated them unfairly and had engaged in racially discriminatory practices. The ruling in favor of the plaintiffs in the Edcouch-Elsa school case was an important victory, giving legitimacy to the students' struggle and consolidating MALDEF's role as legal representatives and defenders of Chicano struggles for justice and equality. In the years following the walkout and school case, Edcouch-Elsa experienced a dramatic transformation. The local school system witnessed an unprecedented hiring of more Mexican American administrators and faculty as Chicanos increasingly took part in the district's decision-making processes. Within five months after the Edcouch-Elsa school protest, Chicano student activists in MAYO began organizing efforts to continue the student movement nearly one hundred miles away in Kingsville, Texas.

5

The 1969 Kingsville School Walkout
Chicano Student and MAYO Activism Spreads to Mid-South Texas

The Kingsville walkout was the third major Chicano student protest in South Texas in April 1969. Student insurgency in Kingsville gained much momentum thanks to the support of Chicano movement activists at Texas A&I University.[1] One former student leader remembered when a strong sense of ethnic pride and collective consciousness was ignited among Kingsville walkout participants and their supporters.[2] Chicano students from Texas A&I and members of MAYO helped local students identify their complaints about the school system, obtain organizational resources for mobilization, and pursue political opportunities. They also actively supported the junior high and high school student walkouts.

Increased student enrollment at Texas A&I University in Kingsville contributed to a population boom in the city, from 16,857 in 1950 to 28,711 in 1970.[3] According to the 1960 census, Kleberg County's population was 30,052, with 12,514 (41 percent) Spanish-surnamed people, and family income of $2,415 for Mexican Americans.[4] By 1970, Kleberg County had a total population of 33,166, with 43 percent Spanish-surnamed people and a per capita income of $2,611.[5] Thus, Kingsville emerged as an industrialized, bustling city in the 1960s, unlike in years past when it was a little-known farm town near the King Ranch.

Chicano Student Activism in Kingsville

Prior to the local walkout in April 1969, Chicano students and members of MAYO met to discuss educational issues. They held informal meetings in students' homes or the local MAYO chapter office building on the corner of Eleventh and Santa Gertrudis Streets.[6] According to Kingsville police captain Darwin Avant and local MAYO member Faustino Erebia, MAYO met with local students for at least two months prior to the walkout.[7] Many of the student activists likely met at a two-day seminar at Texas A&I University that was focused on the need for unity among Mexican Americans. Approximately eighty to one hundred college and high school students in Kingsville attended the seminar, which featured invited speakers such as Chicano community rights organizer Narciso Alemán, state representative Carlos Truan, MAYO leader Efrain Fernández, and Chicano labor leader David López, all men.[8]

The seminar began when Alemán, the main speaker, asked all Anglo-Americans in attendance to leave, asserting that "Chicanos should draw the line somewhere and cut the line of dependency from the Anglo."[9] In short, Alemán maintained that Chicanos could solve their own social and educational problems. This meeting where all Anglos were asked to leave is a clear example of cultural nationalism. Historian Ernesto Chávez explains that the reason Chicanos turned to cultural nationalism is best understood according to the concept of "protonationalism," or consciousness of belonging to Mexico "as a safety valve for the often-harsh realities of the United States" such as racism, inequality, and segregation.[10] Alemán most likely believed that all Anglos were to blame for such harsh realities and therefore called for cultural solidarity among Chicanos who advocated for self-determination and a new political awareness, marking the rise of collective consciousness. However, scholar Maylei Blackwell's book *Chicana Power!* attempts to historicize the complex nature of Chicano nationalism within the context of Chicana feminism:

> Chicano cultural nationalism was forged through the recuperation or rediscovery of a historical legacy suppressed by colonization. More than an act of reclamation, it was a production of a Chicano identity that was crafted through narratives of labor history, migration, and resistance to colonization ... [and] it is vital for us to also understand that identities are not fixed in the past and merely recovered through historical memory.... Remembrance of preconquest narratives of place helped to forge racial and cultural pride, but it was also criticized at the time because women are made invisible through this construction of nationalist patrimony that universalizes masculine subjects through the category "Chicano," encoding a gendered mode of remembrance.[11]

Chicano nationalism reinvigorated a sense of belonging, racial pride, youthful exuberance, and the remembrance of a precolonial past to promote a historical imaginary in the Southwest that developed as part of the revolutionary rhetoric to unite Chicanos. Anglos were perceived as the so-called conquerors or invaders of the land that Chicanos called Aztlán (present-day US Southwest), which included an indigenous past while acknowledging the notion of *mestizaje*, or a hybrid Chicano identity that was neither Mexican nor American but a fusion of two cultures based in the United States and Mexico. This concept of hybridity further depicts the Chicano struggle with biculturalism and social disorientation in the United States as consistent with the opening passage of Corky Gonzales's epic poem "I Am Joaquín": "I am Joaquín, lost in a world of confusion, caught up in the whirl of a gringo society, confused by the rules, scorned by attitudes, suppressed by manipulation, and destroyed by modern society."[12] Chicano nationalism also developed through a historical consciousness that was conceptualized and deployed as a method to decolonize Chicano people, thus expressing a longing for cultural affirmation, liberation, and identity. Chicanos such as Alemán proclaimed *mestizaje* and cultural nationalism as an alternative to assimilation and integration with Anglos.

Truan also emphasized the need to better educate Mexican American children. He further mentioned that state senator Joe Bernal was assisting him in introducing a bilingual education bill, which stated: "The system of education in Texas must change its concept of the Mexican-American child. In an area where the majority of school age children are Mexican, the teacher should conform to the needs of the child, instead of the child conforming to him."[13] Fernández spoke about the use of direct-action protest or "conflict" tactics and strategies to seek redress.[14] This seminar politicized Chicano students and likely engendered a militant fervor and consciousness.

Student activists practiced what they learned within days. They began participating in demonstrations and protests in front of Kingsville City Hall and the Kleberg County Courthouse in late February 1969.[15] The seminar was a valuable resource that mobilized Kingsville student activists to walk out at Gillett Junior High School. College-age activists did not participate directly in the protest but offered moral support, encouragement, advice, and protest signs. Student activism around the country in such places as Denver, Colorado, encouraged activists in Kingsville to form their own grassroots movement. The Chicano Movement occurred in both Kingsville and Denver at almost the same time in the spring of 1969.

The Ongoing Chicano Movement in Denver

In Denver, Rodolfo "Corky" Gonzales, an influential leader of the Chicano Movement at the national level, organized the first-ever national Chicano Liberation Youth Conference, hosted by the group Crusade for Justice, in March 1969. This Chicano rights organization sought to organize Mexican American youth and pushed for social mobilization and action for the economically poor. During the conference, a young poet named Alurista read "El Plan Espiritual de Aztlán," a manifesto that advocated Chicano nationalism and self-determination for young Chicanos.[16] The plan further repudiated the cultural assimilation and integration of Mexican Americans, disputed the myth that Mexican Americans were solely a recent immigrant group, promoted the concept of a separate Chicano homeland known as Aztlán, underscored the significance of Mexican Americans' indigenous ancestral roots, and emphasized the need for Chicano political and economic control. The conference was organized in response to the racism that had shaped the Mexican American experience in the United States. Thus, Chicanos believed they were a colonized people in pursuit of their own revolutionary struggle to achieve a higher level of militancy, political awareness, and organization. Over one thousand passionate supporters and activists, mostly from California, attended this historic conference.[17] The preface summarized the plan's powerful message for autonomy and Chicano separatism:

> In the spirit of a new people that is conscious not only of its proud historical heritage but also of the brutal "gringo" invasion of our territories, we, the Chicano inhabitants and civilizers of the northern land of Aztlán from whence came our forefathers ... declare that ... Aztlán belongs to those who plant the seeds, water the fields, and gather the crops and not to the foreign Europeans. ... Brotherhood unites us, and love for our brothers makes us a people whose time has come and who struggles against the foreigner "gabacho" [Anglo] who exploits our riches and destroys our culture ... we declare the independence of our mestizo nation. We are a bronze people with a bronze culture ... we are a nation, we are a union of free pueblos [people], we are Aztlán.[18]

This celebrated conference marked the first large-scale gathering for Chicano youth, who came away feeling energized and motivated to fulfill their calling for self-determination and nationalism in all spheres of life, subsequently mobilizing student groups to political action. Although no public record confirms the presence of Chicano activists from Kingsville, they likely drew inspiration when they heard about this event from media reports.

Another significant event in the Chicano Movement occurred in Denver when approximately 150 students walked out of West High School on March 19, 1969. Like their counterparts in Texas and in other areas throughout the US Southwest, Chicano students in Denver demanded the implementation of a curriculum reflecting the contributions of ethnic Mexican people in the United States, the hiring of Mexican American faculty, bilingual study options, cultural training for faculty, and the dismissal of racist teachers. One such teacher was Harry Schaffer, who reportedly said in one of his classes, "All Mexicans are stupid because their parents were stupid."[19] Fewer than 1 percent of the school's faculty were Mexican American.[20] The walkout participants and their adult supporters, including Corky Gonzales, were met by local police in riot gear who used tear gas to disperse the crowd. Twenty-five people, including twelve juveniles, were arrested after being teargassed by police. More than half a dozen people and one officer were injured in the melee.[21] A series of neighborhood protests then led to various clashes with police. A jury of mostly white residents later acquitted Gonzales of all assault charges. Shortly after his release, Gonzales spoke at a local rally to explain how the protest symbolized a type of militant revolution for Chicano community control: "What took place ... was a battle between the West Side liberation forces and the occupying army. You kids [young Chicanos] don't realize you have made history. We just talk about revolution, but you act it by facing the shotguns, the billies, the mace. You are real revolutionaries."[22] Indeed, the Denver student walkout inspired Chicano student activism throughout nation, including in Kingsville.

Campus Activism at Texas A&I University

Chicano students at Texas A&I University in Kingsville were politically active on campus and later supported the local walkout. Like many college students around the nation in the 1960s, campus activists at Texas A&I agitated for social and political change. This change involved removing the racial barrier between Anglo-American and Mexican American students. Former campus activist José Angel Gutiérrez comments on the differences between the two groups: "In classes, we Chicanos sat in the back. We did not join nor were we invited to join certain organizations and clubs; we did not star in sports or serve student affairs; we were segregated in dorms; we were not selected to be cheerleaders, twirlers, drum majors, or any other prominent positions in student life. There was little mixing and dating between us and the Anglos."[23] Spanish-surnamed students made up a significant part of the student body.

Three weeks prior to the Kingsville walkout, six members of PASSO at Texas A&I presented university president James C. Jernigan with a list of grievances highlighting the struggles of Mexican American students.[24] In late March 1969, fifteen student activists prepared to travel to a mass demonstration in Del Rio, Texas. This historic protest also featured the presentation of the so-called Mexican-American Manifesto or Bill of Rights.[25] Less than a week before the walkout, Carlos Guerra gave a public speech at the Speaker's Corner on the Texas A&I campus, in which he blamed Anglo-Americans for the societal problems

CARLOS GUERRA BLAMES ANGLO FOR MEXICAN-AMERICAN PROBLEMS
... PASO member at Wednesday Speaker's Corner

Figure 8. MAYO and PAS[S]O member Carlos Guerra speaking at Texas A&I University, circa 1969. Courtesy of *South Texan*, Texas A&M University–Kingsville student newspaper, feature article on the Chicano Movement in Kingsville, October 14, 2020.

impacting Chicanos. He said, "There is no problem with the Chicano; the problem is with the Gringo."[26] Guerra's speech suggested discord between Chicanos and Anglos. His comments further indicated why Chicanos voiced their opposition to housing discrimination, segregation of dormitory housing, lack of academic support services for Mexican American students, exclusion of ethnic minorities in fraternities and sororities, and the Vietnam War.[27] Such events provide a glimpse into the on-campus political activities of local college students.

During the 1967–68 school year, Texas A&I had a Spanish-surnamed enrollment of 25 percent, which increased to 30 percent in 1968–69.[28] In the mid-1960s, Gutiérrez and Carlos Guerra first organized local student chapters of La Raza Unida, the Political Association of Spanish-Speaking Organizations (PASSO), and MAYO.[29] Gutiérrez recalled that Mexican American students at Texas A&I

first became involved in campus activism in the 1960s because of their lack of representation on the student council.[30] Furthermore, he asserted that no representation was given to the majority of Mexican American students living off campus who were members of small organizations and school clubs. Gutiérrez remembered that student activists formed a PASSO chapter at Texas A&I rather informally when they met at a local bar. He comments: "We had the free booze and good-looking women and that's how we started politicizing because after the beer ran out there was always many other dollars that came up for collections to get more beer. So that every Friday night we had a fun meeting and through the girls and throughout conversations over beer and so on we talked about the problems that we have here [Texas A&I]."[31] He would later use this same method of politicization to mobilize Mexican Americans to collective action during the Crystal City school walkout. Women were often sexualized.

Various other students became politically active at Texas A&I throughout the late 1960s as well. They did so after meeting in classes and freely assembling to discuss the educational needs of ethnic-minority students.[32] The era also ushered in unprecedented change at Texas A&I when a coalition of Chicanos and African Americans were elected to the student council for the first time. Gutiérrez claimed that he and fifty to sixty others managed to vote on behalf of 1,108 Mexican American students in order to change the student constitution for campus elections from majority to plurality to decide election winners.[33] Prior to graduating from Texas A&I in 1966, Gutiérrez joined the Alpha Phi Omega fraternity, the Young Democrats, the Newman Club, and the Catholic Student Organization to expand his outreach and recruit of students across campus.[34] He was also instrumental in altering the student government constitution to include new positions for nontraditional students and those attending school part time.[35] Thus, the election and revision to the constitution allowed greater representation.

Another notable accomplishment was the election of a Mexican American homecoming queen and Lantana queen at Texas A&I (the latter named after the annual Lantana Festival held on campus). Prior to the late 1960s, Mexican American females always lost both homecoming queen and Lantana queen elections since they never received a majority vote.[36] In the mid- to late 1960s, the first Mexican American women won these elections shortly after the student election constitution had been altered. Antonio Bill expresses how he and other student activists reflected on this historic moment in school history:

> By an impressive stroke of planning, timing, and resourcefulness student activists revised the by-laws of the student election constitution to read that the Homecoming Queen and Lantana Queen elections were

to be determined by plurality rather than majority. We were elated and became overwhelmed with emotion in the Fall of 1968 when the public address system announced that our own Juanita Alba had been elected the first Chicana Homecoming Queen in the history of Texas A&I. The following Spring Semester we experienced another high when Linda Salinas was elected the first Chicana Lantana Queen.[37]

Despite this change, feminist student activists at Texas A&I later denounced the election of Lantana queen, viewing the contest as a "sexist beauty pageant." For example, the editor of the university student newspaper wrote: "It is a female auction. They parade for the buyers . . . all the elements are there except the bidding."[38] According to a few former Chicana activists, not many Mexican American women students became politically active around feminism.[39] Instead, they concentrated their efforts on ethnicity. This support for ethnicity later became apparent during the 1971 Conferencia de Mujeres por la Raza (or the National Chicana Conference), the first national Chicana feminist conference, in Houston, Texas. During the conference, some Chicana participants called for a walkout to proclaim that their real enemy was not with the macho (Chicano man) but the *gavacho* (slang for "white man").[40]

Chicana scholar Maylei Blackwell's book *Chicana Power!* examines Chicana feminism within student and community-based organizations and underscores the importance of feminist students' resistance toward chauvinism and sexism in the Chicano Movement, as well as the roles of Chicanas within the intersections of gender and sexuality. She notes: "Feminism is part of a larger struggle for justice that historically has emerged in revolutionary and other struggles for freedom, for example, the antislavery, labor, and civil rights movements of the nineteenth and twentieth centuries. This evolving understanding of the interconnectedness of oppressions led to activists working across multiple struggles and across movements. Women of color and Chicana feminisms grounded the struggle in their community's pursuit of freedom and were committed to fighting multiple oppressions."[41] *Chicana Power!* further analyzes the production of Chicana political activism when women activists challenged the gendered confines of Chicano nationalism as part of their vision for liberation and greater autonomy within the movement. Historian Julia Kirk Blackwelder explains the male-centered society and the subservient role of women that were entrenched within the Mexican American community well before the 1960s: "Mexican Americans preserved a culture that emphasized male authority and family authority above other values. . . . Mexican wives were expected to be unquestionably obedient to their husbands, and daughters were expected to defer to the wishes of brothers as well as fathers."[42] Cynthia Orozco also examines Mexican American women's struggles and key roles in civil rights activities in Texas between 1921 and 1965, noting: "Women defined their own political participation and their own brand of citizenship . . . they contested men's patriarchal ideology of empowerment, social citizenship, and organizational membership. Lacking feminist ideology, they could not assert more for women's gendered interests."[43] Such pre-1960s activism paved the way for women who sought to transform their social networks of family and culture into political resources to help their community. Mexican American women's politics during the pre-1960s era served as the precursor for Chicana political activism to oppose gender discrimination during the Chicano Movement. Thus, Chicana feminists sought political participation because of their lack of empowerment and leadership in the movement, and they resisted the traditional role of women as housewives or objects of beauty. Their politics and activism attempted to alter the gendered meaning of politics and promote the collective consciousness and liberation of working-class Chicanas who had been marginalized during the movement.

Throughout the student movement at Texas A&I University, professors offered moral support and external resource mobilization to Chicano students who longed for social acceptance and political representation. These educators included Ward Albro and George Steinmeyer, both professors of history; government professors Bob Rogers, Wayne Johnson, and Charles Cotrell; and Stanley Bittinger, professor of psychology and sociology.[44] While speaking to approximately seventy-five students in a public lecture in March 1969, Bittinger argued that Chicano student insurgency represented a struggle for identity, dignity, and heritage. One of his arguments characterized this struggle as an integral part of student activism: "The most militant Chicano is the one who experiences the most change, the one who has the opportunity to come to college and better himself."[45] Bittinger's remark emphasizes Chicano students' intention to become empowered through education. In the fall of 1969, history professor Ward Albro taught the first Mexican American history course at Texas A&I, "Mexican Americans in the Southwest," the first at a Texas university. Other courses pertaining to Mexican American history and culture were later added to the curriculum after the university approved an ethnic studies program in 1970.[46] Thus, the implementation of ethnic studies courses satisfied one key student grievance.

Renowned Chicana artist Carmen Lomas Garza, a Kingsville native, offers additional insights and recollections of the social conditions and student movement in her hometown. She remembers growing up in the 1950s and 1960s when Kingsville supported institutionalized racism by requiring Mexican Americans to attend segregated elementary and junior high schools and buy homes in the "Mexican" part of town.[47] One oral history describes the adverse conditions and discriminatory treatment Mexican American students faced in South Texas

158 ～ CHAPTER 5

during the 1960s: "This issue about feeling pride in our culture was really crucial because so much damage had been done to us growing up in South Texas in the public schools, in the society in general, being made to feel ashamed of our own culture, our own language, because of discrimination, because of the hardships of being a minority."[48] After her first year in junior high school, Garza expressed her desire to enroll in biology rather than home economics, one of the supposedly gender-appropriate classes pertaining to domestic labor or household chores. After Garza pleaded for assistance at home, her mother eventually intervened to help her circumvent the home economics requirement. She was one of only two females in biology courses during her second and third year of junior high. Recognizing a gender issue, Garza saw the incident as her "first big protest against discrimination" until she noticed how Mexican Americans were treated differently from Anglos at Kingsville High School. As in many schools throughout South Texas, educators in Kingsville prohibited or discouraged Mexican American students from speaking Spanish on school grounds unless they were practicing Spanish in the classroom. Garza explains: "You could take language classes. You could take French, Latin, or Spanish. But if you took Spanish class, the Mexican American kids could not practice their Spanish in the hallways. Only in the classroom. And all the other kids could practice wherever they wanted. If [Mexican American students] spoke Spanish in junior high, in elementary school, and in high school [then they] were paddled. [We] were physically punished."[49] This type of incident reinforced the local Mexican American community's skepticism toward Anglo educators and the public school system, later motivating Chicano students to walk out of school. This situation also led to the rise of collective consciousness, derived in part from Mexican Americans' restriction from speaking Spanish on school grounds.

Prior to her exposure to the Chicano Movement in the late 1960s, Garza's political activism was first influenced by her parents' participation in the American GI Forum in Kingsville, focusing on assisting Hispanic war veterans in fighting discrimination in housing, education, health care, and employment. Both parents vigorously supported the American GI Forum's voter registration drives, endorsed political candidates who promoted the interests of Mexican Americans, and helped raise money for college scholarships for Mexican American students through the organization's Ladies Auxiliary by sponsoring "cakewalks."[50] Garza recalls the effect and impression of her parents' activism on her life:

> I was very much affected by the kinds of stories and happenings and activities that were going [on] around me, not only in school but in my community, with discrimination and racism. Because my parents

were very much involved with the American G.I. Forum, which is a World War II veterans' organization set up to fight for the civil rights of World War II veterans, Mexican-American veterans, that were coming back from the war and still finding discrimination and racism after having served in the war. So I was very much starting to become aware of the fact that things were not correct, and they had to be corrected by civil rights action.[51]

At the age of eight, she also became keenly aware of her mother's skill in creating paintings of *loteria tablas* (bingo cards) and *monitos* (little figures) for lottery games with neighbors. Watching her mother craft handmade art inspired Garza to cultivate her own artistic talent and eventually discover her role within the Chicano Movement as an artist. Garza further underscores the significance of creating Chicano art in the 1960s as a primary outlet to reaffirm her cultural heritage, family background, and willingness to illustrate the history of Mexican Americans through imagery and artistry: "With the Chicano movement there was a big push to get to know our family histories and our historical background. You know, dealing with the Southwest and Mexico because we weren't taught that in the schools. We weren't taught, basically, the history of Mexico. My answer to . . . what I could do within the Chicano movement was to do my artwork."[52] Garza's desire to create her own art as a young adult reflects her connection with the Chicano Movement as a student at Texas A&I University. In December 1969, she was instrumental in organizing a public exhibition featuring the artwork of Chicano students from the university at MAYO's first national conference in La Lomita Catholic Mission in Mission, Texas.[53] However, the student movement had already begun to blossom throughout South Texas in the spring of 1969 after the student walkouts in San Antonio and Edcouch-Elsa. After finishing high school, Garza enrolled in numerous art education courses at the university, where she received formal training in drawing, ceramics, block printing, and print making.[54] During her time as a student from 1967 to 1972, she recalls observing and hearing various Chicano activists on campus leading rallies and discussions by standing on large soapboxes or platforms at noon in front of the Student Union Building and debating major issues pertaining to the Chicano Movement and Mexican American community. One of her art professors, William Renfrow, often invited young movement activists and students to discuss educational issues, regional and national events, and the political philosophy of the Chicano Movement. Such informal gatherings included movement activists such as José Angel Gutiérrez and Carlos Guerra as well as local university students in the art program such as Carlos Truan, Amado Peña, José Rivera, Guadalupe Silva, Billy Nakayama, and Santa Barraza.[55] These meetings served as a forum for participants to express their aspirations for political autonomy, social justice, and public school reform.

Student activism at Texas A&I eventually reverberated outside the university. One such instance occurred during the Gillett Junior High School walkout in 1969. According to a few former movement activists, the Gillett walkout represented the first time Mexican American college students at Texas A&I were involved in so-called barrio or neighborhood politics. Many of these students learned, and put into practice, social protest movement strategies and tactics as campus activists prior to the walkout.[56] On February 28, 1969, approximately twenty students from Texas A&I walked out of their school, demanding the "development of a park at the [city] plaza for public use, paved streets in the Mexican American barrios and maintenance of a drainage ditch on the city's northside," according to participant Antonio Bill.[57] Thus, movement activities at Texas A&I served as the organizational strength for local college students, mobilizing them to support the Kingsville school protest. Texas A&I was the training ground or "experimental lab" for student insurgency in Kingsville. College students served as a valuable mobilizing resource that enhanced community-wide, social movement protest activity in Kingsville. As in other student protests throughout South Texas, college students in Kingsville offered moral support and advice concerning recruitment and organizing but did not participate in the protest.

The Kingsville Student Walkout and Its Aftermath

Unlike for the Edcouch-Elsa student protest, state MAYO leaders traveled to assist student activists in Kingsville. They included José Angel Gutiérrez, Mario Compean, and Carlos Guerra.[58] Kingsville native Faustino Erebia, the local chair of MAYO, emerged as one of the student leaders of the walkout. Erebia, a seventh-grade student at Gillett Junior High School, recalls the harsh treatment he received as a young boy from certain Anglo educators. For instance, substitute teacher Mary Clairehill struck Erebia on the hand with a metal ruler for speaking Spanish in class when he was a fifth-grade student at T. M. Colston Elementary School.[59] According to Erebia, approximately two hundred to three hundred students from Gillett Junior High met at their parents' homes or at Ruben's Daily Grill, a favorite student hangout and hamburger stand, a few weeks prior to the walkout.[60] These informal meetings offered Chicano students the opportunity to discuss their most common educational needs with each other, thus kindling the political spark of collective consciousness. Other key student activists from Gillett included Fred Cuevas, Manuel Treviño, Chico Rojas, Alfredo García, Alfredo Cortez, Cecilia Cortez, Silvia Barrera, and Esther Treviño.[61] Andrés Garza, a former Gillett Junior High School teacher, recalls sensing Chicano students' eagerness for protest a few weeks before the walkout.[62] Students Mateo Vega and José Benavidez, who were part of Garza's after-school study program at Gillett, were also active in the local student movement.[63] However, he does not recall their involvement or exact plans for initiating the movement at Gillett. Former walkout participant Cecilia Cortez remembers students announcing informal meetings by word of mouth to plan the walkout.[64] She also confirms the building of friendships among students engaged in collective action to promote social and political change and develop protest tactics. Campus activists at Texas A&I and Chicano students in the Kingsville public schools met to discuss student issues prior to their protest.[65] During their meetings, MAYO and PASSO members as well as Kingsville Chicano students agreed to seven demands. The key demands were that

- more Mexican American administrators and faculty be hired, including a "Chicano counselor who understands their [Chicano students'] problems";
- there be no punishment for speaking Spanish at school;
- bilingual and bicultural programs be implemented.[66]

School officials were unresponsive to these demands and took no immediate action. Consequently, Chicano students at Gillett Junior High began their walkout shortly after 8:00 a.m. on April 14, 1969. The list of student demands reveals the students' justification for taking such action:

On this day April 14, 1969, we come in hope that our demands will be respectfully heard by the administration and school board. The eyes of Mexican-Americans all over Kingsville are watching and waiting for your decision. If you see this as an act of disrespect or an attempt to disrupt the educational school system by a handful of Revolutionaries instead of a group of young Americans demonstrating for rights that they feel have been denied, then you are depriving them of their right to peaceful assembly guaranteed by the Constitution of the United States of America. We demand Justice!!!!![67]

Shortly after they walked out, the protesters assembled across the street to the west of the school near Ruben's Daily Grill, where they began picketing, clapping, and shouting "Viva la Raza" and "Viva MAYO."[68] MAYO member Rene Treviño described the frustration and angst of the protesters: "We gave them a list of grievances—the principal, that is—and after his failure to meet, or to deal, or to in any way show favor toward these grievances, after that we just walked

162 ~ CHAPTER 5

out, or rather, the students there 'walked out.'"[69] The walkout and subsequent picket-sign protest was orderly and peaceful and occurred west of Gillett Junior High School.[70]

Treviño confirmed that at least thirty to forty MAYO members were at the scene of the protest, and various participants carried signs stating "Who Cares? Kingsville Teachers Should!"[71] An estimated 100 Chicano students boycotted classes on the first day, which MAYO declared was "Chicano Liberation Day."[72] One letter written by MAYO indicates that as many as 220 had walked out on the first day by 3:00 p.m.[73] Approximately 200 students participated in the protest from April 14 to 15.[74] In reaction to the student walkout, school officials held an emergency meeting on the evening of April 15.

During the meeting, officials reaffirmed previous policies regarding student grievances and compulsory school attendance. School policy, released by school board president Nick M. Harrel and unanimously agreed on by school officials, stated: "Any student's grievance or request may be brought before the principal by the parent who has a child attending that school. Any student who has willfully been absent and has not returned to school by Thursday, April 17, 1969 will be subject to suspension or expulsion and a hearing to determine whether he shall be suspended or expelled will be held."[75]

Thus, the implementation of this policy underscores the school board's unwillingness to compromise with the student protesters. Officials approved the April 15 school policy to prevent student activists from continuing their boycott and voicing their grievances against the school system, thus restricting their right to assemble peacefully and exercise their right to free speech. The lack of Mexican American representation or bargaining position in the school system's decision-making process reflects their political powerlessness. While the school board meeting was in session, approximately two hundred student activists initiated a candlelight demonstration outside Gillett Junior High. The protest was short-lived, however, when neighbors quickly notified the local fire department, which arrived within minutes and dispersed the protesters.[76] Not surprisingly, community members in Kingsville felt apprehensive about student insurgency and saw it as controversial and bothersome.

Various parents of local students voiced their disapproval of student militant action as well. Parents such as Mrs. Frank Navarez (first name unknown) and various other parents discouraged students and tried to prevent them from further protest. She expressed her discontent: "We are not trying to say whether the students' demands are right or wrong, but we do not believe this is the right way of going about it at all."[77] The parents of students Cecilia and Alfredo Cortez became upset during the first day of the protest before reprimanding their children for walking out.[78] However, other parents supported the student movement, including parent spokesperson Maria Elena Salinas, who asked to meet with school officials to discuss student demands on Thursday, April 16.[79] The actions of Navarez, Cortez, and Salinas during the walkout indicated that some Mexican Americans opposed the local student movement while others actively supported it. Thus, Kingsville did not witness a rise in collective consciousness among older Mexican Americans because they tended to disagree with Chicano students' recollections of discriminatory and unjust treatment in the local school system.

Other community members voiced their objections to the student movement as well. D. J. Chapa, a local Mexican American community member, mentions, "Can't our poor misguided youth realize that after the out-of-town agitators are long gone from our city, they themselves, will still be living here . . . it may take a long time for some of us to forget to be ashamed of them."[80] One anonymous Mexican American Vietnam soldier expressed his disdain about the movement in a letter to the editor of the local newspaper:

> People in Kingsville (Spanish speaking), I would like to say something to you all. Right now I am in Vietnam. Hearing about this has almost made me ashamed of what you are doing . . . why do you people [Chicano students] that are involved want us to have more problems than the ones we have over here [Vietnam]. I was born in the same town you were born in. I never found anything wrong with it. In high school or junior high, I didn't have any problems. Either you learn the subject or you didn't. . . . Who started this all I don't know, but my guess is that the ones that started it all are not in school.[81]

Another unknown individual, with the initials E. M. J., wrote to the *Kingsville-Bishop Record-News* editor claiming that Chicano students' struggle for civil rights was a farce induced by communism. The letter stated: "Wake up, 'Raza Mia'—you are being used to promote your own downfall and that of this whole country. There is no such thing as 'Civil Rights,' that is only a communist-coined word."[82] Clearly, various community members perceived the local student movement as anti-American and instigated by communists during the peak of the Vietnam War.

Nonetheless, Chicano students at Gillett Junior High School inspired others to participate in the student movement. The boycott soon spread to two other Kingsville schools, including Memorial Junior High and King High School. Two days after the walkout began, the estimated number of student protesters at each school was forty at Gillett Junior High, thirty at Memorial Junior High, and forty-five at King High School.[83] On the morning of Wednesday, April 16, approximately seventy to eighty walkout participants and other local students initiated a protest march within the city at 1:30 p.m. after demonstrating at Gillett Junior High in the morning.[84] They marched twelve blocks to the school administration office downtown, where they demonstrated outside the building.[85] They soon decided to also march and protest outside Memorial Junior High. However, before the protesters arrived at the school, police chief Paul D. Hulsey and fifteen other local officers confronted them, warning them to cease their protest at 2:30 p.m.[86] Prior to this confrontation, approximately seven hundred to eight hundred local student activists and their supporters had joined the march.[87] The marchers were unwilling to comply with the warning, and the police arrested and escorted them to jail. Student participants were charged with "disturbing the peace" and "unlawful assembly."[88] Those arrested walked to jail without incident, having engaged in civil obedience as a means of promoting social and political change.

Later that afternoon, supporters of the walkout, including members of MAYO and students from nearby Texas A&I University, held a rally on campus.

Figure 9. Police Chief Hulsey put demonstrators under arrest. Marchers were halted in the heart of downtown Kingsville, led to jail, and charged. *Corpus Christi Caller*, April 17, 1969.

1969 KINGSVILLE SCHOOL WALKOUT   165

Those present at the rally on April 16 became enraged when they heard about the arrests. Consequently, college students and other young Chicano activists decided to march and protest outside the police station to express their outrage toward the arrests.[89]

After the demonstrators refused to quietly disperse, police chief Hulsey arrested them outside the station, charging them with "disturbing the peace," inciting an "unlawful assembly," and refusing to cooperate with a lawful order of the police.[90] Alberto Luera, a MAYO activist who was among those arrested in the second group, asserts that the police charged him and other college students for "loud and vociferous language."[91] He further claims that the police charged and arrested the first group of Kingsville students for "parading without a permit." Those arrested included 56 juveniles under the age of eighteen and 54 charged as adults, totaling 110.[92] One former Chicano movement activist claimed that the police arrested both Texas A&I students and young adults not enrolled in college in the second group.[93] The exact number and identity of young adult movement activists not attending college is unknown. However, two people arrested in the second group, one former student and one movement activist who did not attend college, recall that they and others incarcerated were placed in four small overcapacity jail cells.[94] Upon learning about the arrests, MAYO and PASSO leader Carlos Guerra contacted MALDEF for legal assistance.[95] Within a matter of hours, MALDEF dispatched attorney and Kingsville native Juan Rocha Jr., a Texas A&I alumnus who had campaigned for student body president in 1958, to secure their release.

Rocha worked with fellow MALDEF attorney Alan Axelrod, police chief Hulsey, corporation court judge Robert Alcorn, and Corpus Christi attorney Rudolph Garza to arrange the incarcerated protesters' release.[96] Reminiscent of what occurred in Edcouch-Elsa, sympathizers gathered outside the jail and held a candlelight vigil to show support. An estimated four hundred people joined the vigil.[97] Some participants carried protest signs with a few popular 1960s-era slogans such as "Justice is a Virtue," "We have waited too long," and "Peace."[98] One MAYO document describes the protesters' situation in jail as follows:

> No one was given a chance to call home until nine o' clock p.m. The young carnales [brothers] outside brought food through the windows to the jailed. Candy, cokes, and cigarettes were also brought.... The cops forgot bringing food to the jailed until ten o'clock. The Chicanos accepted the food, but threw it right back in their faces. No cop was admitted into the jail cells, due to the fact that the guys were armed with cups full of water. They wasted the jail—throwing paper, water and cigarette butts on the hallway.[99]

JAILS FILLED TO OVERFLOWING — Protestors arrested Wednesday numbered 116 on the final count. The cells at police headqurters were originally built to hold 16 people. There were 55 adults crowded into these cells Wednesday.

Figure 10. Kingsville student protestors in jail. *Kingsville-Bishop Record-News*, April 20, 1969.

This further reveals the unjust treatment of those incarcerated by the local police. After they threw food and water at their jailers, the protesters made a "V for victory" sign with their index and middle fingers.[100] According to county juvenile probation officer Mario Salazar, the adolescents under arrest were placed in a separate room in the police station rather than in jail.[101] The juveniles were isolated from the incarcerated adults for their protection. He further mentions that most of those arrested were male, and that females were placed in a separate room.

All juveniles were released to the custody of their parents by 5:00 p.m. the same day.[102] Local law enforcement officials and MALDEF attorneys agreed to allow twelve of the fifty-four young adults imprisoned to pay a fifty-dollar cash bond, while the other forty-two were allowed to leave jail on personal recognizance.[103] The last protester was finally freed shortly after 3:00 a.m. the next morning. MALDEF attorney Juan Rocha Jr. summed up the student protesters' collective feelings regarding their arrests: "So long as the Mexican-American problem is ignored and so long as no solutions are actively sought for the Mexican-American problem, tension will build up. And every day that the Mexican-American problem is ignored is one day closer to the inevitable violence with which oppressed people are force to respond."[104]

Statewide MAYO leader Carlos Guerra further acknowledged the personal sacrifice of those incarcerated: "All people arrested have been released ... [and] have shown their commitment to the cause of the betterment of the Mexican American in education and elsewhere."[105] Shortly after their release from jail, student protesters in Kingsville contemplated whether to return to classes or face expulsion. According to the *San Antonio Express*, only six students failed to return and were expelled.[106] Upon the release of all protesters, Kingsville police chief Paul Hulsey noted, "Everything is real quiet. Of course, I don't know how long that will last."[107] Unknown to Hulsey, the silence would not last long.

On Friday, April 18, Kingsville school officials finally agreed to consider meeting with student activists to hear their demands. Juan Rocha Jr., the attorney representing the protesting students, requested the meeting with the school board after talking to principal Nick M. Harrel Jr., superintendent John S. Gillett, and Kingsville ISD attorney John Stafford.[108] Shortly after their conversation, Kingsville school administrators issued a statement concerning one of the student demands. According to the *San Antonio Express*, the board's statement indicated that Chicano students already had the right to speak Spanish at school: "The school board has not officially received their request, but we understand that they have asked to be allowed to speak their mother tongue on the campus and that bi-lingual education be instituted. There is no school board policy against speaking any language on the campus."[109] On Friday afternoon, a parent-student committee and two lawyers representing the protesting students met with the Kingsville City Commission, supposedly to discuss the demands. The parent-student committee had formed shortly after a rally and meeting at the local MAYO headquarters and initially requested a special school board meeting to discuss the demands, but school officials refused to negotiate.[110] Therefore, the committee and its lawyers soon sought the help of a higher power, the Kingsville City Commission.

The lawyers who accompanied the parent-student committee included Juan Rocha Jr., and Mike González of Del Rio, Texas. They convened to no avail. The committee left because the city commission did not allow MAYO spokesperson

Rene Treviño to explain the grievances. Texas state representative Carlos Truan was disappointed and explained why the committee left the meeting, remarking, "It sort of looked like they were being interrogated."[111] In commenting about the city commission's inability to provide a solution to the grievances of the student protesters, Kingsville mayor J. R. Manning remarked that the commission had no jurisdiction in a school dispute.[112] Later that day, Dr. Hector P. García, representing the US Commission on Civil Rights, visited junior high and high school students to inquire about alleged civil rights violations.

On Saturday, April 19, an estimated four hundred Chicano college students and supporters gathered at an outdoor rally on the Texas A&I University campus. Speaker Carlos Guerra reiterated his insistence that Kingsville school officials seriously consider agreeing to the Gillett Junior High student demands or face the possibility of an unpleasant confrontation. He stated, "If they want to keep this [student protest] non-violent they [school board] are going to have to start listening to us now."[113] Narciso Alemán, a MAYO organizer and graduate student from Colorado State University, expressed the student protesters' sense of urgency. He stated: "The image of the Mexican American is that he leaves everything until tomorrow. The youth who walked out don't want to wait until tomorrow ... [they were] trying to get ... a better education."[114] Such instances indicate that the local student movement was gaining momentum and attention.

Shortly after Alemán made his plea, MAYO Teatro presented a two-act play to reenact the major events of the walkout.[115] It began with Frank Pagana playing the part of an Anglo teacher lecturing to a group of Mexican American students about how and why Texas became the largest state.[116] In making a historical reference to Mexican president Antonio López de Santa Anna, the teacher made racist comments depicting ethnic Mexican people as communist infiltrators in Texas. He said, "Texas became the largest state because a lot of red-blooded white Americans shed their blood. Now Santa Anna was a long-haired Cuban-trained communist outside agitator."[117]

Later in the play, two students suddenly began speaking Spanish. The teacher continued to lecture despite this interruption and further mentioned that "the King Ranch has always been here, and it will always be here. It was put here by God. God said, 'Let there be the ranch and there it was.'"[118] In response to the students who spoke Spanish, the teacher retorted, "If ya all wanna speak Mesking [Mexican] you can go back to Mesko [Mexico]."[119] After the classroom scene, Kingsville school officials acted apathetic and nonchalant toward Chicano students. Another scene showed a re-creation of the Kingsville student walkout. The final part of the play featured a few *vendidos*,[120] or Mexican American community members opposed to the walkout, heckling and ridiculing the protesting students and calling them communists and *estúpidos* (stupid). By staging the play, MAYO intended to dramatize how gringos or Anglos as well as *vendidos* became antagonistic toward Chicanos during the Kingsville student protest.

But MAYO was actively organizing at other sites, such as the University of Texas at Austin. MAYO's growing grassroots support swelled during the period of student walkouts, and its leader José Angel Gutiérrez was boldly advocating for militant resistance. On the night of April 19, Gutiérrez gave his historic "Kill the Gringo" speech at a statewide Chicano youth conference sponsored by the Mexican American Student Association at the University of Texas at Austin. The speech aroused much controversy, and he was both revered and vilified. Thus, this rhetorical symbol of resistance represented an outcry of Chicano nationalism, or what historian Ernesto Chávez theorizes was a type of residual culture or Mexican protonationalism that opposed the exploitative Anglo-American power structure.[121] Approximately 250 students from throughout Texas heard Gutiérrez's speech, which the media misunderstood as advocating violence against Anglo-Americans. One scholar asserts that Gutiérrez spoke out of anger, intended to manipulate the media, targeted the gringo as the focus of attack, and psychologically played on people's fears to instill respect for MAYO.[122] It was further contended that such a verbal attack advocating the destruction of the Anglo power structure—by violence if necessary—had not been made publicly in Texas since the time of insurrectionist Juan Cortina (1859–75) during his raid of Brownsville.[123]

One key part of Gutiérrez's speech spelled out what he actually meant by the phrase "Kill the Gringo": "We [Chicanos] intend to eliminate the gringo first by removing his [Anglos'] base of support, be it economic, political or social. If that doesn't work, then we may have to resort to violence in self-defense. We don't intend to talk forever nor do we intend to march and picket. We intend to change our conditions one way or another."[124] On April 20, before a crowd of approximately four hundred, including walkout participants and their supporters in Kingsville, Gutiérrez clarified his "Kill the Gringo" speech. He reiterated his argument advocating the eradication of the Anglo system or status quo, rather than the death of white people. Moreover, Gutiérrez further explained, "If I am attacked or my person or my family or my property is attacked by a gringo, I will defend myself. I will kill the gringo."[125] One document expressed Gutiérrez's views about the gringo as "a foreigner, a thief, [and] an exploiter" of Chicanos.[126] His speech symbolized the collective feelings of frustration and the development of political consciousness among the Chicano community at the time.[127] The words "Chicano," "Aztlán," and "La Raza" became powerful terms discussed by Gutiérrez, calling for ethnic Mexican unity against those he considered to be at the root of their societal problems, and against Anglo-Americans' economic and political supremacy.[128] While Gutiérrez continued to speak at the rally, local

170 ～ CHAPTER 5

police suddenly converged on scene and reported that they had been alerted to a bomb threat at the MAYO chapter headquarters nearby. Gutiérrez explains that MAYO had premeditated the bomb threat:

> I thought they [police] were trying to get us to disperse and wanted to search our building to see what they could plant inside the building. So I refused to let them have the PA system. I informed the crowd that this pig was trying to break us up and scare us and that . . . bomb threats or no bomb threats we were not going to be dispersed or intimidated . . . I proceeded to turn around saying we are going to have a countdown since Chicanos can't go to the moon, we might just qualify this time. So let's begin our countdown."[129] Thus, one MAYO tactic involved fabricating a bomb threat to excite and arouse supporters, as suggested by Gutiérrez's actions and comments at the time.

Politically Conservative Opposition to Gutiérrez and MAYO

Gutiérrez's historic speech angered many whites and socially conservative Mexican Americans in Texas during the late 1960s and early 1970s. Among those who expressed outrage toward Gutiérrez and MAYO was US congressman Henry B. González of San Antonio, Texas. Born in 1916, González was the first Mexican American elected to the Texas senate in 1956 and to the US House of Representatives in 1961. From 1953 to 1956, González served as a San Antonio city council member and mayor pro tempore best known for speaking out against "segregation in general and specifically against segregation of public facilities."[130]

In 1957, he and Senator Abraham Kazen of Laredo, Texas, gained national attention for their thirty-six-hour filibuster preventing the passage of eight of ten racial segregation bills, the longest such obstructive action in the history of the Texas legislature.[131] His work in Congress often represented the interests of "the poor, the middle-income earners, and small business people."[132] González's first piece of legislation called for the abolition of the poll tax in 1961. This proposal eventually led to the passage of the Twenty-Fourth Amendment to the Constitution prohibiting poll taxes in federal elections, in 1964.[133] Identifying himself as a loyal liberal Democrat, González served as the devoted political voice of San Antonio's predominantly Mexican American West Side, with a sign outside his congressional door that read "This Office Belongs to the People of Bexar County [Texas]." Despite González's popularity among the local Mexican American community, González often claimed to serve the broader public interest. Ignacio M. García indicates: "Beyond pointing out existing federal programs and promoting the Democratic Party, he offered little in the way of addressing the specific grievances of Mexican Americans. By this time [1960s] he sought to be seen as a politician for all the people rather than Mexican Americans particularly."[134]

As a staunch proponent of the Democratic Party, González made a series of antimilitant speeches before the US House of Representatives, referring to Gutiérrez and MAYO as rabble-rousers and racists. One congressional committee hearing investigating the Ford Foundation stated: "MAYO styles itself the embodiment of good and the Anglo-American as the incarnation of evil. That is not merely ridiculous, it is drawing fire from the deepest wellsprings of hate. The San Antonio leader, Jose Angel Gutierrez, may think of himself something of a hero, but he is, in fact, only a benighted soul if he believes that in the espousal of hatred he will find love.... One cannot fan the flames of bigotry one moment and expect them to disappear the next."[135] He specifically criticized MAYO, claiming that its members "adopted the same poisons, the same attitudes, the same tactics of those who have so long offended them . . . using the same sort of distorted logic, deceitful tongues, and hateful words of racists."[136] One television interview shows González accusing young Chicano militants of waging a "campaign of hate" by espousing the same type of racism they were seeking to eradicate.[137] González also feared that the actions of Gutiérrez and MAYO would only escalate hatred toward Anglo-Americans, and therefore González assumed a responsibility to "smoke out and expose these [Chicano activists'] false and mistaken voices of hatred."[138] In short, González did not believe that "racism in reverse is the answer for racism and discrimination [against Mexican Americans]."[139]

Organizations networking with MAYO, including MALDEF, the Southwest Council of La Raza, and PASSO were targets of González's criticisms as well. In 1969, González charged that the $10,000 given by the Ford Foundation to MAYO was a waste of taxpayer money, as it was used to finance the distribution of "hate literature."[140] He further commented that three of the seven organizations associated with MAYO were awarded funding by the Southwest Council of La Raza and the Mexican American Unity Council of San Antonio.[141] González publicized MAYO's acceptance of such funds before the US Congress. On one occasion, he stated: "It is ironic that the self-styled revolutionary head of MAYO [José Angel Gutiérrez], who says he hates gringos [Anglos] and accuses them of being the sole reason for the downtrodden condition of Mexican Americans, doesn't mind accepting in excess of $10,000 gringo Ford Foundation dollars."[142] Thus, liberal politicians such as González publicly rebuked MAYO for accepting such funds and promoting racism.[143] In response to González's allegations of MAYO's endorsement of racism, Gutiérrez argues: "What he [González] did was turn militancy and activism into racism and since he has a large middle class Chicano and white constituency, this was very appealing to them because they are threatened, you know, by our [MAYO's] militancy."[144] But Ford was a "gringo" operation with a liberal bent. Nevertheless, González's condemnation of MAYO likely convinced other politicians including Texas governor Preston Smith to severely cut the organization's financial resources such as grant money.

Smith further accused MAYO of inciting racial tension when he ordered a group of VISTA volunteers to leave the southwest Texas border town of Del Rio in Val Verde County. By calling for the termination of the program, Smith argued: "The abdication of respect for law and order, disruption of democratic process, and provocation of disunity among our citizens will not be tolerated." In response to Smith's dispute, MAYO staged the largest demonstration in town by attaching what it called the "Del Rio Manifesto" to the courthouse door.[145] Congressman O. C. Fisher of San Antonio went even further by urging the House Committee on Internal Security to investigate the activities of MAYO. Fisher accused Gutiérrez of being "deeply involved" in the grape strike at Delano, California, and becoming "a prime agitator" in the "Rio Grande Valley disorders," or farmworkers' movement in Starr County. He wrote to the committee: "Since this is a relatively new organization, it would seem to me that your committee may be interested in exploring the nature of its objectives and involvement which would seem to affect the peace and security of the area involved."[146] This criticism, however, did not measure up to the political attacks levied by Congressman González.[147]

Gutiérrez and MAYO had other critics outside the political arena as well. One week after the Kingsville walkout, one local community member also questioned why MAYO accepted money from the Ford Foundation. Isabel Canales, who heckled speaker Carlos Guerra during a rally at Texas A&I, argued that money received from the Ford Foundation should have been used to free the protesting students who went to jail on April 16. Voicing her suspicion of MAYO's use of $110,000 of the foundation's funds, she retorted: "And you took that money from a Gringo. If you hate gringos so much, why do you take their money"?[148] Guerra responded that the Mexican Unity Council, of which MAYO was only one member, allocated the money from the grant and awarded MAYO only $9,000, to be used solely for staff services.[149]

Kingsville Students Voice Complaints toward the School Board

On April 21, local Chicano high school students and MAYO members waited anxiously to negotiate with the school board. When the board made no attempt to meet with them, protests continued outside the school district's main office. "We [Chicano students] waited for them [board members]. We were here and they were not. That's not our problem. Now we will have to take another course of action," said Carlos Guerra.[150] According to the *Corpus Christi Caller*, one statement MAYO released to the media noted, "Once again they [school board] have refused to do their job, hiding the whole time, behind the bureaucratic procedures that have always been used to keep the Chicano down."[151] Shortly after beginning their demonstration, protesters raised a red and black La Raza flag on the flagpole of the school administration building.[152] Moments later, they lowered the flag and dispersed peacefully.

In an effort to consider student protesters' demands, school board president Nick M. Harrel Jr. reiterated the school district's policy in such instances. He called for parents to present their children's grievances to school principals. Harrell stated in an official school district letter sent to students and their parents, "If you will be kind enough to stay within the School Board Policies your complaint will be given a public hearing before the School Board."[153] Two parents, Mrs. Daniel Salinas and Mrs. Pedro Amador, helped Chicano students comply with the policy by requesting a public meeting with the school board.[154] Thus, the discussion the protesting students desired of a settlement concerning their demands finally took place.

Chicano students presented their grievances to school administrators in a public hearing attended by over four hundred people on Tuesday, April 22. According to the school board record for this day, Maria Elena Salinas spoke on behalf of the students' parents and highlighted their complaints about the school system.[155] It was also during this meeting that students presented an eighth demand, calling for a Mexican American citizens' advisory committee to review school district job applicants, investigate complaints, and serve as a liaison between the board and students.[156] The meeting lasted over two hours, during which Harrel outlined the demands presented by Carlos Guerra. After he had heard from numerous community members, Harrel said that administrators would take the students' demands under advisement but offered no agreeable solution. As in the San Antonio and Edcouch-Elsa school cases, Mexican Americans lacked representation in the school district's governing body (school board and administration), and the Anglo-American power structure made decisions on how it governed the school system.

Various people voiced their opinion for and against the student movement. Moreover, voices of moderation expressed the need for students and administrators to seek a solution at a conference table rather than in the streets.[157] Shortly after the meeting ended, MAYO released a statement expressing remorse over the board's inability to immediately carry out all the demands. Part of it read, "We were told our demands would be taken under advisement and this was a disappointment to the MAYO members. So great a disappointment that a lot of them are sick."[158]

As in Edcouch-Elsa, well-wishers from throughout the nation reaffirmed their support of the student movement mobilization in Kingsville via written correspondence. A telegram from prominent Chicano Movement activist Rodolfo "Corky" Gonzales, chair of the Crusade for Justice, a Chicano social justice organization in Denver, praised student protesters: "The Chicano Movement across the nation is keeping close watch on [the] walkout of Gillett. The Crusade for Justice of Denver, Colorado, fully supports honorable demands of students and expect to see them met. The causes for such student actions are not isolated to Kingsville but affects all of us across the Southwest therefore, we give our brothers full backing in their courageous and inspiring stand."[159] Father James Groppi of Milwaukee, Wisconsin, offered his perspective on why those in Kingsville walked out of their school: "I support your fight to save Mexican Americans from cultural genocide."[160] Another telegram from El Teatro Campesino, a grassroots Chicano theater arts production company, stated: "Gillett Jr. High School carnales [brothers] keep up the struggle in schools que viva nuestra raza hasta la victoria [long live our people until the victory]."[161] Armando Valdez, director of La Causa Student Center in Oakland, California, mentioned in his telegram, "Kingsville walkouts symbolize Chicano solidarity throughout the Southwest for relevant education adelante raza [keep it up people]."[162] Other such correspondence extols the Kingsville walkout participants by exclaiming "Viva la Raza" or "Viva la Causa."

On Sunday, April 27, more than three hundred Chicano junior high, high school, and college students and supporters participated in a protest march to express pride in the walkout. The marchers clearly reflected their ties with MAYO while demonstrating outside the Kleberg County Courthouse by raising a MAYO flag on the flagpole. Moments afterward, a scuffle ensued between MAYO demonstrators and Kleberg County deputy sheriff Jim Martin, who attempted to take down the flag. He failed to do so since various protesters assaulted him and chased him around a few city streets.[163] Student demonstrators also raised this same flag at city hall and the school administration building without incident prior to arriving at the courthouse.[164] According to one student activist who joined the march, Martin opposed the raising of the MAYO flag since he possibly mistook it for the Mexican flag.[165] March organizer Carlos Guerra obtained a parade permit to ensure that the protest would be peaceful and adhere to the law on behalf of Mexican Americans in Kingsville rather than MAYO.[166] During the march, demonstrators posted the list of Kingsville student demands on the front of the city hall and school administration buildings.[167] However, before the march ended, Carlos Guerra spoke to the marchers about the significance of their protest: "We will continue to fight whatever system or persons are oppressing us and keeping from us what is rightfully ours and we will direct any action that is necessary, mostly demonstrations, against these people and institutions until we get what is rightfully ours."[168] Juan Rocha Jr. reminisced about the protest, calling it a "victory march" that reinvigorated Chicano cultural pride and enthusiasm as a result of student activism during the walkout.[169] The march concluded with no arrests or injuries and was the last major Kingsville protest.

After this last demonstration, negotiations between student protesters and school officials resumed but accomplished next to nothing since the two sides failed to reach a suitable resolution. MAYO leader Alberto Luera assessed why negotiations came to a standstill: "Negotiations were held and were continued for two more weeks [after the walkout]. School ended and meetings were supposed to be held during the summer. Committees were set up, thus the whole thing went into committees... the whole thing [negotiations] died, it stayed in committees."[170] According to scholar-activist Armando Navarro, other factors contributing to the demise of the negotiations were that various students who led the walkout graduated in May 1969, and further protest activity ceased during summer.[171] He further argued that the Kingsville walkout failed because of the lack of sustained resource mobilization, which prevented the attainment of movement goals. Additional factors leading to the decline of the movement included failure to gain the unanimous support of local students' parents, the presence of law enforcement officials, the lack of leadership experience of local MAYO members, and minimal support from traditional Chicano organizations. Despite his unfavorable remarks concerning the effectiveness of the walkout, Navarro does reveal one important outcome, the creation of a Chicano studies program in the Kingsville public schools.[172]

Since the walkout, Mexican Americans have been in the majority on the Kingsville School Board and administration thanks to expanding political opportunities and openness of the school's political system.[173] Anglo-Americans were the majority on the school board for sixty-nine years, until 1978. The board has remained predominantly Mexican American (six-to-one majority) since 1990.[174] In the aftermath of the walkout, former MAYO activist and Kingsville protest leader Faustino Erebia recalls the significant increase of Mexican American political activism in the community, the defusing of tension between Anglo educators and Chicano students, and the addition of a new curriculum to reflect the contributions of Mexican Americans in the early 1970s.[175] Whether the local protest of 1969 contributed to this change is difficult to ascertain. Nevertheless, the Kingsville walkout symbolized the student protesters' pursuit of educational reform at their school.

Summary and Conclusion

Kingsville natives, including Carmen Lomas Garza, Faustino Erebia, and Cecilia Cortez remember when Kingsville required Mexican Americans to attend separate "Mexican" elementary and junior high schools during the 1950s and 1960s. Such schools were often plagued by substandard conditions, high dropout rates, and inferior funding. The Chicano student movement in Kingsville began on the campus of Texas A&I University when MAYO organizers José Angel Gutiérrez, Carlos Guerra, and Rene Treviño first ignited the spark of Chicano activism after establishing local chapters of La Raza Unida, PASSO, and MAYO by the late 1960s. A few weeks prior to the Kingsville walkout in April 1969, Chicano students and MAYO members met on various occasions to discuss school issues. They often held informal meetings in students' homes or the local MAYO chapter office building on the corner of Eleventh and Santa Gertrudis Streets. A seminar on community and political activism at Texas A&I University provided valuable information to local college, high school, and junior high students in February 1969. Within days after the seminar, college student movement activists began participating in demonstrations in front of Kingsville City Hall and the Kleberg County Courthouse.

Throughout the late 1960s, Texas A&I University witnessed numerous demonstrations by Mexican American campus activists seeking to combat racial discrimination and gain political empowerment. Texas A&I students encouraged and influenced local student activists at Gillett Junior High to engage in

Figure 11. Hundreds of Chicano students gathered in the streets to fight for equal education and equal rights in Kingsville. Courtesy of *South Texan*, Texas A&M University–Kingsville student newspaper, feature article on the Chicano Movement in Kingsville, October 14, 2020.

nonviolent, direct-action protest at their school. Unlike in the Edcouch-Elsa student walkout, state MAYO leaders, including José Angel Gutiérrez and Carlos Guerra, provided direct assistance and mentorship to student activists in Kingsville, helping local Chicano students draft seven demands calling for educational reform in the Kingsville school system. The walkout gained the support of local MAYO supporters who attended Gillett Junior High, including Faustino Erebia, Fred Cuevas, Manuel Treviño, Chico Rojas, Alfredo García, Alfredo Cortez, Cecilia Cortez, Silvia Barrera, and Esther Treviño. News of Kingsville's protest and activity soon reverberated and influenced similar action at other school sites in the region.

As the Kingsville student movement gained momentum, the boycott spread to Memorial Junior High and King High School. Just as in the Edcouch-Elsa student protest, local school officials and law enforcement authorities conspired to jail the leaders and key activists of the student movement. And not unlike in Edcouch-Elsa, MALDEF also actively defended the incarcerated students and arranged for the release of the protesters through one of its attorneys, Juan Rocha Jr. Rocha also later served as an advocate and resource for Kingsville student activists.

Perhaps the most significant dynamic in this attempt to gain educational reform was MAYO's more direct, overt, and militant participation in the events surrounding the Gillett Junior High School walkout. Since the walkout, Mexican Americans have been in the majority on the Kingsville School Board and in the administration. Whether the local walkout contributed to this remarkable transformation within the local school system is difficult to pinpoint. However, Kingsville witnessed the sudden proliferation of Chicano student insurgency by both college and public school students in the spring of 1969. Despite the inability of school officials to enact immediate educational reform, the Kingsville school walkout emerged as an important part of the overall student movement that attempted to usher in Chicano political empowerment. This objective became more apparent and well known during the Crystal City school protest, which marked the climax of the student movement in South Texas.

6

The 1969–70 Crystal City School Walkout

The Climax and Decline of the Chicano Student Movement in Rural South Texas

One of the most highly publicized and controversial student protests of the Chicano Movement occurred in Crystal City. The Crystal City walkout, the most famous high school student protest in Texas in the 1960s, marked the climax as well as the decline of the regionwide student movement. In December 1969, Crystal City suddenly became a hotbed of student protest activity because Chicano college students, many of whom were active in MAYO, helped local students successfully mobilize collectively and implement a plan for educational reform. However, local Chicano students agreed to initiate a walkout and boycott of classes that spread from the high school to elementary schools after the school board refused to address their grievances. They further contended that the school system had historically denied Mexican American students an equal opportunity to participate in school activities such as cheerleading. This well-organized protest, led by Severita Lara, Mario Treviño, and Diana Serna, served as a galvanizing force in organizing and exerting greater political power among the parents of protesters and other Chicano supporters in Crystal City. This student-led movement also motivated Chicanos to pursue political opportunities and empowerment in the local school system and attracted broader national attention, unlike the previous walkouts in the region. This chapter highlights the forms of political activism and the nature of community involvement, which were unmatched by previous student protests. Thus, this school protest underscores the key issues, student demands, resource mobilization, and political strategies of movement activists in Crystal City's Chicano community. This chapter proposes that the successful unified efforts and collective action of Crystal City's high school students, parents, and community activists ultimately led to the development of La Raza Unida. This movement gained much momentum thanks to the leadership of MAYO and José Angel Gutiérrez.

After the Del Monte Corporation relocated to Crystal City in 1945, it started harvesting crops on approximately 3,200 acres of farmland northeast of town. Before the year ended, Del Monte had planted its first commercial spinach crop.[1] In order to supplement the increased production and marketing of spinach, Del Monte added a new can manufacturing plant in 1958.[2] It became the largest employer of Mexican Americans and Mexican immigrants in Crystal City during the mid- to late twentieth century.[3] Mexican American workers have a long history of struggle in the region. The 1960s are particularly significant for the economic justice and educational reform activism that impacted the local community. Mexican American workers employed at the Del Monte canning plant who had formed a chapter of the Teamsters Union were politically active beginning in the early 1960s. Those who joined the union were instrumental in helping five Mexican American candidates, endorsed by PASSO, win city council elections. They also supported those who participated in the Crystal City school walkout.[4]

The local school district underwent significant changes prior to the walkout. Schooling in the area began when the first one-room schoolhouse was constructed near the county courthouse in 1908.[5] By the late 1920s, the Crystal City School District had segregated students from the first through the fifth grade. There were eight schools designated for whites, eleven for Hispanics, and one for African Americans in 1939.[6] Moreover, elementary schools for Anglos had twice the amount of equipment and facilities as predominantly Mexican American schools.[7] Throughout the first half of the twentieth century, the Crystal City School District enrolled Mexican Americans on school census lists to raise state revenues to fund predominantly Anglo schools.[8] The US census documents educational attainment and reveals the median education of Spanish-speaking people in Crystal City: 1.8 years in 1950 and 2.3 years in the 1960s.[9] Such data reflect the local school district's inability to educate most of its Mexican American residents. Shortly after the mid-1950s, when the famous *Brown v. Board of Education* case outlawed school segregation, the city's predominantly Anglo elementary school slowly began to integrate ethnic-minority students.

Even after the outcome of this historic landmark case, Mexican American students continued to experience discrimination and various educational disparities well into the 1960s. According to former Crystal City school superintendent Angel Noe González, only 9 percent of the Mexican American students who began the first grade together graduated from high school in 1951, and only 17 percent graduated in 1958.[10] According to the Texas Education Agency, 87 percent of all students enrolled in the Crystal City School District in the fall of 1969 were Mexican American.[11] This record further reveals that 376 Anglo-Americans,

12 African Americans, and 2,906 Mexican Americans attended Crystal City schools in the 1968–69 school year. The school district employed 91 Caucasian and 30 Mexican American teachers during the same period.

According to a few former student activists, some Anglo educators at Crystal City High School regarded Mexican American students as racially, culturally, and intellectually inferior.[12] The local school district segregated Mexican American and Caucasian students according to different grade classifications. José Angel Gutiérrez recalled: "Those of us [Mexican Americans] who did ultimately enter a 'white' school, such as the grammar school in 'Cristal,' were further segregated within the school building by 'grade.' There was a fifth year grade-one class, a fifth year grade-two class, and a fifth year grade-three class; the 'one' was all Anglo, the 'two' was mostly Mexican students with a few Anglos, and the 'three' was all Mexican. This practice continued into the junior high grades, and in another modified fashion, into the high school."[13] An investigation of Crystal City High School by the US Commission on Civil Rights in 1970 indicates that Mexican Americans faced discrimination in school:

> Generally, it was discovered that the percentage of Mexican American students receiving academic awards was unusually low when compared with the student population. This is the case especially where the school alone has the power of selection.... The selection process of students for popularity/social honors tends to reveal a conflict in the attitude of the teachers and those of the students regarding the just recipients of the popularity and social honors. In those cases where the selection is done strictly by the students the recipients are usually Mexican American, but when the teachers or others participate in the selection, the recipients are usually Anglo.... Mexican American student participation in drama, speech and debate, and similar activities is usually low.[14]

The commission's findings further indicated that properly accented pronunciation and mastery of the English language were essential for participation in school activities. Former student and walkout participant Diana Palacios remembers having to "go to a grade that they [Crystal City school officials] invented for you [Mexican American students] called zero" before enrolling in the first grade.[15] The school system placed students in certain grade levels depending on their ability to pass a competency test, which most could not pass because they were native Spanish speakers and had limited proficiency in English. Palacios further underscores the blatant disregard and unfair treatment of students of Mexican origin in their local school system. In one oral interview record, she states: "Once we saw that discrimination, you begin to notice it. You become aware of it. And so you see it in other things—in the kind of teachers you have, in the kind of school board you have, in the kind of counselors you have, the way that they direct you. For example, most of our kids, the counselors really didn't prepare us for college. They felt that we didn't have the brains to really attend a college, so we should attend some kind of vocational school."[16] Chicano students who participated in the Crystal City school walkout made such disparities known during their student movement of 1969–70.

Prior to the 1960s, Anglo-American newcomers acquired much wealth and status by governing the city and owning much of its land, while Mexicans served mainly as the subservient labor force. Historian John Staples Shockley theorizes that Crystal City's history in the early to mid-twentieth century was closely linked to the shift from ranching to farming and was thus a product of the social, political, and economic relationships that characterized South Texas at the time.[17] In short, these relationships reflected Anglo domination and control of city and county politics, school systems, businesses, and workplaces. One news report commented on the race relations between Anglos and Mexican Americans in Crystal City in 1971: "Although Crystal City has always had a certain number of open, straight-forward bigots, it has not been the kind of place in which Anglo control is maintained by violence or even by denying Mexican-Americans the right to vote.... [They have] taken political as well as economic control more or less for granted."[18] José Angel Gutiérrez, however, maintained that Crystal City was rigidly segregated, remarking that "it was illegal for a Mexican to join the Crystal City Country Club, to swim at the city pool on the Anglo swim days, to be buried in the Anglo cemetery, to join the service clubs . . . or join an Anglo Boy Scouts troop."[19] Gutiérrez also recalls the early period of his life when Anglos bought homes in affluent neighborhoods with paved streets, sidewalks, and electric lamps, while most Mexican Americans remained in abject poverty in the poorest area of town where polio and tuberculosis were rampant.[20] As in other places in South Texas, most Mexican Americans in Crystal City voted at the behest of their Anglo jefes, or bosses. Gutiérrez also recalls this longtime political relationship between Anglos and Mexican Americans: "The process of participating in elections was a nightmare for most Mexicans. You could lose your job by voting for the wrong person—such as another Mexican—if there was one running for office; you could also lose your job for not voting when the patron, the employer, took you to vote."[21] This circumstance was first evident in a 1926 election to determine whether the county courthouse should be moved from Batesville to Crystal City. According to former school superintendent R. C. Tate, Crystal City eventually won the right to move the courthouse by "voting its Mexicans" two years later.[22] This type of arrangement remained unchallenged until the 1960s.

182   ~   CHAPTER 6

Crystal City's "First Revolt"

The 1960s marked the local Mexican American community's first major attempt to thwart Anglo political rule. Early in the decade, resident Juan Cornejo, a representative of the Teamsters Union at the Del Monte Corporation (spinach-canning plant), who had only a few years of formal education in elementary school and was involved with the armed forces and PASSO, organized a political movement to elect five Mexican Americans to the city council.[23] However, the announcement that five Mexican Americans intended to run for city council was initially a rumor. Those who ran for the election in 1963 included Cornejo, Manuel Maldonado, Antonio Cárdenas, Reynaldo Mendoza, and Mario Hernández, all known collectively as *los cinco candidatos* (the five candidates). Aside from Cornejo, the other candidates' occupations included photographer, car salesman, truck driver, and store clerk.[24] José Angel Gutiérrez commented about the role of PASSO in mobilizing the organizational resources of Mexican Americans when they initiated their own self-run political campaign. "PAS[S]O had support from Anglo liberals and from organized labor in the San Antonio area, namely the teamster union. The leadership of PASSO was comprised of Democratic Party stalwarts from across the state but predominantly south Texas. PASSO sought to take power into areas where Mexican Americans were a majority."[25] His commentary reveals that Mexican Americans gained political support from outside Crystal City to mount an effective campaign.

Chicano scholar-activist Armando Navarro describes what he calls the endogenous phenomena (internal preconditions emanating from within the Chicano community) that sparked this revolt in the late 1950s and early 1960s. They included a local government scandal involving the fraudulent sale of land to ethnic Mexican war veterans; E. C. Muñoz's failed attempt to become the first Hispanic school board member; the Mexican American community's protest against de facto segregation in the city's elementary schools; and political pressure exerted by Mexican Americans to implement a surplus commodities program in the county.[26] One seemingly bizarre and restrictive political practice during this time was that anyone who wanted to vote in the city council election of 1963 had to pay a poll tax between October 1, 1962, and January 31, 1963, the time preceding the filing deadline for candidates.[27]

To legitimize their campaign, los cinco candidatos and PASSO members mainly from San Antonio engaged in a poll-tax drive for voter registration in Crystal City in 1962 and 1963. Gutiérrez, who had begun attending Southwest Texas Junior College in nearby Uvalde, assisted in this drive by going door to door to recruit potential voters and collect poll-tax receipts for the registrar.[28] He recalled that supporters of los cinco candidatos included women who sponsored and held numerous fundraisers (tamale sales, cakewalks, and dances) to help Mexican Americans from low-income families afford the poll tax.[29] This type of resource mobilization enabled the members of such families to exercise their right to vote. Furthermore, the grassroots campaign served to unify the local working-class and migrant communities while providing the initial training ground in the barrio (ethnic Mexican neighborhood) for a new generation of emerging young activists such as Gutíerrez.[30] These activists gained valuable experience in enhancing their organizational skills and learning the procedures of the electoral process, which had a lasting impact on the development of their political strategies during the Chicano Movement in Crystal City. According to historian Marc Simon Rodríguez, the Los Cinco campaign evolved as a social movement on two levels, the first involving the supporters and organizers of PASSO and the Teamsters, and the second including the participation and recruiting efforts of young activists and women who were devoted to promoting the campaign.[31] Political organizers used the money from the fundraisers to purchase Spanish-language radio advertising, print sample ballots, and buy gasoline to transport voters to the polls.[32] The poll-tax drive achieved unprecedented success when more Mexican Americans were eligible to vote than Anglos.

By the end of January 1963, an astounding 1,139 Mexican Americans had paid their poll taxes, while only 542 Anglos had done so.[33] These figures for the previous year also reflect the success of the poll-tax drive: 795 Mexican Americans and 538 Anglos.[34] However, the poll-tax drive did encounter challenges, such as voter intimidation by A. Y. Allee and other Texas Ranger law enforcement officers in Crystal City. In April 1963, Texas governor John Connally sent Allee's Rangers to prevent any potential outbreak of unrest. When Allee and the Rangers observed the local campaign, they accused Gutiérrez and other young Chicano activists of collaborating with the "PASSO Communist bunch."[35] PASSO leader and San Antonio native Albert Peña Jr. also became a target of unjust criticism when Allee accused him of being a communist and an outside agitator. In response to Allee's outrageous assertion, Peña simply stated, "I am an American citizen."[36] Additional opposition included intimidation of Mexican American voters at polling places by clerks and precinct judges, lack of Spanish-language assistance, and economic reprisal or the threat of job loss by Anglo employers.[37] Despite such difficulties, los cinco candidatos achieved an unprecedented victory by winning the election, replacing the old white American political elite and marking the first time an all–Mexican American slate of candidates swept a city council election in a US city.[38] Although Manuel Maldonado won the most votes (864), Juan Cornejo, who received 818 votes, became the first Mexican American mayor of Crystal City. This so-called electoral revolt attracted national publicity in a few major publications across the country, including the *New York Times*, the *Wall Street Journal*, *Life* magazine, and the *Los Angeles Times*.[39] Although the ethnic

Mexican community of Crystal City succeeded in its political "takeover," this historic moment did not last long.

In 1965, a coalition of Anglo and middle-class Mexican Americans succeeded in winning the city council elections, thus ousting los cinco candidatos. The coalition formed a group known as the Citizens Association Serving All Americans (CASAA).[40] This group opposed los cinco candidatos, viewing them as dominated by "outside interests," a reference to the supportive roles of PASSO and the Teamsters Union from San Antonio. Historians refer to the electoral campaign and subsequent victory of los cinco candidatos as Crystal City's "First Revolt."[41] They also consider the local student movement of 1969–70 to be Crystal City's "Second Revolt." The 1963 transition in city politics would later serve as an inspiration, catalyst, and mobilizing influence for Chicano students. In remembering the achievements of los cinco candidatos, local students waged their own campaign for political and institutional control of the local public school system. Examining Crystal City's "Second Revolt" provides a better understanding of how and why this small, dusty city became a breeding ground for Chicano Movement protest activism.

The Emergence of Crystal City's "Second Revolt"

During the spring of 1969, Chicano students at Crystal City High began organizing themselves against the city's schools, which they claimed were discriminatory and unequal. One allegation concerned the method of selecting cheerleaders at the high school, which had been in place for many years prior to 1969. The students specifically opposed the unofficial selection of cheerleaders and homecoming queen by a committee of teachers appointed by the principal.[42] This committee chose three Anglo girls and one Mexican American girl, normally favoring the Anglo girls since they attended gymnastics training schools and were viewed as more competent and athletic.[43]

This controversy represented the catalyst of the Chicano student movement and Crystal City school walkout during the 1969–70 school year. Historian John Staples Shockley underscores the reasons for the Chicano students' discontent: "In the Spring of 1969 the normal routine practice [of cheerleader selection] again occurred. This time, however, two of the Anglo cheerleaders had graduated leaving vacancies, and a [Mexican American], Diana Palacios was considered by the student body to be as good as any of the Anglos trying out. The [Mexican Americans], however, already had their quota in Diana Perez, so the faculty judges again chose two Anglos to fill the vacancies."[44]

Two local students who would eventually emerge as leaders of the Crystal City student movement, Severita Lara and Mario Treviño, presented a petition of seven grievances before the school board.[45] The petition, signed by approximately 150 students, concerned not only the cheerleading squad issue but also educational inadequacies impacting Mexican American students at Crystal City High School. Among the key demands were that no student receive punishment who demonstrated for better education, that teachers be prohibited from "preaching" political agendas to their students, and that the student body elect homecoming candidates and cheerleaders.[46] The petition was initially presented to Crystal City High School principal John B. Lair, who refused to negotiate with the students.[47] Therefore, student leaders approached Crystal City school superintendent John Billings, who agreed to certain concessions regarding the petition.

One important concession called for a quota system for cheerleader selection: three Anglos and three Mexican Americans. Another part of the settlement mandated the selection of one Mexican American and one Anglo for each class-favorite position. Historian Shockley contends that the concessions were based on the 1896 Supreme Court decision of *Plessy v. Fergusson*, mandating "separate but equal" facilities. However, former student leader Severita Lara argued that Chicano students were agitating for equal representation of Mexican Americans on the school's cheerleading squad rather than seeking a "separate but equal" Mexican American squad.[48] Lara further recalled that assistant principal Paulino Mata suspended her from school for distributing flyers highlighting the unfairness of the election procedure.[49] According to Lara, Mata and principal John B. Lair physically grabbed her by the elbows and lifted her into the air to stop her from distributing any more flyers to students. Both administrators sought to stop Lara from publicizing her cause and inciting a protest. Furious, Lair suspended her from school and called her a "rabble-rouser."[50] She was readmitted to school after missing two days upon receiving assistance from MALDEF. What seemed like a major students' rights victory for Chicanos was short-lived since school officials reneged on the concessions in June 1969.[51] Moreover, the Anglo-dominated school board approved a policy stipulating that any student would lose all credit for taking part in a protest or disturbance at school.[52] The board later annulled Billings's agreement with the students since school was not in session and their families migrated north during the summer.

Two former students, Mario and Blanca Treviño, reveal that local Chicano students discussed plans for a protest once again in the summer when they learned about the school board's decision.[53] Severita Lara, like numerous other Mexican American students, migrated during the summer for work. In San Jose, California, Lara began planning a protest at her school after learning about the East Los Angeles school walkouts that occurred in March 1968.[54] According to one historian, the migrant labor network between Crystal City and the vegetable-growing

186 ∼ CHAPTER 6

region near San Jose provided her and other Crystal City migrant students exposure to the development of the Chicano Movement in California.[55] Acquiring knowledge about the movement inspired Lara to plan a protest at her school.

Before the end of summer, Gutiérrez returned to Crystal City to lend leadership and support. The school board met and adopted a policy to revise the election procedures for various student positions, including cheerleaders. The new board policy stated that people from outside the school district would judge and select cheerleaders.[56] However, the policy failed to mention the process of choosing the judges, who could have been chosen by school officials favoring the selection of Anglo females. As in the previous three school cases, Mexican Americans lacked representation on the school board and in the decision-making process for setting educational policies.

In October 1969, the Crystal City High School Ex-Student Association coordinated a plan to crown its own homecoming queen during the football season. However, only former students who were parents of female students could vote. Most of the school board members agreed to endorse these selection criteria for judges.[57] Out of twenty-six eligible girls, only five were Mexican American.[58] However, one published memoir of Lara appears to refute this figure, stating that "only 6 out of 280 Chicana students were eligible [for election]."[59] The criteria for determining the number of qualified candidates were in fact restrictive, and Gutiérrez acknowledged this requirement as a "grandfather clause," which he viewed as discriminatory toward Mexican American female students trying out for their school's cheerleading squad. One anonymous letter to the editor of the *Zavala County Sentinel* contended that seven hundred (64 percent) Mexican Americans graduated from Crystal City High School between 1939 and 1968 and therefore could have joined the Ex-Student Association and voted for homecoming queen.[60] The writer contradicted Gutiérrez's argument that few Mexican Americans had graduated from the school prior to 1968. Meanwhile, the local school board called a meeting to discuss student grievances against the Ex-Student Association's intent to elect its own homecoming queen.

At a crowded school board meeting on November 10, approximately 450 people, including Gutiérrez, Chicano students, and their attorney Jesse Gámez, objected to the use of school property for the crowning of the association's own homecoming queen. They presented a petition of fourteen demands, some of which were the same as those listed in a petition given to the board the previous spring semester. Board minutes state that 139 students and 91 parents signed the petition listing the demands. Key demands in the second, revised petition included

- selecting of cheerleaders, school favorites, and band twirlers by the student body and band, respectively;

- prohibiting teachers from calling students "names like animals, stupid idiots, ignorant";
- designating September 16 as a school holiday;
- hiring a Mexican American school counselor;
- instituting a bilingual program and adding a Mexican American history course to the curriculum;
- ensuring the right to organize peacefully;
- organizing a student group at school to help the local poor;
- publishing a school newspaper with diverse viewpoints.[61]

Before the meeting adjourned, Gutiérrez and Chicano students vowed to stop the coronation unless the board took action.[62] Succumbing to the pressure exerted by student activists and their supporters, the board reluctantly denied the association the use of the football field.

Word of the board's decision angered many in the local Anglo community, especially those belonging to the Ex-Student Association. Letters to the editor of the local newspaper revealed different perspectives. One association member, Larry C. Volz, expressed outrage over the alleged coercion of the board by Gutiérrez, Gámez, and Chicano students, including the "threat of violence" against the school's affairs.[63] One 1966 Mexican American woman graduate, Trinidad Rubio, contends that the group confronted the board to "straighten out this discrimination matter."[64] The Chicano student movement in Crystal City gained greater momentum as a result of this meeting.

Upon recruiting supporters for the student movement, Gutiérrez successfully mobilized people, particularly adult males, in the Mexican American community. Men recruited by Gutiérrez, many of whom were the fathers of students, pressured and heckled the board the most. He often recruited these men at local bars during the afternoon and late-night hours. While conversing with them, Gutiérrez employed a mobilization technique he had used when forming a PASSO chapter at Texas A&I University; he keyed in on Mexican American men's machismo (manhood) to persuade them to attend the school board meeting. He suggested that school officials viewed their daughters as too unattractive for homecoming queen and mentioned that educators disrespected their wives and children.[65] Did most Mexican American men shift the responsibility of dealing with their children's problems at school to their wives? During the student movement, the men became convinced to support the school protest in order to show honor and loyalty toward their families and reaffirm their ethnic pride. This situation highlights the collective consciousness or sense of belonging and ethnic identity of Chicano men who sought to help their families overcome their status as a socially marginalized group.

In the pre–women's movement era, Gutiérrez was not able to see mothers as more political.

The Climax of Chicano Student Activism in Crystal City

In December 1969, Chicano students increased their list of demands to eighteen. They also began planning a walkout, anticipating that the school board would reject them.[66] At a meeting on December 8, the school board made one "last ditch" effort to discourage Chicano students from protesting. Students, parents, and supporters waited an hour and a half for the meeting to finally begin. They also had to stand throughout the entire meeting since the room had no chairs for the audience.[67] As they did during the last board meeting, all the men recruited by Gutiérrez, mostly fathers of Mexican American students, stood in front near the school trustees.

In his autobiography, Gutiérrez mentions the tension felt by the board. His eyewitness recollection indicates that the board remained uncooperative with student activists and supporters: "They [school board] should have had chairs! Their tactic of making us feel uncomfortable by standing backfired."[68] Former student activist Diana Serna also reveals that she and others in attendance "surrounded the board members and breathed down their necks."[69] After the meeting began, the school board approved a motion claiming that no instance of discrimination was found, as suggested by the students' list of demands.[70] Furthermore, the board considered the matters stated in the demands to be "administrative" rather than board problems and therefore would take no action. The board approved the motion by a vote of three to one despite three board members' absences.[71] Gutiérrez alleges that one of the two Mexican American trustees, Eddie Treviño, voted against the motion since he sympathized with the student protesters' situation.

Toward the end of the meeting, student leaders Severita Lara and Mario Treviño presented additional demands before the board. This detailed list of demands had been revised a third time and mentioned instances of discrimination by certain school educators, suggested four books for a Mexican American history course, and identified specific students' rights.[72] While Lara distributed copies to board members, president Ed Mayer told her that the matter had already been discussed, and she should consult the principal. Treviño then accused Mayer of giving students the runaround. "You're out of order, boy," responded Mayer, before calling for a motion to adjourn the meeting. Without warning, the board members left the meeting room and refused to respond to the students and their supporters. Later, during an interview with a news reporter, Billings admitted that "the board chose not to hear their demands a second time."[73]

When the students assembled outside, disillusionment and outrage over the situation fueled their fervor for protest as they shouted, "Let's walk out! Walk out! Walk out!"[74] Many parents felt emboldened to support the protest as well. Diana Serna's father commented: "We have to boycott the schools. Spread the word to everybody to keep their children out of school. They're [board members] going to have to hear us out."[75] Many Chicano students and their parents were discussing walking out and boycotting classes as their next course of action within an hour after the board meeting.[76] To ensure participation in the walkout, students went from house to house recruiting others throughout the night.[77] The local student movement had reached its peak.

The Crystal City Student Walkout and Its Aftermath

Before the start of school on December 9, an estimated two hundred Chicano students and their parents assembled in front of Crystal City High. Their number swelled to over five hundred by late morning, including Chicano junior high school students.[78] By employing his "crescendo effect" strategy, Gutiérrez encouraged some students to return and remain in school before rejoining the protest to show that their demonstration was growing in numbers. He had not used this strategy in previous student protests in South Texas. Throughout the rest of the day, he carefully orchestrated the protest to convince Anglos that it was the coming of the "second Mexican Revolution."[79] Before the morning ended, student leaders including Lara, Treviño, Diana Serna, Richard Espinoza, and Ester Ynosencio requested a meeting with Principal Lair. Assistant Principal Mata agreed to negotiate with the students but said that Lair was absent.[80] The students refused to accept this and instructed him to summon the principal and school superintendent John Billings for a 3:00 p.m. meeting.

Just before the meeting, student protesters marched around the high school before traveling twenty-five blocks through downtown. As they marched, student leader Mario Treviño recorded on cassette tape a few community members' remarks about the walkout. Housewife Irma Benavides stated: "I think that if the school board had listened to these students in the first place, they wouldn't have this situation on their hands." Ester Mandujano, mother of one walkout participant, commented in Spanish: "All this that we are doing is a reasonable thing. What we want is equality for all Mexicans in this town of Crystal City." Reynaldo Maldonado, another parent commenting in Spanish, praised the students' manner of protest: "All of this is very well done. I am proud that there has been no violence and all of that. Everything is in order. I believe that the students are right ... always be united."[81] One handwritten letter from Severita Lara's father to the Texas Education Agency expressed his discontent with the school system as

190 ～ CHAPTER 6

Figure 12. Students outside high school during boycott, Crystal City, Texas, 1969. L-4148-A, San Antonio Light Photograph Collection, MS 359 / UTSA Special Collections.

well. It read: "We have tried to work through the school establishment, but they [school officials] would not listen to us, and our children have had to walk out of school. If you would investigate the situation, we feel you could help solve the problem."[82] In another letter, written to Assistant Principal Mata, Lara further reaffirmed approval of his daughter's participation in the protest: "Severita has my full support in what she is doing because I think and I know she is doing right."[83] Such statements reveal that various parents supported their children's right to protest at school. Gutiérrez described Crystal City as "well politicized" and announced that many parents approved of their children's decision to protest.[84] He further stated that the school boycott was organized effectively because most Chicanos rallied to support the common goal of educational reform and ethnic Mexican cultural awareness. In summing up his prediction of the boycott's outcome, Gutierrez asserted, "We [Chicanos] have never gotten this far before. It looks like ... [the protest is] going all the way."[85] Some parents even mobilized resources to show their support for the school boycott by providing food and beverages.[86] Documentary evidence suggests an outpouring of support and resource mobilization, both material and nonmaterial, from the local Chicano community.

Figure 13.
Women serving food outside high school during boycott, Crystal City, Texas, 1969.
L-4148-K, San Antonio Light Photograph Collection, MS 359 / UTSA Special Collections.

A few hours after the walkout, student leaders agreed to begin negotiations for a mutual settlement with school officials to end the boycott. Just prior to the meeting, walkout leader Mario Treviño led a small group of students toward the entrance of the school and said a prayer. In describing the significance of this courageous act, Gutiérrez suggests that Treviño's "performance made it seem that God himself was going up the steps with them [student leaders] to the negotiating session."[87] During the meeting, student leaders discussed their demands with Superintendent Billings, Principal Lair, and Assistant Principal Mata, but with no success. Frustrated with the negotiations, Lara finally told administrators that Chicano students would continue their protest and return to school only to retrieve their books. Later in the evening, protesters and their parents met publicly at Salón Campestre, a local dance hall, where student leaders discussed their strategy to prolong the protest.[88] As a result of their series of informal meetings with students, parents formed a local grassroots political organization known as Ciudadanos Unidos (United Citizens). They formed this group to help the students plan their strategy during the first week of the school boycott.[89] This organization was instrumental in helping Mexican American adult community members participate in local elections.

Figure 14. Students posed around high school sign during boycott, Crystal City, Texas, 1969. L-4148-B, San Antonio Light Photograph Collection, MS 359 / UTSA Special Collections.

During the next four days, Chicano students continued to protest, increasing their numbers and pressuring school officials to meet their demands. The protest spread from the high school to the junior high and elementary schools. On the second day of the protest, approximately 500 students missed classes, including junior high school students.[90] By the third day an estimated 416 were absent out of a total enrollment of 673 at the high school.[91] To prevent more students from joining the protest, the school board publicized its policy on student demonstrations: "Students missing classes to participate in the demonstration will receive unexcused absences and two points off their grades for each day's absence."[92] While continuing their picket protest, students reported acts of intimidation against them by observers, including verbal threats, obscene gestures, spitting, and cars purposely being driven close to the street curb to frighten them.[93] Unable to reach a settlement to end the school boycott, the school board contacted the Texas Education Agency (TEA) for assistance.

On the second day of the walkout, TEA officials Gilbert Conoley and Juan Ibarra arrived in Crystal City to investigate the situation. During their brief stay in town (December 10–12), they interviewed both administrators and student leaders. Investigative findings revealed that superintendent John Billings viewed the students' protest as peaceful and nondisruptive toward the operation of the school system.[94] Upon completing their investigation, Conoley and Ibarra recommended to the board that the high school close early for the Christmas holidays because tension was "building up by the hour."[95] Conoley argued, "Our sole interest is getting the children back in school.... When the children aren't in school we've got real problems."[96] Despite Conoley and Ibarra's recommendation, school officials took their own course of action by intending to negotiate a settlement to the school boycott with parents rather than students. They also mandated that students return to classes the following Monday. The administrators' decision troubled students since they, not their parents, drafted the demands and attended the school. Moreover, students feared that the board would not negotiate fairly with their parents because their parents lacked knowledge of the school system and feared economic reprisal or the loss of their jobs.[97] Not surprisingly, the parents sided with their children and refused the board's offer.

In a further attempt to resume negotiations, a committee of churchmen formed to offer assistance in mediating the dispute. Clergymen from Catholic, Methodist, and Baptist churches met in separate sessions with students and school board members to find common ground for compromise. One clergyman who attempted to serve as mediator recalled the stigma associated with holding discussions with students: "One of my church members saw me talking with the student demonstrators the first day of the walkout in the morning. She reported to others in the community that I had taken the part of the students, when in fact I was asking student leaders what was going on."[98] Despite good intentions, the churchmen's committee failed to bring about a resolution. The inability to form a consensus and resentment by school officials prevented the group from achieving its purpose.[99] Another factor that hindered unity pertained to the ethnic makeup of each clergyman's congregation. Most church congregations in Crystal City were either predominantly Mexican American or Anglo.[100] Thus, differences of opinion and approaches among church congregations regarding how to end the school boycott likely influenced certain clergymen's strategies for aiding students and school officials.

Utilizing a more sophisticated and drawn-out strategy, on December 13, Chicano students decided to extend their protest outside the school. They called for a consumer boycott throughout the city by targeting Speers Mini-Max, an Anglo-owned grocery store that had a predominantly Mexican American clientele. Coincidently, store owner J. L. Speers immediately fired two local students employed at the store for participating in the walkout two days earlier.[101] Gutiérrez noted that Chicano students' reaction to the arrests was in keeping with the spirit of the motto of the Three Musketeers and LULAC: "All for one and one for all."[102] At the end of a protest march on December 12, student Cleofas Tamez

194 ∼ CHAPTER 6

alleged that the sheriff's officers arrested and later harassed him on his way to a rally shortly after the walkout began.[103] The firing of two students and Tamez's incident of coercive intimidation by the police further increased anger toward the Anglo community. Gutiérrez describes the effectiveness of the protest against the Speers Mini-Max grocery store: "The owner [of the Mini-Max] usually sold some three hundred pounds of ground beef per weekend. Within a few days, it was down to ten pounds."[104] Thus, the store boycott exerted economic pressure on the Anglo establishment and forced school officials to reconsider negotiations with students.

Protest activity momentarily ceased on Sunday, December 14. The next day, Chicano students organized a rally at a park just south of Crystal City. A spokesperson for the student protesters estimated that at least a thousand people attended the rally, preceded by a march through downtown.[105] The march began with five hundred people and then swelled to approximately one thousand when the rally began. A host of speakers greeted the marchers when they reached the park. Speakers included Bexar county commissioner Albert Peña of San Antonio, state chair of PASSO; Gutiérrez, leader of MAYO; and Rev. Henry Casso, a Mexican American Catholic priest from San Antonio.[106] This rally galvanized greater support for the local student movement from those residing outside Crystal City.

The walkout continued to drastically reduce attendance throughout the school system in Crystal City on Monday, December 15. Approximately 400 students missed classes at all local elementary schools on this day.[107] This action resulted after an estimated 300 parents decided to purposely keep their children out of school in support of the Chicano high school students' demands.[108] According to Crystal City School District absentee records, 1,026 out of 2,201 students did not attend school from December 17 to 18.[109] On the last day of the fall semester, over 1,700 out of 2,850 students missed classes.[110] Thus, Chicano students successfully used Gutierrez's "crescendo" strategy to gradually keep increasing the number of students out of school.

During the last two days of the semester, TEA officials Gilbert Conoley and Juan Ibarra revisited Crystal City to inquire about recent developments in the school dispute. When they met with superintendent John Billings, Conoley and Ibarra learned that school officials had failed to contact parents and therefore were "still in the dark" regarding how to arrange a meeting with them,[111] which was a problem because the school board insisted on negotiating with parents only. When they learned that Chicano students refused to allow only parent negotiation with the school board, school officials reconsidered and allowed both students and parents to meet with them. However, Treviño indicated that he was unable to arrange a meeting convenient for both parties to resume negotiations. Community member Frank Benavides and school board member Eddie Treviño served as liaisons for school officials and Chicano students.[112] Meanwhile, a team of investigators from the US Department of Health, Education, and Welfare traveled to Crystal City to determine whether there was segregation in the local public school system.

At the beginning of the second week of the school boycott, Gutiérrez announced an impending trip by three students to Washington, DC, to meet with government officials. US senators Ralph Yarborough (Democrat), John Tower (Republican), and George McGovern (Democrat) expressed an interest in meeting with the students.[113] Those who attended a December 15 student protest rally chose Severita Lara, Diana Serna, and Mario Treviño. Senator Yarborough's office and supporters in Crystal City partially paid the trip's expenses while the students themselves raised money.[114] Gutiérrez arranged for the students' arrival and pickup, as well as lodging with a Yarborough staff member.[115] The students' trip to Washington was the talk of the town. The students said that they "made Washington listen to us."[116]

During their two-day visit in Washington, the student leaders met with various federal officials including Senators Yarborough and Edward Kennedy, and Chris Roggerson, an official in the Department of Health, Education, and Welfare (HEW).[117] The student leaders urged the government to withhold federal aid from their school system.[118] Roggerson promised an investigation into the school district's possible violation of Title VI of the Civil Rights Act of 1964, which allowed HEW to cut funds from segregated school systems.[119] Before the students returned home, an HEW investigative team arrived in Crystal City to meet with community members and administrators. On the evening of December 19, a large crowd greeted and praised the returning students, crediting them for publicizing the school protest to the entire nation. Gutiérrez summarized his perspective on the attention Crystal City received during the students' trip to Washington: "The whole world knew what was happening in Crystal City, Texas. The town was on the map."[120] Crystal City suddenly became the most well-known site of the Chicano Movement in Texas, despite its small population and its remote location in rural southwest Texas. Crystal City became the focal point of national attention, further publicizing the students' plight.

Over the Christmas holidays, Chicano students who boycotted classes had the opportunity to participate in a "teach-in" to make up missed schoolwork. Josué M. González, director of the Texans for the Educational Advancement of Mexican Americans (TEAM), announced that his organization had offered to provide class instruction for the boycotting students. Around fifty members of TEAM, who were high school and college educators from San Antonio, Austin, San Angelo, and Del Rio, taught courses to all Crystal City students who were boycotting their school system. College students from San Antonio and throughout South Texas served as volunteer teachers as well. Parents of the protesting

196 ~ CHAPTER 6

students requested the assistance of TEAM. These volunteers held classes at private homes, city parks, Sacred Heart Catholic Church, the Mexican Chamber of Commerce building, Salón Campestre, and Hidalgo Hall.[121] Commenting about the mediocre conditions of these places, González expressed optimism: "Sometimes the conditions aren't the best, but we're making it all right. . . . But they [students] want to learn. That's what they're here for, and we'll make it all right."[122] Members of TEAM, both Mexican American and Anglo, taught during the morning and early afternoon hours for two weeks.

Some teachers chose to stay temporarily in Crystal City while others traveled to and from their hometowns. Teacher Helen Bernal commented about the deficiency in reading comprehension of numerous students: "It's pathetic what they don't know. It's clear they've had a shortcoming in class, that they do not understand what they are reading, even those on the sixth-grade level. I believe the quality of education they are getting is the issue. Working with Mexican American kids requires knowledge of their values system, their needs, their problems."[123] Bernal's statement clearly indicates that many Mexican American students lagged behind in meeting the educational standards for their grade level. Furthermore, she attributes students' poor academic performance to their school system's failure to consider their linguistic and cultural differences. Such an issue was one main reason why Chicano students boycotted classes, even though the conflict may have arisen from the cheerleader selection controversy. However, volunteer teachers provided walkout participants with valuable instruction that enabled them to remain on par with their studies and avoid falling behind.[124]

Additional pressure to resolve the school dispute occurred shortly after TEAM members began teaching classes, when a two-person mediating team of the Community Relations Service of the US Department of Justice arrived in Crystal City.[125] According to historian John Shockley, Justice Department officials Bob Greenwald and Tom Mata worked with the school, Chicano students, and local community members to draft a final resolution. However, he also indicated that Greenwald and Mata came close to losing their "mediator" status by favoring the students' demands and allegedly castigating or pressuring the school board to work out an agreement with the students.[126] During the last two weeks of December 1969, the Chicano community held rallies, meetings, and solidarity marches as part of the local student movement. Students did not have classes on New Year's Day 1970.

Negotiations for a settlement to end the school boycott resumed in early January 1970. The school board, US Department of Justice mediators, and a negotiating committee comprising five parents and five students met in three lengthy sessions to decide on a resolution in the first few days of January. These students achieved unprecedented success in the Chicano student movement during those negotiations. Nearly all eighteen student demands were approved by the school board.[127] School officials agreed to make the following concessions: "No disciplinary procedures were taken against the striking students and they did not receive unexcused absences resulting in grade penalties. The board agreed to establish bilingual and bicultural programs in the school system, agreed to implement new testing methods for pre-school children, and allowed the student body to elect the cheerleaders and school favorites. Institute a review of dress codes and the censoring of the student newspaper. The board consented to the establishment of an assembly period on September 16, Mexican Independence Day."[128] After this historic settlement was reached, the protest ended on January 6, 1970, when students agreed to return to class. The school board also allowed the walkout participants to make up missed exams and to retain their course grades prior to December 9.[129]

Although the agreement heavily favored Chicano students, walkout leader Mario Treviño expressed mixed emotions. He remarked: "We [students] got what we wanted and we are satisfied with the outcome, but we're just hoping that the school board will keep its word."[130] Students and their parents concluded negotiations with the school board after three long meetings to approve the five-page list of agreements supported by over 1,500 residents.[131] The end of the Crystal City school walkout marked the beginning of significant institutional and political change in this small, obscure town, a change that involved the transfer of political power within the school system from Anglos to Chicanos.

The Crystal City School Protest's Long-Term Impact

Profound changes occurred in the Crystal City school system after the local walkout. Jesse Gámez, a young San Antonio lawyer, native of Crystal City, and friend of José Angel Gutiérrez, was hired as the school district attorney. The ethnic makeup of the faculty and administration changed substantially. Mexican Americans made up 40 percent of the faculty, the highest proportion in the school district's history.[132] Out of sixty-eight new teachers and administrators hired during the 1970–71 school year, forty-one were Mexican American.[133] Former Crystal City teacher's aide Rebecca Pérez remarked about the influx of newly hired Mexican American teachers after the local walkout: "Some of the teachers that came in were a lot different. They were younger teachers and they treated the kids [students] a lot better. And we got quite a few Mexican Americans from outside [Crystal City]."[134] According to one former Crystal City schoolteacher, most of the Anglo principals and faculty resigned or left the school district within months after the walkout.[135] The number of Mexican American teacher's aides and cafeteria workers increased considerably, from fifteen to eighty-five.[136]

198 ∼ CHAPTER 6

Mexican Americans had greater opportunity for employment in the local school system after the walkout.

The Crystal City school administration also changed. School superintendent John Billings, blamed by the local Anglo community for conceding to the walkout participants' demands, resigned in the spring of 1970. Gutiérrez and running mates Mike Pérez and Arturo González succeeded in winning positions on the local school board, capturing approximately 55 percent of the vote.[137] Gutiérrez served as the president. Thus, changes in the schools followed the election of La Raza Unida leadership that favored Chicano political ideology. This leadership implemented bilingual education from kindergarten to the third grade, and a Mexican American history course. The new school administration also spent an estimated $350 to acquire Mexican American literature.[138]

The new Chicano-dominated school system received a significant monetary boost from federal funding, which increased from $417,000 in the 1969–70 school year to $720,000 the following year.[139] The early student demands of the Crystal City walkout were met when school officials changed the procedures for selecting cheerleaders in the early 1970s. Five of the six cheerleaders elected were Mexican American, with Diana Palacios as head cheerleader.[140] This issue initially engendered solidarity among local Chicano student activists and paved the way for substantial long-term improvement in the schools.

Changes in educational activities took place outside the schools as well. A new fight song, "Jalisco," was added to the school band repertoire and was played during football games. Other actions that infuriated some Anglo community members included the band spelling the word "RAZA" on the football field at halftime, and band director Elpidio Lizcano making announcements in both English and Spanish.[141] White residents who were opposed "got up and booed [during the football games]" and "were very, very ugly" about such alterations to halftime activities.[142] Former Crystal City school superintendent Angel Noe González further asserts that many local Anglos behaved in this manner because they regarded Spanish as a "dirty language."[143] However, supporters of La Raza Unida leadership expressed a strong preference for speaking Spanish in private group gatherings, school board meetings, and the schools. Former schoolteacher Joyce Langenegger commented that freely conversing in Spanish "seemed to be a very real part of Crystal City."[144] No known historical documents substantiate whether local Anglo residents publicly criticized Mexican Americans for speaking Spanish at other school-related activities besides football games.

The Crystal City school system witnessed another significant change within months after the walkout. Over two hundred Mexican American student dropouts reportedly returned to school voluntarily after Mexican American candidates, sponsored by the newly formed La Raza Unida, won school board and administrative positions.[145] In the aftermath of the school board elections, numerous Anglo students transferred to neighboring school districts (white flight) such as Uvalde or Carrizo Springs. In a letter to FBI director J. Edgar Hoover, one anonymous community member voiced his or her distrust of the new school administration under the direction of La Raza Unida. The writer commented: "The radical leadership of the school board has instituted a plan of education that is contrary to the American way of life. The indiscriminate discharge of qualified teachers and replacing them with persons of questionable character is deplored by parents. While many people are pleased with this change, it is plain to see that the heart of our community, its schools, are being destroyed."[146] Consequently, the activities of the Raza Unida–dominated school administration became a subject of FBI investigation. Various Anglo educators in Crystal City voiced their discontent with the new school administration, alleging reverse discrimination. These included R. C. Tate, Ann Lander, Pamela Seymour, John Briggs and his wife, and Judy Perkins. They claimed that their termination of employment with the Crystal City school system violated their civil rights and involved discriminatory treatment against Anglos, according to FBI documents.[147] However, Chicano school officials, including Gutiérrez and Angel Noe González, the main targets of the FBI investigation, did not face indictment.

R. C. Tate, Crystal City school superintendent during the 1950s, recalled an important change in the school system in the early 1970s. He mentioned that six principals, two assistant principals, and two counselors resigned from the school district.[148] He further claimed that the Raza Unida school administration "fired, retired, or just ran off" more than forty Anglo teachers who did not agree to work under its policies.[149] White administrators and teachers most likely left the school district because they found it difficult to adapt to the different educational philosophy and school structure under a Chicano school administration. Nevertheless, information provided by FBI files and R. C. Tate suggests how the Chicano-controlled administration restructured the local school system.

The actions of the administration tended to reflect its radical political ideology, focusing on Chicano representation from the highest to lowest employment position, bilingual and bicultural education, and teaching in the Spanish language. In addition, changes occurred at various levels of school life. Former Crystal City teacher's aide Rebecca Pérez noted that numerous Mexican American schoolchildren did not receive lunch at school prior to the arrival of the Raza Unida–dominated school administration. She further attested that the new administration implemented a free-lunch program for Mexican American students from low-income homes.[150] Overall, Chicano control of the schools meant mobilizing resources and providing increased funding, programming, and staffing to better meet the educational needs of ethnic Mexican students.

One important book by scholar Armando Trujillo, *Chicano Empowerment and Bilingual Education: Movimiento Politics in Crystal City, Texas* (1998), indicates that the Crystal City walkout and local teachers' years of schooling significantly influenced their teaching methodology. He underscores how postwalkout educators espoused a different attitude from that of prewalkout educators.[151] Trujillo highlights that educational restructuring under the Raza Unida school officials was different from what it had been under the Anglo system. Prewalkout teachers had been successful students under the Anglo administration and received their college degrees before the walkout. Postwalkout teachers "felt a sense of empowerment and vindication from a discriminatory system."[152] The student movement influenced their approaches to teaching, with an emphasis on bilingual education, Mexican cultural identity, and ethnic pride in being Chicano. Teachers of the postwalkout era of the early 1970s further recalled a change in attitude about schooling reflected in the increasing number of young Chicanos who wanted to further their education by earning college degrees.

According to Trujillo, the Raza Unida Party (RUP), a grassroots Chicano-based political party that was a product of 1960s Chicano student militancy advocating for equitable schooling, initiated a political campaign to elect Chicano candidates to the Crystal City school board, city council, and county-level offices. His main argument is that La Raza Unida endorsed the election of Chicanos to public office to gain political autonomy for the local school system, which led to the adoption of bilingual and bicultural educational programs in the school district. Trujillo concludes: "As part of the strategy for instituting schooling reforms, Chicanos used the 1968 federal legislation on bilingual education to implement a comprehensive kindergarten through twelfth grade maintenance bilingual/bicultural education program as an integral part of their plan for Chicano self-determination and cultural revitalization."[153] Thus, local Chicano activists' Movimiento in Crystal City promoted bilingual and bicultural education as an expression of Chicano militant philosophy and was an example of a historical counterforce that lasted until the early 1980s.

Trujillo examines the development of bilingual education in Crystal City by analyzing the emergence of Chicano militant ideology unique to those who lived in Crystal City. Regarded as a "die-hard Chicano stronghold cultivating radical ethnic consciousness through schooling," the Crystal City school system faced challenges by Chicano activists, whose key issue was educational reform.[154] Discontent with the Crystal City school system led to Chicano grassroots activism among students. Local Chicano activists achieved political autonomy through successful campaigning and elections of Raza Unida candidates to the school board and city council, and they advocated for the inauguration of bilingual and bicultural education in Crystal City schools. Thus, Trujillo illustrates the workings of ethnic mobilization and Chicano political activism as a means to ensure bilingual education, as well.

Like most other Chicano scholars, Trujillo argues that differences in political identity and ideology between the younger and older generations of the Mexican American community during the Chicano Movement resulted in factionalism and disharmony between them. Thus, they prevented themselves from extending grassroots political activism involving educational reform on a larger scale at both the state and national levels. Trujillo astutely points out that implementing bilingual education meant much more than linguistic development; it was also related to community empowerment. It further correlated with the level of consciousness raising in the development of community-wide Chicano political activism.

One article that attributes the rise of Chicano activism after 1960 to the maintenance of migrant social networks between Texas and Wisconsin is Marc Simon Rodríguez's "A Movement Made of 'Young Mexican Americans Seeking Change': Critical Citizenship, Migration, and the Chicano Movement in Texas and Wisconsin, 1960–1975." This revisionist account indicates that Chicano Movement activism was not restricted to one location, as suggested by traditional one-place-bound community studies that focus on the development of the movement. Thus, Rodríguez maintains, "by linking the activism of Crystal City to Wisconsin's migrant community, the Chicano Movement of the period emerged as part of a unified interstate youth-directed social movement."[155] Moreover, the article examines youth activism in Crystal City pertaining to local politics and civil rights advocacy.

The second part of the article includes insights concerning the second Crystal City "revolt" that occurred during the local walkout of 1969. This further highlights the historical information regarding the protest and reviews Chicano student issues articulated before and during the walkout. Rodríguez reveals that migrant labor networks existed among local activists who participated in the protest such as walkout leader Severita Lara, who spent the summer of 1969 visiting family members in California, where she first learned about the 1968 East Los Angeles walkouts. Thus, Lara and another Crystal City native (name unknown) were inspired by this event and formulated a plan of action to mobilize Chicano students at their school later in the year.[156] Therefore, Rodríguez's work offers a revisionist history and analysis of the Crystal City walkout.

Another noticeable change occurred in the early 1970s when the Chicano school leaders arranged for the painting of a Mexican mural at Zapata Elementary School to give symbolic representation to their political takeover and the Chicano Movement. However, certain images were painted over by the late 1970s shortly after the city elected new school leaders.[157] This symbolic act suggested how political ideology among Mexican Americans in Crystal City had deviated from the radicalism of the late 1960s. After the early 1970s, the decline of the Chicano student movement in South Texas became apparent. Many of the same student activists from throughout the region left their schools to engage in electoral politics under the Raza Unida Party. Consequently, student militancy in the region gave birth to ethnic Mexican third-party politics that transformed the Texas political arena with the election of numerous Mexican American politicians and judges. Crystal City emerged as an important stronghold of Chicano Movement insurgency that provided a blueprint for achieving educational reform and political empowerment that was unique for its time.

Summary and Conclusion

The Crystal City school boycott became one of the most important yet contentious student protests of the Chicano Movement. The year 1963 marked the local Mexican American community's first major political victory over Anglo government rule with the election of los cinco candidatos. However, in 1965, a coalition of Anglo and middle-class Mexican Americans won the city council elections, thus ousting los cinco candidatos. Nevertheless, the 1963 transition in city politics later served as a model for Chicano students to launch their own campaign for political control of the local public schools. Crystal City's so-called Second Revolt referred to the emergence of Chicano student insurgency and marked a time of political change as well.

During the spring of 1969, Chicano students at Crystal City High School began organizing themselves to combat unequal treatment in the public school system. They sought to change a discriminatory practice regarding the method of selecting cheerleaders at the high school. Expressing this grievance mobilized Chicano students to formulate a broader and more comprehensive list of demands outlining educational reform.

After the beginning of the Crystal City school walkout, José Angel Gutiérrez and MAYO activists employed an important protest strategy known as the "crescendo effect," which had not been used in previous student protests in South Texas. This strategy greatly enhanced the momentum of the local student movement by drastically reducing the average daily attendance as a means to pressure school officials to consider protesters' demands. While the boycott spread from the high school to the junior high and elementary schools, the local walkout gained outside attention and state officials were brought in to investigate the situation. Others in the local community such as clergy from different church denominations attempted to assist students and school board members to find common ground for compromise. But the students availed themselves of a strategy that would exert increased pressure on the school board: they conducted an economic boycott throughout the city. The boycott of an Anglo store marked the first time that student activists extended their protest outside the school. By boycotting the store, Chicano student activists and their supporters pressured the local Anglo community into considering the Chicano students' demands.

In addition, the Crystal City school boycott attracted national attention when protest leaders Severita Lara, Diana Serna, and Mario Treviño traveled to Washington, DC. Their trip helped them seek the sympathy and support of federal officials such as Senators Yarborough and Edward Kennedy, and Chris Roggerson, an official in the Department of Health, Education, and Welfare. Government officials from the Justice Department became aware of the educational needs of Mexican Americans in South Texas and worked with the school system, Chicano students, and local community members to draft a final resolution to the school dispute. As a result of their negotiations, the school board approved nearly all eighteen student demands.

In the years after the walkout, the makeup of the school board, faculty, and administration changed completely. Former walkout participant Diana Palacios remembered: "It was very exciting because we had new teachers. We had Mexican American teachers. We had counselors who were encouraging us to go to universities. . . . People here [at Crystal City High School] who understand us and who encourage us. People who think we really have a brain."[158] Mexican Americans suddenly gained political power in the school system and implemented their own public school reform plan that favored Chicano movement activists. The student movement in Crystal City fostered community-wide political activism, leading to structural and administrative changes in city government. On January 10, 1970, Severita Lara and those active in Ciudadanos Unidos began discussing the expansion of their political organizing work throughout Zavala County.[159] Mexican American political dominance began in one locale. Thus, the local student movement ultimately culminated in the rise of the Raza Unida Party in Texas by the early 1970s.

7

Conclusion

The push for educational reform in Texas began during the Mexican American Civil Rights Movement of the 1930s–1950s. At this time, organizations such as LULAC and the American GI Forum, headed by middle-class Mexican American activists, promoted desegregation and improved educational facilities for ethnic Mexican students but focused on the idea that they were Americans and must assimilate. The Chicano Movement of the 1960s rejected the Mexican American Generation's focus on assimilation and its political brand of gradualism, instead focusing considerable attention on influencing the formation of education policies directly applicable to the Mexican American experience as one of its key goals. Yet this movement emerged from a foundation of earlier struggles as students began to play a more central role in the Chicano fight for justice. The Chicano Movement became part of a national movement that allowed young Mexican American activists to voice their concerns about the US public school system.

Chicano students came of age during the African American Civil Rights Movement, Third World struggles, women's liberation movement, Chicano and antiwar movements, and other mass protests for equal rights in the 1960s. The leaders and historic protests of these movements that inspired such students include César Chávez's farmworkers' strike and Martin Luther King Jr.'s campaign for nonviolent civil disobedience protests to combat racial segregation in cities. These leaders and movements emboldened Chicano students across the region to contest discriminatory practices and institutional deficiencies within their school systems. Throughout US history, activists have conducted "walkouts" in places they were not allowed to sit, whether at racially segregated lunch counters or in the offices of politicians. These actions deliberately broke the rules and thus caused disruptions. In the most successful cases, the disruptions put pressure on the people who claimed to control those spaces. But since the main requirement for students is that they sit in their classrooms, the most logical (and popular) method of protest has been to do the exact opposite, to refuse to cooperate and walk out of school. Thus, actions by Chicano students reflected the societal changes and political climate of the late 1960s and early 1970s. These students further challenged the educational system by demanding social justice, political access, and the same educational opportunities as Anglo-American students.

Throughout their movement, students adopted a new ethnic identity of "Chicano," which often included revolutionary goals and militant organizational strategies. Chicano cultural nationalism developed in response to adverse conditions including the psychological, emotional, and political barriers supported by white supremacy and segregation while attempting to promote political unity transcending regional, class, and ideological boundaries at the height of this movement.[1] Student protesters participated in nonviolent, peaceful demonstrations to press their grievances against the school system. They demanded that school administrators and trustees, who were mostly Anglo, be more attentive to their academic needs and accommodate accordingly. Charismatic Chicano Movement leaders like José Angel Gutiérrez and student movement groups such as MAYO helped engender a political/militant consciousness among Chicano students, but they lacked a feminist consciousness. They also taught students direct-action tactics, strategies, and organizing methods that enhanced their effectiveness, thus offering the necessary resource mobilization during this student-led movement. This activist training further reveals how much thought and planning went into these protests. They did not "just happen" but were planned to have maximum effect.

This book has analyzed the congruence and divergence of four important Chicano school walkouts in South Texas. It has reconstructed the major events of each protest and revealed the nature of Chicano student educational experiences in each school, describing the student protesters' roles, motives, and strategies. It has also explored how school officials viewed the educational deficiencies faced by Chicano students and examined the interactions between school administrators, students, and parents, revealing Movimiento leaders and the reactions of local, state, and federal leaders to the protests.

Chicano student activism emerged as a 1960s-type mass movement in the United States. This book does not presume to represent the experience of the entire Chicano student movement in the United States but rather focuses on four key sites in rural South Texas. Chicano students' demand for public school reform and ethnic Mexican cultural awareness brought forth a greater awareness of educational issues as an important element of political and cultural struggle within the Chicano Movement. In the tumultuous environment of the 1960s, Chicano students heard the rhetoric of social protest and adopted it in order to improve school conditions. Chicano student insurgency culminated in one of the most important movements for social and political change of the era, ultimately leading to the creation of one of the most significant Mexican American political parties of the twentieth century, La Raza Unida.

This book identifies the inequities and discontent that motivated both Chicanos and Chicanas in San Antonio's West Side, Edcouch-Elsa, Kingsville, and Crystal City to protest and formulate their own grievances against their school system. Their most common demands included access to college preparatory courses at their schools, academic advising informing them of the application process for college, the adoption of textbooks or curricula focusing on the contributions of people of Mexican origin, the hiring of more Mexican American faculty and administrators, allowing students to speak Spanish freely on school grounds, and granting students the opportunity to nominate and vote for their own class representatives on the student council. Students also sought political power in determining the method of selecting representatives in extracurricular activities such as cheerleading, a major factor leading to one of the most famous student protests in US civil rights history, the Crystal City walkout of 1969. The four case studies further reveal how students became influenced, organized, and encouraged to walk out. Thus, ethnic Mexican student activism developed into a grassroots social movement across rural communities in South Texas.

The San Antonio and Kingsville cases demonstrate that Chicano empowerment evolved over the years. However, Chicanos gained considerable political control of the public schools in the years immediately following the walkouts, especially in Edcouch-Elsa and Crystal City. The student movement in the region was not an isolated outburst of an irrational form of insurgency, but rather part of an ongoing historical process of social and political change. Student protesters gained a renewed sense of empowerment and made known their desire for better educational opportunities through their commitment to unity, ethnic pride, and nonviolent protest. They also learned how power is attained within the school system and sought to gain inclusion within it as well. Moreover, movement activists negotiated collectively yet competed for control in making the decisions that impacted educational policy.

Chicano students also faced a variety of structural challenges in their schools. School board members, superintendents, principals, counselors, and teachers made all the decisions that shaped these students' educational experiences and future pathways as adults. Such decisions included allocating funding or setting local school budgets, designating school boundaries or determining who students' classmates would be, adopting school textbooks, and establishing school rules and standards for extracurricular activities. Some of these decisions were made by teachers, others by teachers' supervisors: principals, superintendents, and other administrators. Still other policies were determined by federal and state government officials. District school boards and city councils typically set local policies, while state-level governments decided on legislative budgets and common curricula. Federal officials, meanwhile, set national education policies (Congress), ruled on the constitutionality of laws (the US Supreme Court), and enforced those decisions (the president). High schoolers could not vote for any of these officials, however, and as this book has demonstrated, Chicano students sought to make their collective voices heard and influence school policies in other ways.

High school students used whatever means were available to try to shape their worlds by confronting and challenging people in power to reconsider the school system's decision-making process. In some cases, students opposed certain teachers and administrators. In other cases, students joined forces with both sympathetic parents and community members as they took on school officials. Sometimes, simply being organized during their protest was enough for students to promote their desire for change in their schools. Some policies existed not because anyone specifically opposed a change, but because no one had ever tried to make a change. For example, many schools adopted bilingual education and college preparatory courses when students said they wanted them. In other cases, however, students encountered substantial resistance and employed various means of protest.

"We Want Better Education!" has also revealed that the student movement was self-directed by community-based, school-issue politics. This movement significantly influenced the electoral process and hiring practices of public schools, beginning in the major areas of contestation in South Texas. Chicano students organized and participated in one of the most important social and political change movements in US history. Student movement participants developed strategies, asserted new political activist identities, and formed a student movement organization that mobilized and unified different activists. However, the movement declined when student participants ceased their activities or became focused on broader national concerns.[2] This book underscores the conditions and factors evident in the political process model, including expanding political opportunities, the rise of collective consciousness (cognitive liberation), and resource mobilization.

Expanding Political Opportunities

My work assesses the process by which student activists and their supporters sought political empowerment by using the electoral and hiring systems of their school districts to their advantage to carry out this reform. School boards and

208 ～ CHAPTER 7

their members, superintendents and central office administrators, and teachers strategically used their power to affect the outcomes of decision-making and protect their interests. They maintained their influence by controlling who was allowed to participate in decision-making, and what items or issues became part of the agenda. Because they did not act on or fully implement the demands of students and their supporters, policy making was skewed to benefit a few at the expense of the majority. Therefore, Chicanos explored their political opportunities to advance their interests, level their bargaining position, and negotiate on par with school officials. Negotiations between student protesters and school officials deteriorated when the two sides failed to reach a mutual resolution during the student movement, except for Crystal City.

Educational deficiencies and the lack of Mexican American participation in the school system's power structure motivated students to walk out, challenge their school system through collective action, and promote expanding political opportunities for Mexican Americans. Political opportunities resulting from the student movement included school board members favoring the interests of Chicanos, increased numbers of Mexican American administrators and faculty, and implementation of bilingual education and other culturally sensitive school curricula. The four cases in this book indicate that the student protests led to the increased hiring of Mexican American educators and administrators in South Texas, as the makeup of the school boards in the communities where the walkouts occurred changed dramatically. Mexican Americans occupied the majority of school board positions in the years immediately following the protests and remain the majority to this day.

The 1968 Edcouch-Elsa school case filed by protest leaders Javier Ramírez, Raúl Arispe, Mirtala Villareal, José Luis Chávez, and Artemio Salinas provided the legal resolution that ended the local walkout. This case challenged the validity of the school board's policies and punishment, impacting the protesters by suing the Edcouch-Elsa School District in US federal district court. The plaintiffs and defendants reached a landmark court settlement when Chicano student protesters agreed to end their protest once the Edcouch-Elsa School District readmitted them to classes in January 1969. This legal victory for Chicano students represented the mitigation of student protest activism in Deep South Texas. Although this ruling took place outside the school, it had legal ramifications in upholding students' right to free speech and peaceful assembly on school grounds.

Chicano students and their supporters in Crystal City took advantage of expanding political opportunities within their school system as well. Most significantly, those of Mexican ancestry who favored Chicano political ideology formed the Raza Unida leadership and gained control of the school board and administration shortly after the walkout. Candidates endorsed by the Raza Unida leadership, including José Angel Gutiérrez, later won school board positions in local elections. This leadership implemented bilingual education from kindergarten to third grade and included Mexican American history curricula. The new school administration also spent an estimated $350 to acquire more Mexican American literature. These opportunities provided material conditions for organized change that subsequently reduced the need for protest.

Political opportunities were not as evident immediately after the protests in the San Antonio case. Chicano students in that case agreed to cease their protest activities only after local school officials agreed to meet with the protesters to hear and consider their demands. The student movement in San Antonio's West Side ended when school authorities supposedly granted certain demands such as the upgrading of school facilities and the hiring of qualified teachers. However, these changes were not immediate and took years to come to fruition. Although unsuccessful, the 1971 *Rodriguez v. San Antonio ISD* case represented another political opportunity for Chicano students and their parents. This landmark case, ultimately decided by the Supreme Court after a federal district court ruled in favor of the plaintiffs, attempted to implement reform within the Texas school finance system. By suing the school system and ultimately availing themselves of Supreme Court justice, the plaintiffs sought to alleviate the financial inequities impacting Mexican American students in economically poor school districts.

No significant political gains were made in the Kingsville case. Local school authorities agreed to meet with Chicano students and their supporters a few days after the walkout began, and administrators agreed to take the students' demands under advisement but made no effort to offer an agreeable solution. By the end of the 1968–69 academic year, negotiations between student protesters and school officials resumed but eventually deteriorated when the two sides failed to reach a mutual resolution. As mentioned before, increasing numbers of Mexican American school board members, administrators, and teachers enabled the gradual restructuring of the school system in the years after the walkout. Nevertheless, Chicano students throughout South Texas could not have initiated their movement without the sufficient mobilization of resources.

Resource Mobilization

Chicano students mobilized a variety of resources during their movement. Acquiring sufficient resources was essential to initiating and sustaining the student movement. Chicano rights organizations such as MAYO and MALDEF were in their early stages of development yet provided Chicano students with organizational resources (both material and nonmaterial) to support movement goals. Student protesters utilized resources such as the friendships formed between their parents and local movement supporters, community fundraising, the support of college students, and the assistance of community-based groups.

Chicano movement leader José Angel Gutiérrez and MAYO played an important role by assisting and advising Chicano high school students in conducting peaceful, nonviolent protests. The activism of MAYO throughout South Texas stimulated a politically radical consciousness among such students and offered them advice in drafting their list of demands. MAYO also taught students protest strategies and tactics including the economic boycott, and organizing methods that would publicize the purpose of their protest. The formation and activism of numerous MAYO chapters throughout the region represented an important student movement resource and provided a forum to discuss educational issues important to ethnic Mexican students. Many MAYO members were college students or community activists who gave of themselves to meet and advise Chicano high school students during the movement. These young adult activists volunteered to assist because many of them came from similar conditions and had confronted the same institutional deficiencies when they attended high school in South Texas.

According to movement historian Armando Navarro, MAYO gained its purpose by focusing on using "the boycott to flex [the organization's] developing mobilization muscle."[3] MAYO cofounder José Angel Gutiérrez asserts that this group often directed students and their parents into action and required the backing of parents and the formation of support networks before school walkouts could occur.[4] As this book has suggested, MAYO helped establish social support networks among student activists and their supporters that fostered mutual cooperation and solidarity. Moreover, MAYO members donated or purchased resources themselves, such as materials for protest signs, and small food and beverage items for other student activists.

As indicated in this book, the social and political climate engendered by the African American, Chicano, and antiwar movements influenced Chicano students to seek opportunities for change. Mexican Americans possess a rich organizational heritage dating back to the early twentieth century. Moreover, the prior context of protest in South Texas before the 1960s and during these movements served to stimulate Chicano student insurgency. Pre-1960s challenges to inequity were a launching pad for El Movimiento. Chicano activists modified and utilized the strategies of Mexican American Generation activists to suit their needs, albeit in a more vociferous and aggressive manner. Such strategies included community-wide activism, filing occasional school lawsuits such as *Ramirez v. Edcouch-Elsa ISD* and *Rodriguez v. San Antonio ISD*, and drafting well-defined grievances to promote reform within the US educational system.

The Chicano Generation radicalized the Mexican American movement for civil rights and, "inspired by the racial pride of the Black Power movement . . . came to embrace a politics of cultural distinctiveness and to view themselves as members of a brown race."[5] Like other civil rights protesters, Chicano students opposed the status quo and power structure or "establishment" that had marginalized them. The successes of various movements convinced students of the effectiveness of nonviolent civil disobedience protests. Further, students also focused on the gains that African Americans had achieved by legal means. Landmark legislation reflected the progress effected by civil rights activists. Two significant laws that reflected these gains were the 1964 Civil Rights Act (banning racial discrimination in public establishments) and the Voting Rights Act of 1965 (providing federal supervision of voter registration and elections). The conditions and events of the 1960s strengthened Chicano activists' faith in the power of protest to initiate change and reform. Such conditions and events transmitted a sense of collective consciousness and ethnic pride among Chicano students.

Rise of Collective Consciousness

This book revealed the status of Mexican Americans as socially marginalized and economically poor, which led to a rise of their collective consciousness during the Chicano Movement. This movement promoted a new political consciousness, called for new leadership in the school system to influence decision-making, and enhanced Mexican Americans' legitimacy and voice. The rise of collective consciousness was derived mainly from Chicano students' experiences of discriminatory or unjust treatment in school, as suggested by all four case studies. This treatment included restrictions on speaking Spanish on school grounds; the lack of curricula that accurately reflected Mexican American history; the inability to enroll in college preparatory classes because of discouragement from their school counselor; and the lack of educational opportunities that were afforded to Anglo students only. Students argued that their school's lack of curricula focusing on Mexican Americans indicated educators' disregard of them. Tracking Mexican American students into low-level curricula served to reinforce the racial stereotypes of certain educators who viewed students of Mexican origin as intellectually inferior or incapable of completing college. Although most public high schools in South Texas were ethnically mixed institutions, most Chicano students were social outcasts from their Anglo classmates.[6] They were isolated because of differences in socioeconomic class, ethnic culture, and language preference. The personal recollections of former students indicated that they endured humiliation, criticism, and harsh punishment by certain educators for a variety of infractions. Chicano students felt disrespected and angered by the unequal treatment at their schools.

During each of the protests, school administrators and educators failed to seriously consider and immediately carry out Chicano students' demands for reform. Instead, administrators and educators were often evasive, uncooperative, and socially distant from Chicano students. School boards refused to consider and resolve the grievances of the students until well after the walkout in each case study. School administrators in the Edcouch-Elsa and Kingsville case studies called for the arrests of key student leaders and protesters in order to quell the protest. Additionally, most Anglo school officials did not understand the ethnic culture or language of students of Mexican origin, which hampered their ability to effectively compromise with students to prevent the protests.

Chicano students' experiences in and outside their schools influenced the formation of their collective consciousness. The Chicano student movement in Texas epitomized the acceptance of a new ethnic identity. The use of the term "Chicano" reflected a new sense of ethnic pride that rejected the dominance of Eurocentric views and emphasized a greater appreciation of ethnic Mexican cultural roots. Numerous ethnic Mexican students endured discriminatory and unequal treatment in their schools over generations. This treatment, and their dissatisfaction with certain school educators and other educational inadequacies, shaped the collective consciousness, attitude, and behavior of Chicano students throughout their social protest movement.

Legacy and Retrospective of the Chicano Student Movement

The Chicano student movement in South Texas underscores similar real-life struggles and adversities that ethnic-minority communities face in education today. Examining this history reveals how the past causes or shapes the present day, our lives, and so the future. Assessing this history is essential to understanding the importance of practicing good citizenship, achieving social justice, overcoming cultural misunderstandings, and learning from the mistakes of the past. This history reveals the educational inequities facing Chicano and other Latino students as well as their hopes and dreams to achieve educational success over time. Indeed, the study of this movement offers some important lessons concerning the years of struggle for equality, institutional reform, and self-determination.

By 1968, this movement had suddenly burst onto the national stage and emerged as one of the most significant social protest movements of the civil rights era in US history. Within the context of this upheaval, the Chicano Movement established a new and revolutionary orientation leading to the rise of young participants committed to the quest for better-quality education. Chicano students protested at their schools throughout South Texas in such notable places as San Antonio's West Side, Edcouch-Elsa, Kingsville, and Crystal City. Former movement activist Mario Compean underscores how Chicano students achieved social and political change in the region. He noted:

> The Movement's assault on the system was on three fronts: electoral politics, activist social protest, and litigation. The Chicano Student Movement was active in all three fronts, a strategy that partially accounts for its effectiveness and success. The young Chicano activists energized this broad alliance of people and leaders working for social and institutional change, and helped create great optimism and hope for meaningful, profound social transformation. It was the collective effort of this broad alliance that greatly shortened the life of the racial wall that had kept Chicanos in the tight grip of cultural, racial, and economic oppression that began with the annexation of northern Mexico (the American southwest) to the United States.[7]

Thus, Chicano students engaged in social protest activism to call attention to various educational inequalities at their schools. Many of these same student activists participated in electoral politics under the Raza Unida Party in the 1970s. The Chicano student movement in South Texas began to tear away the "racial wall" that Compean claimed had oppressed Chicanos in North America since the time Mexico lost the southwest territories after the Mexican-American War of 1846–48.

In 2006, the HBO channel released a motion picture highlighting the historic events of the East Los Angeles school walkouts of 1968. For younger generations of Mexican Americans, the movie offers an important awareness of ethnic Mexican student participation in the 1960s Chicano Civil Rights Movement. Unfortunately, many people, including Mexican Americans and other Latinos today, do not know or understand the significance of what the Chicano student movement sought to achieve. Present-day students might view a short video at school about the walkouts, but not much else is taught about the movement. Only a few who participated in the movement regularly discuss their experiences in public, while others have passed away. Another reason for the lack of community engagement among adolescents is that the social and political reality of contemporary society has changed since the 1960s, especially since 9/11. Whereas in the past, high school students would have been involved in political activities and addressed educational issues, today schools are no longer viewed as political arenas, and most believe it is no longer a time for such politicking, with the exception of the gun reform movement based at Marjory Stoneman Douglas High

School in Parkland, Florida. This latest political youth movement began shortly after the tragic school shooting that claimed seventeen lives in February 2018 and continues to harness the power of teenage anger to demand action.

"We Want Better Education!" contributes to a greater understanding of the legacy of the Chicano student movement in US history. Although the movement in South Texas did not immediately transform the educational system throughout the United States, it did change the lives of its participants. An entire new generation of Chicano/Latino professionals and scholars came out of the movement. Presently, numerous former student activists work as doctors, lawyers, school administrators, teachers, media journalists, and in other professions. A few of them include Edgar Lozano, owner of the Atlas Pallet Company in San Antonio; Homer D. García, professor of sociology at Texas Southern University; Severita Lara, former council member and former mayor of Crystal City, and former educator at Crystal City High School; Maricela Rodríguez Lozano, administrative secretary in the Edcouch-Elsa School District; the late Carlos Guerra, who was a news columnist for the *San Antonio Express-News* before his death in 2009; and José Angel Gutiérrez, former trustee and president of the Crystal City Independent School District (1970–73), former county judge of Zavala County (1974–81), and founder of a national third party, La Raza Unida. These former students' protest movement represented ethnic Mexican people's desire for equal opportunity in the US public school system that was unique for its time. Another notable achievement of the Chicano Movement was the launching of the Mexican American Legal Defense and Educational Fund, the first major group representing the political and legal interests of ethnic Mexican people across the United States. Not long after the resolution of the Crystal City school protest in 1970, the newly formed Raza Unida Party began to endorse candidates in various South Texas counties. The party often campaigned in areas with predominantly ethnic Mexican populations, including Hidalgo, Zavala, Dimmit, and La Salle Counties. It went on to inspire Mexican Americans to vote, use their voting rights to change things for themselves, and reshape Texas politics, and it led to the inclusion of Mexican Americans in the Democratic Party. This political activism extended beyond the schools and into electoral politics and catapulted the Chicano activists into national prominence well into the 1970s.

The Chicano student movement in South Texas was an integral part of broader 1960s political activity and educational reform. Thus, political and ethnic unity was intrinsic to the Chicano Movement in the region by building cultural awareness and exposing the inequities of the school system affecting Mexican American students. By participating in the Chicano Movement, the protesters sensitized others to their social and political barriers in the local community and in Texas and helped pave the way for future generations to gain academic acceptance in high school and college. Forming their own mass movement showed students that their education was not simply their individual responsibility; through collaboration and collective action, they sought to make their schools and communities accountable for improving educational opportunities for everyone regardless of race, color, gender, or national origin. Activists established a strong political legacy and a new political consciousness inherited from the struggles of the 1960s. Education has improved significantly for Mexican Americans, in large part because of the impact and ramifications of the movement, despite systemic forces associated with lingering school inequities. The Chicano student movement across South Texas was one of the most important facets of the larger Chicano Movement because of how students contributed their time, energy, and passion with the hope of improving their schools and enriching their lives.

In 2014, the Texas State Board of Education reached a historic vote (eleven to three) to allow school districts the option to add Mexican American studies as part of the curriculum at the high school level, and it approved the creation or adoption of instructional material for such classes.[8] This historic achievement is a testament to the efforts of so many former activists, politicians, civic leaders, educators, parents, and students who organized a statewide campaign to add such an important course at the time of the walkouts and school boycotts of the 1960s. Many view the Chicano Movement as an outgrowth of the Civil Rights Movement, yet the movement was heterogeneous and involved not only students but hundreds of activists from diverse populations and regions across the nation, both men and women who were active in leadership or supported the protests in their own unique ways. The larger Civil Rights Movement also inspired Chicano activists to unite behind one singular cause, thus changing how Anglo-Americans viewed others and how Mexican Americans redefined their status and role in society. With major institutional changes evolving after the 1960s, the foundation of society became altered as the educational disparities affecting racial minority students and the hierarchy of white racial domination began to break down. At the very least, Chicano Movement activists in South Texas and in most other places began to grapple with how to reform education in ways that would preserve its strengths while removing its systemic problems, such as the lack of access to quality resources and well-balanced curricula. More than fifty years after the walkouts, the challenge now lies in identifying how Latinos play a vital role in the educational life, society, and politics of the state, as they now make up the majority of the student population (51.8 percent) in Texas public schools.[9] As Latinos remain the fastest-growing ethnic group in Texas, the public school system must now adapt to this demographic change and incorporate teaching methodologies that promote the knowledge, awareness, and acceptance of diverse cultures. While Latinos possess more political power than they did in the 1960s, educational reform remains of key importance to the community.

The walkouts that occurred during the Civil Rights Movement have been recognized as a standard manifestation of grievance and protest in African American as well as Latino movements. An estimated thirty-nine high school walkouts supported by MAYO from 1968 to 1969, especially those in San Antonio's West Side, Edcouch-Elsa, Kingsville, and Crystal City, attracted media attention. From Edcouch-Elsa in Deep South Texas to San Antonio, in middle schools and high schools, ethnic Mexican students transformed themselves from a disenchanted and rather obscure minority class to actively involved agents of change in Texas education and society. Calling themselves Chicanas and Chicanos, these immigrant and lower-income teenagers not only organized their own protests but collaborated with adult professionals in their local communities and the courts. Their mass movement also drew followers and ultimately precipitated years of federal court cases and major educational reforms in Texas. In case after case throughout this book, students maintained their dignity and their credible arguments to attract the attention of the community at large and of the nation. Indeed, the history of the 1960s Chicano student movement in South Texas serves to broaden our understanding of the importance of collective action in promoting educational reform, empowered by the spirit of the popular rallying cry "We Want Better Education!" May this worthwhile desire for better-quality education help ensure equal access and opportunities for all, as well as further collaboration between schools and the larger community for years to come.

Appendix A

Lanier High School Walkout Demands

SAN ANTONIO INDEPENDENT SCHOOL DISTRICT
OFFICE OF SUPERINTENDENT
SAN ANTONIO, TEXAS 78210

On April 15, 1968, the Superintendent, Mr. Oscar E. Miller and Mr. A. W. Norton, Assistant Superintendent in charge of secondary schools, met with representatives of the student body of the Sidney Lanier High School, with representatives of the administration and faculty and with representatives of the Parent Teacher Association to discuss the twelve demands made by some of the students of the Sidney Lanier High School.

The following is an answer to these demands:

1. "We demand that no action be taken against any teacher or student who may have taken part in this movement for the betterment of our education, and that all suspended students be re-instated along with their positions. That the school records of these students be cleared."

   So long as these people who have participated in the movement have conducted themselves according to the rules and regulations of the San Antonio Independent School District no action will be taken against them. However, any student who is insubordinate and defiant to his superiors must suffer the consequences. The first prerequisite of a good school is law and order and a respect for authority and to this end the Superintendent will support the teachers and the administration.

2. "We demand more and effective counselling to prepare us for college."

   Lanier school, like some of our other schools has been short of counselors. This Spring we added an additional counselor and there are two more counselors in the budget for the next school year. This will make it possible to give the boys and girls an effective counselling program. However, students must show some initiative by responding to the requests of counselors to come in for counselling.

3. "We demand more academic courses to correspond with other schools, some of which are:
   a.) Chemistry, Physics, Algebra (beginning at 9th grade)
   b.) Trigonometry and Calculus
   c.) Computer programming
   d.) History dealing with the Mexican culture
   e.) Up-dated printing and photographic shops. An evaluation of present Vocational and Technical training in accordance with the technical skills needed for the community.
   f.) Electronics
   g.) Cosmetology

   Regarding the request for more academic courses Biology, chemistry and physics are offered at Lanier High School this year and they will be part of the curriculum next year. Algebra I will be offered at the 9th grade level; trigonometry and calculus will be offered at the 12th grade level to give Lanier a complete math program. Computer math will NOT be offered next year, if practicable it may be offered in the future. History dealing with the Mexican culture will not be offered until the Texas Education Agency includes it in its course offerings at the State level. The print and photography shops are

-2-

modern shops with excellent equipment .but they do need larger working areas. Electronics and cosmetology would be fine additions to the course offerings at Lanier, when more space is made available.

4. "We demand that the Student Council be the voice of the students."

In general the Student Council should be the voice of the students. However, such a policy should not prevent minority groups or individual students from being heard.

5. "We demand more assemblies on the various careers available to the students."

Plans should be implemented to broaden the scope of career information for the students.

6. "We demand that a committee be formed consisting of faculty members to listen and investigate and act upon complaints from students."

We can not concur with the request to form a faculty committee to hear student complaints. This is and should be the responsibility of the administration of the school.

7. "We demand to have the right to comment on any school policy without being silenced."

Students should be permitted to comment on school policies if done in the proper spirit and in a constructive manner.

8. "We demand the right to use democratic principles and procedures at all meetings, particularly in the Student Council."

Democratic principles and procedures should be encouraged in all student organizations but it should be understood that the teacher or sponsor in charge of a group has the authority which takes precedence over the constitution of each organization.

9. "We demand a copy of the constitution of each organization be made available to that club either to be displayed or easily referred to."

It is recommended that each organization revise and update their constitution and by-laws and make them available to students, teachers, and parents.

10. "We demand that a moment of silent prayer be observed at the beginning of every Student Council meeting, rather than to recite the LORD'S PRAYER, which is unconstitutional."

The prayer request seems to be rather minor. It is suggested that the student council let the members vote to see which type of prayer to use.

11. "We demand more information regarding scholarships, and other higher education assistance programs."

By having more counselors on the staff it is felt certain that more

-3-

information regarding scholarships and higher education will be available to the students. However, the students must remember they must use some initiative of their own if they are to benefit from this service.

12. "We demand, as Mexican-Americans, the right to speak our native tongue, Spanish, in our school."

It is recommended that students be required to use English in the classrooms and in the presence of teachers. It is also recommended that students be encouraged to use English in the halls, on the yard and in the cafeteria, but they should not be punished if they do not choose to do so.

OSCAR E. MILLER
Superintendent

OEM:kr

Appendix B

Edgewood High School Walkout Demands

EDGEWOOD HIGH SCHOOL STUDENT BODY GRIEVANCES

The following deficiencies in the physical plants, grounds and the administrative system at Edgewood High School constitute a basis for grievance by the student body. We propose that the administration, faculty and students work together to improve these deficiencies which presently exist.

1) <u>Inadequate discipline:</u> We request a more strict disciplinary system. Teachers must make all possible efforts to control students. If these efforts fail, the administration must take necessary steps to insure that infractions of school rules do not recur. As of the present time, the administration has been extremely lax with respect to enforcement of school policies.

2) <u>Inadequate policing of buildings and grounds, restroom supplies:</u> We request more adequate janitorial service that that presently available. <u>Two janitors are inadequate for the area to be kept clean and policed. Many of the restroom facilities lack running water, toilet tissue and/or soap.</u> This deficiency is a health hazard and must be remedied. Plaster in many rooms falls in chunks while classes are in session, and heavy rains have caused many leaks which have not been repaired.

3) <u>Inadequate qualified teachers:</u> Many teachers are not fully qualified to teach the subjects which they have been hired to teach. We request that this inadequacy be remedied, and that periodic inspection by school officials of the classrooms while in session be made to observe the material being taught and the methods being used. Teachers who fail to meet the standards with respect to their respective fields should be dismissed. The educational standards for our student body must be improved to the maximum extent.

4) <u>Inadequate control of monetary records of various clubs and general fund:</u> We request that monetary records be audited by a commitee of qualfied parents and administrators and that club monies be entered in the names of the respective clubs for which they have been collected.

5) <u>Inadequate level of academic courses and facilities for teaching:</u> We ask for higher standards with respect to academic courses, as well as a wider variation of such courses to obtain comparability, with those of other schools to better prepare those students planning college study on graduation. Examples are: Chemistry, Physics, Algebra, Computer Programming, Updated Printing and Photography Shops. (an evaluation of present vocational and technical training should be in accord with the technical skills need for the local community); more speakers on various career opportunities should be engaged. Professional counseling should be made available to all students, as well as counseling on scholarships, loans, grants and other high education assistance programs.

6) <u>Grievance Board:</u> We ask that a committee of faculty members be formed to listen to, investigate, and act upon complaints of the student body.

7) _Freedom to express views:_ We request the right to comment upon any school policy or policies felt to be detrimental to the student body without fear of being silenced, ignored or reproved.

8) _Student Council to be Voice of Student Body:_ We request that the Student Council be the voice of the student body. Such meetings held by the Council should be open to the faculty and the student body to hear complaints which may be solved by the Student Council in accord with the administration.

9) We further and finally request that no action be taken against any student or any teacher who has taken part in this non-violent student movement for the improvement of school conditions and the betterment of our educational standards.

Appendix C

Edcouch-Elsa High School Walkout Demands

LIST OF DEMANDS

We, the student body of Edcouch-Elsa Junior and Senior High School, demand of the officials and administrators:

1. That no diciplinary action be taken against any student or teacher that has taken part in this movement and that all suspended students and teachers be re-instated to their previous post or office and that any mention of such action omitted from school records. Also all intimidations should stop.

2. That no threats, intimidation or penalties be made against any student by teachers or administrators for membership or attendance of meetings of any club or organization outside of school.

3. That the students be allowed to select their own candidates for Student Council --- it should be the students Student Council.

4. That excessive and unfair penalties and punishments stop being given students for minor infractions or completely ridiculous reasons, for example:
    a) student suspended <u>three days</u> for failure to keep appointment with teacher after school.
    b) student suspended for <u>three days</u> for failing to stand at school pep rally!
    c) if something (shorts, tennis shoes,) are stolen from lockers the students are punished (paddled or sent to do manual labor) <u>for not being able to suit up!</u>
    Likewise, that due process be followed in cases of suspension or expulsion of students, that is, that a student be given opportunity to defend himself and that evidence be presented to both administrators and parents. Also no paddling should be given student until explanation for punishment be given to parents, if students request such explanation.

5. That no teacher or administrator shall use profanity or abusive language in presence of students and in no case shall any teacher or administrator lay a hand on a student.

6. That, in the case of tardy or absent students, the students be allowed to re-enter class and no points taken off <u>until</u> his excuse is verified or not. Students should not be kept out of class till parents call school.

7. That either the price of the cafeteria lunch be lowered to a more reasonable price or that more and better foods be served.

8. That, as Chicano students, we be allowed to speak our mother tongue, Spanish, on school premises without being subjected to humiliating or unjust penalties.

9. That courses be introduced, as a regular part of the curriculum, to show the contributions of Mexicans and Mexican Americans to this state and region. For instance, factual accounts of the history of the Southwest and Texas, courses in Mexican history and culture. Also, that qualified, certified teachers be hired to teach these courses.

(2)

10. That all college preparatory courses be signalled out for students by the time they enter high school.

11. That more effective counseling be given students from understanding counselors that are able to relate to students. Present student-counselor ratio is too great, we need more counselors. Likewise, more assemblies on career opportunities, availability of scholarships, grants, loans, college entrance requirements, etc.

12. Finally that the blatant discrimination against the Mexican American students in this school stop immediately. We demand Justice.

13. That regulations for "passes" be set down clearly and defined so that no question remains as to when passes are needed or not. The present system, or lack of it, is ridiculous.

14. That special attention be given the situation a great number of Edcouch-Elsa students find themselves in--that is, they are migrant workers.
   a) Student choices of subjects in spring registration be respected and adopted in the fall term, these subject forms are often disregarded. -
   b) Migrants leave school early, they take part in an accelerated program Advance tests are supposed to be given before they leave. Often teachers do not let migrants take tests or do not send tests to students up north after them. All tests should be given to migrant students before they leave.

15. That school facilities be improved, renovated, replaced or installed where appropriate. For example:
   a) Fans-teachers often use fans only for their own comfort, ignoring students.
   b) Heaters-The heaters are for the most part outdated and not in working order. We need new heaters.
   c) Restrooms-Some of the restrooms and toilets are not cleaned and inoperable; constantly out of repair.
   d) Windows-Fix broken windows.
   e) Walls-repair holes in wall. Give school buildings a face-lifting.
   f) How about Hot water for the showers.

We want to be proud of our school.

Recommendations

1. Teachers have been driving buses for the district up till now. We recommend that either students, senior students, or townspeople be hired to fill these positions.

2. We recommend that longer periods of time be given to get to classes between classes. Five minutes would be sufficient.

STUDENT COMMITTEE
November 7, 1968

APPENDIX C ～ 225

Appendix D

Kingsville Gillett Junior High School Walkout Demands

Non-Militant Protest for Demand

April 14, 1969

We the Chicano student body of Gillett Junior High make the following demands to all the school teachers and administrators.

1. Any student or teacher taking part in this justified demonstration be allowed back in school without retalatory backlash from administrators or school board. We don't want teachers taking sides.

2. We demand that all Chicanos be allowed to speak their mother tongue; Spanish, without harrassment and humiliation from school faculty.

3. We also demand intregation of school library with books on Mexican-American culture.

4. In a school which is predominantly Mexican-American, you should have a Chicano counselor who understands their problems. We demand you hire one immediately.

5. Our dignity and pride has been spiritually and mentally hurt. You and your racist history books which genocide us from history must be changed immediately. We demand equal representation.

6. We also demand that a bilingual and bi-culture program be taught by qualified instructors.

7. A minority of your faculty have been taking political views and are preaching them on the students. We believe that this is an invasion of their individual rights, and must stop.

8. In a region where the majority is Mexican-American we recommend and demand that you make it a practice to hire more qualified chicano principal and teachers, that understand the barrio problems and are willing to help the students.

We also want to be proud of our school!

On this day April 14, 1969 we come in hope that our demands will be respectfully heard by the administration and school board. The eyes of Mexican-Americans all over Kingsville are watching and waiting for your decision. If you see this as an act of disrespect or an attempt to disrupt the educational school system by a handful of Revolutionaries instead of a group of young Americans demonstrating for rights that they feel have been denied, then you are depriving them of their right to a peaceful assembly guaranteed by the Constitution of the United States of America.

We demand Justice!!!!!

Appendix E

Crystal City High School Walkout Demands

1. That all elections concerning the school be conducted by the student body. Concerning class representatives, the petition asked that the qualifications such as personality, leadership, grades be abolished. These factors do not determine whether the student is capable of representing the student body. The students are capable of voting for their own representatives. The representatives are representing the students, not the faculty. All nominating must be done by the student body, and the election should be decided by a majority vote.

2. The present method of electing most handsome, beautiful, most popular, and most representative is elected [sic] by the faculty. The method of cumulative voting is unfair.

3. National Honor Society—the grades of the students eligible must be posted on the bulletin board well in advance of selection. The teachers should not have anything to do with electing the students.

4. An advisory board of Mexican American citizens should be a part of the school administration in order to advise on the needs and problems of the Mexican American.

5. No other favorites should be authorized by school administrators or board members unless submitted to the student body in a referendum.

6. Teachers, administrators and staff should be educated; they should know our language—Spanish—and understand the his-tory, traditions and contributions of Mexican culture. How can they expect to teach us if they do not know us? We want more Mexican American teachers for the above reason.

7. We want immediate steps taken to implement bilingual and bi-cultural education for Mexican Americans. We also want the school books revised to reflect the contributions of Mexicans and Mexican Americans to the U.S. society, and to make us aware of the injustices that we, Mexican Americans, as a people have suffered in an "Anglo" dominant society. We want a Mexican American course with the value of one credit.

8. We want any member of the school system who displays prejudice or fails to recognize, understand and appreciate us, Mexican Americans, our culture, our heritage removed from Crystal City's schools. Teachers shall not call students any names.

9. Our classes should be smaller in size, say about 20 students to one teacher to insure more effectiveness. We want parents from the

a teacher who may disagree politically or philosophically with administrators will not be dismissed or transferred because of it. Teachers should encourage students to study and should make class more interesting, so that students will look forward to going to class.

10. There should be a manager in charge of janitorial work and maintenance details and the performance of such duties should be restricted to employees hired for that purpose. In other words, no more students doing janitorial work.

11. We want a free speech area plus the right to have speakers of our own.

12. We would like September 16 as a holiday, but if it is not possible we would like an assembly, with speakers of our own. We feel it is a great day in the history of the world because it is when Mexico had been under Spanish rule for about 300 years. The Mexicans were liberated from the harsh rule of Spain. Our ancestors fought in this war and we owe them tribute because we are Mexicans, too.

13. Being civic minded citizens, we want to know what the happenings are in our community. So, we request the right to have access to all types of literature and to be able to bring it on campus. The newspaper in our school does not carry sufficient information. It carries things like the gossip column, which is unnecessary.

14. The dress code should be abolished. We are entitled to wear what we want.

15. We request the buildings open to students at all times.

16. We want Mr. Harbin to resign as Principal of Fly Jr. High.

17. We want a Mexican American counselor fully qualified in college opportunities.

18. We need more showers in the boy's and girl's dressing rooms.

Source: MAYO document, Jose Angel Gutiérrez Files, Crystal City, Texas, 1973, cited from Armando Navarro, *Mexican American Youth Organization: Avant-Garde of the Chicano Movement in Texas* (Austin: The University of Texas Press, 1995), 251-252.

Notes

FRONTMATTER

1. South Texas newspaper articles on the walkout offer different estimates of how many students walked out and picketed. Some of these figures are not accurate. The *McAllen Monitor* reported that 140 students began the walkout, while the *Edinburg Daily Review* and *Corpus Christi Caller* estimated that 150 did so. The *Valley Morning Star* (Harlingen, TX) estimated that as many as 160 to 175 Chicano students started the protest.
2. "Student Demographics," Texas A&M University Accountability, accessed March 27, 2023, https://accountability.tamu.edu/all-metrics/mixed-metrics/student-demographics.
3. "Pharr (Texas) Man Plays Key Role in Viet Security," *McAllen Monitor*, April 25, 1969. This article is about my father serving as an engineer for Brown and Root.
4. The University of Texas–Pan American is now the University of Texas Rio Grande Valley. This school was originally founded in 1927 and named Pan American College.
5. Nicolas "Nic" González, the principal of McAllen Memorial High School when I attended it in the early 1990s, later served as the administrator for high school programs and services at South Texas College (STC), where I currently work as an associate professor of history. We were colleagues for fourteen years before González's retirement in 2019.
6. McKittrick, "Daniel 'Rudy' Ruettiger."

INTRODUCTION

1. I use the term "Chicano" interchangeably with "Mexican American" when referring to people of Mexican ancestry born and/or raised in the United States. It is gender inclusive, acknowledging the roles of both male and female Mexican Americans as major participants in the Chicano Movement. "Chicano" was a popular identity label chosen by young Mexican Americans who gained a strong sense of ethnic solidarity, community identity, and political consciousness from the Civil Rights Movement that challenged the conventional views or stereotypes of racial inferiority in America during the 1960s. The word "Chicano" also expressed ethnic and cultural pride in one's Mexican ancestry and indigenous roots dating back to the Aztec civilization in central Mexico. However, "Chicana" is a separate term that had a different meaning among women activists who sought to establish social, political, and cultural identities for themselves by the early 1970s. Such activists also expressed pride in their ethnic Mexican culture and heritage but opposed Chicano patriarchal authority, machismo, and sexism within the movement. Thus, they struggled to gain recognition and respect even within their own ethnic community.
2. Arreola, *Tejano South Texas*, 9–22. A discussion of the varying scholarly interpretations of South Texas boundaries can be found in Menchaca, *Naturalizing Mexican Immigrants*, 13–14.
3. I use the term "insurgency" to describe Chicano students who engaged in peaceful, nonviolent protest action to seek immediate resolution of various educational deficiencies faced by ethnic Mexican students at their schools. I further contend that the 1960s Chicano student protests in South Texas and in other places throughout the US Southwest resembled a type of "revolt" to "overthrow" the Anglo-dominated school system.

4. I use the terms "protester" and "activist" interchangeably, although some activists may not have participated in the walkouts. Activists, often the relatives or friends of protesters, played more low-key yet supportive roles by offering moral support and encouragement, donating material items such as food, and making picket signs. However, both activists and protesters shared similar socioeconomic backgrounds, cultural values, language usage, and educational settings. These commonalities enabled them to agree on the effectiveness and meaning of the protests.

5. For further analysis of the historical influences of 1960s Chicano social protest activism, see Chávez, *"¡Mi Raza Primero!"*; Echeverría, *Aztlán Arizona*; García, *Chicanismo*; Gómez-Quiñones, *Mexican Students Por la Raza*; Muñoz, *Youth, Identity, Power*; Navarro, *Mexican American Youth Organization*; San Miguel, *Brown, Not White*; and Trujillo, *Chicano Empowerment*.

6. García, *Chicanismo*, 8.

7. Ibid., 2.

8. "Social Movements and Culture.".

9. McAdam, *Political Process*, 50–51.

10. Sekhon, "Social Movement Theory.".

11. McAdam, *Political Process*, 48–50.

12. Oberschall, *Social Conflicts*, 28.

13. Friedman and McAdam, "Collective Identity and Activism," 163–64.

14. Braschayko, "Sybil Ludington"; Roberts, *Founding Mothers*, 81.

15. "History of American Women"; Roberts, *Founding Mothers*, 81.

16. See Alvarez, *Power of the Zoot*; Rodríguez, *Tejano Diaspora*. Alvarez examines the development of the multiracial, gendered, transregional zoot suit culture among young men and women from the East to West Coast before and during World War II. Rodríguez analyzes how Chicano political and social movements evolved at both ends of the migratory farmworker network that existed between Crystal City, Texas, and Wisconsin during the 1960s and 1970s. The migration of young workers from Crystal City became the backbone of a grassroots movement spreading Mexican American activism that was connected to a larger movement via the Tejano diaspora, or the transregional, interstate migrant labor stream of Texas residents of Spanish and Mexican ancestry.

17. Abrams, *Oral History Theory*, 78.

18. Ibid., 84.

19. *McAllen Monitor*, July 27 and December 14, 1998.

20. Sánchez offered legal counsel to students who were suspended and expelled during the protest, according to the *McAllen Monitor*, November 18 and 19, 1968, and July 27, 1998. The 1998 article revealed Lozano's occupation at the time, secretary of the Edcouch-Elsa School District main office.

21. Major works on the history of the Chicano educational experience and student activism in the twentieth century include Blanton, *Strange Career*; Chávez, *"¡Mi Raza Primero!"*; Donato, *Other Struggle*; Echeverría, *Aztlán Arizona*; García, *Blowout!*; Gómez-Quiñones, *Mexican Students Por la Raza*; Sonia A. López, "The Role of the Chicana within the Student Movement," in *Essays on La Mujer* (Los Angeles: UCLA Chicano Studies Center, 1977), 16–29, cited from García, *Chicana Feminist Thought*, 100–106; Ruiz, *From Out of the Shadows*, 102–3, 116; Muñoz, *Youth, Identity, Power*; Navarro, *Mexican American Youth Organization*; San Miguel, *"Let All of Them"*; San Miguel, *Brown, Not White*; San Miguel, *Chicana/o Struggles*; and Trujillo, *Chicano Empowerment*.

22. Major studies that specifically explore the Chicano struggle for better education during the 1960s and 1970s in the US Southwest include Donato, *Other Struggle*; Echeverría, *Aztlán Arizona*; Gómez-Quiñones, *Mexican Students Por la Raza*; González, *Chicano Education*; Muñoz, *Youth, Identity, Power*; Navarro, *Mexican American Youth Organization*; San Miguel, *Brown, Not White*; San Miguel, *Chicana/o Struggles*; and Trujillo, *Chicano Empowerment*.

23. Donato, *Other Struggle*, 20.

24. González, *Chicano Education*, 45.

25. González, "Segregation and the Mexican Children," 80. Quote is from Joseph M. Sniffen, "The Senior High School Problem Boy," *Los Angeles School Journal* 11, no. 32 (1928): 187–88.
26. Donato, *Other Struggle*, 30.
27. González, *Chicano Education*, 99.
28. Carter, *Mexican Americans in School*, 146.
29. Echeverría, *Aztlán Arizona*, 5.
30. Ibid., 7.
31. San Miguel and Valencia, "From the Treaty of Guadalupe-Hidalgo," 353–413.
32. Gutiérrez, *Making of a Chicano Militant*, 126–27.
33. San Miguel, *Brown, Not White*, 20.
34. Ibid., xii.
35. San Miguel, *Chicana/o Struggles*, 5.
36. Ibid., 139.
37. Ibid., 5.
38. Ibid., 142.
39. Ibid., 142.
40. Blanton, *Strange Career*, 59–73.
41. Ibid., 69.
42. Blanton, "Rise of the English-Only Pedagogy," 59.
43. Blanton, *Strange Career*, 54.

CHAPTER 1

1. Major works that discuss the development of the early ranching community and farming society, changing ethnic and political identities, transnational cultural practices, kinship ties, and the tradition of Tejano landholding in South Texas include Alonso, *Tejano Legacy*; Tijerina, *Tejano Empire*, and Valerio-Jiménez, *River of Hope*. The term "Tejano" refers to people of Spanish/Mexican ancestry born and raised in Texas, including those whose ancestors lived in Texas prior to Anglo-/Euro-American settlement in 1821.
2. For detailed information on Native American tribes that resided in South Texas during the colonial period, see Newcomb, *Indians of Texas*; and La Vere, *Texas Indians*.
3. Paredes, *With His Pistol*; Cotera, *Life along the Border*.
4. Horsman, *Race and Manifest Destiny*, 210.
5. Ibid., 9.
6. De León, *They Called Them Greasers*, 63.
7. Martínez, *Mexican-Origin People*, 56.
8. Noah Smithwick, *The Evolution of a State: Recollections of Old Texas Days* (1900; repr., Austin: 1935), 35, cited from Weber, *Myth and History*, 154.
9. De León, *They Called Them Greasers*, 6.
10. Calderón, "Tejano Politics.".
11. Ibid.
12. Ibid.
13. Ibid.; Segovia, "Botas and Guaraches.".
14. Segovia, "Botas and Guaraches.".
15. Weber, *From South Texas*, 18; also see Falcón, "Force and the Search for Consent," 107–34.
16. Weber, *From South Texas*, 18.
17. Ibid., 85.
18. Ibid., 79–80.
19. Montejano, *Anglos and Mexicans*, 162, 195–96.
20. Anders, *Boss Rule in South Texas*, 34–37.
21. Cotera, *Life along the Border*, 76–77.
22. For further information on the development of political bossism in South Texas, see Anders, *Boss Rule in South Texas*.

NOTES TO PAGES 17–28 ⁓ 233

23. Cotera, *Life along the Border*, 77.
24. See De León and Stewart, *Tejanos and the Numbers Game*, table 3.6, 43.
25. Ibid.
26. Ibid., 35.
27. De León and Stewart, *Tejanos and the Numbers Game*, table 3.6, 43.
28. Montejano, *Anglos and Mexicans*, 110.
29. V. O. Key, *Southern Politics* (New York: Random House, 1949), 271, cited from Shockley, *Chicano Revolt*.
30. Shockley, *Chicano Revolt*.
31. Preuss, *To Get a Better School System*, 41–49.
32. Maril, *Poorest of Americans*, 31.
33. Ibid.
34. Ibid.
35. Blanton, *Strange Career*, 24–31; Barragán Goetz, *Reading, Writing, and Revolution*, 1–47.
36. Blanton, *Strange Career*, 28.
37. Ibid., 29. For further information on the cultural impact, settlement, legal traditions, labor patterns, and contributions of Tejanos during the nineteenth century, see Tijerina, *Tejanos and Texas*; De León, *Tejano Community*.
38. Blanton, *Strange Career*, 30–31; De León, *Tejano Community*, 188–90.
39. De León, *Tejano Community*, 188.
40. Ibid., 187–94.
41. Cotera, *Life along the Border*, 94.
42. Ibid.
43. Sánchez, *Shared Experience*, 69–71.
44. *Texas Almanac and U.S. Census, Population of Valley Counties, 1850–1980*, cited from Maril, *Poorest of Americans*, 33–34.
45. Taylor, "Mexican Labor in the United States," 389.
46. Richard Littleton, interview by Paul Taylor, April 16, 1929, series 3, carton 12, folder 14, Paul S. Taylor Collection, Bancroft Library, University of California, Berkeley, cited from Weber, *From South Texas*, 87.
47. Eby, "Education in Texas," 130.
48. Berger and Wilborn, "Education.".
49. Eby, "Education in Texas," 151–52.
50. Ibid., 130–99; Berger and Wilborn, "Education," 1–22.
51. Berger and Wilborn, "Education." .
52. MacDonald, *Latino Education in the U.S.*, 250; Berger and Wilborn, "Education." .
53. Eby, "Education in Texas," 250; Berger and Wilborn, "Education." .
54. Eby, "Education in Texas," 336.
55. Gammel, *Laws of Texas*, 998–99.
56. Berger and Wilborn, "Education." .
57. Eby, "Education in Texas," 540. Also see De Gress, *First Annual Report*, 4; and Eby, *Development of Education*.
58. Blanton, *Strange Career*, 20.
59. *Second Annual Report of the Superintendent*, 25.
60. *Fifth Biennial Report of the Superintendent*.
61. Montejano, *Anglos and Mexicans*, 160.
62. I use the terms "Anglo-American," "Anglo," "white American," or "white" to refer to non-Hispanic white people whose mother tongue or native language is English, not limited to those of English or British ancestry. The term "European American" is sometimes used interchangeably to indicate all non-Hispanic white people of European origin who speak English as their first language.
63. Blanton, *Strange Career*, 59–73.
64. González, *Chicano Education*, 30.

65. Blanton, "Rise of the English-Only Pedagogy," 59.

66. San Miguel, *"Let All of Them,"* 33.

67. Ellwood P. Cubberley, *Changing Conceptions of Education* (Boston: Houghton Mifflin, 1909), 15; and Emory S. Bogardus, *Essentials of Americanization* (Los Angeles: University of Southern California Press, 1920), 13–14, both cited from Blanton, "Rise of the English-Only Pedagogy." For further details on the history of the origins and implementation of Americanization/English-only mandates affecting Mexican Americans during the Progressive Era, see San Miguel, *"Let All of Them,"* chap. 2; and Blanton, *Strange Career*, chaps. 3 and 4.

68. Annie Webb Blanton, *A Handbook of Information as to Education in Texas, 1918–1922*, Bulletin 157 (Austin: Texas State Department of Education, 1923), 22–23, cited from San Miguel, *"Let All of Them"*; Blanton, "Rise of the English-Only Pedagogy."

69. Everett E. Davis, "A Report on Illiteracy in Texas," *University of Texas Bulletin* no. 2328 (July 22, 1923), 35, cited from González, *Chicano Education*, 56.

70. González, *Chicano Education*, 46.

71. Ibid., 33.

72. Císneros, *Borderlands*, 140, 141. One of Císneros's pictures shows an Anglo patrón supervising two Mexican rail workers.

73. "Hidalgo Pumphouse Heritage."

74. Vigness and Odintz, "Rio Grande Valley."

75. Císneros, *Borderlands*, 144.

76. Gonzáles, "World of Mexico Texanos"; Gonzáles, "Mexican Revolution," 108–9.

77. Fehrenbach, "San Antonio, TX."

78. Ibid.

79. Odintz, "Crystal City, TX."

80. Ibid.

81. Rosales, *Testimonio*, 63–65.

82. Ibid.

83. Zamora et al., *Mexican Americans in Texas History*, 106. For detailed information on the Plan of San Diego revolt and the bloody counterinsurgency waged by the Texas Rangers against people of Mexican origin in South Texas, see Johnson, *Revolution in Texas*.

84. Maril, *Poorest of Americans*, 44.

85. "Photos from Elsa, Texas."

86. Isabel Gutiérrez, interview by Francisco Guajardo, 1997, unpublished oral history archive manuscript, Llano Grande Center Oral History Collection II, Edcouch-Elsa High School, Elsa, Texas, cited from Guajardo, "Narratives of Transformation," 5–6.

87. Luisa Garza, interview by Francisco Guajardo, 1998, unpublished oral history archive manuscript, Llano Grande Center Oral History Collection II, Edcouch-Elsa High School, Elsa, Texas, cited from Guajardo, "Narratives of Transformation," 123.

88. "Photos from Elsa, Texas."

89. See "Illustration 2: Map of Sale of Elsa, March 2, 1927" in Guajardo, "Narratives of Transformation," 132.

90. Nájera, *Borderlands of Race*, 37.

91. Esperanza Salinas, interview by Francisco Guajardo, 1998, unpublished oral history archive manuscript, Llano Grande Center Oral History Collection II, Edcouch-Elsa High School, Elsa, Texas, cited from Guajardo, "Narratives of Transformation," 131.

92. Ezequiel Granado, interview by Francisco Guajardo, 1998, unpublished oral history archive manuscript, Llano Grande Center Oral History Collection II, Edcouch-Elsa High School, Elsa, Texas, cited from Guajardo, "Narratives of Transformation," 131.

93. Garza, "History of Vahl'sing," 14–15.

94. *Reader's Digest*, 1947, cited from Guajardo, "Narratives of Transformation," 128.

95. Ibid.

96. R. Beane, "A Brief History of the Educational Development of Hidalgo County, Texas" (master's thesis, Texas A&M University, 1942), cited from Guajardo, "Narratives of Transformation,"

120. I contacted the Franklin D. Roosevelt Presidential Library to inquire about material related to the Edcouch-Elsa School District desegregation in 1942. Library archivist Dara Baker searched a few records of the collections most likely to include the correspondence I was seeking but did not locate anything relevant. According to Baker, none of the material related to Texas or education addressed the school district of Edcouch-Elsa or the concept of Mexican American students' integration. Therefore, I was unable to find archival documentation to further verify this claim.

97. Ibid.

98. Lupita Guzman, interview by Francisco Guajardo, 1997, unpublished oral history archive manuscript, Llano Grande Center Oral History Collection II, Edcouch-Elsa High School, Elsa, Texas, cited from Guajardo, "Narratives of Transformation," 140.

99. *Now and Then in Zavala County*, 1. The county was created when it became part of the municipality of San Antonio de Béxar shortly after Texas gained its independence from Mexico in 1836. Thus, Zavala County can trace its history to the establishment of the independent Republic of Texas, formed under Sam Houston before Texas became a US state in 1845.

100. Ibid.

101. Ibid., 6.

102. Ibid., 5–9.

103. Ibid., 61.

104. Odintz, "Crystal City, TX.".

105. Taylor, *American-Mexican Frontier*, 184.

106. Gutiérrez, *Making of a Chicano Militant*, 34 (italics in original).

107. *Now and Then in Zavala County*, 60.

108. Ibid.

109. Shockley, *Chicano Revolt*, 5.

110. Odintz, "Crystal City, TX.".

111. Rodríguez, *Tejano Diaspora*, 17.

112. Selden C. Menefee, *Mexican Migratory Workers of South Texas* (Washington, DC: US Government Printing Office, 1941), 52, cited from Cortés, *Mexican Labor in the United States*.

113. Ibid.

114. Ibid., xiii; *Now and Then in Zavala County*, 3.

115. The 1930 US census indicates the ethnic groups in Zavala County, including 2,617 Native Whites, 52 foreign-born Whites, 7,660 Mexicans, and 19 Negros. William McKinley Pridgen, "Survey and Proposed Plan of Reorganization of the Public Schools in Zavala County" (master's thesis, University of Texas at Austin, 1939), 7, cited from Shockley, *Chicano Revolt*.

116. Ochoa, "Zavala County.".

117. Selden C. Menefee, *Mexican Migratory Workers of South Texas* (Washington, DC: US Government Printing Office, 1941), xv, 37, cited from Cortés, *Mexican Labor in the United States*.

118. Ibid., xv.

119. Ibid., 52.

120. *Now and Then in Zavala County*, 29–31.

121. Zamora, *Claiming Rights*, 79; Weber, *From South Texas*, 193–99.

122. Weber, *From South Texas*, 194.

123. Meier and Ribera, *Mexican Americans*, 176.

124. Zamora, *Claiming Rights*, 81.

125. De León, *Mexican Americans in Texas*, 120.

126. Zamora, *Claiming Rights*, 80–81.

127. George Sánchez to Senator Ralph Yarborough, April 12, 1954, box 3, folder 4, Ed Idar Papers, Nettie Lee Benson Latin American Collection, University of Texas Libraries, University of Texas at Austin, cited from Weber, *From South Texas*, 197.

128. Weber, *From South Texas*, 196.

129. Meier and Ribera, *Mexican Americans*, 183–84.

130. Coalson, "Kingsville, Texas.".

131. *Kleberg County, Texas*, 174.
132. Monday and Colley, *Voices from the Wild Horse Desert*, chap. 3.
133. Ashton and Sneed, "King Ranch.".
134. Ibid.
135. For further general background information, see Coalson, "Kingsville, Texas." .
136. *Kleberg County, Texas*, 174.
137. Hunter and Hunter, *Historic Kingsville, Texas*, 8; "Organization of First Railroad Here Recalled by Long-Time Resident," article in a scrapbook titled "Kingsville, Texas," scrapbook collection, Robert J. Kleberg Public Library, Kingsville, Texas.
138. *Corpus Christi Caller-Times*, July 12, 1953.
139. Ibid.; Allison, *Images of America*, 7.
140. Hunter and Hunter, *Historic Kingsville, Texas*, 8; "Organization of First Railroad Here Recalled by Long-Time Resident," article in a scrapbook titled "Kingsville, Texas," scrapbook collection, Robert J. Kleberg Public Library, Kingsville, Texas.
141. *Kleberg County, Texas*, 174.
142. Ibid.
143. Coalson, "Kingsville, Texas.".
144. Raúl G. Garza, interview by the author, Kingsville, Texas, February 12, 2005; hand-drawn map of Kingsville by Raúl G. Garza.
145. Allison, *Images of America*, 55.
146. Hunter and Hunter, *Historic Kingsville, Texas*, 10.
147. Coalson, "Kingsville, Texas.".
148. Hunter and Hunter, *Historic Kingsville, Texas*, 11.
149. Coalson, "Kingsville, Texas."

CHAPTER 2

1. Orozco, "Mexican American Women.".
2. Zamora, "Sáenz, José de la Luz"; also see Zamora's translation of Sáenz's diary, *The World War I Diary of José de la Luz Sáenz*.
3. Rupert N. Richardson, Adrian Anderson, and Ernest Wallace, *Texas: The Lone Star State*, 7th ed. (Upper Saddle River, NJ: Prentice Hall, 1997), 336, cited from Ramírez, *To the Line of Fire*, 22.
4. Zamora, "Sáenz, José de la Luz.".
5. Ramírez, *To the Line of Fire*, 23–30; Morales, "Hijos de la Gran Guerra," 9–10.
6. Morales, "Hijos de la Gran Guerra," 16.
7. Ramírez, *To the Line of Fire*, 91.
8. Ibid.; Orozco and León, "Vento, Adela Sloss.".
9. For further information on the formation and activism of LULAC, see Márquez, *LULAC*; and Orozco, *No Mexicans*.
10. "LULAC History." .
11. Ibid.
12. Márquez, *LULAC*, 3.
13. Orozco, "League of United.".
14. Ibid.; "LULAC History.".
15. Orozco, *No Mexicans*, 11. Orozco explores two key concepts of racial identity—racial formation and racialization—and further assesses the construction of the term "Mexican" as a racialized imaginary. See her work for further details.
16. Ibid.
17. LULAC constitution, article II, cited from Rosales, *Testimonio*, 165.
18. LULAC constitution, article II, section 4, cited from San Miguel, *"Let All of Them,"* 73.
19. Alonso S. Perales, "My Message to the League of United Latin American Citizens," *El Paladin*, July 5, 1929, 1–2, cited from San Miguel, *"Let All of Them,"* 74.

20. Historian Mario T. García was among the first scholars to use the term "Mexican-American Generation" in his work *Mexican Americans*. This term was first used by sociologist Rodolfo Alvarez to refer to a biological generation rather than a historical political generation, as García indicates. See Alvarez, "Psycho-Historical and Socioeconomic Development.".

21. García, *Mexican Americans*, 19–20.

22. García, *Chicanismo*, 9.

23. Meier and Ribera, *Mexican Americans*, 201.

24. Quoted in García, *Rise of the Mexican American*, 75. For a profile of Tranchese and his work on the West Side, see George Sessions Perry, "Rumpled Angel of the Slums," *Saturday Evening Post*, August 21, 1948, 32–33, 43–44, 47; and *San Antonio Express-News*, July 26, 2017.

25. American Public Welfare Association, Public Welfare Survey of San Antonio, *Texas: A Study of a Local Community* (Chicago: American Public Welfare Association, 1940), 27, cited from Weber, *From South Texas*, 131.

26. Meier and Ribera, *Mexican Americans*, 149–50.

27. Ibid., 153.

28. Croxdale, "Pecan-Shellers' Strike.".

29. Meier and Ribera, *Mexican Americans*, 135.

30. Blackwelder, *Women of the Depression*, 81, 95.

31. Croxdale, "Pecan-Shellers' Strike.".

32. Ibid.

33. Ibid.

34. Blackwelder, *Women of the Depression*, 143.

35. Croxdale, "Pecan-Shellers' Strike.".

36. Blackwelder, *Women of the Depression*, 143.

37. For further information on this protest, see Menefee and Cassmore, *Pecan Shellers of San Antonio*.

38. Gómez-Quiñones, *Chicano Politics*, 34.

39. Ibid., 41.

40. Haney-López, "White Latinos," 2.

41. Romo, *East Los Angeles*, 167–68.

42. *Justice for My People*. According to the video, the American GI Forum adopted a logo with thirteen stripes and stars resembling the US flag to reflect their pride and patriotism toward the United States.

43. Carroll, *Felix Longoria's Wake*, 209.

44. Two outstanding works analyzing the ethnic tensions and controversy that resulted from the incident are Carroll, *Felix Longoria's Wake*; and *The Longoria Affair* (DVD).

45. For an excellent detailed analysis of this incident, see Carroll, *Felix Longoria's Wake*.

46. Ibid.

47. Gómez-Quiñones, *Chicano Politics*, 88–89.

48. Orozco, *No Mexicans*, 183–95.

49. Ibid.

50. Emory Bogardus, *American G.I. Forum and What It Stands For*, America G.I. Forum Papers, Mary and Jeff Bell Library, Texas A&M University–Corpus Christi, cited from San Miguel, *"Let All of Them,"* 117.

51. Allsup, *American G.I. Forum*, 79–80.

52. For further details on the case, see San Miguel, *"Let All of Them,"* 77–82; Allsup, *American G.I. Forum*, 82; and Montoya, "Brief History," 159–72.

53. Everett E. Davis, "A Report on Illiteracy in Texas," *University of Texas Bulletin* no. 2328 (July 22, 1923), 30, cited from González, *Chicano Education*, 33; Montejano, *Anglos and Mexicans*, 228.

54. Carter, *Mexican Americans in School*, 67, 69.

55. "The Grove Case," *San Diego Union Tribune*, May 18, 2004.

56. Haney-López, "White Latinos," 2.

57. For a more detailed analysis of these two cases, see San Miguel, *"Let All of Them,"* chap. 5; Allsup, *American G.I. Forum,* chap. 7.

58. For further details on the Lemon Grove case, see Balderrama, *In Defense of La Raza;* and Weinberg, *Chance to Learn.*

59. Valencia, *Chicano Students,* 59; Blanton, *George I. Sánchez,* 247.

60. Blanton, *George I. Sánchez,* 247. Blanton's book includes a wealth of data from the George I. Sánchez Papers in the Nettie Lee Benson Latin American Collection, University of Texas Libraries, University of Texas at Austin.

61. Blanton, *George I. Sánchez,* 247; Allsup, "Hernández v. State of Texas.".

62. Allsup, "Cisneros v. Corpus Christi ISD.".

63. Lessoff, *Where Texas Meets the Sea,* 131.

64. Ibid.; Valencia, *Chicano Students,* 60.

65. Valencia, *Chicano Students,* 60–61; Allsup, "Cisneros v. Corpus Christi ISD.".

66. Valencia, *Chicano Students,* 61. Valencia's book offers a very detailed explanation of the legal proceedings of the case based on court records.

67. Císneros v. Corpus Christi Independent School District, 324 F. Supp. at 606 (Southern District of Texas, 1970), cited from Valencia, *Chicano Students,* 62; Blanton, *Strange Career,* 147.

68. *Císneros v. Corpus Christi,* 324 F. Supp. at 607, cited from Valencia, *Chicano Students,* 62.

69. *Císneros v. Corpus Christi,* 324 F. Supp. at 617.

70. Allsup, "Cisneros v. Corpus Christi ISD.".

71. Blanton, *Strange Career,* 147–48.

72. *Corpus Christi Caller,* August 15, 1972.

73. The San Felipe Independent School District and Del Rio ISD, neighboring school districts near the Texas-Mexico border, agreed to consolidate in 1971 in the aftermath of *United States of America v. State of Texas* after Judge Justice supported an integration plan for East Texas schools. The US Department of Health, Education, and Welfare approved the plan to desegregate "all Negro" school districts. Part of this plan also supported the inclusion of bilingual instruction, depending on the child's preferred language system (English, Spanish, or both), in order to develop proficiency in one or more additional language systems.

74. United States of America v. State of Texas et al., 28, cited from Blanton, *Strange Career,* 148.

75. J. Stanley Pottinger, "Memorandum to School Districts with More Than Five Percent National Origin-Minority Group Children" (Washington, DC: Department of Health, Education, and Welfare, Office for Civil Rights, May 25, 1970), cited from San Miguel, "Conflict and Controversy," 507.

76. San Miguel discusses more details concerning the major legal suits filed by Mexican American activists against the Texas public school system from the 1940s to 1960s ("Compelled to Litigate" in *"Let All of Them,"* 113–34). For additional information on school desegregation cases and the status of Mexican American litigation to the early 2000s, see Valencia, *Chicano Students,* 64–71.

77. Gómez-Quiñones, *Chicano Politics,* 91.

78. Boyd, *We Shall Overcome,* 39–45; Sargent, *Civil Rights Revolution,* 11–12; Weisbrot, *Freedom Bound,* 11–13.

79. Boyd, *We Shall Overcome,* 47–53; Sargent, *Civil Rights Revolution,* 18–23, 72–74.

80. Boyd, *We Shall Overcome,* 147–57; Sargent, *Civil Rights Revolution,* 85–86; Weisbrot, *Freedom Bound,* 76–85.

81. Johnson, "We Shall Overcome.".

82. Johnson, "Annual Message to the Congress.".

83. Johnson, "Address to a Joint Session of Congress"; "Cotulla, Texas," YouTube video.

84. Pycior, *LBJ and Mexican Americans,* 6; Kearns, *Lyndon Johnson,* 28–31; Caro, *Years of Lyndon Johnson,* 45.

85. Preuss, "Cotulla Revisited," 21.

86. Ibid., 27.

87. Pycior, *LBJ and Mexican Americans,* 21.

88. Johnson, "Remarks at the Welhausen Elementary School.".

89. García, *Blowout!*, 6.

90. Cunningham, *Operation Wetback*.

91. Sánchez, *Becoming Mexican American*, 129–44.

92. Gómez-Quiñones, *Chicano Politics*, 101–5.

93. "Story of César Chávez.".

94. Ibid.

95. Rendón, *Chicano Manifesto*, 13.

96. Gómez-Quiñones, *Chicano Politics*, 101.

97. De León and del Castillo, *North to Aztlán*, 158–59.

98. Muñoz, *Youth, Identity, Power*, 130.

99. García, "'The Best Bargain,'" 248. This article focuses on García's recollections of the key testimonies and the significance of the Civil Rights Commission hearing for Chicano students at Lanier and Edgewood High Schools. Additionally, he underscores other testimonies from a few scholars and educators, including San Antonio mayor Walter McAllister and Texas Ranger officer A. Y. Allee.

100. De León and del Castillo, *North to Aztlán*, 158–59; Gonzales, "I Am Joaquin." In 1967 Chicano movement leader and poet Rodolfo "Corky" Gonzales wrote "I Am Joaquin," which was widely circulated among Chicano activists, to express the struggles of ethnic Mexican people seeking economic justice and equal rights in the United States, as well as to proclaim an identity as part of a hybrid mestizo society.

101. Gutiérrez, "Community, Patriarchy," 45.

102. Anderson, *Imagined Communities*, 6–7.

103. Gutiérrez, "Community, Patriarchy," 45.

104. *El Plan de Santa Barbara*, 51.

105. "Chicano Fighting for Political Power," YouTube video.

106. Hammerback et al., *War of Words*, 141.

107. Mario Compean, interview by Ignacio M. García, Tucson, Arizona, September 10, 1985, cited from García, *United We Win*, 18–19.

108. Ibid.

109. José Angel Gutiérrez, "Notes from José Angel Gutiérrez: Presently in Self-Imposed Exile" (unpublished position paper, January 1969), 2, cited from Navarro, *Mexican American Youth Organization*, 81.

110. De León, *Mexican Americans in Texas*, 127.

111. Carlos Guerra, interview by the author; Alberto Luera, interview by the author; Ignacio M. García, interview by the author; Mario Compean, interview by the author.

112. Major works that discuss Chicano student activism in detail include Gómez-Quiñones, *Mexican Students Por La Raza*; Muñoz, *Youth, Identity, Power*; Muñoz and Barrera, "La Raza Unida Party," 101–20; and Barrera, "The 1968 Edcouch-Elsa High School Walkout," 93–122.

113. "Chicano Fighting for Political Power," YouTube video.

114. Carlos Guerra, interview by the author; Viviana Santiago Cavada, interview by the author.

115. Montejano, *Quixote's Soldiers*, 154; Carlos Guerra, interview by Armando Navarro, September 1, 1993, quoted in Navarro, *Mexican American Youth Organization*, 110.

116. Rudy Rodríguez, interview by Armando Navarro, September 6, 1993, quoted in Navarro, *Mexican American Youth Organization*, 110–11.

117. Gutiérrez, "Community, Patriarchy," 47.

118. del Castillo, "Mexican Women in Organization," 10.

119. Gutiérrez, "Community, Patriarchy," 47.

120. The term "Xicanisma" emphasized the distinctly Mexican-origin sound of the word. It was first coined by scholar Ana Castillo in *Massacre of the Dreamers*.

121. *La Raza* 2 (ca. November–December 1969), courtesy of Ernesto Chávez, cited from Ruiz, *From Out of the Shadows*, 111–12.

122. "Chicano Fighting for Political Power," YouTube video.

123. Gutiérrez, *Making of a Chicano Militant*, 108–9; anonymous Chicano Movement activist, interview by the author; Juan Rocha Jr., interview by the author; Albro, "Gringo at the Awakening," 134. The conference had no relation to or affiliation with the Raza Unida Party organized under José Angel Gutiérrez in the early 1970s. Ward Albro was a professor emeritus of history at Texas A&I University (now Texas A&M University–Kingsville), where he spent most of his academic career. He taught one of the first Mexican American history classes in Texas and sympathized with student activists in the Kingsville student movement at Texas A&I because some of them were his students. After retiring from A&I, he moved to Castroville, Texas, where he passed away in 2022.

124. Anonymous Chicano Movement activist, interview by the author; Juan Rocha Jr., interview by the author; Albro, "Gringo at the Awakening," 134.

125. US Commission on Civil Rights, *Demographic, Economic, and Social Characteristics*, 6.

126. Ibid.; Texas Advisory Committee to the US Commission on Civil Rights, *Civil Rights in Texas*, 4.

127. Office of Economic Opportunity, Texas Department of Community Affairs, *Poverty in Texas, 1973*, 49.

128. Ibid., 51.

129. Texas Advisory Committee to the US Commission on Civil Rights, *Civil Rights in Texas*, 4.

130. Ibid.

131. US Commission on Civil Rights, staff report, *The Mexican American Population*, table 5, "Median Years of School Completed by Anglo, Nonwhite, and Mexican American Populations of Texas, 1950 and 1960," 10, box 66, folder 4, Joe J. Bernal Papers, Nettie Lee Benson Latin American Collection, University of Texas Libraries, University of Texas at Austin.

132. Homer D. García, "The Reluctant Spiritualist: Adventures of an Academic in the World of Curanderos" (unpublished manuscript, 2013), Homer D. García Academic Files, Humble, Texas.

133. Texas Advisory Committee to the US Commission on Civil Rights, *Civil Rights in Texas*, 5.

134. García, *Mexican American Youth Organization*, 3.

135. Castro, *Chicano Power*, 148.

136. Gutiérrez, *Making of a Chicano Militant*, 31. Gutiérrez also recalls that various Anglo community members told his mother to sell his father's medical equipment and either "return to her Mexican world or leave town." His mother chose to remain in Crystal City after her husband's death, despite being shunned by the local Anglo community.

137. Gutiérrez, *Making of a Civil Rights Leader*, 6.

138. Robert Clyde Tate, interview by Lyle C. Brown.

139. Gutiérrez, *Making of a Chicano Militant*, 58–59. Texas A&I University is now Texas A&M University–Kingsville. In consulting numerous sources for this study, I discovered that some documents list the organization's acronym as PASSO, while others use PASO.

140. Ibid. The term "bloc voting" refers to voting to elect several representatives from a single multimember constituency, otherwise known as at-large voting, plurality voting, or winner-take-all voting, meaning that the winner does not need the majority of votes to win the election. Thus, no run-off election is necessary, regardless of whether the vote count between candidates is close. Gutiérrez believed that plurality voting favored Chicano students who ran for student body positions at his college since most of them lost to Anglo candidates in runoff elections.

141. Gutiérrez, *Making of a Chicano Militant*, 12.

142. Ibid., 111, 142, 175.

143. "Chicano Fighting for Political Power," YouTube video.

144. Ibid.

145. Gutiérrez, *Making of a Chicano Militant*, 33.

146. Ibid., 126–27.

147. García, *United We Win*, 15–17.

148. García, *Mexican American Youth Organization*, 1.

149. Ibid., 4–5.
150. García, *United We Win*, 17.
151. Palomo Acosta, "Mexican American Youth Organization.".
152. Ibid.
153. Gutiérrez, *Making of a Civil Rights Leader*, 120.
154. "Requirement for New Members, MAYO," n.d., José Angel Gutiérrez Papers, 1954–1990, Nettie Lee Benson Latin American Collection, University of Texas Libraries, University of Texas at Austin. Hereafter cited as José Angel Gutiérrez Papers, 1954–1990.
155. Carlos Guerra, interview by the author.
156. "Organizational Development of MAYO," *La Voz: Juvenil de la Raza* (MAYO statewide letter, 1978), José Angel Gutiérrez Papers, 1954–1990.
157. Navarro, *Mexican American Youth Organization*, 22–44.
158. Ibid., 118–48.
159. Ibid., 95.
160. Ibid., 85–103. Saul Alinsky was a community organizer from Chicago, Illinois, who trained leftist organizers, taught his views on achieving mass power, and was credited with laying the foundation for confrontational political tactics that dominated during the 1960s.
161. Ibid., 119.
162. Gutiérrez, *Making of a Chicano Militant*, 128.
163. Navarro, *Mexican American Youth Organization*, 118.
164. For detailed information on MAYO, see Navarro, *Mexican American Youth Organization*; and García, *United We Win*.
165. Palomo Acosta, "Mexican American Youth Organization.".
166. Congressional Record, April 15, 1969, 9059.
167. Rosales, *Chicano!*, 184–90; *Walkout*. The movie *Walkout* portrays the major events of the 1968 East Los Angeles student protests and reveals the roles of the adult organizers who met and advised Chicano students before and during the walkout. Executive producer Montezuma Esparza was one of the adult leaders and a student activist at the University of California, Los Angeles who assisted in organizing the East Los Angeles "blowouts.".
168. Gómez-Quiñones, *Mexican Students Por La Raza*, 3.
169. Ibid., 43.
170. Muñoz, *Youth, Identity, Power*, 15.
171. Ibid., 70–71.
172. Chávez, "¡Mi Raza Primero!," 47.
173. Historian Mario T. García relied on data from oral history recordings of feedback from Sal Castro and others who knew Castro in the East Los Angeles community. For further information on Castro's teaching methods and role in the Chicano student movement in East Los Angeles, see García, *Blowout!*.
174. *Chicano!*, videocassette.

CHAPTER 3

1. According to my research, very few secondary sources offer detailed information on the Lanier High School walkout of 1968. The only books that provide general information on the protest include García, *United We Win*; and Navarro, *Mexican American Youth Organization*. However, one insightful source chronicles the schooling of Mexican American students at Lanier High School during the World War II era (Rivas-Rodríguez, *Mexican Americans and World War II*, chap. 3). This includes data from oral interviews by Rivas-Rodríguez with Julio Noboa and a few former students who attended the school in the 1940s. In his memoir, Noboa mentions that Lanier High School, named for American author Sidney Lanier, was originally founded as a vocational junior high school in 1929 and housed both junior and high school students during its early years.

2. García, *United We Win*, 30; García, *Rise of the Mexican American*, 38; Rivas-Rodríguez, *Mexican Americans and World War II*, 71; Ignacio M. García, interview by the author.

3. Ignacio M. García, interview by the author; Edgar G. Lozano, interview by the author.

4. Romo, "World of Our Fathers.".

5. Homer D. García, interview by the author.

6. Weber, *From South Texas*, 88.

7. David R. Johnson, John A. Booth, and Richard J. Harris, *The Politics of San Antonio: Community, Progress, and Power* (Lincoln: University of Nebraska Press, 1983), vii–xi, 3–71; and Rodolfo Rosales, *The Illusion of Inclusion: The Untold Political Story of San Antonio* (Austin: University of Texas Press, 2000), 1–33, both cited from Weber, *From South Texas*, 89.

8. "San Antonio: A City Already Desegregated," *St. Petersburg (FL) Times*, October 6, 1963, cited from La Rotta, "'Talk to Me.'".

9. García, *Rise of the Mexican American*, 38; Weber, *From South Texas*, 89–91. Weber's book provides historical information on the devastating impact of flooding, substandard housing, and the death rate that resulted from such circumstances in San Antonio's West Side beginning in the early 1920s.

10. Montejano, *Anglos and Mexicans*, 265.

11. San Antonio Public Service Company, *Economic and Industrial Survey* (1942), 6, 31, 32, 169–70; San Antonio Chamber of Commerce, *Manufacturing for Less in San Antonio*, 11; and Michael Garland Landolt, "The Mexican-American Workers of San Antonio, Texas" (PhD diss., University of Texas at Austin, 1965), all cited from García, *Rise of the Mexican American*, 29.

12. García, *Chicano while Mormon*, 9, 11.

13. Ibid., 61.

14. García, *United We Win*, 30.

15. García, "Reluctant Spiritualist," chap. 4, section "Describe Race Relations." Homer D. García's personal biographical account in "The Reluctant Spiritualist" offers more specific details concerning his mistreatment at the school. All citations of "Reluctant Spiritualist" include chapters and section headings since the source does not include page numbers.

16. Robert Coles and Harry Huge, "Thorns on the Yellow Rose of Texas," *New Republic*, April 19, 1969, 13–17; and Robert Garland Landolt, *The Mexican American Workers of San Antonio, Texas* (New York: Arno Press, 1976), 320, 326, both cited from Acuña, *Occupied America*, 297.

17. Edgar G. Lozano, interview by the author.

18. CBS news anchor Charles Kuralt narrates the film and first mentions statistics from the *Citizens' Board of Inquiry into Hunger and Malnutrition in the United States*, a comprehensive and scholarly report investigating various conditions of chronic hunger across the United States. Kuralt quotes statistics stating that out of a total population of 200 million in the United States, 30 million remained impoverished, yearly family income was below $3,000, and 5 million received assistance from at least two federal food programs in 1968. This report received national attention and widespread publicity through the broadcast of the "Hunger in America" television documentary.

19. "CBS Documentary Hunger in America." "Hunger in America" originally aired as an episode of the program *CBS Reports* on May 21, 1968. The first nineteen minutes of this one-hour program feature a study of hunger in San Antonio's West Side and the city's preoccupation with the opening of HemisFair '68. According to statistics on hunger and poverty cited in a *San Antonio Express-News* article dated March 18, 2013, approximately 96 percent of West Side residents were Latino, an estimated 40 percent lived below the poverty line, and about 35 percent of all households received food stamps, more than three times the national average.

20. Ibid.

21. Davies, "'Hunger in America.'".

22. Orozco, "School Improvement League.".

23. Eleuterio Escobar, autobiographical notes (typescript), box 1, folder 2, Eleuterio Escobar Papers, Nettie Lee Benson Latin American Collection, University of Texas Libraries, University of Texas at Austin. Hereafter cited as Escobar Papers.

24. Eleuterio Escobar, "Final Autobiography, 1894–1958" (typescript), box 1, folder 5, Escobar Papers.

25. Darder et al., *Latinos and Education*, 400. For more in-depth information on the role of Escobar and the Liga, see Mario García's excellent chapter, "Education and the Mexican American: Eleuterio Escobar and the School Improvement League of San Antonio," in Darder et al., *Latinos and Education*.

26. Eleuterio Escobar, "Final Autobiography, 1894–1958" (typescript), box 1, folder 5, Escobar Papers; Darder et al., *Latinos and Education*, 400.

27. Eleuterio Escobar, "Final Autobiography, 1894–1958" (typescript), box 1, folder 5, Escobar Papers; Darder et al., *Latinos and Education*, 401.

28. See Board of Education documents, October 23, 1934, box 2, folder 3, and undated document apparently written in 1934, "Escobar Archives," box 1, cited from Darder et al., *Latinos and Education*, 402; San Miguel, *"Let All of Them,"* 83; Orozco, "School Improvement League.".

29. Undated document apparently written in 1934, "Escobar Archives," box 1, cited from Darder et al., *Latinos and Education*, 402.

30. See Board of Education documents, October 23, 1934, box 2, folder 3, and undated document apparently written in 1934, "Escobar Archives," box 1, cited from Darder et al., *Latinos and Education*, 402.

31. Escobar to A. B. Stevens, San Antonio, May 4, 1934, folder "Escobar Archives," box 1; see pamphlet "More and Better Schools for the Western Section," in "Escobar Archives," box 1, cited from Darder et al., *Latinos and Education*, 402.

32. Orozco, "School Improvement League.".

33. Ibid.

34. Ibid., According to García's chapter in Darder et al., *Latinos and Education*, Escobar personally contacted the San Antonio school board to present the LULAC committee's case for promoting educational improvements on the West Side. In response to the committee's proposal, the board purchased and approved the transfer of fifteen abandoned frame rooms to Lorenzo de Zavala School. The committee criticized the board's action by stating, "The said frame dwellings are inadequate and unsafe. . . . We do not want shacks." The committee began to solicit public support and recruit civic organizations to achieve its objectives after the board's refusal to make substantial improvements to predominantly Mexican American schools.

35. Darder et al., *Latinos and Education*, 405.

36. Eleuterio Escobar, "Final Autobiography, 1894–1958" (typescript), box 1, folder 5, Escobar Papers; Escobar to José Rendón, San Antonio, November 7, 1934, "Escobar Archives," box 1; *La Prensa*, October 24, 1934, Miscellaneous Newspapers, all cited from Darder et al., *Latinos and Education*, 405.

37. Hammerback et al., *War of Words*, 142. In chap. 7 of *War of Words*, coauthor José Angel Gutiérrez mentions LULAC and María Hernández's participation in the 1934 San Antonio rally as part of his discussion of LULAC's assimilationist approach to educational issues.

38. L. A. Woods to Escobar, Austin, September 17, 1934, "Escobar Archives," box 1, cited from Darder et al., *Latinos and Education*, 404.

39. Eleuterio Escobar, "Respetable auditores," 1–2 (English translation), cited from San Miguel, *"Let All of Them,"* 85.

40. Eleuterio Escobar, "Respetable auditores," 6–7 (English translation), cited from San Miguel, *"Let All of Them,"* 85.

41. Darder et al., *Latinos and Education*, 406.

42. "What the School Improvement League Has Done, What Remains to Be Done, and How to Do It," circa 1949, box 6, folder 2, Escobar Papers.

43. School Improvement League letter, ca. 1949, box 6, folder 2, Escobar Papers.

44. See "Constitución general de la Liga Pro-Defensa Escolar," 4, for a list of these organizations. The Liga's constitution was written in Spanish; cited from San Miguel, *"Let All of Them,"* 86; Orozco, "School Improvement League.".

45. Orozco, "School Improvement League.".

46. "'La Gran Junta' de la Liga Pro-Defensa Escolar," Eleuterio Escobar Papers, University of Texas Libraries. University of Texas at Austin.

47. Orozco, "School Improvement League.".

48. Rivas-Rodríguez, *Mexican Americans and World War II*, 68.

49. Ibid., 72–75.

50. Gilbert G. González, "Crisis of Urbanization: Racism, Education and the Mexican Community in Los Angeles, 1920–1930" (School of Social Science, University of California, Irvine, 1976), 1, 5, cited from García, *Rise of the Mexican American*, 175. Also, for further information on school districts promoting an English-only, vocationally oriented curriculum in San Antonio and throughout Texas, see San Miguel, *"Let All of Them,"* 39–47.

51. García, *Rise of the Mexican American*, 176.

52. *Los Recuerdos: Sidney Lanier High School Yearbook*, 34–39. The yearbook shows pictures of various vocational courses featuring mostly Mexican American students. This record also reveals that the San Antonio School District approved a $35 million school improvement bond on January 27, 1968, but does not indicate how the money was spent.

53. García, *Rise of the Mexican American*, 177.

54. "50th Anniversary.".

55. US Commission on Civil Rights, *Hearing Before the United States Commission*, 12. Hereafter cited as San Antonio transcript.

56. Orozco, "Hernández, María L. de.".

57. García, *Chicano while Mormon*, 69.

58. San Antonio transcript, 188–89.

59. González, *Chicano Education*, 45.

60. US Commission on Civil Rights, *Excluded Student*, 13–20.

61. For the original copy of Lanier High School's Spanish detention violation slip, see exhibit 12, "Violation Slip," in San Antonio transcript, 881; García, "'The Best Bargain,'" 250.

62. US Commission on Civil Rights, *Excluded Student*, 16.

63. San Antonio transcript, 190.

64. Joe J. Bernal, interview by Valentino Mauricio.

65. Ibid.

66. Rivas-Rodríguez, *Mexican Americans and World War II*, 81.

67. *San Antonio Express-News*, April 13, 2008.

68. García, "Reluctant Spiritualist," chap. 4, section "HS Conformity.".

69. San Antonio transcript, 181.

70. García, "Reluctant Spiritualist," chap. 4, section "Describe Lanier.".

71. García, *United We Win*, 4.

72. Rafael Castillo, interview by the author. Castillo explained how the military recruiter's speech in the movie *Born on the Fourth of July* reminded him of the recruiters who were key speakers in some of the student assemblies at Lanier.

73. Ignacio M. García, interview by the author.

74. San Antonio transcript, 269–70.

75. Ibid., 180.

76. Ibid., 823. For the official report assessing the conditions of Mexican Americans in San Antonio–area schools in the 1960s, see exhibit 11, US Commission on Civil Rights, *Demographic, Economic, and Social Characteristics*.

77. Donato, *Other Struggle*, 20.

78. San Antonio transcript, 180.

79. Homer D. García, interview by the author.

80. García, *Chicano while Mormon*, 74.

81. Rafael Castillo, interview by the author.

82. Ibid.

83. Carlos Cortes, "A Bicultural Process for Developing Mexican American Heritage Curriculum," in *Multilingual Assessment Project: Riverside Component, 1971–1972, Annual Report*, eds. Alfredo

Castañeda, Manuel Ramirez, and Leslie Herold (Riverside, CA: Systems and Evaluations in Education, 1972), 5, cited from *Toward Quality Education for Mexican Americans*, 7.

84. De León, *They Called Them Greasers*, 12.
85. García, *When Mexicans Could Play Ball*, 76.
86. García, "'The Best Bargain,'" 251.
87. Rosie Peña and Irene Yañez, interview by the author.
88. García, "'The Best Bargain,'" 263; San Antonio transcript, 135.
89. This celebration commemorates the Texan victory in the Battle of San Jacinto when Mexican general Antonio López de Santa Anna surrendered to General Sam Houston in April 1836.
90. Daniel Hernández, interview by the author.
91. San Antonio transcript, 71, 77.
92. Ibid., 71–73.
93. Homer D. García, email to the author.
94. Ibid.
95. García, "Reluctant Spiritualist," chap. 4, section "Precognition.".
96. Ibid.
97. The Inman Christian Center is a community center of the Central Christian Church serving as a low-income outreach agency that continues to provide educational and recreational programs, emergency food assistance, and affordable housing to those in the inner city and in San Antonio's West Wide. For further details, see https://www.inmancenter.org. According to one official letter from the center, the median income of the neighborhood around Inman was $2,080 during the late 1960s. See copy of letter titled "Inman Christian Center and Central Christian Church Crisis in the Nation Proposals Narrative" in the Joe J. Bernal Papers, box 32, folder 16, Nettie Lee Benson Latin American Collection, University of Texas Libraries, University of Texas at Austin. Hereafter cited as Bernal Papers.
98. Edgar G. Lozano, interview by the author.
99. Ibid.
100. Homer D. García, interview by the author. García did not know the exact reason why the organizers refused to invite him.
101. Irene Yañez, interview by the author.
102. Typewritten list of community leaders and student leaders supporting the Lanier Student demands/grievances, copy obtained from Homer D. García, Humble, Texas.
103. García, "Reluctant Spiritualist," chap. 4, section "Leaflet Distribution.".
104. Homer D. García, interview by the author.
105. Ibid.; García, "Reluctant Spiritualist," chap. 4, section "Frisking." This embarrassing incident in the principal's office reminded García of the time he saw his father pulled over and frisked by INS agents as a young child growing up in San Antonio. He remembers seeing his father, a veteran of World War II, cry as the agents were frisking him because they most likely assumed that he was not a citizen or somehow thought he resembled a criminal.
106. Palomo Acosta, "Mexican American Legal Defense.".
107. *San Antonio Express*, April 11, 1968. Also see appendix A.
108. *San Antonio Express*, April 11, 1968.
109. *San Antonio Express-News*, April 13, 2008; Edgar G. Lozano, interview by the author; *Inferno* 2, no. 3 (May 1968): 8.
110. *San Antonio Express-News*, April 13, 2008; García, "Reluctant Spiritualist," chap. 4, section "Student Council Presentation"; Homer D. García, interview by the author.
111. San Antonio transcript, 190.
112. *Inferno* 2, no. 3 (May 1968): 8.
113. *San Antonio Express-News*, April 13, 2008; García, "Reluctant Spiritualist," chap. 4, section "Student Council Presentation"; Homer D. García, interview by the author.
114. Homer D. García, interview by the author,.
115. *San Antonio Express*, April 11, 1968.
116. Irene Yañez, interview by the author.

117. Edgar G. Lozano, interview by the author.
118. García, "Reluctant Spiritualist," chap. 4, section "Walkout." García's memoir also reveals that the faculty sponsor and the student council members wrote down the names of the twelve to fifteen students who walked out of the meeting, but this record no longer exists.
119. García, "Reluctant Spiritualist," chap. 4, section "I Protest"; Homer D. García, interview by the author.
120. García, "Reluctant Spiritualist," chap. 4, section "Walkout.".
121. García, *Chicano while Mormon*, 65.
122. García, "Reluctant Spiritualist," chap. 4, section "Human Rights Violation," chap. 5, section "Name Calling.".
123. García, "Reluctant Spiritualist," chap. 5, section "Post Protest Threats.".
124. García, "Reluctant Spiritualist," chap. 4, section "Pressure on Me.".
125. *Inferno* 2, no. 3 (May 1968): 8.
126. Edgar G. Lozano, interview by the author; Homer D. García, interview by the author; García, "Reluctant Spiritualist," chap. 4, section "Protest Activities"; García, "'The Best Bargain,'" 249; *Alamo Messenger*, April 19, 1968, box 32, folder 16, Bernal Papers.
127. Homer D. García, interview by the author. García could not recall all the names of the other students who were suspended from school.
128. Edgar G. Lozano, interview by the author.
129. García, *Chicano while Mormon*, 60.
130. García, *United We Win*, 30; Sepúlveda, *Life and Times of Willie Velásquez*.
131. Ignacio M. García, interview by the author. García explained that this group of student activists was politically active even before the walkout by endorsing candidates for student council, including student leader Homer D. García, who favored social and political change within the school.
132. Edgar G. Lozano, interview by the author.
133. Ibid.
134. For the complete list of Lanier High School student demands, see *San Antonio Express*, April 11, 1968; exhibit 15, letter, San Antonio Independent School District, in San Antonio transcript, 888–90; also see appendix A of this book.
135. García, "'The Best Bargain,'" 250. Former student Ignacio M. García briefly mentions his support of the Lanier student movement: "Adding my own contribution to the protests, I passed out leaflets and engaged in a grassroots 'speaking circuit' by rank-and-file students promoting the demands of the student leaders" (249).
136. Stephen Castro, interview by the author.
137. *San Antonio Express*, April 11, 1968.
138. *San Antonio Light*, April 12, 1968.
139. Ibid.
140. Exhibit 11, San Antonio transcript, exhibit 11, table 18, 861.
141. Ibid.
142. Rivas-Rodríguez, *Mexican Americans and World War II*, 85–86.
143. Ignacio M. García, interview by the author; Carlos Guerra, interview by the author; Rivas-Rodríguez, *Mexican Americans and World War II*, 68–72.
144. *San Antonio Express*, April 11, 1968.
145. Ibid.
146. *San Antonio Express*, April 12, 1968.
147. Ibid.
148. *San Antonio Express*, April 11, 1968; *Alamo Messenger*, April 19, 1968, box 32, folder 16, Bernal Papers.
149. García, *United We Win*, 31.
150. From an unfinished autobiography by Ignacio M. García that deals in depth with Sidney Lanier High School and the West Side of San Antonio, cited from García, *United We Win*, 31.
151. *San Antonio Express*, April 11, 1968.

152. *Alamo Messenger*, April 19, 1968, box 32, folder 16, Bernal Papers.
153. *San Antonio Light*, April 12, 1968.
154. Ibid.
155. *Alamo Messenger*, April 19, 1968, box 32, folder 16, Bernal Papers.
156. Ibid.
157. Rosales, *Chicano!*, 143–44; Bender, *One Night in America*, 31.
158. Paul Schrade (United Auto Workers western director), interview with Mariah Kennedy Cuomo, Providence, RI, March 27, 2017, cited from Kennedy Cuomo, "Robert F. Kennedy," 57.
159. Ferris and Sandoval, *Fight in the Fields*, 116.
160. "Robert Kennedy Took On Kern County Sheriff," YouTube video.
161. *San Antonio Light*, April 16, 1968.
162. Lanier protest leaflet, n.d., box 32, folder 16, Bernal Papers.
163. *San Antonio Express*, April 16, 1968.
164. Stephen Casanova, "The Movement for Bilingual/Bicultural Education in Texas: School Boycotts and the Mexican American Youth Organization," unpublished text, n.d., 11, cited from García, *United We Win*, 31–32.
165. *San Antonio Express*, April 18, 1968.
166. Ibid.
167. Homer D. García, interview by the author.
168. Ibid. García could not remember how the television news networks were notified of his situation. He speculates that Pete Tijerina or another lawyer from MALDEF likely contacted the local news stations.
169. Ibid.; Edgar G. Lozano, interview by the author.
170. García, "Reluctant Spiritualist," chap. 4, section "HS Admins Confronted"; Homer D. García, interview by the author.
171. Homer D. García, interview by the author. García believes school officials reneged on their promise to prevent the school district and its officials from facing legal action.
172. Ibid.
173. García, "Reluctant Spiritualist," chap. 4, section "Kidnap Attempted."
174. Homer D. García, interview by the author.
175. Ibid.
176. García, "Reluctant Spiritualist," chap. 4, section "Superintendent Threatened."
177. Homer D. García, interview by the author; García, "Reluctant Spiritualist," chap. 4, section "Superintendent Threatened."
178. García, "Reluctant Spiritualist," chap. 4, sections "Superintendent Threatened" and "We Win."
179. *Alamo Messenger*, April 19, 1968, box 32, folder 16, Bernal Papers.
180. Ruben Lucio, interview by the author.
181. Richard and Diana Herrera, interview by Dick Gordon.
182. *Edgewood: The Story—The People*, 8.
183. Ibid. According to *Edgewood: The Story—The People*, the south San Antonio area of Edgewood extended west beyond the present Loop 410, which was part of School District 15. After the Bexar county commissioner's court granted permission to divide District 15, the eastern part of District 15 became the Lake View Gardens School District 41, which enrolled students in one-room, wooden-frame schoolhouses. Edgewood residents voted in favor of becoming an independent school district on January 20, 1950.
184. *Edgewood: The Story—The People*. The Edgewood School, originally built in 1915, expanded to include four new classrooms and a gymnasium to accommodate high school students by 1936. The Edgewood School District issued $40,000 in bonds to finance the construction of Edgewood High School and received assistance from the Works Progress Administration, part of President Franklin D. Roosevelt's New Deal program, in 1938.
185. *Edgewood: The Story—The People*, 10.
186. Ibid.

187. Cárdenas, *Texas School Finance Reform*, 21.
188. Richard and Diana Herrera, interview by Dick Gordon; Richard and Diana Herrera, interview by the author; *San Antonio Express-News*, April 13, 2008. Other former Edgewood students who also met and spoke to me to discuss the major educational deficiencies at an informal meeting and interview on July 18, 2013, include Ruben Elizondo, Rey Flores, Henry N. García, Raymond A. Ortega Jr., Ramon Ríos, Silvia Cortez Rodríguez, and Herlinda Martínez Sifuentes.
189. Richard and Diana Herrera, interview by the author.
190. *Edgewood High School Walkout '68*, DVD.
191. *San Antonio Express-News*, July 27, 1998.
192. Rebecca Campos Ramirez, email message to the author, July 4, 2013.
193. Rebecca Campos Ramirez, interview by the author.
194. *Edgewood High School Walkout '68*, DVD.
195. Fernández, "Edgewood High School Walkouts.".
196. Mario Compean, interview by the author.
197. Fernández, "Edgewood High School Walkouts"; Mario Compean, interview by the author. Compean mentioned that he did not know about the availability of counseling at Edgewood until the week before he graduated, which suggests that not all students received adequate counseling at the school.
198. Fernández, "Edgewood High School Walkouts." .
199. *San Antonio Express-News*, July 27, 1998.
200. For the complete list of Edgewood High School student demands, see exhibit 16, San Antonio transcript, exhibit 16, 891–92; also see appendix B of this book.
201. San Antonio transcript, 192.
202. Rosendo T. Gutiérrez, interview by the author; Richard Herrera, interview by the author. Both Gutiérrez and Herrera revealed that students at Edgewood had to pay a twenty-five-cent poll tax in order to vote for representatives on the student council from the freshman to senior class. According to Gutiérrez, Edgewood student council elections and meetings taught Chicano students to become more aware of the significance of political activism and exercising civil disobedience during the walkout.
203. Diana Herrera, interview by the author.
204. San Antonio transcript, 193.
205. San Antonio transcript, exhibit 8, table 10, 782.
206. García, *Mexican American Youth Organization*, 13.
207. Ibid.
208. San Antonio transcript, exhibit 11, table 18, 868.
209. Mario Compean, interview by the author. Regarding the poor condition of the high school building, the second student demand listed in the "Edgewood High School Student Body Grievances" reveals that two janitors serviced and cleaned the entire school, and most of the restroom facilities lacked running water, toilet tissue, and soap.
210. *San Antonio Express-News*, July 27 and 29, 1998; Reynaldo Anaya Valencia et al., *Mexican Americans and the Law*, 30; Richard R. Valencia, *Chicano Students*, 95–97.
211. Reynaldo Anaya Valencia et al., *Mexican Americans and the Law*, 30; Richard R. Valencia, *Chicano Students*, 96.
212. Mario Compean, interview by the author. Compean also explained that Mexican Americans employed by Kelly Air Force Base received meager wages and had little opportunity for significant advancement or promotion.
213. San Antonio transcript, exhibit 11, table 18, 831. According to this source, the assessed property valuation per student in the Edgewood School District for the 1967–68 school year was $2,208, compared to $11,414 spent in the Northwest ISD the same year.
214. *San Antonio Evening News*, August 4, 1965; Mario Compean, interview by the author.
215. See the fifth student demand in San Antonio transcript, "Edgewood High School Student Body Grievances." Another part of this demand states the need for better counseling for all students.

NOTES TO PAGES 110–114 ❧ 249

216. See the fifth student demand in San Antonio transcript, "Edgewood High School Student Body Grievances." Compean also states that the parents of Chicano students were very supportive of their children during the Edgewood High School walkout. Unfortunately, Compean does not recall how many students participated in the walkout but believes the number of protesters may have been in the hundreds.

217. *San Antonio Express-News*, July 27, 1998; Mario Compean, interview by the author. Compean was unable to tell me the whereabouts of the parents and presumes that many of them have passed away over the years.

218. Rosendo T. Gutiérrez, interview by the author.

219. *San Antonio News*, May 17, 1968.

220. *San Antonio Express*, May 16 and 17, 1968.

221. *San Antonio Express-News*, April 13, 2008.

222. *Edgewood High School Walkout '68*, DVD.

223. Richard and Diana Herrera, interview by Dick Gordon; Richard and Diana Herrera, interview by the author. During his interview with Dick Gordon, Richard Herrera claims that Mrs. Mooney attempted to discourage her students from walking out.

224. Gamboa, "Forgotten History.".

225. Rosendo T. Gutiérrez, interview by the author; *Edgewood High School Walkout '68*, DVD.

226. Gamboa, "Forgotten History." .

227. Rosendo T. Gutiérrez, interview by the author; *Edgewood High School Walkout '68*, DVD; *San Antonio Express-News*, April 13, 2008.

228. *San Antonio News*, May 17, 1968.

229. *Edgewood High School Walkout '68*, DVD.

230. *San Antonio News*, May 17, 1968; Orozco, "Rodriguez v. San Antonio ISD." Also see the newspaper photograph of the Edgewood student protest in figure 2.

231. Richard Herrera, interview by the author.

232. *San Antonio News*, May 17, 1968, and April 13, 2008; Richard Herrera, interview by the author.

233. Ibid.

234. *San Antonio Express*, May 17, 1968. Willie Velásquez was a Chicano community organizer from San Antonio who helped José Angel Gutiérrez establish MAYO, and Father Henry Casso was a San Antonio parish priest who expressed concern about the educational deficiencies impacting Mexican American students in the United States. Casso later served as a member of the advisory committee of the US Commission on Civil Rights.

235. *Edgewood: The Story—The People*, 25.

236. *San Antonio Express*, May 18, 1968.

237. *San Antonio News*, May 17, 1968.

238. *San Antonio News*, May 18, 1968.

239. *San Antonio Express*, May 17, 1968.

240. *San Antonio News*, May 17, 1968.

241. *San Antonio Light*, May 23, 1968.

242. *San Antonio Light*, May 20, 1968.

243. Ibid. According to former Edgewood students who participated in the walkout, neither Sabater nor Hilgen was ever reinstated, and both left the school after the end of the school year. One article in the *San Antonio Express* on May 14, 1968, reveals the controversy regarding the Edgewood school board's failure to renew the teaching contract of Albert Sabater. The article does not mention whether Janie Hilgen's name was omitted from the list of Edgewood teachers receiving new contracts for the following school year.

244. *San Antonio News*, May 18, 1968.

245. *San Antonio Light*, May 21, 1968.

246. Richard and Diana Herrera, interview by Dick Gordon. Also, see the fifth student demand in San Antonio transcript, "Edgewood High School Student Body Grievances." Richard and Diana Herrera were among the many Chicano students to notice major renovations at their

school after resuming classes in the fall of 1968. They believe the school district made the renovations in response to the students' demands for improved conditions, and to avoid further protest activity publicizing the deterioration of the school.

247. Cárdenas, *Texas School Finance Reform*, 17.

248. *San Antonio Express-News*, July 27, 1998.

249. Sracic, San Antonio v. Rodriguez, 20.

250. *San Antonio Express-News*, July 28, 1998; Sracic, San Antonio v. Rodriguez, 21.

251. Valencia, *Chicano Students*, 92–93; Sracic, San Antonio v. Rodriguez, 20; Orozco, "Rodriguez v. San Antonio ISD.".

252. Valencia, *Chicano Students*, 92–93; Sracic, San Antonio v. Rodriguez, 20; Pratt, "Review of *Brown v. Board of Education*," 145.

253. Valencia, *Chicano Students*, 93; Sracic, San Antonio v. Rodriguez, 20–21; Orozco, "Rodriguez v. San Antonio ISD.".

254. Pratt, "Review of *Brown v. Board of Education*," 145; Soltero, *Latinos and the American Law*, 79.

255. Raymond, "Snid, Alberta Zepeda.".

256. *San Antonio Light*, May 21, 1968.

257. *Rodríguez v. San Antonio Independent School District*, 337 F. Supp. at 281, 284 (Western District of Texas, 1971), cited from Valencia, *Chicano Students*, 94. Valencia's book mentions two separate cases, not as *Rodriguez I* (case filed in federal district court) and *Rodriguez II* (Supreme Court case), but as *Rodríguez v. San Antonio Independent School District* (1971) and *San Antonio Independent School District v. Rodríguez* (1973) for ease of communication. Also see Soltero, *Latinos and the American Law*, 80.

258. *San Antonio Express-News*, July 28, 1998; Reynaldo Anaya Valencia et al, *Mexican Americans and the Law*, 30–31; Richard R. Valencia, *Chicano Students*, 96.

259. Deposition of Jose Cardenas, October 20, 1971, *Rodriguez v. San Antonio Independent School District*, 337 F. Supp. at 280 (Western District of Texas, 1971), cited from Sracic, San Antonio v. Rodriguez, 47, and Yudof and Morgan, "*Rodriguez v. San Antonio*," 392.

260. Sracic, San Antonio v. Rodriguez, 47.

261. Ibid., 51, 52. Table 4.4 on p. 52 lists data on district wealth and educational quality, comparing the percentage of teachers with college and master's degrees and the percentage of total staff with emergency permits in five San Antonio–area school districts, including Edgewood.

262. For specific data on the financial disparities and selected indicators of educational quality comparing the Edgewood and Alamo Heights School Districts for 1968, see Valencia, *Chicano Students*, 96–97, tables 2.5 and 2.6.

263. *San Antonio Independent School District v. Rodríguez*, 411 U.S. at 12 (1973), cited from Valencia, *Chicano Students*, 93, 96.

264. *San Antonio Independent School District v. Rodríguez*, 411 U.S. at 12–13 (1973), cited from Valencia, *Chicano Students*, 96.

265. US Commission on Civil Rights, *Mexican American Education in Texas*, 25.

266. Ibid., 27.

267. J. Berke and J. Callahan, "*Serrano v. Priest*: Milestone or Millstone for School Finance," *Journal of Public Law* 21 (1972): 33, cited from Valencia, *Chicano Students*, 92.

268. Preuss, *To Get a Better School System*, 82–92; Yudof and Morgan, "*Rodriguez v. San Antonio*," 386–87.

269. Preuss, *To Get a Better School System*, 82–92; Yudof and Morgan, "*Rodriguez v. San Antonio*," 386–87; Soltero, *Latinos and the American Law*, 81–82; Cárdenas, *Texas School Finance Reform*, 1. The Gilmer-Aikin Committee proposed the Minimum Foundation Program, calling for a school finance formula allowing the state to pay 80 percent of the costs of the program, with local school districts responsible for the remaining 20 percent. The "economic index" was intended to provide additional funds to be redistributed to poorer school districts in order to cover all or part of their required 20 percent, thereby enabling such low-income school districts to maintain the state-established minimum.

270. Cárdenas, *Texas School Finance Reform*, 31.

271. Valencia, *Chicano Students*, 93; Yudof and Morgan, "*Rodriguez v. San Antonio*," 391–92.

272. Yudof and Morgan, "*Rodriguez v. San Antonio*," 392.

273. *San Antonio Independent School District v. Rodríguez*, 411 U.S. at 4 (1973), cited from Valencia, *Chicano Students*, 94.

274. *San Antonio Independent School District v. Rodríguez*, 411 U.S. at 11, cited from Valencia, *Chicano Students*, 95.

275. For the total revenues per student, see Sracic, San Antonio v. Rodriguez, 50, table 4.3, "District Wealth and School Revenue.".

276. *Rodríguez v. San Antonio Independent School District*, 337 F. Supp. at 282, 284 (Western District of Texas, 1971), cited from Valencia, *Chicano Students*, 95; *San Antonio Independent School Dist. v. Rodriguez*, 411 U.S. at 15, cited from Yudof and Morgan, "*Rodriguez v. San Antonio*," 392–93.

277. *Rodríguez v. San Antonio Independent School District*, 337 F. Supp. at 282, 284 (Western District of Texas, 1971), cited from Valencia, *Chicano Students*, 95.

278. Yudof and Morgan, "*Rodriguez v. San Antonio*," 393.

279. *San Antonio Express-News*, July 27, 1998; Reynaldo Anaya Valencia et al., *Mexican Americans and the Law*, 29–37; Richard R. Valencia, *Chicano Students*, 97; Yudof and Morgan, "*Rodriguez v. San Antonio*," 393; Orozco, "Rodriguez v. San Antonio ISD." .

280. Soltero, *Latinos and the American Law*, 78.

281. *Rodríguez v. San Antonio Independent School District*, 337 F. Supp. at 286 (Western District of Texas, 1971), cited from Valencia, *Chicano Students*, 98; Soltero, *Latinos and the American Law*, 78–79.

282. Sracic, San Antonio v. Rodriguez, 53, 60. Assistant attorney general Pat Bailey, who represented the defendants, argued that the plaintiffs' case was part of a conspiracy that amounted to an endorsement of communism and socialism as a means to equalize school funding in Texas. According to Sracic, Supreme Court justice Lewis F. Powell Jr. later expressed this same sentiment when the case went before the Supreme Court after the state filed an appeal (67–68). Bailey's argument against increased centralization over education most likely influenced Justice Powell's decision on the case since Powell feared that such centralized authority would affect every state-supported public school, including colleges and universities, across the nation.

283. Deposition of Jose Cardenas, October 20, 1971, *Rodriguez v. San Antonio Independent School District*, 337 F. Supp. 280 (Western District of Texas, 1971), cited from Yudof and Morgan, "*Rodriguez v. San Antonio*," 392.

284. Yudof and Morgan, "*Rodriguez v. San Antonio*," 393. The "Aftermath" section of the article (393–99) provides insightful information on the reactions to the lower court's decision from the general public, education community, Texas politicians, and three study groups that presented school resource allocation plans (as distinguished from tax reform proposals) with a legitimate chance for public debate.

285. Yudof and Morgan, "*Rodriguez v. San Antonio*," 399.

286. Ibid., 400.

287. Valencia et al., *Mexican Americans and the Law*, 32–35.

288. Soltero, *Latinos and the American Law*, 81–92; Sracic, San Antonio v. Rodriguez, 113–17; Valencia, *Chicano Students*, 99–100.

289. Sracic, San Antonio v. Rodriguez, 67–68.

290. Orozco, "Rodriguez v. San Antonio ISD"; Sracic, San Antonio v. Rodriguez, 119; Valencia, *Chicano Students*, 100–103.

291. Quoted in Soltero, *Latinos and the American Law*, 91. In 1946, Heman M. Sweatt, an African American, applied for admission to the University of Texas School of Law but was denied entry because of his race, despite meeting all eligibility requirements. Sweatt sued the university in state court on the grounds that the Texas State Constitution prohibited integrated education. The defendant was university president Theophilus Painter. The lower court later dismissed the case when the state supposedly established a "separate but equal" law school.

Sweatt appealed the dismissal to the US Supreme Court, claiming that the admissions criteria violated the Equal Protection Clause of the Fourteenth Amendment. The court ultimately ruled that the Equal Protection Clause required Sweatt's admission since Texas' equality of treatment without integration was insufficient. Furthermore, the decision allowed Sweatt and other African American applicants the opportunity to pursue graduate and professional degrees that were not available at historically black universities in Texas, such as Prairie View or Texas Southern.

292. Jeffrey S. Sutton, "San Antonio Independent School District.".

293. Soltero, *Latinos and the American Law*, 93.

CHAPTER 4

1. Valencia, *Chicano Students*, 47–48. Valencia includes sets of photographs reprinted from Calderón's thesis showing the differences in the quality of the facilities at the two schools. One set features the well-kept indoor drinking fountain with an electric cooler for South Edcouch Elementary School (Anglo), and the poorly maintained outdoor drinking fountains at North Edcouch Elementary School (Mexican American). For photos of the elementary schools, see pp. 44–47.

2. Carlos Calderón, "The Education of Spanish-Speaking Children in Edcouch-Elsa, Texas" (master's thesis, University of Texas at Austin, 1950), cited from Valencia, *Chicano Students*, 48.

3. Ibid., 43.

4. Kopel, *Border Life*, 114.

5. I was able to determine the approximate enrollment and ethnic composition of the school by studying the 1968–69 *La Avispa: Edcouch-Elsa High School Yearbook*. Edcouch-Elsa High School was, and remains, the only high school in the area. Students in grades seven to twelve attended the school during the period in question. The school continues to have a majority ethnic Mexican student population today.

6. Garza, "Edcouch TX"; Garza, "Elsa, TX." During my research, I discovered that very few published or unpublished works offer a comprehensive examination of small, rural cities in South Texas such as Edcouch-Elsa.

7. Jacinto González, interview by Francisco Guajardo, 1998, unpublished oral history archive manuscript, Llano Grande Center Oral History Collection II, Edcouch-Elsa High School, Elsa, Texas, cited from Guajardo, "Narratives of Transformation," 140.

8. I refer to Maricela Rodríguez Lozano by her maiden name since she was known by this name at the time of the walkout.

9. Rodríguez Lozano, interview by the author.

10. Ibid.

11. The *Edcouch-Elsa Walkout Clips* video shows Uvaldo Vásquez discussing the incident in which Coach Kachtik scolded him for speaking Spanish during class. The incident occurred before the walkout, but Vásquez does not mention the date.

12. González, *Chicano Education*, 45.

13. Kopel, *Border Life*, 114.

14. Frank Vallejo, interview by the author.

15. Eddy González, interview by the author.

16. Freddy Sáenz, interview by the author.

17. Raúl Arispe, interview by Francisco Guajardo.

18. Bene Layton, interview by the author.

19. Felix Rodríguez, interview by the author.

20. Carter, *Mexican Americans in School*, 19.

21. Nelda Villareal Treviño and Mirtala Villareal, interview by the author.

22. *Edcouch-Elsa Walkout Clips* video. This video shows Porfirio González speaking in Spanish about his recollections of the conversation with his daughter's teacher and his discovery of

how this teacher segregated Mexican Americans from Anglos in the classroom. González does not mention the teacher's name, what subject the teacher taught, or the date of his visit to the school; it presumably occurred days or weeks before the walkout.

23. Eugene Gutiérrez, interview by the author.

24. Geneva García, interview by Francisco Guajardo, 1998, unpublished oral history archive manuscript, Llano Grande Center Oral History Collection II, Edcouch-Elsa High School, Elsa, Texas, cited from Guajardo, "Narratives of Transformation," 158.

25. Homero Díaz, interview by the author.

26. Francis Anderson, interview by Francisco Guajardo, 1998, unpublished oral history archive manuscript, Llano Grande Center Oral History Collection II, Edcouch-Elsa High School, Elsa, Texas, cited from Guajardo, "Narratives of Transformation," 158.

27. Willie Ruth Foerster, interview by Francisco Guajardo, 1998, unpublished oral history archive manuscript, Llano Grande Center Oral History Collection II, Edcouch-Elsa High School, Elsa, Texas, cited from Guajardo, "Narratives of Transformation," 158.

28. Billie Cellum, interview by the author.

29. Nelda Villareal Treviño and Mirtala Villareal, interview by the author.

30. Freddy Sáenz, interview by Francisco Guajardo, 1998 and 2001, unpublished oral history archive manuscript, Llano Grande Center Oral History Collection II, Edcouch-Elsa High School, Elsa, Texas, cited from Guajardo, "Narratives of Transformation," 150–51.

31. Ibid.

32. Gómez-Quiñones, *Mexican Students Por La Raza*, 2.

33. Arturo Salinas, interview by the author.

34. Ibid.

35. For newspaper coverage suggesting MAYO's involvement in this process, see *Valley Morning Star* (Harlingen, TX), November 13, 1968; *McAllen Monitor*, November 13, 1968.

36. Information quoted from the list of demands drafted by the student committee, November 7, 1968.

   Also see an article on the walkout in the *McAllen Monitor*, November 14, 1968, for a complete list of the student demands and recommendations; and appendix C in this book.

37. Guajardo, "Narratives of Transformation," 146. I believe that Ramírez may have spoken to labor leaders in secret during and after work hours but cannot verify whether Ramírez participated in labor organizing in Detroit. For further details on Ramírez's time in Detroit, consult Francisco Guajardo's research.

38. Nelda Villarreal Treviño of Elsa, Texas, made these notes available to me. She most likely collected them from her sister Mirtala and other student leaders who were more active in the student movement. These notes offer important details on the student meetings but are rather sketchy regarding student interactions with school officials. The precise actions, names, and meeting times with such officials are not listed.

39. See handwritten notes by Javier Ramírez, n.d., Edcouch-Elsa, Texas, copies obtained from Nelda Villarreal Treviño, Elsa Texas. The notes by Ramírez do not indicate how or when he recorded the feedback from the Edcouch-Elsa school educators opposed to the walkout. His notes do not provide any positive or supportive commentary from teachers. Ramírez most likely used the educators' criticisms of the student movement to motivate Chicano students to walk out during his informal conversations with student activists.

40. Neal Galloway, interview by the author.

41. *McAllen Monitor*, November 7, 1968.

42. See Edcouch-Elsa School Board meeting minutes, November 4, 1968, copies obtained from Nelda Villarreal Treviño, Elsa, Texas; *McAllen Monitor*, November 6, 1968; letter sent to parents from school board, November 5, 1968. A copy of the letter is in the author's possession. However, the main contents of the school board policy written in the letter can be found in the *McAllen Monitor*, November 6, 1968.

43. See letter sent to parents from school board, November 5, 1968.

44. Javier Ramírez, interview by the author.

45. *McAllen Monitor*, November 14, 1968; Billie Cellum, interview by the author.
46. See handwritten notes by Javier Ramírez.
47. *Edinburg Daily Review*, November 12, 1968.
48. Ibid.
49. Ibid.
50. Ibid.
51. Nelda Villareal Treviño and Mirtala Villareal, interview by the author.
52. Felix Rodríguez, interview by the author.
53. Ibid.
54. *Valley Morning Star* (Harlingen, TX), November 14, 1968.
55. South Texas newspaper articles on the walkout offer different estimates of how many students walked out and picketed. Some of these figures are not accurate. The *McAllen Monitor* reported that 140 students began the walkout, while the *Edinburg Daily Review* and *Corpus Christi Caller* estimated that 150 did so. The *Valley Morning Star* (Harlingen, TX) estimated that as many as 160 to 175 Chicano students started the protest. Also see the newspaper photograph of the Edcouch-Elsa student protest in figure 4.
56. *Brownsville Herald*, November 15, 1968.
57. Ibid.
58. Navarro, *Mexican American Youth Organization*, 121.
59. *Edcouch-Elsa Walkout Clips* video. This video shows Maricela Rodríguez Lozano discussing how she was reprimanded by her mother for walking out of school.
60. An article in the *McAllen Monitor*, November 14, 1968, mentions Rebecca González urging student protesters to return to school but does not say whether her children participated in the walkout.
61. Eloy Zavala, interview by the author.
62. Former teacher Eugene Gutiérrez helped identify these principals and faculty members when I showed him a copy of a *McAllen Monitor* newspaper photo. Gutiérrez could not identify one person in the photo, who he believed was a faculty member.
63. *McAllen Monitor*, November 14, 1968.
64. Ibid.
65. Ibid. Also see García, *Mexican American Youth Organization*, 21.
66. *Corpus Christi Caller-Times*, November 15, 1968.
67. Arturo Salinas, interview by the author.
68. I was unable to locate the arrest records of the six student leaders, as Hidalgo County Sheriff's Department personnel informed me that they could not verify the existence or whereabouts of such records.
69. Eloy Zavala, interview by the author.
70. *McAllen Monitor*, November 15, 1968.
71. Freddy Sáenz, interview by the author.
72. *McAllen Monitor* and *Valley Morning Star* (Harlingen, TX), November 17, 1968.
73. Artemio Salinas, interview by the author.
74. *Edinburg Daily Review*, November 17, 1968.
75. Although the *Valley Morning Star* (Harlingen, TX), November 17, 1968, states that R. M. González and Rafael Yarrito signed the surety bond, their relationship to Sustaita is not indicated.
76. *Edinburg Daily Review* and *McAllen Monitor*, November 17, 1968.
77. *McAllen Monitor*, November 17, 1968.
78. One *McAllen Monitor* article, "E-E Campus Quiet Saturday after Six Arrested" (November 17, 1968), quotes Pipkin making this statement. However, the 1968–69 *La Avispa: Edcouch-Elsa Yearbook* refers to a total of fifty-six faculty members rather than forty-five.
79. For details concerning the proceedings of this meeting and the decisions made by the school board, see Edcouch-Elsa School Board meeting minutes, November 18, 1968, copies obtained from Nelda Villarreal Treviño, Elsa, Texas.

80. *Edinburg Daily Review*, November 19, 1968.
81. *McAllen Monitor*, November 19, 1968.
82. Eddy González, nephew of board member Gilbert G. González, told me that his uncle often fell asleep during board meetings and did not show support or sympathy toward those who walked out of school, which suggests his apathy concerning the walkout.
83. Nelda Villareal Treviño, interview by the author.
84. *McAllen Monitor*, November 19, 1968.
85. Edcouch-Elsa School Board meeting minutes, November 19, 1968, copies obtained from Nelda Villarreal Treviño, Elsa, Texas. .
86. Ibid., November 29, 1968. .
87. Billie Cellum, interview by the author.
88. Nelda Villareal Treviño and Mirtala Villareal, interview by the author.
89. The Edcouch-Elsa School Board meeting minutes for November 19–21 and 29, 1968, offer the most detailed account of student hearings conducted by school officials. They state that school officials expelled 58 students and allowed 134 to return to classes, totaling 192.
90. Eddy González, interview by the author.
91. Billie Leo, interview by the author.
92. Raúl Arispe, interview by Frank Guajardo; *Edcouch-Elsa High School Walkout Clips* video. In the video, walkout supporter Rubén Rodríguez describes how various Mexican American community members conveyed their sympathy with the protesters by donating spare change as gas money for the bus.
93. Raúl Arispe, interview by Frank Guajardo. In the interview, Arispe did not elaborate on whether local or state law enforcement officials followed the bus as it traveled to La Joya High School, or how many police officers observed the bus.
94. Nelda Villareal Treviño and Mirtala Villareal, interview by the author.
95. Ibid.
96. Western Union telegram to Javier Ramirez, November 15, 1968, photocopy obtained from Nelda Villarreal Treviño, Elsa, Texas.
97. Western Union telegram to Javier Ramirez, November 16, 1968, photocopy obtained from Nelda Villarreal Treviño, Elsa, Texas.
98. Western Union telegram to Javier Ramirez, November 27, 1968, photocopy obtained from Nelda Villarreal Treviño, Elsa, Texas.
99. *McAllen Monitor*, November 24, 1968.
100. US Federal District Court for the Southern District of Texas, Brownsville Division, *Xavier Ramirez*.
101. Navarro, *Mexican American Youth Organization*, 158–59.
102. San Miguel, "Let All of Them," 173.
103. Blanton, *George I. Sánchez*, 247; Kaplowitz, *LULAC*, 131.
104. I obtained a photocopy of the case docket from the US federal district court clerk's office in Brownsville, Texas. Further analysis of the case can be found in Barrera, "1968 Edcouch-Elsa High School Walkout," chap. 3.
105. Also see *McAllen Monitor*, November 20, 1968.
106. Reynaldo G. Garza, a native of Brownsville, Texas, was the first Mexican American chief judge of a federal district court in the United States. In 1979, he became the first Mexican American to serve on the US Court of Appeals. President Jimmy Carter offered him the position of attorney general, which would have made him the first Mexican American to serve on a presidential cabinet had he chosen to accept the appointment.
107. US Federal District Court for the Southern District of Texas, Brownsville Division, photocopy of plaintiffs' complaint for civil case *Xavier Ramirez*, 1. Also see *McAllen Monitor*, November 20, 1968.
108. See US Federal District Court for the Southern District of Texas, Brownsville Division, photocopy of Defendants' Motion to Sever the Issue of Damages and Demand for Jury on Such Issue from civil case *Xavier Ramirez*.

109. *McAllen Monitor*, December 17, 1968.
110. *McAllen Monitor*, December 19, 1968.
111. *McAllen Monitor*, December 20, 1968.
112. R. P. "Bob" Sánchez, interview by the author.
113. *McAllen Monitor*, December 19, 1968.
114. US Federal District Court for the Southern District of Texas, Brownsville Division, photo-copy of judgment for civil case *Xavier Ramirez*, 1–2.
115. *McAllen Monitor*, December 19, 1968.
116. Ibid.
117. Sánchez to Mario Obledo, December 19, 1968, box 5, folder 14, R. P. "Bob" Sánchez Papers, 1921–2005, Nettie Lee Benson Latin American Collection, University of Texas Libraries, University of Texas at Austin.
118. *Edcouch-Elsa Walkout Clips* video; Rubén Rodríguez, interview with the author. Sadly, Rubén Rodríguez died within a year after this interview. A newly constructed elementary school in the Edcouch-Elsa School District was named in Rodríguez's honor shortly after his death.
119. Felix Rodríguez, interview by author, 2010.

CHAPTER 5

1. Texas A&I University is now Texas A&M University–Kingsville. This school was originally founded in 1925 and named South Texas Teachers College.
2. Faustino Erebia, interview by the author.
3. Coalson, "Kingsville, Texas.".
4. Texas Advisory Committee to the US Commission on Civil Rights, *Civil Rights Status of Spanish-Speaking Americans*, ii.
5. Office of Economic Opportunity, Texas Department of Community Affairs, *Poverty in Texas, 1973*, 235. The $2,611 per capita income figure is presumably for Mexican American residents.
6. Raúl Garza, interview by the author; Faustino Erebia, interview by the author.
7. *San Antonio Express*, April 15, 1969.
8. *South Texan* (Texas A&M University–Kingsville student newspaper), February 21, 1969, South Texas Archives and Special Collections, James C. Jernigan Library, Texas A&M University–Kingsville, Kingsville, Texas.
9. Ibid.
10. Chávez, "¡Mi Raza Primero!," 5.
11. Blackwell, *Chicana Power!*, 95.
12. Gonzales, "I Am Joaquín.".
13. *South Texan* (Texas A&M University–Kingsville student newspaper), February 21, 1969, South Texas Archives and Special Collections, James C. Jernigan Library, Texas A&M University–Kingsville, Kingsville, Texas.
14. Ibid.
15. *South Texan*, February 21 and 28, 1969; *Corpus Christi Caller*, April 15, 1969. The newspaper articles provide the only information regarding these demonstrations and reveal only a few details. The *San Antonio Express* and *Corpus Christi Caller* indicate that student activists who demonstrated outside city hall presented a list of demands to city officials almost exactly like the one issued to school administrators during the Gillett Junior High School walkout. However, the *South Texan* mentions that activists submitted four demands to city leaders regarding civic improvements such as the construction of a public park, pavement of city streets in predominantly Mexican American neighborhoods, maintenance of a drainage ditch running through the north side of town, and the forgoing of plans to build a new sports stadium.
16. Rosales, *Chicano!*, 182.
17. Ibid., 181.
18. Quoted in Navarro, *Mexican American Youth Organization*, 67.
19. Quoted in Rosales, *Chicano!*, 181.

20. *Denver Post*, March 21, 2009.

21. Ibid.

22. Quoted in Marín, *Spokesman of the Mexican American Movement*, 10.

23. Gutiérrez, *Making of a Chicano Militant*, 86.

24. *South Texan*; see article "President Receives Grievances from Six Mexican-Americans," March 28, 1969, South Texas Archives, Texas A&M University–Kingsville. Key student grievances called for lowering the admissions standards for Mexican Americans applying to Texas A&I University, offering bilingual programs in all fields of study, increased hiring of Mexican American professors, establishing a Chicano Studies Department, publicizing on-campus jobs, and establishing low-rent housing at the university.

25. *South Texan*; see article "PASO Seeking Funds to Help Sunday Protest," March 28, 1969, South Texas Archives, Texas A&M University–Kingsville. This mass demonstration, which was orderly and peaceful, reportedly included approximately two thousand to three thousand people from throughout the nation and protested the removal of the Volunteers in Service to America (VISTA) program in Del Rio by Texas governor Preston Smith. County officials in Del Rio requested the closure of the program, claiming that VISTA workers became too active in Chicano politics. José Angel Gutiérrez and state senator Joe Bernal spoke to those assembled during the march, reiterating their opposition to Preston's decision to discontinue the VISTA program in Del Rio. For further information on this historic event, see documents in the Hector P. García Papers in the Special Collections and Archives of Texas A&M University–Corpus Christi.

26. *South Texan*, April 11, 1969. Carlos Guerra did not mention giving this speech prior to the Kingsville walkout during my interview with him on December 2, 2004.

27. Gutiérrez, *Making of a Chicano Militant*, 86; Hunter and Hunter, *Texas A&M University–Kingsville*, 143–45.

28. Registrar's Office, "Local Reports," South Texas Archives, Texas A&M University–Kingsville; "Proposal for Ethnic Studies," in "Ethnic Program 1970," UA, A1992–036.043, South Texas Archives, Texas A&M University–Kingsville, cited from Hunter and Hunter, *Texas A&M University–Kingsville*, 154.

29. Ward Albro, interview by the author; Antonio and Diana Bill, interview by the author; Carlos Guerra, interview by the author; Alberto Luera, interview by the author; anonymous Chicano Movement activist, interview by the author; Hunter and Hunter, *Texas A&M University–Kingsville*, 139. Also see numerous articles documenting Chicano Movement activities at Texas A&I University during the late 1960s and early 1970s in the *South Texan* student newspaper collection in the South Texas Archives at Texas A&M University–Kingsville.

30. José Angel Gutiérrez, interview by Lyle C. Brown.

31. Ibid.

32. Antonio and Diana Bill, interview by the author; Carlos Guerra, interview by the author; Alberto Luera, interview by the author.

33. José Angel Gutiérrez, interview by Lyle C. Brown. This oral memoir documents how Gutiérrez and a group of fifty to sixty unknown people, presumably other students, collected and borrowed the identification cards of 1,108 Mexican American students at Texas A&I University in order to vote on their behalf when the election was held on a Saturday (exact date unknown). According to Gutiérrez, the 1,108 students could not vote on that day since they did not remain on campus on the weekends. He further indicates that the election was won by a margin of fewer than ten votes. Gutiérrez's technique involved persuading Mexican American students to vote in unison during elections, which later became one of his most popular techniques for voting in school board and city government elections. He first tried it when he ran unsuccessfully for student body president at Southwest Texas Junior College in Uvalde in 1963.

34. Gutiérrez, *Making of a Civil Rights Leader*, 119–20.

35. Ibid.

36. Antonio and Diana Bill, interview by the author; Carlos Guerra, interview by the author; Alberto Luera, interview by the author.

37. Antonio and Diana Bill, interview by the author; Antonio Bill, email message to the author, July 22, 2005.

38. *South Texan*, March 1, 1974, cited from Hunter and Hunter, *Texas A&M University–Kingsville*, 152.

39. Antonio and Diana Bill, interview by the author; Viviana Santiago Cavada, interview by the author.

40. Blackwell, *Chicana Power!*, 161–91. Chapter 5 of Blackwell's book discusses the details of the walkout of Chicana activists during the 1971 Conferencia de Mujeres por la Raza.

41. Blackwell, *Chicana Power!*, 209.

42. Blackwelder, *Women of the Depression*, 36.

43. Orozco, *No Mexicans*, 228–29.

44. Antonio and Diana Bill, interview by the author; Carlos Guerra, interview by the author; Alberto Luera, interview by the author.

45. *South Texan*, March 14, 1969.

46. Ward Albro, interview by the author; Hunter and Hunter, *Texas A&M University–Kingsville*, 141.

47. Cortez, *Carmen Lomas Garza*, 6.

48. Carmen Lomas Garza, interview by Paul J. Kalstrom.

49. Ibid.

50. Cortez, *Carmen Lomas Garza*, 7–9. The illustration of Carmen Lomas Garza's *Cakewalk* on p. 9 shows people of all ages participating in the cakewalk game, consuming food and beverages, and socializing with each other. The painting shows fifteen participants walking over squares with numbers (1–17) forming a large circle drawn by chalk while music plays in the background. Those playing the game must halt and stand still on one of the squares when the music suddenly ends. One of the organizers of the fundraiser announces a random number after the music stops, and the person who landed on that number wins a cake. The game resumes as soon as the music starts again. This type of fundraiser was common among other American GI Forum chapters in the 1960s.

51. Carmen Lomas Garza, interview by Paul J. Kalstrom.

52. Ibid.

53. For specific details on Carmen Lomas Garza's involvement with the MAYO exhibit and Chicano Movement, see Cortez, *Carmen Lomas Garza*, 15–20.

54. Carmen Lomas Garza, interview by Paul J. Kalstrom.

55. Ibid.

56. Antonio and Diana Bill, interview by the author; Carlos Guerra, interview by the author; Alberto Luera, interview by the author; Viviana Santiago Cavada, interview by the author.

57. "1969: Student Walkouts." .

58. Navarro, *Mexican American Youth Organization*, 125.

59. Faustino Erebia, interview by the author.

60. Faustino Erebia, interview by the author; Cecilia Cortez, interview by the author. According to walkout participants Erebia and Cortez, most former local student activists had either moved out of the community or passed away since the walkout. Both interviewees also recalled the names of a few other former students from Gillett Junior High who remain hesitant to speak of their experiences during the protest.

61. Faustino Erebia, interview by the author.

62. Andrés Garza, interview by the author. Garza, former head of the Records Department at Kingsville ISD, remembered some of his former students participating in the walkout. Garza also discussed sponsoring an after-school tutoring program at Gillett Junior High School that assisted these students with their schoolwork.

63. Ibid.

64. Cecilia Cortez, interview by the author.

NOTES TO PAGES 156–162 ◆ 259

65. Antonio and Diana Bill, interview by the author. Former campus activists Antonio and Diana Bill mentioned that Chicano Movement participant and Texas A&I alumnus Efrain Fernández and his younger brother Homer, a local high school student, helped arrange meetings between activists at Texas A&I and Chicano students in the Kingsville public schools prior to the walkout. However, neither they nor other former student activists interviewed for this book could recall whether other such siblings helped facilitate meetings between Texas A&I and public school students in Kingsville. I managed to contact Efrain Fernández, but he declined to be interviewed. I was also unable to locate Homer Fernández to request an interview.

66. Antonio and Diana Bill, interview by the author; Kingsville student grievances, "Non-militant Protest for Demand," April 14, 1969, 1, folder 12.22, Hector P. García Papers, Mary and Jeff Bell Library, Texas A&M University–Corpus Christi. Also see appendix D in this book.

67. Kingsville student grievances, "Non-militant Protest for Demand," April 14, 1969, 2, folder 12.22, Hector P. García Papers, Mary and Jeff Bell Library, Texas A&M University–Corpus Christi.

68. Raúl G. Garza, interview by the author; *Corpus Christi Times*, April 15, 1969.

69. *San Antonio Express*, April 15, 1969.

70. Faustino Erebia, interview by the author.

71. *San Antonio Express*, April 15, 1969.

72. Ibid.; *Kingsville-Bishop Record-News*, April 16, 1969.

73. MAYO letter, "This Is What Has Happened So Far, This Is to Keep You Informed," n.d., José Angel Gutiérrez Papers, 1954–1990.

74. Faustino Erebia, interview by the author; *Kingsville-Bishop Record-News*, April 16, 1969; Navarro, *Mexican American Youth Organization*, 126.

75. Kingsville School Board meeting minutes, April 15, 1969, Department of Records, Kingsville Independent School District; *Kingsville-Bishop Record-News*, April 16, 1969.

76. MAYO letter, "This Is What Has Happened So Far"; *Kingsville-Bishop Record-News*, April 16, 1969.

77. *Corpus Christi Caller*, April 15, 1969; *Kingsville-Bishop Record-News*, April 16, 1969.

78. Cecilia Cortez, interview by the author. Former student Cecilia Cortez further reveals that the Gillett Junior High School principal first notified her parents of the walkout by phone and believes other students' parents may have received similar phone calls from the school as well.

79. *Kingsville-Bishop Record-News*, April 16, 1969.

80. *Kingsville-Bishop Record-News*, April 30, 1969.

81. Ibid.

82. Ibid.

83. MAYO letter, "This Is What Has Happened So Far." Figures also cited in Navarro, *Mexican American Youth Organization*, 126.

84. MAYO letter, "This Is What Has Happened So Far"; *Corpus Christi Caller*, April 17, 1969. I cannot confirm whether all the students who marched had participated in the walkout. Most if not all of them likely walked out of the school.

85. *Corpus Christi Caller*, April 17, 1969; *San Antonio Express*, April 17, 1969; *South Texan*, April 18, 1969.

86. MAYO letter, "This Is What Has Happened"; *Kingsville-Bishop Record-News*, April 16, 1969; *San Antonio Express*, April 17, 1969; Faustino Erebia, interview by the author.

87. Faustino Erebia, interview by the author.

88. Alberto Luera, interview by the author, January 17, 2005; anonymous Chicano Movement activist, interview by the author; Faustino Erebia, interview by the author; *McAllen Monitor*, April 18, 1969.

89. Alberto Luera, interview by the author; anonymous Chicano Movement activist, interview by the author.

90. *Corpus Christi Caller*, April 17, 1969; *San Antonio Express*, April 17, 1969; *South Texan*, April 18, 1969.

91. Alberto Luera, interview by the author.

92. *Corpus Christi Caller*, April 17, 1969; *Corpus Christi Times*, April 17, 1969; *San Antonio Express*, April 17, 1969; MAYO letter, "This Is What Has Happened.".

93. Anonymous Chicano Movement activist, interview by the author.

94. Alberto Luera, interview by the author; anonymous Chicano Movement activist, interview by the author. Also, see newspaper photograph of the incarcerated Kingsville student protesters in figure 10.

95. Carlos Guerra, interview by the author; *San Antonio Express*, April 17, 1969.

96. Juan Rocha Jr., interview by the author; *Corpus Christi Caller*, April 17, 2005.

97. *Corpus Christi Caller*, April 18, 1969; *Corpus Christi Times*, April 17, 1969; *San Antonio Express*, April 17, 1969; *South Texan*, April 18, 1969.

98. *San Antonio Express*, April 17, 1969.

99. MAYO letter, April 23, 1969, cited from Navarro, *Mexican American Youth Organization*, 127.

100. Alberto Luera, interview by the author, January 17, 2005; anonymous Chicano Movement activist, interview by the author; *San Antonio Express*, April 18, 1969.

101. Mario Salazar, interview by the author.

102. Anonymous Chicano Movement activist, interview by the author; Mario Salazar, interview by the author; Juan Rocha Jr., interview by the author; *Corpus Christi Caller*, April 17, 2005. Scholar Armando Navarro claims that all juveniles had been released to their parents by 6:00 p.m. (*Mexican American Youth Organization*, 127).

103. *Corpus Christi Caller*, April 17, 2005; *Corpus Christi Times*, April 17, 1969; *San Antonio Express*, April 18, 1969; *South Texan*, April 18, 1969; Navarro, *Mexican American Youth Organization*, 128. Only the *Corpus Christi Times* article and Navarro's text indicate that twelve young adult protesters posted bond. The *South Texan* article indicates that Texas A&I University professor Ronald Sommers donated the students' bond money. Unfortunately, former MALDEF attorney Juan Rocha Jr. and former student activists interviewed for this book failed to remember whether certain student protesters paid bonds while police freed others on their own recognizance without having posted bond.

104. *South Texan*, April 18, 1969.

105. *San Antonio Express*, April 17, 1969.

106. Ibid.

107. *San Antonio Express*, April 18, 1969.

108. *San Antonio Express*, April 19, 1969; *Corpus Christi Caller*, April 19, 1969. During an interview with me, Rocha did not recall arranging this meeting.

109. *San Antonio Express*, April 19, 1969.

110. Navarro, *Mexican American Youth Organization*, 128.

111. *Corpus Christi Caller*, April 19, 1969; Navarro, *Mexican American Youth Organization*, 128.

112. *San Antonio Express*, April 19, 1969.

113. *Corpus Christi Caller*, April 19, 1969; Navarro, *Mexican American Youth Organization*, 128.

114. *San Antonio Express*, April 20, 1969.

115. MAYO Teatro was an artistic theatrical arm of MAYO, which, like Teatro Campesino, was used as an educational, organizational, and agitational tool.

116. MAYO Teatro–Gillett Junior High School Walkout two-act play, April 18, 1969, José Angel Gutiérrez Papers, 1954–1990.

117. Ibid.

118. Ibid.; *San Antonio Express*, April 20, 1969.

119. MAYO Teatro–Gillett Junior High School Walkout two-act play, April 18, 1969, José Angel Gutiérrez Papers, 1954–1990.

120. The term *vendidos*, which means "sellouts" in Spanish, refers to Mexican Americans who fail or refuse to acknowledge their ethnic identity or Mexican cultural roots. The *vendidos* were heckling and ridiculing the Kingsville student protesters.

121. Chávez, *"¡Mi Raza Primero!,"* 5.

122. Navarro, *Mexican American Youth Organization*, 173.

123. Ibid., 173–74.

124. *Corpus Christi Caller*, April 20, 1969.

125. José Angel Gutiérrez, interview by Lyle C. Brown.

126. *Manifesto Addressed to the President of the United States*, 66.

127. Jensen and Hammerback, "Interview with José Angel Gutiérrez," 208. The interview states that many in the Mexican American community were grateful to hear Gutiérrez's "Kill the Gringo" speech since they felt anger and bitterness toward Anglos. During the interview, Gutiérrez recalls receiving a large amount of mail and numerous phone calls from both educated professionals and working-class Mexican Americans commending him for the speech.

128. Hammerback et al., *War of Words*, 86–96. Chapter 5 explains how Gutiérrez used rhetoric to convince his followers of Mexican origin that they shared a common struggle and were continually repressed by Anglo-Americans. Gutiérrez used the term "Chicano" to acknowledge people of Mexican origin under one racial/ethnic label; "Aztlán" referred to the US Southwest as Chicanos' ancestral homeland that was once inhabited by their Indian ancestors; and "La Raza" meant that all Mexican Americans could unite to gain their political rights as US citizens against the political, social, and economic structures of Anglo-American hegemony.

129. José Angel Gutiérrez, interview by Armando Navarro, May 16, 1973, Crystal City, Texas, cited from Navarro, *Mexican American Youth Organization*, 129–30.

130. Kohout, "González, Henry Barbosa"; Eugene Rodríguez Jr., *Henry B. González: A Political Profile* (New York: Arno Press, 1976), 71, cited from Hammerback et al., *War of Words*.

131. Kohout, "González, Henry Barbosa"; Dugger, "Segregation Filibuster of 1957," 46–47.

132. Eugene Rodríguez Jr., *Henry B. González: A Political Profile* (New York: Arno Press, 1976), 124, cited from Hammerback et al., *War of Words*.

133. "Texas Politics: Henry B. González." Also see McKenzie, *Mexican Texans*, 110.

134. García, "'The Best Bargain,'" 253.

135. *Congressional Record*, April 3, 1969, 8590.

136. Congressional Record, April 15, 1969, 9058.

137. *Latino Americans: The 500-Year Legacy*; Montejano, *Quixote's Soldiers*, 104–8.

138. *Latino Americans: The 500-Year Legacy*.

139. Congressional Record, April 22, 1969, 9952.

140. *San Antonio Light*, April 18, 1969.

141. Congressional Record, April 22, 1969, 9953; Congressional Record, April 29, 1969, 10779–80.

142. *Corpus Christi Caller*, April 8, 1969; *San Antonio Light*, April 18, 1969.

143. For further information on Henry B. González's denunciation of the Ford Foundation's funding of MAYO, see García, *United We Win*, 27–29; Navarro, *Mexican American Youth Organization*, 168–71.

144. José Angel Gutiérrez, interview by Lyle C. Brown.

145. *San Antonio Express and News*, March 31, 1969.

146. *San Antonio Express and News*, April 23, 1969.

147. For more specific details on González's criticisms of MAYO and the Ford Foundation and other types of political opposition, see Navarro, *Mexican American Youth Organization*, 168–71; García, *United We Win*, 26–29.

148. *Kingsville-Bishop Record-News*, April 20, 1969.

149. Ibid.

150. *San Antonio Express*, April 22, 1969.

151. *Corpus Christi Caller*, April 22, 1969.

152. *San Antonio Express*, April 22, 1969.

153. Kingsville School Board meeting minutes, April 21, 1969, Department of Records, Kingsville Independent School District; *Corpus Christi Times*, April 21, 1969; *San Antonio Express*, April 22, 1969.

154. *Corpus Christi Times*, April 22, 1969.

155. Kingsville School Board meeting minutes, April 21, 1969, Department of Records, Kingsville Independent School District.
156. Ibid.; *San Antonio Express*, April 23, 1969.
157. *San Antonio Express*, April 23, 1969.
158. *Kingsville-Bishop Record-News*, April 23, 1969.
159. Western Union telegram to Rene Treviño, April 16, 1969, José Angel Gutiérrez Papers, 1954–1990.
160. Western Union telegram to Kingsville chapter of MAYO, April 18, 1969, José Angel Gutiérrez Papers, 1954–1990.
161. Western Union telegram to Kingsville chapter of MAYO, April 17, 1969, José Angel Gutiérrez Papers, 1954–1990.
162. Western Union telegram to Kingsville chapter of MAYO, April 16, 1969, José Angel Gutiérrez Papers, 1954–1990.
163. Anonymous Chicano Movement activist, interview by the author.
164. *Kingsville-Bishop Record-News*, April 30, 1969.
165. Anonymous Chicano Movement activist, interview by the author.
166. *Kingsville-Bishop Record-News*, April 30, 1969.
167. Navarro, *Mexican American Youth Organization*, 131.
168. *Kingsville-Bishop Record-News*, April 30, 1969.
169. Juan Rocha Jr., interview by the author, January 28, 2005.
170. Alberto Luera, interview by Armando Navarro, Crystal City, Texas, April 18, 1973, cited from Navarro, *Mexican American Youth Organization*, 131.
171. Navarro, *Mexican American Youth Organization*, 131.
172. Ibid.
173. Raúl G. Garza, interview by the author. Garza was able to provide a written summary of statistics indicating the increased numbers of Mexican Americans serving on the Kingsville School Board and administration before and after 1969.
174. Ibid.
175. Faustino Erebia, interview by the author.

CHAPTER 6

1. *Now and Then in Zavala County*, 32.
2. Ibid.
3. Viviana Santiago Cavada, interview by the author.
4. Ibid.; *Now and Then in Zavala County*, 4.
5. *Now and Then in Zavala County*, 64.
6. Ochoa, "Zavala County."
7. Shockley, *Chicano Revolt*, 11.
8. Ochoa, "Zavala County."
9. Statistics on Crystal City and Zavala County from *U.S. Census Reports, Statistical Profile of the Spanish-Surname Population of Texas*, José Angel Gutiérrez Papers, 1954–1990.
10. Angel Noe González, interview by John Staples Shockley, November 11, 1970, Crystal City, Texas, cited from Shockley, *Chicano Revolt*.
11. Gilbert Conoley and Juan Ibarra, interoffice memorandum, Texas Education Agency, December 22, 1969, 1, Hector P. García Papers, Special Collections and Archives, Mary and Jeff Bell Library, Texas A&M University–Corpus Christi.
12. Severita Lara, interview by the author; Diana Palacios, interview by the author.
13. Gutiérrez, *Making of a Chicano Militant*, 24.
14. US Commission on Civil Rights, Issue Presentation for Education Conference, March 7, 1970, Crystal City, Texas, José Angel Gutiérrez Papers, 1954–1990.
15. Diana Palacios, interview by Priscilla Martinez, July 19, 2012, interview 1, transcript, Oral History Memoir, Baylor University Institute for Oral History, Waco, Texas.

16. Ibid.
17. Shockley, *Chicano Revolt*, 13.
18. Trillin, "U.S. Journal," 102.
19. Gutiérrez, *Making of a Chicano Militant*, 24.
20. *Latino Americans: The 500-Year Legacy.*
21. Gutiérrez, *Making of a Chicano Militant*, 36.
22. R. C. Tate, "History of Zavala County, Texas" (unpublished master's thesis, Southwest Texas State College, San Marcos, Texas, 1942), 88, cited from Shockley, *Chicano Revolt.*
23. Gutiérrez, *Making of a Chicano Militant*, 41; Rodríguez, *Tejano Diaspora*, 47.
24. Rodríguez, *Tejano Diaspora*, 47.
25. Ibid.
26. Navarro, *Cristal Experiment*, 20–25. Ethnic Mexican war veterans were either American citizens or legal residents living in the United States.
27. Gutiérrez, *Making of a Chicano Militant*, 36–37.
28. Ibid.
29. Ibid., 37–39.
30. Rodríguez, *Tejano Diaspora*, 47.
31. Ibid., 48; José Angel Gutiérrez, interview in "Chicano Fighting for Political Power," YouTube video.
32. Gutiérrez, *Making of a Chicano Militant*, 39.
33. *San Antonio Express*, April 14, 1963; Shockley, *Chicano Revolt*, 26; Rodríguez, *Tejano Diaspora*, 51.
34. *San Antonio Express*, April 14, 1963; Shockley, *Chicano Revolt*, 26.
35. Gutiérrez, *Making of a Chicano Militant*, 43.
36. Albert J. Peña Jr., interview by José Angel Gutiérrez, July 2, 1996, CMAS 15, TVOH, cited from Rodríguez, *Tejano Diaspora.*
37. Gutiérrez, *Making of a Chicano Militant*, 39.
38. "Latin Ticket Wins Council Race," *Zavala County Sentinel*, April 5, 1963; "New Council Takes Office Apr. 16," *Zavala County Sentinel*, April 5, 1963; *Texas Observer*, April 18, 1963, 7; Robert A. Cuellar, "Social and Political History of the Mexican American Population, 1929–1963" (master's thesis, North Texas State University, 1969), all cited from Rodríguez, *Tejano Diaspora.*
39. Rodríguez, *Tejano Diaspora*, 1; also see the excellent analysis of the los cinco campaign and election outcome, 46–59.
40. For detailed information on the formation and political activism of CASAA and its subsequent victory in the 1965 county elections, see Shockley, *Chicano Revolt*, chaps. 3 and 4.
41. Major works that discuss the election of los cinco candidatos as the "First Revolt" in Crystal City in 1963 include García, *United We Win*; Gutiérrez, *Making of a Chicano Militant*; Navarro, *Cristal Experiment*; Shockley, *Chicano Revolt*; Trujillo, *Chicano Empowerment.*
42. Severita Lara, interview by the author; Diana Palacios, interview by the author.
43. John Staples Shockley, "Crystal City: La Raza Unida and the Second Revolt," in *Chicano: The Evolution of a People*, ed. Renato Rosaldo, Robert A. Calvert, and Gustav L. Seligmann (Minneapolis: Winston Press, 1973), cited from Navarro, *Mexican American Youth Organization.*
44. Shockley, *Chicano Revolt*, 120.
45. Severita Lara, interview by the author; Navarro, *Mexican American Youth Organization*, 134.
46. *San Antonio Express*, April 30, 1969.
47. Severita Lara, interview by the author.
48. Severita Lara, interview by the author. Activist-scholar Armando Navarro agrees with Shockley's contention about Chicano students arguing that Mexican American students in Crystal City were plagued by "separate but equal" education. See Navarro, *Mexican American Youth Organization*, 134.
49. Severita Lara, interview by the author.
50. José Angel Gutiérrez, *We Won't Back Down!*, 57.

51. Severita Lara, interview by the author; Diana Palacios, interview by the author; Ray Espinoza, interview by the author; Carlos Guerra, interview by the author; Alberto Luera, interview by the author; Viviana Santiago Cavada, interview by the author.

52. Crystal City School Board minutes, May 12, 1969, José Angel Gutiérrez Papers, 1954–1990.

53. Mario and Blanca Treviño, interview by John Staples Shockley, December 5, 1970, Crystal City, Texas, cited from Shockley, *Chicano Revolt*.

54. Severita Lara, interview by the author.

55. Rodríguez, "Movement Made of 'Young Mexican Americans,'" 284. This article offers a revisionist account refuting the traditional one-place-bound community studies in Chicano Movement historiography. Rodríguez further argues that examining Mexican American migrant social networks reveals the interconnection and development of Chicano Movement activism across the migrant stream after 1963 from Texas to Wisconsin.

56. Crystal City School Board minutes, August 11, 1969, José Angel Gutiérrez Papers, 1954–1990. The school board policy includes revisions for the selection of school favorites, including most beautiful and most handsome, twirlers, and most representative boy and girl.

57. Gutiérrez, *We Won't Back Down!*, 54.

58. *Zavala County Sentinel*, November 20, 1969.

59. Gutiérrez et al., *Chicanas in Charge*, 116.

60. Ibid.

61. Crystal City School Board minutes, November 10, 1969, José Angel Gutiérrez Papers, 1954–1990. Also see Shockley, *Chicano Revolt*, appendix 3.

62. *Zavala County Sentinel*, November 13, 1969.

63. *Zavala County Sentinel*, November 20, 1969.

64. *Zavala County Sentinel*, November 27, 1969.

65. José Angel Gutiérrez, "The Walkout of '69: A Diary of Events," n.d., 2, José Angel Gutiérrez Papers, 1954–1990; José Angel Gutiérrez, interview by Lyle C. Brown; Navarro, *Mexican American Youth Organization*, 137; Gutiérrez, *Making of a Chicano Militant*, 144–45.

66. Severita Lara, interview by the author; Ray Espinoza, interview by the author.

67. José Angel Gutiérrez, "The Walkout of '69: A Diary of Events," n.d., 3, José Angel Gutiérrez Papers, 1954–1990.

68. Gutiérrez, *Making of a Chicano Militant*, 147.

69. Diana Serna, "Growing Up in Cristal: A Chicano Perspective," 15 (undergraduate student paper, Government 312 course, Professor Armando Gutiérrez, University of Texas at Austin, summer 1974).

70. Crystal City School Board minutes, December 8, 1969, José Angel Gutiérrez Papers, 1954–1990.

71. Ibid.

72. Revised Petition Presented by High School Students to the School Board, December 1969, José Angel Gutiérrez Papers, 1954–1990; Shockley, *Chicano Revolt*, appendix 3.

73. *San Antonio Express*, December 10, 1969.

74. José Angel Gutiérrez, "The Walkout of '69: A Diary of Events," n.d., 3, José Angel Gutiérrez Papers, 1954–1990.

75. Diana Serna, "Growing Up in Cristal: A Chicano Perspective," 16 (undergraduate student paper, Government 312 course, Professor Armando Gutiérrez, University of Texas at Austin, summer 1974).

76. Ibid.

77. José Angel Gutiérrez, interview by Armando Navarro, May 16, 1973, Crystal City, Texas, cited from Navarro, *Mexican American Youth Organization*.

78. José Angel Gutiérrez, "The Walkout of '69: A Diary of Events," n.d., 4–5, José Angel Gutiérrez Papers, 1954–1990; Navarro, *Mexican American Youth Organization*, 140. Also, see newspaper photographs of the Crystal City school boycott in figures 12 and 14.

79. Gutiérrez, *Making of a Chicano Militant*, 149.

80. José Angel Gutiérrez, "The Walkout of '69: A Diary of Events," n.d., 4, José Angel Gutiérrez Papers, 1954–1990; Gutiérrez, *Making of a Chicano Militant*, 149.

81. Gutiérrez, *Making of a Chicano Militant*, 150–51.

82. José M. Lara to Leon Graham, December 9, 1968, transcript in the hand of Leon Graham, handwritten manuscript copy, José Angel Gutiérrez Papers, 1954–1990.

83. José M. Lara to Mr. Mata, n.d., transcript in the hand of Paulino Mata, handwritten manuscript copy, José Angel Gutiérrez Papers, 1954–1990.

84. *Houston Post*, December 21, 1968, José Angel Gutiérrez Papers, 1954–1990.

85. Ibid.

86. Diana Serna, "Growing Up in Cristal: A Chicano Perspective," 17 (undergraduate student paper, Government 312 course, Professor Armando Gutiérrez, University of Texas at Austin, summer 1974). Also see photograph of mothers and volunteers serving food to striking students in figure 13.

87. Gutiérrez, *Making of a Chicano Militant*, 151.

88. Ibid., 154.

89. Ibid.

90. Armando Navarro, "El Partido de la Raza Unida in Crystal City: A Peaceful Revolution" (PhD diss., University of California, Riverside, 1974), 113–15, cited from García, *United We Win*; Shockley, *Chicano Revolt*, 133.

91. Armando Navarro, "El Partido de la Raza Unida in Crystal City: A Peaceful Revolution" (PhD diss., University of California, Riverside, 1974), 113–15, cited from García, *United We Win*.

92. *Zavala County Sentinel*, December 11, 1969.

93. Gutiérrez, *Making of a Chicano Militant*, 155.

94. Gilbert Conoley and Juan Ibarra, interoffice memorandum, Texas Education Agency, December 22, 1969, 1, Hector P. García Papers, Special Collections and Archives, Mary and Jeff Bell Library, Texas A&M University–Corpus Christi.

95. Ibid., 4.

96. *Houston Post*, December 21, 1968, José Angel Gutiérrez Papers, 1954–1990.

97. Severita Lara, interview by the author; Ray Espinoza, interview by the author.

98. Rev. Kenneth Newcomer, "A Progress Report on the Churchmen's Committee of Crystal City, Texas" (mimeographed paper, Crystal City, Texas, 1970), 1, cited from Shockley, *Chicano Revolt*.

99. Shockley, *Chicano Revolt*, 135.

100. Most Protestant and Catholic churches remain segregated in Crystal City. For further information, see *Now and Then in Zavala County*.

101. See typewritten sheet listing educational and economic statistics for Crystal City (1950 and 1960), which mentions J. L. Speers's firing of the two student employees as an example of economic racism, José Angel Gutiérrez Papers, 1943–1990.

102. Gutiérrez, *We Won't Back Down!*, 61.

103. Gutiérrez, *Making of a Chicano Militant*, 156–58. A copy of Tamez's affidavit detailing his arrest and harassment is on p. 158.

104. José Angel Gutiérrez, "Aztlán: Chicano Revolt in the Winter Garden," *La Raza* 1, no. 4 (1971), 34–35, cited from Navarro, *Mexican American Youth Organization*.

105. *San Antonio Express*, December 15, 1969.

106. Ibid.

107. *Zavala County Sentinel*, December 18, 1969.

108. *Corpus Christi Caller*, December 17, 1969; *Zavala County Sentinel*, December 18, 1969.

109. Crystal City ISD Attendance Record, December 17–18, 1969, Hector P. García Papers, Special Collections and Archives, Mary and Jeff Bell Library, Texas A&M University–Corpus Christi.

110. George Sánchez, "The Crystal City School Boycott: 1969" (unpublished paper), 10, cited from Navarro, *Mexican American Youth Organization*.

111. Texas Education Agency, "Second Visit to Crystal City ISD, Crystal City, Texas," December 17–18, 1969, Hector P. García Papers, Special Collections and Archives, Mary and Jeff Bell Library, Texas A&M University–Corpus Christi. Conoley and Ibarra's report on their second visit to Crystal City states that they met with five members of the school board, three parents, one reporter, and Superintendent Billings.

112. Ibid.

113. *Corpus Christi Caller*, December 17, 1969; *Zavala County Sentinel*, December 18, 1969.

114. José Angel Gutiérrez, interview by Armando Navarro, May 24, 1973, cited from Navarro, *Mexican American Youth Organization*. Gutiérrez's autobiography, *The Making of a Chicano Militant*, further reveals that Ciudadanos Unidos helped raise money for the Washington trip by encouraging those who attended a December 15 rally to donate money (162).

115. Gutiérrez, *Making of a Chicano Militant*, 162.

116. Ibid.

117. Severita Lara, interview by the author.

118. *New York Times*, December 19, 1969.

119. Ibid.

120. Gutiérrez, *We Won't Back Down!*, 63.

121. *San Antonio Evening-News*, December 24, 1969; *Zavala County Sentinel*, December 25, 1969.

122. *San Antonio Evening-News*, December 24, 1969.

123. Ibid.

124. Severita Lara, interview by the author. Lara further mentions that certain teachers incorporated lessons on Mexican American history and culture in addition to teaching the curriculum.

125. Shockley, *Chicano Revolt*, 13. Shockley reveals that the Justice Department report compiled by Greenwald and Mata is confidential and not available for public viewing.

126. Ibid.

127. For a full list of all student demands made during the course of the Crystal City school boycott, see appendix E in this book.

128. Agreement between the Crystal City School Board and the Negotiating Committee of Student Boycott Spokesmen and Representative Parents, January 4, 1970, 1, José Angel Gutiérrez Papers, 1954–1990.

129. Ibid.

130. *San Antonio Express*, January 6, 1970.

131. *San Antonio Light*, January 6, 1970.

132. Shockley, *Chicano Revolt*, 161.

133. *La Verdad*, March 31, 1971, 14, cited from Shockley, *Chicano Revolt*.

134. Rebecca Pérez, interview by Joyce Langenegger, October 4, 1972, transcript, Mexican American Project, Texas Collection, Baylor University, Waco, Texas.

135. Joyce Langenegger, interview by Lyle C. Brown, August 15, 1972, transcript, Mexican American Project, Texas Collection, Baylor University, Waco, Texas.

136. *La Verdad*, March 31, 1971, 14, cited from Shockley, *Chicano Revolt*.

137. *Zavala County Sentinel*, April 9, 1970. The newspaper indicated that Gutiérrez, Pérez, and González received 1,344, 1,397, and 1,344 votes, respectively.

138. *La Verdad*, March 18, 1971, 5, cited from Shockley, *Chicano Revolt*.

139. Angel Noe González, interview by John Staples Shockley, Crystal City, Texas, November 11, 1970, cited from Shockley, *Chicano Revolt*.

140. Shockley, *Chicano Revolt*, 164.

141. Ibid., 165.

142. Rebecca Pérez, interview by Joyce Langenegger, October 4, 1972, Texas Collection, Baylor University, Waco, Texas.

143. Angel Noe González, interview by Lyle C. Brown, August 26, 1972, transcript, Mexican American Project, Texas Collection, Baylor University, Waco, Texas.

144. Joyce Langenegger, interview by Lyle C. Brown, August 15, 1972, transcript, Mexican American Project, Texas Collection, Baylor University, Waco, Texas.

145. Shockley, *Chicano Revolt*, 165.

146. Anonymous letter to J. Edgar Hoover, September 16, 1971, transcript in the hand of anonymous writer, typewritten manuscript copy, José Angel Gutiérrez Papers, Institute of Texan Cultures, University of Texas at San Antonio.

147. For the files on the FBI investigation of the Crystal City School District obtained via the Freedom of Information Act, see box 23, folder 2 of the José Angel Gutiérrez Papers, Institute of Texan Cultures, University of Texas at San Antonio. These files are quite intriguing and document certain Anglo educators' complaints against the Chicano-dominated school system, alleging unlawful termination from their jobs during the early 1970s. One of the files indicates that two professional teacher organizations, the Texas State Teachers Association and Texas Classroom Teachers Association, initiated an investigation regarding the activities of school superintendent Angel Noe González to determine whether he violated the civil rights of certain teachers.

148. Robert Clyde Tate, interview by Lyle C. Brown, August 24, 1972, transcript, Mexican American Project, Texas Collection, Baylor University, Waco, Texas.

149. Ibid.

150. Rebecca Pérez, interview by Joyce Langenegger, Texas Collection, Baylor University.

151. Trujillo, *Chicano Empowerment*, 107–18.

152. Ibid., 115.

153. Ibid., 37.

154. Ibid., 6.

155. Rodríguez, "Movement Made of 'Young Mexican Americans,'" 276.

156. Ibid., 292.

157. Ibid., 176.

158. Diana Palacios, interview by Priscilla Martinez, July 19, 2012, interview 1, transcript, Oral History Memoir, Baylor University Institute for Oral History, Waco, Texas.

159. Gutiérrez, *We Won't Back Down!*, 72.

CHAPTER 7

1. Martinez, "Struggles of Solidarity," 524.

2. Friedman and McAdam, "Collective Identity and Activism," 163–64.

3. Navarro, *Mexican American Youth Organization*, 118.

4. Gutiérrez, *Making of a Chicano Militant*, 128.

5. Haney-López, "White Latinos," 4.

6. Carter, *Mexican Americans in School*, 81–86.

7. Mario C. Compean, email to the author, "Questionnaire on Role of MAYO during the Chicano High School Walkouts of the 1960s–1970s," May 31, 2005.

8. Planas, "Why Mexican-American Studies.".

9. Ramsey, "Analysis: Texas Schools."

Bibliography

ARCHIVAL COLLECTIONS

Edcouch-Elsa High School Library Collection. *La Avispa: Edcouch-Elsa High School Yearbook.* Edcouch, Texas, 1960, 1965–69, 1971, 1975.

Eleuterio Escobar Papers. Nettie Lee Benson Latin American Collection, University of Texas Libraries, University of Texas at Austin.

Hector P. García Papers. Mary and Jeff Bell Library, Texas A&M University–Corpus Christi, Corpus Christi, Texas.

Joe J. Bernal Papers. Nettie Lee Benson Latin American Collection, University of Texas Libraries, University of Texas at Austin.

José Angel Gutiérrez Papers, 1954–1990. Nettie Lee Benson Latin American Collection, University of Texas Libraries, University of Texas at Austin.

José Angel Gutiérrez Papers. Special Collections, University of Texas at San Antonio.

R. P. "Bob" Sanchez Papers, 1921–2005. Nettie Lee Benson Latin American Collection, University of Texas Libraries, University of Texas at Austin.

Scrapbook Collection. Robert J. Kleberg Public Library, Kingsville, Texas.

University Archives Collection. South Texas Archives and Special Collections, James C. Jernigan Library, Texas A&M University–Kingsville.

GOVERNMENT DOCUMENTS

Baker, Benjamin M. *Fifth Biennial Report of the Superintendent of Public Instruction for the Scholastic Years Ending August 31, 1885, and August 31, 1886.* Austin: State Printing Office, 1886.

De Gress, Jacob C. *First Annual Report of the Superintendent of Public Instruction of the State of Texas, 1871.* Austin: J. G. Tracy, State Printer, 1872.

Menefee, Selden, and Orin C. Cassmore. *The Pecan Shellers of San Antonio: The Problem of Underpaid and Unemployed Mexican Labor.* Washington, DC: US Government Printing Office, 1940.

Office of Economic Opportunity, Texas Department of Community Affairs. *Poverty in Texas, 1973.* Austin: Texas Department of Community Affairs, 1974.

Second Annual Report of the Superintendent of Public Instruction of the State of Texas for the Year 1872. Austin: James P. Newcomb, 1873).

Texas Advisory Committee to the US Commission on Civil Rights. *Civil Rights in Texas.* Washington, DC: Government Printing Office, 1970.

———. *The Civil Rights Status of Spanish-Speaking Americans in Kleberg, Nueces, and San Patricio Counties, Texas.* Washington, DC: Government Printing Office, 1967.

———. *Texas: The State of Civil Rights, Ten Years Later, 1968–1978.* Washington, DC: Government Printing Office, 1980.

US Commission on Civil Rights. *Demographic, Economic, and Social Characteristics of the Spanish Surname Population of Five Southwestern States.* Staff report. Washington, DC: US Government Printing Office, 1970.

———. *The Excluded Student: Educational Practices Affecting Mexican Americans in the Southwest.* Report 3. Washington, DC: US Government Printing Office, May 1972.

———. *Hearing Before the United States Commission on Civil Rights, Hearing Held in San Antonio, Texas, December 9–14, 1968.* Transcript of proceedings. Washington, DC: US Government Printing Office, 1969.

———. *Mexican American Education in Texas: A Function of Wealth.* Report 4, Mexican American Education Study: A Report of the U.S. Commission on Civil Rights. Washington, DC: Government Printing Office, August 1972.

———. *Toward Quality Education for Mexican Americans.* Report 6, Mexican American Education Study: A Report of the U.S. Commission on Civil Rights. Washington, DC: Government Printing Office, 1974.

US Congress, Senate Select Committee on Equal Educational Opportunity. *Equal Educational Opportunity: Hearings, Part IV, Mexican American Education.* Washington, DC: US Government Printing Office, 1971.

US Federal District Court for the Southern District of Texas, Brownsville Division. *Xavier Ramirez, by his next of friend Pablo Ramirez, et al. v. Edcouch-Elsa Independent School District Board of Trustees,* et al. Civil action file 68-B-116. Federal Records Center, Fort Worth, Texas.

NEWSPAPERS

Brownsville (TX) Herald
Corpus Christi (TX) Caller
Corpus Christi (TX) Caller-Times
Corpus Christi (TX) Times
Denver Post
Edinburg (TX) Daily Review
Houston Post
Inferno (underground newspaper in San Antonio, TX)
Kingsville-Bishop Record News (Kingsville, TX)
Los Angeles Gazette
McAllen (TX) Monitor
San Antonio Express
San Antonio Express and News
San Antonio Express-News
San Antonio Light
San Antonio News
San Diego Union Tribune
Saturday Evening Post
South Texan (Texas A&M University–Kingsville student newspaper)
Valley Morning Star (Harlingen, TX)
Zavala County Sentinel (Crystal City, TX)

YEARBOOK PUBLICATION

Los Recuerdos: Sidney Lanier High School Yearbook. Vol. 29. San Antonio, Texas, 1968.

ORAL HISTORY INTERVIEWS

Arispe, Raúl. Interview by Frank Guajardo, July 28, 1998. Interview tape 82, transcript. Oral History Collection, Llano Grande Center for Research and Development, Edcouch-Elsa High School, Edcouch, Texas.

Bernal, Joe J. Interview by Valentino Mauricio, February 12, 2006. Interview summary by Erin Peterson. Voces Oral History Center, US Latino and Latina World War II Oral History Project Collection, University of Texas Libraries, University of Texas at Austin. Accessed July 23, 2013. http://www.lib.utexas.edu/voces/templatestoriesindiv.html?work_urn=urn%3Autlol %3Awwlatin.533&work_title=Bernal%2C+Joe

Garza, Carmen Lomas. Interview by Paul J. Kalstrom, April 10–May 27, 1997. San Francisco, CA. Transcript. Smithsonian Archives of American Art, Washington, DC. https://www.aaa.si.edu/collections/interviews/oral-history-interview-carmen-lomas-garza-13540#transcript

González, Angel Noe. Interview by Lyle C. Brown, August 26, 1972. Transcript. Mexican American Project, Texas Collection, Baylor University, Waco, Texas.

Gutiérrez, José Angel. Interview by Lyle C. Brown, 1973. Transcript. Mexican American Project, Texas Collection, Baylor University, Waco, Texas.

Herrera, Richard and Diana Herrera. Interview by Dick Gordon. "To Walk or Not Walk." WUNC Public Radio, October 31, 2008.

Langenegger, Joyce. Interview by Lyle C. Brown, August 15, 1972. Transcript. Mexican American Project, Texas Collection, Baylor University, Waco, Texas.

Palacios, Diana. Interview by Priscilla Martinez, July 19, 2012. Interview 1. Transcript. Oral History Memoir, Baylor University Institute for Oral History, Waco, Texas.

Pérez, Rebecca. Interview by Joyce Langenegger, October 4, 1972. Transcript. Mexican American Project, Texas Collection, Baylor University, Waco, Texas.

Tate, Robert Clyde. Interview by Lyle C. Brown, August 24, 1972. Transcript. Mexican American Project, Texas Collection, Baylor University, Waco, Texas.

ORAL INTERVIEWS BY THE AUTHOR

Albro, Ward. Phone interview, digital voice recording. January 11, 2005.

Anonymous. Digital voice recording. McAllen, Texas, February 1, 2005.

Bill, Antonio, and Diana Bill. Digital voice recording. Alice, Texas, February 12, 2005.

Campos Ramirez, Rebecca. Digital voice recording. San Antonio, Texas, July 30, 2016.

Castillo, Rafael. Digital voice recording. San Antonio, Texas, September 17, 2016.

Castro, Stephen. Digital voice recording. San Antonio, Texas, September 16, 2016.

Cavada, Viviana Santiago. Digital voice recording. Corpus Christi, Texas, March 24, 2005.

Cellum, Billie. Pharr, Texas, June 16, 2000.

Compean, Mario. Phone interview, digital voice recording. June 16, 2005.

Cooper, Janet. Phone interview, digital voice recording. January 7, 2005.

Cortez, Cecilia. Kingsville, Texas, February 21, 2015.

Díaz, Homero. Tape recording. Monte Alto, Texas, June 19, 2000.

Erebia, Faustino. Digital voice recording. Kingsville, Texas, February 21, 2015.

Espinoza, Ray. Phone interview, digital voice recording. January 7, 2005.

Galloway, Neal. Tape recording. Elsa, Texas, June 5, 2000.

García, Homer D. Digital voice recording. Humble, Texas, August 13, 2016.

García, Ignacio M. Phone interview, digital voice recording. April 21, 2005.

Garza, Andrés. Digital voice recording. Kingsville, Texas, February 28, 2005.

Garza, Raúl G. Digital voice recording. Kingsville, Texas, February 12, 2005.

González, Eddy. Tape recording. Elsa, Texas, June 27, 2000.

Guerra, Carlos. Digital voice recording. San Antonio, Texas, December 2, 2004.

Gutiérrez, Eugene. Tape recording. Edinburg, Texas, July 14, 2000.

Gutiérrez, Rosendo T. Digital voice recording. San Antonio, Texas, July 30, 2016.

Hernández, Daniel. Digital voice recording. San Antonio, Texas, January 7, 2017.

Herrera, Richard, and Diana Herrera. Digital voice recording. San Antonio, Texas, August 18, 2016.

Lara, Severita. Digital voice recording. Crystal City, Texas, November 10, 2004.

Layton, Bene. Tape recording. Elsa, Texas, July 12, 2000.

Lehman, Annette Guerrero. Digital voice recording. Crystal City, Texas, November 8, 2004.

Leo, Billie. Tape recording. La Joya, Texas, July 6, 2000.

Lozano, Edgar G. Digital voice recording. San Antonio, Texas, July 29, 2016.

Lucio, Ruben. Digital voice recording. San Antonio, Texas, June 23, 2013.

Luera, Alberto. Phone interview. Digital voice recording. January 17, 2005.

Palacios, Diana. Digital voice recording. Crystal City, Texas. November 9, 2004, and January 10, 2005.

Peña, Rosie. Digital voice recording. San Antonio, Texas, September 30, 2016.
Ramírez, Javier. Phone interview, tape recording. July 23, 2000.
Rocha, Juan, Jr. Digital voice recording. McAllen, Texas, January 28, 2005.
Rodríguez, Felix. Edinburg, Texas, November 12, 2010.
Rodríguez Lozano, Maricela. Tape recording. Edcouch, Texas, May 17, 1999.
Rodríguez, Rubén. Tape recording. July 12, 2000.
Sáenz, Freddy. Tape recording. Weslaco, Texas, May 18, 1999.
Salazar, Mario. Digital voice recording. Kingsville, Texas, February 18, 2005.
Salinas, Artemio. Phone interview, tape recording. August 3, 2000.
Salinas, Arturo. Tape recording. Weslaco, Texas, July 21, 2000.
Sánchez, R. P. "Bob". Tape recording. McAllen, Texas, December 31, 1998.
Treviño, Nelda Villareal, and Mirtala Villareal. Tape recording. Elsa, Texas, June 3, 2000.
Vallejo, Frank. Tape recording. McAllen, Texas, July 25, 2000.
Yañez, Irene. Digital voice recording. San Antonio, Texas, September 30, 2016.
Zavala, Eloy. Tape recording. Elsa, Texas, July 11, 2000.

BACHELOR'S THESIS

Kennedy Cuomo, Mariah. "Robert F. Kennedy and the Farmworkers: The Formation of Robert F. Kennedy and Cesar Chavez's Bond." Bachelor's thesis, Brown University, 2017. Accessed July 24, 2018. https://doc.uments.com/s-robert-f-kennedy-and-the-farmworkers-the-formation -of-robert.pdf (site discontinued)

MASTER'S THESIS

Barrera, James Baldemar. "The 1968 Edcouch-Elsa High School Walkout: Chicano Student Activism in a South Texas Community." Master's thesis, University of Texas at El Paso, 2001.
La Rotta, Alex. "'Talk to Me': The Story of San Antonio's West Side Sound." Master's thesis, Texas State University, 2013.

DOCTORAL DISSERTATIONS

Barrera, James Baldemar. "'We Want Better Education!': The Chicano Student Movement for Educational Reform in South Texas, 1968–1970." PhD diss., University of New Mexico, 2007.
Gonzáles, Trinidad. "The World of Mexico Texanos, Mexicanos and Mexico Americanos: Transnational and National Identities in the Lower Rio Grande Valley during the Last Phase of United States Colonization, 1900 to 1930." PhD diss., University of Houston, 2008.
Guajardo, Francisco Javier. "Narratives of Transformation: Education and Social Change in Rural South Texas." PhD diss., University of Texas at Austin, 2003.
Morales, Ralph Edward, III. "Hijos de la Gran Guerra: The Creation of the Mexican American Identity in Texas, 1836–1929." PhD diss., Texas A&M University, 2015.

ELECTRONIC SOURCES

"1969: Student Walkouts at Texas A&I and Robstown High School." South Texas Rabble Rousers History Project. Accessed January 15, 2016. https://southtexasrabblerousers.wordpress .com/2014/04/16/1969-student-walkouts-at-texas-ai-and-robstown-high-school/
"50th Anniversary of the US Commission of Civil Rights Hearing on Mexican-Americans in the Southwest." Accessed October 5, 2018. https://www.50yearslater.org/history/ (site discontinued)
Allsup, V. Carl. "Cisneros v. Corpus Christi ISD." *Handbook of Texas Online*. Texas State Historical Association. Accessed July 17, 2018. https://tshaonline.org/handbook/online/articles/jrc02
——. "Hernández v. State of Texas." *Handbook of Texas Online*. Texas State Historical Association. Accessed July 17, 2018. https://tshaonline.org/handbook/online/articles/jrh01

Ashton, John, and Edgar P. Sneed. Revised by Bob Kinnan. "King Ranch." *Handbook of Texas Online*, Texas State Historical Association. Accessed July 1, 2015. https://www.tshaonline.org/handbook/entries/king-ranch

Berger, Max, and Lee Wilborn. "Education." *Handbook of Texas Online*. Texas State Historical Association. Accessed June 15, 2018. https://tshaonline.org/handbook/online/articles/khe01

Braschayko, Karen. "Sybil Ludington and Her Horse Star, Heroes of the American Revolution." Equitrekking, July 3, 2017. Accessed July 10, 2018. http://www.equitrekking.com/articles/entry/sybil-ludington-and-her-horse-star-heroes-of-the-american-revolution/

Calderón, Roberto R. "Tejano Politics." *Handbook of Texas Online*. Texas State Historical Association. Accessed June 17, 2013. http://www.tshaonline.org/handbook/online/articles/wmtkn

"CBS Documentary Hunger in America." YouTube video. 51:24. Posted by "Garry J." Accessed August 28, 2016. https://www.youtube.com/watch?v=h94bq4JfMAA

"Chicano Fighting for Political Power." YouTube video. 56:38. Posted by "National Brown Berets." Accessed March 15, 2017. https://www.youtube.com/watch?v=Tukgadlabjc

Coalson, George O. "Kingsville, Texas." *Handbook of Texas Online*. Texas State Historical Association. Accessed August 4, 2005. https://www.tshaonline.org/handbook/entries/kingsville-tx

"Cotulla, Texas." YouTube video. 2:03. Posted by "TheLBJLibrary." Accessed March 15, 2017. https://www.youtube.com/watch?v=gdNEOtGRi_w

Croxdale, Richard. "Pecan-Shellers' Strike." *Handbook of Texas Online*. Texas State Historical Association. Accessed December 26, 2006. https://www.tshaonline.org/handbook/entries/pecan-shellers-strike

Cunningham, Jerry. *Operation Wetback: The "Brown Scare" and Mass Deportation during the Cold War*. Amazon Digital Services, 2017. Kindle.

Davies, David Martin. "'Hunger in America': The 1968 Documentary That Exposed San Antonio Poverty." Texas Public Radio, June 8, 2018. Accessed July 29, 2021. https://www.tpr.org/san-antonio/2018-06-08/hunger-in-america-the-1968-documentary-that-exposed-san-antonio-poverty/

"Dicey Langston, South Carolina Revolutionary War Patriot." History of American Women, Women in the American Revolution. Accessed July 10, 2018. http://www.womenhistoryblog.com/2009/04/dicey-langston-springfield.html

Eby, Frederick, comp. "Education in Texas Source Materials." University of Texas Bulletin no. 1824 (April 25, 1918). Hathi Trust Digital Library, Harvard University. Accessed June 15, 2018. https://babel.hathitrust.org/cgi/pt?id=hvd.32044030221683;view=1up;seq=7

Fehrenbach, T. R. "San Antonio, TX." *Handbook of Texas Online*. Texas State Historical Association. Accessed July 15, 2013. http://www.tshaonline.org/handbook/online/articles/hds02

Fernández, Isa. "Edgewood High School Walkouts of '68." *La Prensa Texas*. Last modified August 29, 2019. Accessed October 28, 2021. https://laprensatexas.com/edgewood-high-school-walkouts-of-68/

Gamboa, Suzanne. "Forgotten History: Chicano Student Walkouts Changed Texas, but Inequities Remain." NBC News, November 23, 2019. Accessed July 21, 2021. https://www.nbcnews.com/news/latino/forgotten-history-chicano-student-walkouts-changed-texas-inequities-remain-n1090071

Gammel, H. P. N., comp. and arr. *The Laws of Texas, 1822–1897*. Austin: Gammel Book Company, 1898. Hathi Trust Digital Library, Harvard University. Accessed June 25, 2018. https://babel.hathitrust.org/cgi/pt?id=hvd.hl3grq;view=1up;seq=1006

Garza, Alicia A. "Edcouch, TX." *Handbook of Texas Online*. Texas State Historical Association. Accessed March 31, 2023. https://www.tshaonline.org/handbook/entries/edcouch-tx

———. "Elsa, TX." *Handbook of Texas Online*. Texas State Historical Association. Accessed March 31, 2023. https://www.tshaonline.org/handbook/entries/elsa-tx

Gonzales, Rodolfo "Corky." "I Am Joaquín." Latin American Studies.org. Accessed November 13, 2016. http://www.latinamericanstudies.org/latinos/joaquin.htm

Guzmán, Venecia. "Examining 'La Familia' in Relation to the Chicana." Undergraduate paper, University of Texas at Austin. Accessed March 13, 2017. http://www.academia.edu/10463151/Examining_La_Familia_in_Relation_to_the_Chicana

"Hidalgo Pumphouse Heritage and Discovery Park/World Birding Center." Texas Historical Commission. Accessed July 15, 2013. http://texastropicaltrail.com/plan-your-adventure/historic-sites-and-cities/sites/hidalgo-pumphouse-heritage-and-discovery-park

Inman Christian Center. San Antonio, Texas. Accessed September 10, 2016. https://www.inmancenter.org

Johnson, Lyndon B. "Annual Message to the Congress on the State of the Union." January 8, 1964. The American Presidency Project. Accessed March 16, 2023. https://www.presidency.ucsb.edu/documents/annual-message-the-congress-the-state-the-union-25

———. "Remarks at the Welhausen Elementary School, Cotulla, Texas." November 7, 1966. The American Presidency Project. Accessed March 16, 2023. https://www.presidency.ucsb.edu/documents/remarks-the-welhausen-elementary-school-cotulla-texas

———. "We Shall Overcome." Address to a joint session of Congress on voting legislation. American Rhetoric Top 100 Speeches, March 15, 1965. Accessed March 14, 2017. http://www.americanrhetoric.com/speeches/lbjweshallovercome.htm

Kemerer, Frank R. "United States v. Texas." *Handbook of Texas Online*. Texas State Historical Association. Accessed July 19, 2018. https://tshaonline.org/handbook/online/articles/jru02

Kohout, Martin Donell. "González, Henry Barbosa (1916–2000)." *Handbook of Texas Online*. Texas State Historical Association. Accessed July 13, 2015. https://tshaonline.org/handbook/online/articles/fgo76

"LULAC History—All for One and One for All." League of United Latin American Citizens. Accessed July 7, 2014. http://lulac.org/about/history/#

Martinez, Nydia A. "The Struggles of Solidarity: Chicana/o-Mexican Networks, 1960s–1970s." *Social Sciences* 4, no. 3 (July 2015): 520–32. MDPI open access journal. Accessed December 17, 2018. https://www.mdpi.com/2076-0760/4/3/520

McKittrick, Chris. "Daniel 'Rudy' Ruettiger and Notre Dame Football." True.Sports.Movies, June 26, 2016. Accessed March 6, 2017. http://truesportsmovies.com/football/rudy-ruettiger-notre-dame-football/.

Ochoa, Ruben E. "Zavala County." *Handbook of Texas Online*. Texas State Historical Association. Accessed September 8, 2005. https://www.tshaonline.org/handbook/entries/zavala-county

Odintz, Mark. "Crystal City, TX." *Handbook of Texas Online*. Texas State Historical Association. Accessed July 15, 2013. https://www.tshaonline.org/handbook/entries/crystal-city-tx

Orozco, Cynthia E. "Hernández, María L. de (1896–1986)." *Handbook of Texas Online*. Texas State Historical Association. Accessed October 15, 2016. https://tshaonline.org/handbook/online/articles/fhe75

———. "League of United Latin American Citizens." *Handbook of Texas Online*. Texas State Historical Association. Accessed July 7, 2014. http://www.tshaonline.org/handbook/online/articles/wel01

———. "Mexican American Women." *Handbook of Texas Online*. Texas State Historical Association. Accessed March 12, 2017. https://tshaonline.org/handbook/online/articles/pwmly

———. "Rodriguez v. San Antonio ISD." *Handbook of Texas Online*. Texas State Historical Association. Accessed March 15, 2006. https://www.tshaonline.org/handbook/entries/rodriguez-v-san-antonio-isd

———. "School Improvement League." *Handbook of Texas Online*. Texas State Historical Association. Accessed June 12, 2015. https://www.tshaonline.org/handbook/entries/school-improvement-league

Orozco, Cynthia E., and Jazmin León. "Vento, Adela Sloss (1901–1998)." *Handbook of Texas Online*. Texas State Historical Association. Accessed November 13, 2016. https://tshaonline.org/handbook/online/articles/fve19

Palomo Acosta, Teresa. "Mexican American Legal Defense and Educational Fund." *Handbook of Texas Online*. Texas State Historical Association. Accessed August 16, 2013. http://www.tshaonline.org/handbook/online/articles/jom01

———. "Mexican American Youth Organization." *Handbook of Texas Online*. Texas State Historical Association. Accessed August 4, 2005. https://www.tshaonline.org/handbook/entries/mexican-american-youth-organization

"Photos from Elsa, Texas." Accessed January 28, 2002. https://kenanderson.net/delta/elsa.html

Planas, Roque. "Why Mexican-American Studies Is 'Going to Spread Like Wildfire' in Texas." *Huffington Post*, Latino Voices. Accessed June 11, 2016. http://www.Huffingtonpost.com/2014/04/10/texas-mexican-american-studies-vote_n_5126215.html

Ramsey, Ross. "Analysis: Texas Schools, by the Numbers." *Texas Tribune*, July 13, 2015. Accessed January 22, 2016. https://www.texastribune.org/2015/07/13/analysis-texas-schools-numbers/

Raymond, Virginia. "Snid, Alberta Zepeda (1919–1994)." *Handbook of Texas Online*. Texas State Historical Association. Accessed July 30, 2018. https://tshaonline.org/handbook/online/articles/fsn12

"Robert Kennedy Took On Kern County Sheriff United Farm Workers." YouTube video. Posted by United Farm Workers. August 18, 2015. Accessed July 24, 2018. https://www.youtube.com/watch?v=G66myWragTg

Romo, Ricardo. "The World of Our Fathers Westside Life 1920–1950." *La Prensa Texas*, June 14, 2019. Accessed August 4, 2021. https://laprensatexas.com/the-world-of-our-fathers-westside-life-1920-1950/

Sanchez, Joseph P. "Palo Alto, Battle of." *Handbook of Texas Online*. Texas State Historical Association. Accessed July 10, 2014. http://www.tshaonline.org/handbook/online/articles/qep01

Segovia, Jose Francisco. "Botas and Guaraches." *Handbook of Texas Online*. Texas State Historical Association. Accessed March 31, 2018. https://tshaonline.org/handbook/online/articles/pqb01

Sekhon, Jas S. "Social Movement Theory: Political Opportunity Structure." Accessed December 18, 2006. http://macht.arts.cornell.edu/jss13/apsa95/node4.html (site discontinued)

"Social Movements and Culture: Glossary of Terms Used to Study Social Movements." Accessed January 24, 2005. http://www.wsu.edu/~amerstu/smc/glossary.html (site discontinued)

"The Story of César Chávez: The Beginning." United Farm Workers. Accessed January 15, 2016. https://ufw.org/research/history/story-cesar-chavez/

"Student Demographics." Texas A&M University Accountability. Accessed March 27, 2023. https://accountability.tamu.edu/all-metrics/mixed-metrics/student-demographics.

"Texas Politics: Henry B. González." Accessed August 1, 2005. http://www.Loper.org/~george/archives/2001/Jan/99.html (site discontinued)

Vigness, David, and Mark Odintz. "Rio Grande Valley." *Handbook of Texas Online*. Texas State Historical Association. Accessed July 15, 2013. http://www.tshaonline.org/handbook/online/articles/ryr01

Zamora, Emilio. "Sáenz, José de la Luz (1888–1953)." *Handbook of Texas Online*. Texas State Historical Association. Accessed November 13, 2016. https://tshaonline.org/handbook/online/articles/fsa97

VIDEO RECORDINGS

Chicano!: History of the Mexican American Civil Rights Movement. Videocassette. Vol. 3, *The Blowouts: The Struggle for Educational Reform*. Produced by National Latino Communications Center and Galán Productions, 1996.

Edcouch-Elsa Walkout Clips. Videocassette. Produced and directed by Frank Guajardo. Oral History Collection, Llano Grande Center for Research and Development. Edcouch-Elsa High School, Edcouch, Texas, 1998.

The Edgewood High School Walkout '68. DVD. 11th Annual Scholarship and Awards Gala. San Antonio TX: San Antonio Association of Hispanic Journalists, 2009.

Justice for My People: The Dr. Hector P. Garcia Story. DVD. Produced by KEDT–Corpus Christi. Corpus Christi, TX: South Texas Public Broadcasting System, 2002.

Latino Americans: The 500-Year Legacy That Shaped a Nation. Episode 5, "Prejudice and Pride." Disk 2. DVD. Directed by David Belton and Sonia Fritz. WETA-TV. Washington, DC: Busch and Co., and Latino Public Broadcasting, 2013.

The Longoria Affair. DVD. Produced and directed by John J. Valadez. Burbank, CA: Latino Public Broadcasting, 2010.

Walkout. DVD. Executive producers Montezuma Esparza and Robert Katz. HBO Films, 2007.

BOOKS

Abrams, Lynn. *Oral History Theory*. 2nd ed. Abingdon, England: Routledge, 2016.

Acuña, Rodolfo F. *Occupied America: A History of Chicanos*. 8th ed. New York: Pearson, 2015.

Allison, Pat. *Images of America: Kingsville*. Charleston, SC: Arcadia, 2011.

Allsup, Carl. *The American G. I. Forum: Origins and Evolution*. Austin: University of Texas, Center for Mexican American Studies, 1982.

Alonso, Armando. *Tejano Legacy: Rancheros and Settlers in South Texas, 1734–1900*. Albuquerque: University of New Mexico Press, 1998.

Alvarez, Luis. *The Power of the Zoot: Youth Culture and Resistance during World War II*. Berkeley: University of California Press, 2008.

Anders, Evan. *Boss Rule in South Texas: The Progressive Era*. Austin: University of Texas Press, 1982.

Anderson, Benedict. *Imagined Communities: Reflections on the Origin and Spread of Nationalism*. Rev. ed. New York: Verso, 2006.

Arreola, Daniel D. *Tejano South Texas: A Mexican American Cultural Province*. Austin: University of Texas, 2001.

Balderrama, Francisco E. *In Defense of La Raza: The Los Angeles Mexican Consulate and the Mexican Community, 1929 to 1936*. Tucson: University of Arizona Press, 1982.

Barragán Goetz, Philis M. *Reading, Writing, and Revolution: Escuelitas and the Emergence of a Mexican American Identity in Texas*. Austin: University of Texas Press, 2020.

Bender, Steve. *One Night in America: Robert Kennedy, César Chávez, and the Dream of Dignity*. Boulder, CO: Paradigm, 2008.

Blackwelder, Julia Kirk. *Women of the Depression: Caste and Culture in San Antonio, 1929–1939*. College Station: Texas A&M University Press, 1984.

Blackwell, Maylei. *Chicana Power! Contested Histories of Feminism in the Chicano Movement*. Austin: University of Texas Press, 2011.

Blanton, Carlos Kevin. *George I. Sánchez: The Long Fight for Mexican American Integration*. New Haven, CT: Yale University Press, 2015.

———. "The Rise of the English-Only Pedagogy: Immigrant Children, Progressive Education, and Language Policy in the United States, 1900–1930." In *When Science Encounters the Child: Education, Parenting, and Child Welfare in 20th-Century America*, edited by Barbara Beatty, Emily D. Cahan, and Julia Grant, 56–76. New York: Teachers College Press, 2006.

———. *The Strange Career of Bilingual Education in Texas, 1836–1981*. College Station: Texas A&M University Press, 2004.

Boyd, Herb. *We Shall Overcome: The History of the Civil Rights Movement as It Happened*. Naperville, IL: Sourcebooks Media Fusion, 2004.

Cárdenas, José A. *Texas School Finance Reform: An IDRA Perspective*. San Antonio, TX: Intercultural Development Research Association, 1997.

Caro, Robert. *The Years of Lyndon Johnson: The Path to Power*. New York: Knopf, 1982.

Carroll, Patrick J. *Felix Longoria's Wake: Bereavement, Racism, and the Rise of Mexican American Activism*. Austin: University of Texas Press, 2003.

Carter, Thomas P. *Mexican Americans in School: A History of Educational Neglect*. New York: College Entrance Examination Board, 1970.

Castillo, Ana. *Massacre of the Dreamers: Essays on Xicanisma*. Albuquerque: University of New Mexico Press, 1994.

Castro, Tony. *Chicano Power*. New York: Saturday Review Press, 1974.

Chávez, Ernesto. *"¡Mi Raza Primero!": Nationalism, Identity, and Insurgency in the Chicano Movement in Los Angeles, 1966–1978*. Berkeley: University of California Press, 2002.

Císneros, José. *Borderlands: The Heritage of the Lower Rio Grande Valley through the Art of José Císneros*. Edinburg, TX: Hidalgo County Historical Museum, 1998.

Cortés, Carlos E. *Mexican Labor in the United States*. New York: Arno Press, 1974.

Cortez, Constance. *Carmen Lomas Garza*. A Ver: Revisioning Art History, vol. 5. Los Angeles: UCLA Chicano Studies Research Center Press, 2010.

Cotera, María E., ed. *Life along the Border: A Landmark Tejana Thesis by Jovita González*. College Station: Texas A&M University Press, 2006.

Darder, Antonia, Rodolfo D. Torres, and Henry Gutiérrez, eds. *Latinos and Education: A Critical Reader*. New York: Routledge, 1997.

del Castillo, Adelaida R. "Mexican Women in Organization." In *Mexican Women in the United States: Struggles Past and Present*, edited by Magdalena Mora and Adelaida R. del Castillo, 7–16. Los Angeles: Chicano Studies Research Center Publications, University of California, 1980.

del Castillo, Richard G. *The Treaty of Guadalupe Hidalgo: A Legacy of Conflict*. Norman: University of Oklahoma Press, 1990.

De León, Arnoldo. *Mexican Americans in Texas: A Brief History*. 2nd ed. Wheeling, IL: Harlan Davidson, 1999.

——. *The Tejano Community, 1836–1900*. Albuquerque: University of New Mexico Press, 1982. Reprint, Dallas: Southern Methodist University Press, 1997.

——. *They Called Them Greasers: Anglo Attitudes toward Mexicans in Texas, 1821–1900*. Austin: University of Texas Press, 1983.

De León, Arnoldo, and Richard Griswold del Castillo. *North to Aztlán: A History of Mexican Americans in the United States*. 2nd ed. Hoboken, NJ: Wiley-Blackwell, 2012.

De León, Arnoldo, and Kenneth L. Stewart. *Tejanos and the Numbers Game: A Socio-Historical Interpretation from the Federal Censuses, 1850–1900*. Albuquerque: University of New Mexico Press, 1989.

Donato, Rubén. *The Other Struggle for Equal Schools: Mexican Americans during the Civil Rights Era*. Albany: State University of New York Press, 1997.

Eby, Frederick. *The Development of Education in Texas*. New York: Macmillan, 1925.

Echeverría, Darius V. *Aztlán Arizona: Mexican American Educational Empowerment, 1968–1978*. Tucson: University of Arizona Press, 2014.

Edgewood: The Story—The People. San Antonio, TX: Community Relations Office, Edgewood Independent School District, 1986.

El Plan de Santa Barbara: A Chicano Plan for Higher Education. Oakland, CA: La Causa Publications, 1969.

Falcón, Romana. "Force and the Search for Consent: The Role of the Jefaturas Políticas of Coahuila in National State Formation." In *Everyday Forms of State Formation: Revolution and the Negotiation of Rule in Modern Mexico*, edited by Gilbert M. Joseph and Daniel Nugent, 107–34. Durham, NC: Duke University Press, 1994.

Ferris, Susan, and Ricardo Sandoval. *The Fight in the Fields: Cesar Chavez and the Farmworkers Movement*. Boston: Houghton Mifflin Harcourt, 1997.

Friedman, Debra, and Doug McAdam. "Collective Identity and Activism: Networks, Choices and the Life of a Social Movement." In *Frontiers in Social Movement Theory*, edited by Aldon D. Morris and Carol McClurg Mueller. New Haven, CT: Yale University Press, 1992.

García, Alma M., ed. *Chicana Feminist Thought: The Basic Historical Writings*. New York: Routledge, 1997.

García, Ignacio M. *Chicanismo: The Forging of a Militant Ethos among Mexican Americans*. Tucson: University of Arizona Press, 1997.

———. *Chicano while Mormon: Activism, War and Keeping the Faith*. Madison, NJ: Fairleigh Dickinson University Press, 2015.

———. *Mexican American Youth Organization: Precursors of Change in Texas*. Tucson: University of Arizona, Mexican American Studies and Research Center, 1987.

———. *United We Win: The Rise and Fall of La Raza Unida Party*. Tucson: University of Arizona Press, 1989.

———. *When Mexicans Could Play Ball: Basketball, Race and Identity in San Antonio, 1928–1945*. Austin: University of Texas Press, 2013.

García, Mario T. *Blowout! Sal Castro and the Chicano Struggle for Educational Justice*. Chapel Hill: University of North Carolina Press, 2011.

———. *Mexican Americans: Leadership, Ideology, and Identity, 1930–1960*. New Haven, CT: Yale University Press, 1989.

García, Richard A. *Rise of the Mexican American Middle Class: San Antonio, 1929–1941*. College Station: Texas A&M University Press, 1991.

Gómez-Quiñones, Juan. *Chicano Politics: Reality and Promise, 1940–1990*. Albuquerque: University of New Mexico Press, 1990.

———. *Mexican Students Por La Raza: The Chicano Student Movement in Southern California, 1967–1977*. Santa Barbara, CA: Editorial La Causa, 1978.

Gonzáles, Trinidad. "The Mexican Revolution, Revolución de Texas, and Matanza de 1915." In *War along the Border: The Mexican Revolution and Tejano Communities*, edited by Arnoldo De León, 107–33. College Station: Texas A&M University Press, 2011.

González, Gilbert G. *Chicano Education in the Era of Segregation*. Philadelphia: Balch Institute Press, 1990.

———. "Segregation and the Education of Mexican Children: 1900–1940." In *The Elusive Quest for Equality: 150 Years of Chicano/Chicana Education*, edited by José F. Moreno, 53–76. Cambridge, MA: Harvard Educational Review, 1999.

Gutiérrez, José Angel, Michelle Melédez, and Sonia Adriana Noyola. *Chicanas in Charge: Texas Women in the Public Arena*. Lanham, MD: AltaMira Press, 2007.

———. *The Making of a Chicano Militant: Lessons from Cristal*. Madison: University of Wisconsin Press, 1998.

———. *The Making of a Civil Rights Leader: José Angel Gutiérrez*. Houston, TX: Arte Público Press, 2005.

———. *We Won't Back Down! Severita Lara's Rise from Student Leader to Mayor*. Houston, TX: Arte Público Press, 2005.

Hammerback, John C., Richard J. Jensen, and José Angel Gutiérrez. *A War of Words: Chicano Protests in the 1960s and 1970s*. Westport, CT: Greenwood Press, 1985.

Horsman, Reginald. *Race and Manifest Destiny: The Origins of American Racial Anglo-Saxonism*. Cambridge, MA: Harvard University Press, 1981.

Hunter, Cecilia Aros, and Leslie Gene Hunter, eds. *Historic Kingsville, Texas: Guide to the Original Townsites*. Vol. 2. Kingsville, TX: Kingsville Historical Development Board, 2001.

———. *Texas A&M University–Kingsville*. Chicago: Arcadia Press, 2000.

Johnson, Ben. *Revolution in Texas: How a Forgotten Rebellion and Its Bloody Suppression Turned Mexicans into Americans*. New Haven, CT: Yale University Press, 2003.

Kaplowitz, Craig A. *LULAC: Mexican Americans and National Policy*. College Station: Texas A&M University Press, 2005.

Kearns, Doris. *Lyndon Johnson and the American Dream*. New York: Harper and Row, 1976.

Kleberg County, Texas: A Collection of Historical Sketches and Family Histories. Austin, TX: Hart Graphics, 1979.

Kopel, Hal, ed. *Border Life in the Rio Grande Valley: Essays of Remembrance and Research*. Edinburg, TX: Hidalgo County Historical Society, 1996.

La Vere, David. *The Texas Indians*. College Station: Texas A&M University Press, 2004.

Lessoff, Alan. *Where Texas Meets the Sea: Corpus Christi and Its History*. Austin: University of Texas Press, 2015.

MacDonald, Victoria-María, ed. *Latino Education in the U.S.: A Narrated History from 1513–2000*. New York: Palgrave-Macmillan, 2004.

Maril, Robert Lee. *Poorest of Americans: The Mexican Americans of the Lower Rio Grande Valley of Texas*. Notre Dame, IN: University of Notre Dame Press, 1989.

Marín, Christine. *A Spokesman of the Mexican American Movement: Rodolfo "Corky" Gonzales and the Fight for Chicano Liberation, 1966–1972*. San Francisco: R and E Research Associates, 1977.

Márquez, Benjamin. *LULAC: The Evolution of a Mexican American Political Organization*. Austin: University of Texas Press, 1993.

Martínez, Oscar J. *Mexican-Origin People in the United States: A Topical History*. Tucson: University of Arizona Press, 2000.

McAdam, Doug. *Political Process and the Development of Black Insurgency, 1930–1970*. Chicago: University of Chicano Press, 1982.

McKenzie, Phyllis. *The Mexican Texans*. College Station: Texas A&M University Press, 2004.

Meier, Matt S., and Feliciano Ribera. *Mexican Americans/American Mexicans: From Conquistadors to Chicanos*. New York: Hill and Wang, 1993.

Menchaca, Martha. *Naturalizing Mexican Immigrants: A Texas History*. Austin: University of Texas Press, 2011.

Monday, Jane Clements, and Betty Bailey Colley. *Voices from the Wild Horse Desert: The Vaquero Families of the King and Kenedy Ranches*. Austin: University of Texas Press, 1997.

Montejano, David. *Anglos and Mexicans in the Making of Texas, 1836–1986*. Austin: University of Texas Press, 1987.

———. *Quixote's Soldiers: A Local History of the Chicano Movement, 1966–1981*. Austin: University of Texas Press, 2010.

Muñoz, Carlos. *Youth, Identity, Power: The Chicano Movement*. New York: Verso, 1989.

Nájera, Jennifer R. *The Borderlands of Race: Mexican Segregation in a South Texas Town*. Austin: University of Texas Press, 2015.

Navarro, Armando. *The Cristal Experiment: A Chicano Struggle for Community Control*. Madison: University of Wisconsin Press, 1999.

———. *Mexican American Youth Organization: Avant-Garde of the Chicano Movement in Texas*. Austin: University of Texas Press, 1995.

Newcomb, W. W., Jr. *The Indians of Texas: From Prehistoric to Modern Times*. Austin: University of Texas Press, 1969.

Now and Then in Zavala County: A History of Zavala County, Texas. Crystal City, TX: Zavala County Historical Commission, 1986.

Oberschall, Anthony. *Social Conflicts and Social Movements*. Englewood Cliffs, NJ: Prentice Hall, 1973.

Orozco, Cynthia E. *No Mexicans, Women or Dogs Allowed: The Rise of the Mexican American Civil Rights Movement*. Austin: University of Texas Press, 2009.

Paredes, Américo. *With His Pistol in His Hands*. Austin: University of Texas Press, 1958.

Preuss, Gene B. *To Get a Better School System: One Hundred Years of Education Reform in Texas*. College Station: Texas A&M University Press, 2009.

Pycior, Julie Leininger. *LBJ and Mexican Americans: The Paradox of Power*. Austin: University of Texas Press, 1997.

Ramírez, José A. *To the Line of Fire: Mexican Texans and World War I*. College Station: Texas A&M University Press, 2009.

Rendón, Armando B. *Chicano Manifesto: The History and Aspirations of the Second Largest Minority in America*. Berkeley, CA: Ollin and Associates, 1996.

Richardson, Rupert N., Adrian Anderson, and Ernest Wallace. *Texas: The Lone Star State*. 7th ed. Upper Saddle River, NJ: Prentice Hall, 1997.

Rinzler, Alan, ed. *Manifesto Addressed to the President of the United States from the Youth of America*. New York: Macmillan, 1970.

Rivas-Rodríguez, Maggie. *Mexican Americans and World War II*. Austin: University of Texas Press, 2005.

Roberts, Cokie. *Founding Mothers: The Women Who Raised Our Nation*. New York: William Morrow, 2004.

Rodríguez, Marc Simon. *The Tejano Diaspora: Mexican Americanism and Ethnic Politics in Texas and Wisconsin*. Chapel Hill: University of North Carolina Press, 2011.

Romo, Ricardo. *East Los Angeles: History of the Barrio*. Austin: University of Texas Press, 1983.

Rosales, F. Arturo. *Chicano! History of the Mexican American Civil Rights Movement*. Houston: Arte Público Press, 1996.

———. *Testimonio: A Documentary History of the Mexican American Struggle for Civil Rights*. Houston: Arte Público Press, 2000.

Ruiz, Vicki L. *From Out of the Shadows: Mexican Women in Twentieth-Century America*. New York: Oxford University Press, 1997.

Sánchez, George J. *Becoming Mexican American: Ethnicity, Culture and Identity in Chicano Los Angeles, 1900–1945*. New York: Oxford University Press, 1993.

Sánchez, Mario L., ed. *A Shared Experience: The History, Architecture and Historic Designations of the Lower Rio Grande Heritage*. Austin: Los Caminos del Rio Heritage Project and Texas Historical Commission, 1994.

San Miguel, Guadalupe. *Brown, Not White: School Integration and the Chicano Movement in Houston*. College Station: Texas A&M University Press, 2001.

———. *Chicana/o Struggles for Education: Activism in the Community*. College Station: Texas A&M University Press, 2013.

———. *"Let All of Them Take Heed": Mexican Americans and the Campaign for Educational Equality in Texas, 1910–1981*. Austin: University of Texas Press, 1987.

Sargent, Frederic O. *The Civil Rights Revolution: Events and Leaders, 1955–1968*. Jefferson, NC: McFarland, 2004.

Sepúlveda, Juan A., Jr. *Life and Times of Willie Velásquez: Su Voto Es Su Voz*. Houston: Arte Público Press, 2005.

Shockley, John Staples. *Chicano Revolt in a Texas Town*. Notre Dame, IN: University of Notre Dame Press, 1974.

Soltero, Carlos R. *Latinos and the American Law: Landmark Supreme Court Cases*. Austin: University of Texas Press, 2006.

Sracic, Paul A. *San Antonio v. Rodriguez and the Pursuit of Equal Education: The Debate over Discrimination and School Funding*. Lawrence: University Press of Kansas, 2006.

Stewart, Charles J., Craig Allen Smith, and Robert E. Denton Jr. *Persuasion and Social Movements*. 4th ed. Prospect Heights, IL: Waveland Press, 2001.

Taylor, Paul S. *An American-Mexican Frontier*. Durham, NC: Duke University Press, 1934.

———. *Mexican Labor in the United States: Dimmit County, Winter Garden District, South Texas*. Berkeley: University of California Press, 1930.

Tijerina, Andrés. *Tejano Empire: Life on the South Texas Ranchos*. College Station: Texas A&M University Press, 2008.

———. *Tejanos and Texas under the Mexican Flag, 1821–1836*. College Station: Texas A&M University Press, 1994.

Trujillo, Armando. *Chicano Empowerment and Bilingual Education: Movimiento Politics in Crystal City, Texas*. New York: Garland, 1998.

Uschan, Michael V. *The 1960s Life on the Front Lines: The Fight for Civil Rights*. Farmington Hills, MI: Lucent Books, 2004.

Valencia, Reynaldo Anaya, Sonia R. García, Henry Flores, and José Roberto Juárez Jr. *Mexican Americans and the Law: ¡El Pueblo Unido Jamás Será Vencido!* Tucson: University of Arizona Press, 2004.

Valencia, Richard R. *Chicano Students and the Courts: The Mexican American Legal Struggle for Educational Equality*. New York: New York University Press, 2008.

Valerio-Jiménez, Omar S. *River of Hope: Forging Identity and Nation in the Rio Grande Borderlands*. Durham, NC: Duke University Press, 2013.

Weber, David. *Myth and History of the Hispanic Southwest.* Albuquerque: University of New Mexico Press, 1998.

Weber, John. *From South Texas to the Nation: The Exploitation of Mexican Labor in the Twentieth Century.* Chapel Hill: University of North Carolina Press, 2015.

Weinberg, Meyer. *A Chance to Learn: A History of Race and Education in the United States.* Cambridge: Cambridge University Press, 1977.

Weisbrot, Robert. *Freedom Bound: A History of America's Civil Rights Movement.* New York: W. W. Norton, 1990.

Zamora, Emilio. *Claiming Rights and Righting the Wrongs in Texas: Mexican Workers and Job Politics during World War I.* College Station: Texas A&M University Press, 2009.

———, ed. *The World War I Diary of José de la Luz Sáenz.* College Station: Texas A&M University Press, 2014.

Zamora, Emilio, Cynthia Orozco, and Rodolfo Rocha, eds. *Mexican Americans in Texas History.* Austin: Texas State Historical Association, 1999.

ARTICLES

Albro, Ward. "A Gringo at the Awakening: The Origins of the Chicano Movement at Texas A&I." *Journal of South Texas* 29, no. 1 (2015): 128–35.

Alvarez, Rodolfo. "The Psycho-Historical and Socioeconomic Development of the Chicano Community in the United States." *Social Science Quarterly* (March 1973): 920–42.

Barrera, James B. "The 1968 Edcouch-Elsa High School Walkout: Chicano Student Activism in a South Texas Community." *Aztlán: A Journal of Chicano Studies* 29, no. 2 (Fall 2004): 93–122.

Dugger, Ronnie. "The Segregation Filibuster of 1957." *Texas Observer* 66 (December 27, 1974): 46–47.

García, Ignacio M. "'The Best Bargain . . . Ever Received': The 1968 Commission on Civil Rights Hearing in San Antonio, Texas." *Southwestern Historical Quarterly*, 122, no. 3 (January 2019): 246–76.

Garza, Israel, Jr. "The History of Vahl'sing." *Llano Grande Journal* 2, no. 1 (Fall 1998): 14–15.

Gutiérrez, Ramón A. "Community, Patriarchy and Individualism: The Politics of Chicano History and the Dream of Equality." *American Quarterly* 45, no. 1 (1993): 44–72.

Haney-López, Ian F. "White Latinos." *Latino Law Review* 6 (2003): 1–7.

Jensen, Richard J., and John C. Hammerback. "An Interview with José Angel Gutiérrez." *Western Journal of Speech Communication* 44 (Summer 1980): 203–13.

Martínez, Oscar J. "On the Size of the Chicano Population: New Estimates, 1850–1900." *Aztlán: A Journal of Chicano Studies* 6 (Spring 1975): 43–67.

Montoya, Margaret E. "A Brief History of Chicana/o School Segregation: One Rationale for Affirmative Action." *La Raza Law Journal* 12 (2001): 159–72.

Muñoz, Carlos, and Mario Barrera. "La Raza Unida Party and the Chicano Student Movement in California." *Social Science Journal* 19, no. 2 (April 1982): 101–19.

Pratt, Robert A. "Review of *Brown v. Board of Education: A Civil Rights Milestone and Its Troubled Legacy*, by James T. Patterson." *Reviews in American History* 30, no. 1 (March 2002): 141–48.

Preuss, Gene P. "Cotulla Revisited: A Reassessment of Lyndon Johnson's Year as a Public School Teacher." *Journal of South Texas* 10, no. 1 (1997): 20–37.

Rodriguez, Marc Simon. "A Movement Made of 'Young Mexican Americans Seeking Change': Critical Citizenship, Migration, and the Chicano Movement in Texas and Wisconsin, 1960–1975." *Western Historical Quarterly* 34 (Autumn 2003): 275–99.

San Miguel, Guadalupe. "Conflict and Controversy in the Evolution of Bilingual Education in the United States—An Interpretation." *Social Science Quarterly* 65 (June 1984): 505–18.

San Miguel, Guadalupe, and R. R. Valencia. "From the Treaty of Guadalupe-Hidalgo to Hopwood: The Educational Plight and Struggle of Mexican Americans in the Southwest." *Harvard Educational Review* 68, no. 3 (1998): 353–413.

Sutton, Jeffrey S. "San Antonio Independent School District v. Rodriguez and Its Aftermath." *Virginia Law Review* 94, no. 8 (December 2008): 1963–86.

Trillin, Calvin. "US Journal: Crystal City, Texas." *New Yorker*, April 17, 1971.

Yudof, Mark G., and Daniel C. Morgan. "*Rodriguez v. San Antonio Independent School District*: Gathering the Ayes of Texas—The Politics of School Finance Reform." *Law and Contemporary Problems* 38 (1974): 383–414.

Index

activist: commonalities with protester 226n4; defined, 226n4; used interchangeably with protester, 226n4. *See* Chicano student movement

Acuña, Rodolfo (Rudy): historian, 78; impact of student movement, 78

Aguilar, Elida, 98, 99, 104, 109; expelled from Lanier High School, 103, 104, 105; ignored demand to be silent, 98–99; on low quality of education, 98; parental support, 103, 104; part of committee drafting grievances, 97; selection of student officers, 98

Alemán, Narciso: community rights organizer, 151; MAYO organizer, 169; on Chicanos solving their own problems, 151; views on mestizaje and cultural nationalism, 152

Alvarez v. Lemon Grove School District: first successful desegregations case, 54; served as precedent, 54

American Indian Movement. *See* political movements (1960s)

Americanization, 33–34; accelerated by military service, 51; aimed at cultural and linguistic assimilation, 20; and vocational training, 88; as English-only policies, 17, 22; in Texas schooling policies, 32–33; reinforced marginalization of Mexicans, 33; subtractive, 1, 22

Anglo: as Caucasian, 181; some viewed as conquerors or invaders, 151–52; used interchangeably with Anglo American, white American, European American, and white, 228n62

Arispe, Raúl, 147, 209; attended Edcouch-Elsa High School, 130; attended meeting with Principal Pipkin, 137; community meetings at the house of, 130; deficient school counseling of, 128; drove protesters' school bus to La Joya high school, 143; expelled from school board meeting, 142; father helped purchase school bus, 143; involvement with Chicano student activism, 130; Mexican American teachers sought to discourage local student movement, 132; plaintiff in suit against school district, 145; plaintiff witness in suit against school district, 146

Axelrod, Alan: attorney with MALDEF, 146; in suit against Edcouch-Elsa High School, 146

Avena, Richard: attended Elsa Community Center meeting (1968), 134; member of the US Commission on Civil Rights, 134

Aztlán, 65; academic journal, 23; as present day US Southwest, 152; Chicano homeland, 153; mythical homeland of the Pre-Columbian Mexican indigenous civilization, 64. *See* El Plan Espiritual de Aztlán, 78

Barragán Goetz, Philis: on feasibility of bilingual instruction in private schools, 29; research on *escuelitas* (small-community based schools), 29

Bazan, Gutiérrez, Luz: Chicana activist, 67; Chicanas asked to perform menial tasks, 68; Chicanas not allowed leadership roles in MAYO/Chicano student movement, 67–68; Chicanas who assumed leadership roles denigrated by Chicano males, 68; former spouse of Gutiérrez, José Ángel, 67

Benavides, Santos: Confederate Army colonel, 26; county judge, 26; opposed the *Botas* (Boots, political organization), 26; supported the *Guaraches* (Sandals, citizens party), 26; Texas State Representative, 26

Bernal, Joe J. (Texas Senator): attended Elsa Community Center meeting (1968), 134; bilingual education bill, 152; distribution of high school ribbons "I'm an American, I speak English," 91; graduated from Lanier High School, 91; organized a political training for male Lanier High School student, 97; praised Chicano students after the start of protest, 103; ribbons taken away from Mexican American students, 91; sought to connect with the Chicano Movement, 134; training for junior high school students, 97

Blackwell, Maylei: feminist challenges within Chicano movement, 157

Blanton, Carlos Kevin, 16; ambiguity of Texas two hour non-English rule; 32; basis of segregated schools, 56; bilingual schooling as key demand, 22; on Americanization, 22, 29; on bilingual education, 22; on feasibility of bilingual instruction in private schools, 29; on importance of *Cisneros* case, 55; the basis of segregated schools, 56; use of IQ tests, 33; use of Spanish in the classroom, 29

Brown Berets, 77, 144; encouraged walkouts in Los Angeles, 79; Medina's, Tony, telegram to Edcouch-Elsa students, 144

Brown v. Board of Education of Topeka (1954), 54, 119, 121, 125: focus on African American school segregation, 53; US Supreme Court outlawed school racial segregation, 58, 82, 180

Canales, Isabel: critical of Chicano acceptance of Ford Foundation monies, 173

Canales, J.T. (Representative): collaborated with Sáenz, José de la Luz, 47; investigation of Texas Rangers, 35

Cantú, Martín: graduate of Edgewood High School, 89, 112; gave testimony to the US Commission on Civil Rights , 89, 89f; drafting of nine demands, 112; on non-degree teachers at Edgewood High School, 112, 113; support of parents, 114; suspended for participating in the walkout, 117

Cárdenas, José: advised not to testify, 120; called for equalized school funding, 122; founded the Intercultural Development Research Association (IDRA), 118; provided disparity data for lawsuit, 119; superintendent of Edgewood ISD, 118; vice principal at Edgewood High School, 110. See also *Rodriguez v. San Antonio ISD*

Carter, Thomas P.: on success of Mexican American students, 128–29; schooling and demands of the socioeconomic and labor systems, 18

Castro, Sal: biography of, 79; important leader in the Chicano student movement, 79–80; role in student walkout and mentor, 79; teacher at Lincoln High School, 77

Castro, Stephen: critical of school invitation of prisoners, 92; part of committee drafting grievances, 97; participated in drafting demands, 101

Caucasian Race Resolution (Texas): House Concurrent Resolution 105, 42; outlawed discrimination, 42

Chapa v. Odem (1967), 55: ended segregation of Mexican students, 54. *See also* De Anda, James

Chávez, César, 58, 63, 75, 78; farmworker strike's impact on student movement, 205

Chávez, José Luis, 145, 146, 209; attended Edcouch-Elsa High School, 130; community meetings at the house of, 130; parent support for, 135, 137, 137f, 146

Chicana/Chicano: adoption of Hispanic or Latino, 6; as expression of ethnic and cultural pride in Mexican ancestry, 225n1; defined, 225n1; opposition to Hispanic and Latino, 5; student movement gave value to the term, 5; used interchangeably with Mexican American, 225n1

Chicana feminism: and opposition to Chicano patriarchal authority, machismo, and sexism, 225n1; description of male-centeredness within Mexican American community, 157; examined by Blackwell, Maylei, 157; on the universalization of masculine subjects and women's invisibility, 151; some women did not want to create divisions within MAYO, 67; sought political participation, 158. *See also* Conferencia de Mujeres por La Raza

Chicano Liberation Youth Conference (1969): Alurista read *El Plan Espiritual de Aztlán* at, 153; hosted by Crusade for Justice, 152; first national meeting of Chicano youth, 152–53. *See also* Gonzales, Rodolfo (Corky)

Chicano Movement (Chicano Civil Rights Movement/*El Movimiento*): activists in, 61–69; and emergence of MALDEF, 215; as *El Movimiento*, 18; began by youth in 1968, 2, 23; cultural nationalism within, 5, 6, 151–152; decline in the 1970s, 202–3;

emergence in Denver, 152–54; favored a direct and aggressive approach, 5; gave rise to new and revolutionary orientation, 213; importance of Crystal City events to, 13; inspired by Civil Rights Movement, 61, 76, 216; La Raza Unida Party as culmination of, 204; made possible by increased Mexican migration, 62; militant ethos of *chicanismo*, 5; nationalism fostered belonging, racial pride, and youthful exuberance, 151; parallel emergence in Denver and Kingsville, 152; presentation of Mexican American Manifesto (Bill of Rights), 154; reference and value of the label Chicano, 5; refrain from use of Hispanic or Latino, 5, 177f; rejection of past political strategies, 205; studies of, 8, 16–17, 20–23, 52, 74–77; rise of collective consciousness, 212; within tradition of civil rights and social protest, 2. *See also* Compean, Mario C.; Gonzales, Rodolfo (Corky); Guerra, Carlos; Gutiérrez, José Angel; Velásquez, Willie C.

Chicano student movement: absence of comprehensive understanding of, 8; academic assessment in the 1960s, 69–70; activism at Texas A&I University, 154–61; broader political context, 4, 5, 57–61; disharmony with older Mexican American community, 202; formation of Chicano Generation, 61–69; demand for better accommodation of educational needs, 5, 7; links across communities, 202; opposed school policies and advocated for cultural awareness, 7; part of a broader political and social transformation, 4; pursued power through collective action, 7; research on activism in education, 19–23; sought political-clout, 5–6; struggle for better education, 16–19; studies of Chicano activism in education in California, 78–80

Cisneros v. Corpus Christi ISD (1970): first case to extend ruling in *Brown v. Board of Education*, 54; Mexican Americans as an identifiable, ethnic-minority class, 54–55; previously Mexicans considered an "other white" group, 56

Citizens Association Serving All Americans (CASAA), 185; coalition of Anglo and middle-class Mexicans to reverse 1963 Crystal City election, 185

Ciudadanos Unidos (United Citizens), 204; parent organization (Crystal City), 192; raised funds for student trip to Washington, D.C., 261n114

Civil Rights Movement: African American activists and the, 125; and bilingual education, 22; aspirations in, 2; campaigns of nonviolence in, 2; Chicano activists inspired by the, 61, 63; civil disobedience in, 2; coinciding movements with the, 58, 76, 205; manifestation of grievances, 3; tensions with, 1; view of Chicano Movement as outgrowth of the, 216. *See* Chicano Movement; Chicano student movement

Compean, Mario C., 13, 74, 113, 161; Chicano leader from San Antonio, 66; deficiencies in Edgewood schools, 113; explanation of school financing disparities, 113; importance of Black Movement, 66; integration of Alinsky, Saul, methods, 66; liaison between Chicano students and MAYO, 111; on "racial wall," 214; role in linking Chicano students and MAYO, 77, 124; summary of Chicano student strategies, 214

Conferencia de Mujeres por la Raza (National Chicana Conference, 1971): first national Chicana feminist conference, 157; held in Houston (Texas), 157

Cornejo, Juan: among the *los cinco candidatos* election campaign in 1963, 183; a Teamsters Union representative, 183; first Mexican American mayor of Crystal City, 184; worked at the Del Monte Corporation, 183

Cortez, Cecilia, 164; 176, 178; attended Gillett Junior High School (Kingsville), 13, 161; building of friendships, 162; informal student meetings spread by word of mouth, 162; key Chicana student activist, 161; recollection of walkout, 13, 162; view of parents on activism, 163

Cortina, Juan N. (1859-75): Mexican insurrectionist, 170; led raid on Brownsville, 57, 170

Crystal City school walkouts (1969-70), 4; aftermath of student protest, 198–03; cheerleader controversy, 185–89; Chicano student movement as Second Revolt, 185-89; contested selection of

INDEX ∼ 285

homecoming queen, 187–88; decision to walk out, 190; educational inequities, 180; efforts and success in raising funds for poll tax for low-income Mexicans, 183–84; emphasis to enroll Mexican student to raise revenues for Anglo schools, 180; first revolt and strategies to win 1963 local elections, 183–85; forms of Jim Crow rules in the City, 182; highly publicized and controversial student protest, 179; history of city, 39–42; investigators from the US Department of Health, Education, and Welfare traveled to Crystal City, 196; local activism led to formation of La Raza Unida Party, 179; low high school graduation rates for Mexican students, 180; MAYO assisted local students, 179; Mexicans as subservient labor force in the city, 182; Mexicans segregated within the same school, 181; parents mobilized to support students, 192–93; required poll tax to vote, 183; role of PASSO in first revolt, 183; school board agreed to most of the student demands, 198; school board refused to address student grievances, 179; school board rule to remove class credits of protesters, 186; school officials invented the level "zero" for Mexican students, 181; school officials sought to reach a settlement only with parents, but parents rejected offer, 194; segregation of students, 180; slow integration of schools after 1954 *Brown v. Board of Education*, 180; some Anglo teachers considered Mexican students as inferior, 181; students called for a consumer boycott, 194; student grievances presented to the principal, 185–86; tracking of Mexican students into vocational schools, 182; US Commission on Civil Rights report on Crystal City High School, 181; voter intimidation by Texas Rangers, 184; walkouts spread from high school to junior high, and elementary schools, 179, 193, 195. *See also* Cornejo, Juan; Del Monte Corporation; Gutiérrez, José Ángel; *los cinco candidatos*

Davis, Edmund J. (Texas Governor): creation of a state board of education, 32; enacted creation of a state public school system (1871), 32

De Anda, James (attorney): class apart legal argument, 54; co-counsel in *Cisneros v. Corpus Christi ISD*, 55; Corpus Christi civil rights attorney, 146; litigated *Chapa v. Odem* (1967), 54; litigated *Hernandez v. State of Texas* (1954), 54; co–counsel in Edcouch-Elsa High School lawsuit, 146

De León, Arnoldo (historian): interpretation of Chicano militant activism, 66–67; on Anglo stereotype of Mexicans, 94; on countywide ranch schools, 29; racial domination of Tejanos/Mexicans, 25

Delgado v. Bastrop ISD (1948): school desegregation case, 54

Del Monte Corporation: manufacturing plant in Crystal City, 40, 180; grew spinach, 180; previously the California Packing Corporation, 41; relocated to Crystal City in 1945, 41, 180

Del Rio ISD v. Salvatierra (1930): court ruled that segregations could continue if based on "pedagogical wisdom," 53; early desegregation case, 53; litigated before *Brown v. Board of Education* (1954), 53 desegregation cases, 54–57

Donato, Rubén (education scholar), 20, 56: and Mexican schools, 20; the basis of segregated schools, 56; tracking Mexican students into vocational programs, 17, 93; unequal education, 17–18

Dylan, Bob, 1

Echeverría, Darius V. (historian): Arizonan-Mexican education, 18; educational challenges in Arizona, 18–19; long-standing educational discrimination in Arizona, 18–19; student-oriented actions during Chicano Movement, 19

Edcouch-Elsa school walkouts (November 1968): Anglo American high school students encouraged to take college preparatory classes, 128; district agreed to settlement of suit, 147; district expelled activist students and parents filed suit, 145; history of city, 36–39; inferior Mexican schools, 126; junior and senior high school students walked out, 126; La Joya schools admitted expelled students, 143; MALDEF provided legal counsel, 145; Mexican American teachers divide over walkout, 129–30; Mexican high school students encourage to pursue a trade or join the military, 128; origins of student activism, 130–35; parents and expelled students sued the district, 145; parents divided over walkout, 136–37; participants in walkout, 126; school board expelled key activists, 142; school officials and county sheriff's office arrest students, 138–40; student awareness of student absence and school funding, 138; student expressions of patriotism to refute charges of communism, 136; student protest leaders, 145, 209; student protesters suspended, 138; surrounding school districts refused to admit protest students, 143; teachers Raúl Champion, Javier Gutiérrez, and Robert Cunningham were witnesses for the district, 145; walkout commemorated in 1998, 12. *See also* González, Eddy; MALDEF; Rodríguez, Maricela; Sánchez, R. P. (Bob); Vásquez, Uvaldo

El Plan de San Diego (1912): drafted by Mexicans and Tejanos, 35; made public (1915), 35; provisions in the Plan, 35; uprising, 36, 45, 57. *See also* Texas Rangers

El Plan de Santa Barbara, 78

El Plan Espiritual de Aztlán, 78; advocated Chicano nationalism and self-determination, 153. *See also* Chicano Liberation Youth Conference

Elsa Community Center meeting (168): attended by recognized Mexican American leaders, 134; presided by Ramírez, Javier (student), 134

English-only: 29, 32, 33; adverse effect on Mexican students, 38; and Americanization, 17, 22

Erebia, Faustino, 176, 178; attended Gillett Junior High School, 161; chair of local MAYO chapter, 161; commentary on Gillett Junior High School walkout, 13; member of MAYO, 151; met with local students prior to walkout, 151; observation on aftermath of walkout, 176; physical punishment for speaking Spanish, 161; student activist, 13

Escobar, Eleuterio, Jr., 86: aided in organizing LULAC Council #16, 84; assumed presidency of *La Liga Pro-Defensa Escolar*, 86; attended a segregated elementary school, 84; examined the use of temporary frame classrooms, 85; founded *La Liga Pro-Defensa Escolar*

(School Improvement League), 84; hosted rally at Lanier High School, 85; local business owner and community leader, 84; on overcrowded classrooms, 84–85; owner of Escobar Furniture Company, 84; partnered with Perales, Alonso S., 84; resigned from LULAC education committee, 86

estúpidos (stupid), 169; view of Chicano students, 169

European American: defined, 228n62

feminism: Chicana activist limited involvement with feminism, 157; Chicana activists opposed gender discrimination, 158; critique of Chicana Homecoming Queen victory, 156–57; Mexican American community as male-centered, 157; Mexican women's pre-1965 actions, 158. *See also* Blackwell, Maylei

Fernández, Efraín, 69, 152; Anglo residents boycotted parent's restaurant, 69; MAYO leader, 151; organized protest at Humble Oil, 69; parents owned a restaurant in Kingsville, 69

Ford Foundation, 117; and gringo dollars, 172–73; Congressional investigation of, 172; González, Henry B. (Congressman) critical of funding by, 172; grant to MALDEF, 145; grant to MAYO, 172. *See also* Canales, Isabel

García, Hector P., 94; appointed to the US Commission on Civil Rights, 88, 169; Army medic, 51; arrested alongside student activists, 55; attended meeting at Elsa Community Center, 134; explored civil rights violations of Mexican students, 169; founded the American GI Forum, 134; on the Longoria, Felix controversy. 52; physician from Corpus Christi, 51; ribbons taken away from Mexican American students, 91

García, Homer D., 14, 89f, 104; administrators and teachers degraded and threatened, 99–100; admonished for distributing leaflets, 97; allowed to return to school, 107; asserted "All we want is a better education," 102; attended the community meeting in the Guadalupe Catholic Church, 103; catalyst in Chicano student movement, 96–98; confrontation at student council meeting, 98; declared

INDEX   287

that Mexican Americans are as capable as Anglo Americans, 101; expelled from Lanier High School, 105; father was of Mexican and Tap Pilam Coahuiltecan descent, 96; gave testimony to the US Commission on Civil Rights, 89, 92; graduate of Lanier High School, 10; labeled a militant, radical, anarchist, and communist, 100; memories of segregation and racial inequality in San Antonio, 82–83; on students selection of student officers in school council, 98; part of committee drafting grievances, 97; participated in drafting demands, 101; prison inmates invited to school, 92; protagonist in Chicano student movement at Lanier High School, 98; represented by Tijerina, Pete (attorney), 107; school counselors did not encourage college or professional careers, 92; secret interrogation at school district offices, 108; spiritual mission, 96; student council walkout did not foster a school-wide protest, 99; suspended for "having a bad attitude," 100; target of scrutiny and antagonism, 96; was told by principal that students had no human or civil rights in school, 99

García, Ignacio M. (historian), 74, 89, 103; admonishment for students speaking Spanish, 90; attended Lanier High School, 5, 81; Chicano activists' emulation of radical organizations, 74; contrast between older strategies, and those in the Chicano student movement, 64; considered San Antonio a "Mexican" town, 82; did not consider Lanier as an inner-city school, 82; expression of pride, 6; Mexicans as subordinate, 94; militant ethos, 5; on Gutiérrez, José Ángel, 70; presence of teachers without a college degree, 113; prominence of issue related to speaking Spanish, 107; viewed González, Henry B., as offering little to address student grievances, 171–72

García, Irene: part of committee drafting grievances, 97

García, Mario T. (historian): among first scholars to use the term "Mexican American Generation," 232n20; autobiography of Castro, Sal, and Chicano movement, 79; Castro's inspired Chicano students, 79; inequities in East Los Angeles schools, 79; Mexican students ridiculed for speaking Spanish, 79–80; Chicano student pushed to low-wage jobs or Vietnam War, 80

Garza, Ben: participated in the creation of LULAC, 47. See also LULAC

Garza, Carmen Lomas (artist), 160; attended Texas A&I University, 160; born in Kingsville, 158, 176; dual policies on speaking a non-English language in school, 159; parent and American GI Forum, 159–60; recollections about Kingsville, 158; sought to be allowed to take biology, 159

Garza, Reynaldo G. (federal district judge): appointed by President Kennedy, 146; Edcouch-Elsa suit settled, 147; first Mexican American federal judge, 146; presided over Edcouch-Elsa lawsuit, 146–147

gavacho: slang for 'white man,' 157

Gochman, Arthur M. (attorney): legal arguments by, 121, 122; recommended by Velasquez, Willie, 118; represented plaintiffs in Rodriguez v. San Antonio ISD, 119, 122

Gómez-Quiñones, Juan (historian): first academic study of student activism, 78; importance of local student movements, 131; Mexican Americans active in state Democratic Party, 52; not seen as significant in federal elections, 52; promoted Chicano studies, 78

Gonzales, Rodolfo (Corky), 75, 152, 154; arrested then acquitted of assault charges, 154; author of I am Joaquín poem (1967), 152, 234n100; organized the Chicano Liberation Youth Conference (1969), 152–53; supported Denver student walkout (1969), 154; telegram to Edcouch-Elsa protesters, 175

González, Eddy: attended community meeting to address educational issues, 130; attended Edcouch-Elsa High School, 130; elected to Edcouch-Elsa School Board, 126–27, 148; leadership role in protest for better education, 130; paddled by Principal Pipkin, 128; punished for speaking Spanish, 128; suspended from school for violation of rule on sideburns, 128

González, Gilbert G. (historian): Americanization rationalized as assimilation, 34;

288 ～ INDEX

and Mexican schools, 20; analysis of Spanish language and Mexican culture in schools, 17, 90, 127; basis of segregated schools, 56; on migratory students and the economic system, 18; rationales for segregation of Mexican students, 17

González, Henry B. (Congressman): antimilitant speeches in Congress, 172; bill to abolish the poll tax, 171; critical of Gutiérrez's, José Ángel, actions and ideas, 172; criticized MAYO 172; disapproved of Gutiérrez's "Kill the Gringo" speech, 171; elected to San Antonio City Council, 171; first Mexican American elected to the Texas Senate (1956), 171; Ford Foundation criticized by, 172; identification as a voice of San Antonio's West Side, 171; noted contradiction in Chicano acceptance of Ford Foundation monies, 172

González, Jacinto: first Mexican American on Edcouch-Elsa School Board, 126

González, Jovita, description of rural Mexican schools, 30; on Mexican peons, 27

Good Neighbor Commission: minimized extent of discrimination, 41; Sánchez, George I., labeled it a "glorified tourist agency," 42

Great Depression, 81, 84: in South Texas, 49–50

Greenberg, Jack (attorney), 146; Director-Counsel of NAACP Legal Defense Fund, 145

Guerra, Carlos, 154, 155f, 160, 173–74, 215: acknowledgement of patriarchal tendencies among males in MAYO, 67; activist and organizer in MAYO, 13, 67; assisted Kingsville student activists, 161, 178; contacted MALDEF to assist students in Kingsville, 166; Gringos as the problem, 155; heckled by Canales, Isabel, 173; MAYO members active in farmworkers' struggle, 75; native of Robstown, 65; on dissatisfaction with old-line organizations, 65–66; on Gillet Junior High student demands, 169; organized chapters of Chicano organizations, 175, 177; organized march in Kingsville, 175; statewide MAYO leader, 168; Texas A&I University spark, 177

Gutiérrez, José Angel, 124, 154, 160, 177; able to debate in English and Spanish, 70;

authored a biography, 72; completed an MA degree from St. Mary's University, 73; conservative opposition to, 171–73; "crescendo effect" strategy, 190, 195, 203; did not examine the factors that led students to walk out, 73; earned a bachelor's degree from Texas A&I University, 72; earned a Ph.D. from The University of Texas at Austin, 73; emerged as one of the most radical and well-known organizers, 70; father served as a doctor in Pancho Villa's army, 71; graduated from Crystal City High School, 72; impetus for creation of La Raza Unida Party, 72; implemented the political concept of bloc-voting, 72; incorporated "machismo" in recruiting adult males to attend school board meetings, 188; invoked the terms Aztlán, Chicanos, and La Raza, 170; "Kill the Gringo" speech, 170; MAYO presence in Kingsville, 161, 178; native of Crystal City, 70; on Anglo-centered curriculum, 20; on regaining the land by gaining political control, 67; on systematic discrimination in schooling, 20, 181; participated in thirty-nine school boycotts, 73; participation in First Revolt in Crystal City, 183; perplexed about his personal class and racial identifications, 73–74; public school aimed to strip Mexicaness from Mexican students, 71; refused to become a Hispanic, 72; rejected LULAC assimilationism, 66; role in linking Chicano students and MAYO, 77, 124; role in creating and shaping MAYO, 70–77; social and economic segregation in Crystal City, 40, 182; son of a medical doctor, 71

Hernández, Daniel: part of committee drafting grievances, 97; participated in drafting demands, 101

Hernández, María: activist with the San Antonio School Improvement League, 89; presented testimony on racial discrimination against Mexican Americans, 89; witness to the US Commission on Civil Rights (1968), 89

Hernandez v. Texas (1954): challenge to jury exclusion, 54; constitutional rights against class discrimination, 55. *See also* De Anda, James

Herrera, Richard: participated in walkout at Edgewood High School, 10

Hispanic: teachers pressuring student to be good Mexicans, 91;

Huerta, Dolores: labor activist for UFW, 63, 78. *See also* Chávez, César

Hunger in America (documentary, 1968), 83, 95, 237nn18–21; focused on poverty in San Antonio, 83

insurgency: defined, 225n3; resemblance of revolt to overthrow Anglo-dominated schooling, 225n3

Johnson, Lyndon Baines (Senator/President), 57, 60; Americanization, 61; assisted in burial of Longoria, Felix, at Arlington National Cemetery, 52; enacted the Civil Rights Act (1964), 59; enacted the Voting Rights Act (1965), 59; formation of "Viva Johnson" clubs, 57; García, Hector P., sent letter regarding burial of Longoria, Felix, to 52; implemented the War on Poverty, 59–60; taught in Cotulla, 60; labeled as paternalistic and condescending, 60–61

Justice, William Wayne (federal district judge): concluded Texas public schools provided unequal education, 56; presided over *United States of America v. State of Texas* (1971), 57

Kennedy, Edward (Senator), 204; met with Chicano activist students from Crystal City, 196

Kennedy, John F. (President), 57, 59; formation of "Viva Kennedy" clubs, 57; shot in Dallas, 59

Kennedy, Robert (Senator), 105–6; hearing on treatment of agricultural workers, 105

Kingsville school walkouts (1969), 150–78, 167f: aftermath of walkout, 178; arrested students, 165, 167–68; Anglos were asked to leave seminar, 151; Chicano student demonstrations at Texas A&I University, 177; declaration of Chicano Liberation Day, 163; demonstrations at City Hall, 152; emphasis on nonviolent, direct action protests, 177–78; Gillett Junior High student demands, 162; history of city, 42–44; key student-activists, 161, 178; Kingsville operated a 'Mexican' elementary and junior

high school, 176–77; Kingsville residents apprehensive about student insurgency, 163; limited achievements of walkout, 176; MALDEF and local attorneys represented students, 166, 178; MAYO leadership support, 178; MAYO's strategies in, 178; Mexican American veteran opposed student actions, 164; mixed view of student actions by parents, 163–64; number of students participating in marches, 165; PASSO participation in, 162; play by MAYO Teatro, 169; principal given list of grievances, 162–63; protest at police station, 166; Salinas, María Elena, parent spokesperson, 164; school board unwilling to compromise with protesters, 163; school officials and police sought to jail student leaders and activists, 178; segregated schools in Kingsville, 176–77; spread to Memorial Junior High, and King High School, 164, 178; student demands, 162, 178; student movement as a "farce induced communism," 164; Texas A&I University MAYO student support, 150, 161, 163, 177; third walkout in 1969, 4, 150, 152; community and political activism seminar at Texas A&I University, 151, 177; walkout at Gillett Junior High School, 152

Lara, Severita, 13; argued that students were seeking equal representation of cheerleaders, 186; attended Crystal City High School, 179; exposed to Chicano Movement in California, 187; key student organizer at Crystal City High School, 179; presented additional demands at school board meeting, 189; presented student grievances, 185–86; suspended for distributing flyers about elections procedures, 186; visited government officials in D.C., 196

League of United Latin American Citizens (LULAC, 1929): and identifications as México Texano or Mexican Texan, 48; argued that Mexican Americans were of the white race, 54; constitution of, 48; fought educational inequality, 19, 52–53; in creation of *La Liga Pro-Defensa Escolar*, 84; learning English and becoming American, 48; merging of organizations, 47; not seen as a successful civil rights organization, 52; proclaimed English as its official language, 48; promoted education, 57; pushed for civil rights legislation, 41; role in desegregation cases, 53; sought to end the Bracero Program, 42; support for Lanier High School students, 85; viewed as proassimilationist, 64. *See also* Escobar, Eleuterio, Jr.; Orozco, Cynthia E.; Rodríguez, Demetrio

legal cases challenging segregation of Mexican students, 56

Liga Pro-Defensa Escolar, La (School Improvement League), 87, 238n25: disbanded (1935), 86; founding of (1934), 84; reorganized as School Improvement League (1947), 86. *See also* Escobar, Eleuterio, Jr.,

Longoria, Felix: buried at Arlington National Cemetery, 53; controversy on wake and burial of, 52, 57

López, David: Chicano labor leader in Kingsville, 151; participated in seminar for Chicano activist students, 151

los cinco candidatos: Antonio Cárdenas, Juan Cornejo, Mario Hernández, Manuel Maldonado, Reynaldo Mendoza, 183; victory in Crystal City 1963 election, 184; ousted by a coalition of Anglos and middle-class Mexicans (1965), 185

Lozano, Edgar: attended Lanier High School, 89; gave testimony to the US Commission on Civil Rights, 89; participated in drafting student demands, 101; participated in Young Leaders Club, 97; was told Spanish was a filthy language, 91

Luera, Alberto, 13; arrested in Kingsville, 166; charged for "loud and vociferous language," 166; interpretation why students-school officials negotiations failed, 176; MAYO activist, 166

Manifest Destiny: defined, 25

Martínez, Vilma (attorney): part of legal counsel on the Edcouch-Elsa suit, 146

Mendez v. Westminster School District (1946): outlawed the segregation of Mexican children in California, 54

Mexican, ethnic. *See* Chicana/Chicano; Mexican Americans/Mexicans

Mexican-American Betterment Organization, 119

Mexican American Generation, 78; Chicano activists integrated strategies from, 211; Chicanos viewed as passive, ineffectual, and accommodating, 64, 205; coining of term, 232n20; defined, 48; efforts to connect with the Chicano Movement, 134; influence on actions of Chicano activists, 211; insistence on working within the US political system, 134; labeled *vendidos* (sellouts) by some Chicanos, 65–66; periodization of, 21, 48; political strategies of, 21, 48–49

Mexican American Legal Defense and Educational Fund (MALDEF), 210; assisted plaintiffs in Corpus Christi ISD suit, 55; criticized by González, Henry B. (Congressman), 172; Edcouch-Elsa case considered its first court victory, 147–48, 149; filed lawsuit against Edcouch-Elsa School District (1968), 145–49; founded in 1968, 13; important early resource for student activists, 210–11; legal counsel to Kingsville students, 13, 166–69, 178; legal counsel to Crystal City students, 186; represented Lanier High School students, 97–98, 106, 107

Mexican American Unity Council (San Antonio), 172

Mexican Americans/Mexicans: as Caucasian, 31; civil rights and, 2; housing restrictions, 82; some did not support protesting students, 14

Mexican American Youth Organization (MAYO): additional issues of concern, 74; cofounders, 74; Del Rio Manifesto, 173; emerged as an offshoot of older Mexican American political activists, 74; established in 1967, 72, 74, 75; inspired by farmworkers movement, 75; link to La Raza Unida Party, 75–76; membership requirements of, 75; promoted aggressive, confrontational strategies, 74; strategy to impact school funding, 138. *See also* Navarro, Armando; La Raza Unida Party

Mexican schools, 64; as inferior in every respect, 126; as overcrowded, in dilapidated buildings with inadequate resources, and with incompetent teachers, 20; discussed in a master's thesis, 126; first established in Elsa in 1902, 33, 38; Seguin as location of first, 33

INDEX ~ 291

Montalvo, Ray: attended Edgewood High School, 117; suspended for participating in Edgewood walkout, 117

Montejano, David (historian): description of early economy and society in South Texas, 27; discrimination and segregation of Mexicans in San Antonio, 82; 'Mexican town' in San Antonio, 82; on first Mexican school, 33

Muñoz, Carlos, Jr. (political scientist), activist-scholar, 78–79; examined Chicano political activism, 78; participated in the East Los Angeles school walkouts, 78

National Chicano Moratorium (1970), 78

Navarro, Armando (political scientist): activist-scholar, 75; does not examine specific members of MAYO, 76; examines the formation and demise of MAYO, 75; on Gutiérrez, José Ángel, 75. See also MAYO

Obledo, Mario: MALDEF attorney, 146, 148. See also MALDEF

oral histories, 10–11; importance of memory in, 10–11

Orozco, Cynthia E. (historian): broader movements in pre- and post-World War II, 52; Chicano reluctance to acknowledge pre-World War II Mexican American activism, 52; contestation of patriarchal ideology, 158; Mexican American women's political participation, 157–58; México Texano dual identifications, 48

Ortiz, Pablo: part of student committee drafting Edgewood grievances, 97; participated in drafting student demands, 101

PASSO (Political Association of Spanish-Speaking Organizations), 72, 177; chapter at Texas A&I University, 156; chapter in Kingsville, 72; criticized by González, Henry B. (Congressman), 172; endorsed winning candidates in Crystal City council 1963 elections, 180; limited role in Edcouch-Elsa student activism, 131, 149; participated in Crystal City First Revolt, 183–85; participation in Edcouch-Elsa, 131; presented grievances to Texas A&I University president, 154; referred to as "outside agitators," 132.

See also Guerra, Carlos; Gutiérrez, José Ángel; Peña, Albert

Peña, Albert (Bexar County Commissioner), 195; accused of being a communist and outside agitator, 184; contrast between handicapped students, and a handicapped educational system, 103; held leadership role in PASSO, 184, 195; praised Chicano student on the schooling controversy, 103

Peña, Rosie, 14; attended Lanier High School, 95; shame in portrayal of Mexicans in history of Texas Revolution, 95

Perales, Alonso S. (civil rights attorney): attended the rally at Lanier High School, 85; collaborated with Sáenz, José de la Luz, 47; encouraged Mexican Americans to vote, 84; on LULAC's view of education, 48; participated in the creation of LULAC, 47; partnered with Escobar, Eleuterio, Jr., 84; promoted educational reform, 84

Pipkin, Marvin (Principal of Edcouch-Elsa High School), 128, 136, 140, 146; after testimony, defense attorneys agreed to a settlement, 147; arrest of student protesters, 138; disavowed student protest and demands, 130, 137; first witness in the trial, 146; met with Mexican students and parents, 137–38; questioned by Judge Garza, Reynaldo G., 146–47

Plessy v. Ferguson (1896): and the ideology of separate but equal, 20; equal representation goals, 186; overturning of separate but equal principle, 58

political movements (1960s): African Americans, 2; American Indian, 1; Civil Rights, 1, 2; Women's Rights, 1. See also Chicano Movement

Ramírez, Irene, 89f; gave testimony to the US Commission on Civil Rights, 89; paddled for speaking Spanish in school, 90; student at Lanier High School, 89

Ramírez, Javier, 145, 147, 209; arrested, 138–39; attended Edcouch-Elsa High School, 130; attended meeting with Principal Pipkin, 137; community meetings at the house of, 130; Mexican American teachers sought to discourage local student movement, 132; plaintiff in suit against school district, 145; presided at the Elsa Community Center meeting,134

Ramírez, Jesús: attended Pharr-San Juan-Alamo High School, 130; leader within MAYO, 130

Ramírez, Rebecca Campos: Edgewood activist, 14; her father purchased toilet paper for her to take to school, 111; on deplorable conditions in Edgewood schools, 111

Raza Unida Party, La, 204, 214; examined by Trujillo, Armando, 201; fostered the inclusion of Mexican Americans in the Democratic Party, 215; founded in Texas (1972), 76; inspired Mexican Americans to vote, 215; support for Mexican American candidates, 215; student activists and, 203. *See also* Gutiérrez, José Ángel; Mexican American Youth Organization (MAYO); PASSO (Political Association of Spanish-Speaking Organizations)

Rendón, Armando B: *Chicano Manifesto* by, 63–64

Rocha, Juan, Jr. (MALDEF attorney), 13, 168, 176; alumnus of Texas A&I University, 166; represented Chicano students in Kingsville 166, 178

Rodriguez v. San Antonio ISD (1971): challenged Texas' public school funding methods, 124; defendants raised specter of socialism and communism, 122; court concluded that education is not a constitutional right, 122; federal court ruled in favor of plaintiffs, 121–22; US Supreme Court ruling on, 122–23

Rodríguez, Demetrio: member of Mexican American civil rights organizations, 119; parent and plaintiff in *Rodriguez v. San Antonio* case, 119

Rodríguez, Maricela: Junior High School student (Edcouch-Elsa), 127; in the eight-grade, 127; stripped of school awards, 127

Sáenz, Freddy: attended Edcouch-Elsa High School, arrested, 128; deficient school counseling of, 128; expelled from school board meeting, 142

Sáenz, José de la Luz: collaborated with Canales, J. T., Perales, Alonso S., and Vento, Adela Sloss, 47; enlisted in the Army (WWI), 46; published a diary, 46; Zamora, Emilio translated diary of, 231n2

Sáenz, Lali: an aide in the migrant education program, 131; encouraged participation in MAYO, 130–31; graduate of Edcouch-Elsa High School, 130

Salinas, Artemio, 145, 209: arrested, 138; attended Edcouch-Elsa High School, 130; expelled from school board meeting, 142; leadership role in protest for better education, 130; plaintiff in suit against school district, 145; Edinburg jail vigil for, 139

San Antonio walkouts (Edgewood ISD), 98–109; abundance of vocational shop courses at, 102; administrators denigrated and threatened students, 99–100; Bishop's Committee for the Spanish-Speaking supported students, 103; Chicana/o students decide to walk out of student council meeting (1968), 99; Chicano view of the school as humiliating and degrading to Mexican Americans, 103; coercion of student to sign an admission of guilt, 108; coexistence of residential and school segregations, 81; confrontation at student council meeting, 98; counselors denying Mexicans access to an academic curriculum, 94; Edgewood and Lanier High School prepared Mexican students for vocational trades, 88, 94; Edgewood High School student activism and walkout, 109–18; first student demonstration in Texas (April 1968), 81; five students testified at US Commission on Civil Rights hearing, 89–96; frisking and searching students, 97–98; Great Depression, 84-85; hearing by US Commission on Civil Rights, 88–92; history of San Antonio, 82–88; Lanier High School student activism and walkout, 98–109; lawsuit against district, 118–124; lower enrollment in more rigorous courses, 102; officials selected school mascot, Voks, 94; poverty in West Side, 82-84, principal told that students they had no human or civil rights in school, 99; proportion of non-degree teachers, 113; rally outside Lanier High School, 85-86; record keeping system and vocational tracking, 88; reflection of an underprivileged

INDEX ∼ 293

socioeconomic environment, 103; school district officials agree to student demands, 108–9; school officials selected "model" student to defend the school, 103; student demands, 101; study of financing disparities in San Antonio schools, 113; support of Edgewood Concerned Parents Organization, 114; Voks, as short for vocational trades, 94. *See also* Escobar, Eleuterio; García, Homer D.; Hernández, María; *Hunger in America*; Liga Pro-Defensa Escolar/School Improvement League; Lozano, Edgar

Sánchez, George I. (education scholar): aided the creation of MALDEF, 145; educator and civil rights advocate, 42; participated in *Chapa v. Odem* suit, 54; view of Good Neighbor Commission, 42. *See also* Good Neighbor Commission

Sánchez, R. P. (Bob), 141f, 147; attorney in McAllen, 12; letter to MALDEF on victory, 147–48; presented the student demands to the school board, 140–42; provided legal counsel to Edcouch-Elsa student protesters, 12, 145; served as trustee for students after settlement, 147

San Antonio ISD v. Rodriguez (1972). See *Rodriguez v. San Antonio ISD*

San Miguel, Guadalupe, Jr. (historian), 16, 20, 21–22, 33; and Mexican schools, 20; educational discrimination in Texas, 19; MALDEF's early litigation, 145; on aftermath of Chicano Movement, 21; on brown, not white slogan, 20; on Chicano activism in Houston, 20; three major activist strategies, 21; victim-oppressor relationship, 19

school segregation legal cases: 53–57

school walkouts (1968–69): thirty-nine, 217

Serna, Diana: attended Crystal City High School, 179; key student organizer, 179; visited government officials in D.C., 196

Smith, Preston (Texas Governor): accused MAYO of inciting racial tension, 173; cut financial resources for MAYO, 173

social movements, 6; student-led, 6; three key factors of, 7–8; three stages in, 8; limited scholarly attention on the role of youth in, 9

South Texas: contested territory between the Nueces and Rio Grande Rivers, 25; development of public schools,

31–34; counter narratives on Mexicans in Edcouch-Elsa, 36–37; economic expansion in, 34–36; Great Depression in, 49–50; history of Crystal City, 39–42; history of Edcouch-Elsa, 36–39; history of Kingsville, 42–44; labor unrest in the 1930s, 49–50; political bossism in, 26–31; pre-1960s history of, 24–45; segregation within Catholic churches and schools in La Feria, 37; World War II internment camp in Crystal City, 41. *See also* Montejano, David

Southwest Council of La Raza (Phoenix), 144; criticism of, 172; praise for Edcouch-Elsa student movement, 144

Sustaita, Arnulfo: arrested, 138, 142; attended Edcouch-Elsa High School, 130; expelled from school board meeting, 142; leadership role in protest for better education, 130; released from jail on bond, 140

Taylor, Paul S. (economist): banishment of Mexicans, 41; Mexican property obtained cheaply, 40

Tejano, 22, 26, 27, 28; activism, 30; at bottom of economic and social strata, 26; and military enlistment, 46–47; dark-skinned, 26; defined, 25, 227n1; establishment of community schools, 32; limited English among, 22; patronage of, 29; population share and income, 28; ranching community, 24; retention of Spanish, 32–33; schooling conditions, 30

Tenayuca, Emma: key role in San Antonio pecan shellers strike, 50; member of the Workers Alliance, 50

Texans for the Educational Advancement of Mexican Americans (TEAM): members included Anglo and Mexican American educators, 197; schooling for boycotting students, 196–97

Texas Rangers: between three hundred to two-thousand Mexicans killed by, 35–36; voter intimidation in Crystal City by, 184. *See also* Canales, J. T.

Texas State Advisory Committee: advisory to the US Commission on Civil Rights, 70; concluded that Texas failed to educate Mexican American students, 70

Tijerina, Pete, 146; in contact with Greenberg, Jack (attorney), 145; prevented from entering school district office, 108;

represented García, Homer D., 107; San Antonio attorney who assisted expelled students, 104. *See also* Greenberg, Jack

Tio Taco: defined, 97

Treaty of Guadalupe Hidalgo (1848), 25, 26, 36, 62

Treviño, Homero, 138, 140; arrested, 138; attended Edcouch-Elsa High School, 130; expelled from school board meeting, 142; leadership role in protest for better education, 130

Treviño, Mario: attended Crystal City High School, 179; key student organizer, 179; presented additional student demands at school board meeting, 189; presented student grievances, 185–86; visited government officials in D.C., 196

Truan, Carlos F. (Texas Representative/ Senator): attended Kingsville MAYO and Chicano student meeting, 151; bilingual education bill, 152; disappointed with the Kingsville City Commission, 168–69; emphasized the importance of education, 152

United Cannery, Agricultural, Packing and Allied Workers (UCAPAWA), 50

US Commission on Civil Rights, 134, 169: hearing in San Antonio, 88–91; investigation of Crystal City High School, 181; investigation of Edgewood High School, 112; investigation of Lanier High School, 124; report by 102; Texas State Advisory Committee presents conclusion that Texas fails to educate Mexican Americans to, 70

Valencia, Richard: inequalities in Edgewood ISD, 119–20

Vallejo. Frank: attended Edcouch-Elsa High School, 127; suspended for disagreeing with counselor, 127

Vásquez, José, 95, 103: attended Lanier High School, 89; attended the community meeting in the Guadalupe Catholic Church, 103; counselor tracking Mexican students into vocational trades, 93; educational system failed to prepare him for college, 93; gave testimony to the US Commission on Civil Rights, 89, 89f; lack of cultural content on Mexicans, 94; part of committee drafting grievances, 97; poor instruction in English, 93; view that

school curriculum reinforced stereotypes and myths about Mexicans, 95

Vásquez, Uvaldo: attended Edcouch-Elsa schools, 127; experienced discrimination as a student, 127; reprimanded for speaking Spanish, 127

Velásquez, Willie C.: advise to Chicano students, 101, 114; considered a professional agitator, 116; founding co-organizer of MAYO, 74; referred civil rights attorney Gochman, Arthur to Edgewood students and parents, 118; role in linking Chicano students and MAYO, 77, 124

vendidos (sellouts), 65, 169–170; explained, 255n120; Mexican American Generation viewed as, 65

Vento, Adela Sloss: collaborated with Sáenz, José de la Luz, 47; community activist, 144; supported walkout at Edcouch-Elsa High School, 144

Vietnam War, 1, 62, 114, 155, 164; anti-war movements, 7, 58, 76, 77; attending college to avoid draft, 128; draft, 80; Mexican American participation in, 78; soldier's critical letter of Chicano students in Kingsville, 164

Villareal, Mirtala, 145, 209: arrested, 138; attended Edcouch-Elsa High School, 130; community meetings at the house of, 130; dissatisfaction among Mexican students, 135; expelled from school board meeting, 142; inferior and old equipment for Mexican students, 129; plaintiff in suit against school district, 145; released after arraignment, 139; older sister of Villareal Treviño, Nelda, 135

Villareal Treviño, Nelda, 135; attended Edcouch-Elsa High School, 10, view on why trustee abstained from voting, 142; participated in the Edcouch-Elsa walkout, 10; positive view of education at La Joya ISD, 144; younger sister of Villareal, Mirtala, 12, 135

Women's Rights Movement. *See* political movements (1960s)

World War I, Americanization during, 22, 33; as start of cultural assimilation, 46; Tejano males in, 47. *See also* Escobar, Eleuterio, Jr.; Sáenz, José de la Luz:

World War II: Bracero Program, 41; internment camp in Crystal City,

INDEX ~ 295

41; Mexican American veteran's and patriotism, 51; military importance of Kingsville railroad, 44; redefined the citizenship status of Mexican Americans, 50–53; fostering of "Americanness" among Mexican Americans, 51; turning point for Mexican Americans, 50–51. *See also* García, Hector P.

Yáñez, Irene: attended Lanier High School, 95; infringement of faculty sponsor of student council, 99; shame in portrayal of Mexicans in history of Texas Revolution, 95

Xicanisma: coined by Castillo, Ana, 234n120; explained, 234n120; promoted the liberation from oppression, 68

Zamora, Emilio (historian): translated diary of Sáenz, José de la Luz, 231n2